U.S.-Panama Relations, 1903–1978

Westview Replica Editions

The concept of Westview Replica Editions is a response to the continuing crisis in academic and informational publishing. Library budgets for books have been severely curtailed. Ever larger portions of general library budgets are being diverted from the purchase of books and used for data banks, computers, micromedia, and other methods of information retrieval. Interlibrary loan structures further reduce the edition sizes required to satisfy the needs of the scholarly community. Economic pressures on the university presses and the few private scholarly publishing companies have severely limited the capacity of the industry to properly serve the academic and research communities. As a result, many manuscripts dealing with important subjects, often representing the highest level of scholarship, are no longer economically viable publishing projects--or, if accepted for publication, are typically subject to lead times ranging from one to three years.

Westview Replica Editions are our practical solution to the problem. We accept a manuscript in camera-ready form, typed according to our specifications, and move it immediately into the production process. As always, the selection criteria include the importance of the subject, the work's contribution to scholarship, and its insight, originality of thought, and excellence of exposition. The responsibility for editing and proofreading lies with the author or sponsoring institution. We prepare chapter headings and display pages, file for copyright, and obtain Library of Congress Cataloging in Publication Data. A detailed manual contains simple instructions for preparing the final typescript, and our editorial staff is always available to answer questions.

The end result is a book printed on acid-free paper and bound in sturdy library-quality soft covers. We manufacture these books ourselves using equipment that does not require a lengthy make-ready process and that allows us to publish first editions of 300 to 600 copies and to reprint even smaller quantities as needed. Thus, we can produce Replica Editions quickly and can keep even very specialized books in print as long as there is a demand for them.

About the Book and Authors

U.S.-Panama Relations, 1903-1978:
A Study in Linkage Politics
David N. Farnsworth and James W. McKenney

This book traces relations between the United
States and Panama from 1903 to 1978, focusing especially
on the Panama Canal dispute from its origin until ratification of the historic Carter-Torrijos treaties. The
authors' analysis emphasizes the extent to which the
domestic politics of each country influence decisions
about foreign policy and about the canal treaty negotiations, and how these decisions in turn affected internal
political circumstances. Beyond its overall assessment
of issues historically important in relations between
the United States and Panama, the book covers a wide
range of topics: Panama's political system, its domestic
politics, and the importance of the canal; the hostile
yet interdependent relationship between canal-zone residents and other Panamanians; details of the Panama-U.S.
canal dispute, the lengthy negotiating process, and the
negotiating strategies of each country; the treaty-rati-
fication process in the U.S. Senate; and the likely impact of the treaty on future U.S.-Panama relations. The
book is based on interviews with key figures in both
countries and on extensive review of articles, government
documents, and FBIS reports.

David Farnsworth is professor of political science
at Wichita State University where James McKenney is department chairman.

U.S.-Panama Relations, 1903–1978

A Study in Linkage Politics

David N. Farnsworth
and James W. McKenney

Westview Press / Boulder, Colorado

A Westview Replica Edition

Copyright © 1983 by Westview Press, Inc.

Published in 1983 in the United States of America by
     Westview Press, Inc.
     5500 Central Avenue
     Boulder, Colorado 80301
     Frederick A. Praeger, President and Publisher

Library of Congress Cataloging in Publication Data
Farnsworth, David N. (David Nelson), 1929-
     U.S. Panama relations, 1903-1978.

     (A Westview replica edition)
     1. United States--Foreign relations--Panama.
2. Panama--Foreign relations--United States.
I. McKenney, James W. II. Title. III. Title: US
Panama relations.
E183.8.P2F37 1983   327.7307287   83-10368
ISBN 0-86531-969-3

Printed and bound in the United States of America.

10 9 8 7 6 5 4 3

Contents

Acknowledgments ix

1   PROBLEM AND FRAMEWORK 1

2   GENESIS OF THE CANAL 13

3   RIOTS AND AFTERMATH 35

4   THE TWO PANAMAS 59

5   POINTS OF CONFLICT 83

6   SEARCH FOR AN ALTERNATIVE 105

7   INTERNATIONALIZING THE CONFLICT 119

8   EFFORTS TOWARD SETTLEMENT 143

9   THE CANAL AND U.S. DOMESTIC POLITICS 167

10   THE FIGHT FOR RATIFICATION 189

11   AFTERMATH AND POSSIBILITIES 245

Appendix A: Treaty Concerning the Permanent
Neutrality and Operation of the Panama Canal . . . 273

Appendix B: Panama Canal Treaty 277

Selected Bibliography 299

Index 303

Acknowledgments

During the time that this book was in preparation, we accumulated a great many debts which we wish to acknowledge. Without the generous assistance of the following organizations and individuals, we might never have undertaken the project, let alone completed it.

Initially, we would like to acknowledge the financial support of the Social Science Foundation at the University of Denver, which allowed us to travel to Panama and Washington, D.C., to collect materials and conduct interviews for the book. Additional financial assistance was provided by the university research committee of Wichita State University.

Fran Major's contribution to the book went far beyond her responsibility for preparing and typing the final manuscript. With good humor, she also helped us to avoid many mistakes and performed the role of constructive critic whenever we had problems of language or substance. Phyllis Nickel and Barbara Ciboski filled similar roles in earlier stages of the manuscript preparation. Steve Smith was of inestimable value in preparing the index. A special note of appreciation to our wives and families for the support and assistance they so willingly gave.

We wish to thank all those anonymous individuals, both in the United States and Panama, who gave so unselfishly of their time and knowledge during the time when we were doing our research. However, we wish to absolve them and others of any responsibility for any analyses or interpretations which we have made in this study.

David N. Farnsworth
James W. McKenney

June 20, 1983

1
Problem and Framework

On 7 February 1974, Secretary of State Henry
Kissinger visited the Republic of Panama. He arrived at
Tocumen, Panama's single international airport, and drove
to Panama City, where he consulted with Panamanian leaders, including General Omar Torrijos, head of the military government, and Juan Antonio Tack, Kissinger's
Panamanian counterpart. After a few hours, Kissinger and
Tack signed an agreement that was to serve as the basis
for a new treaty between the United States and Panama
concerning the operation of the Panama Canal, its defense, and the administration of the Canal Zone. Kissinger then returned to Tocumen and flew back to the United
States. Throughout his visit, Kissinger was heavily
guarded by the Panamanian National Guard.
    This trip was remarkable for several reasons. For
several months preceding his visit to Panama, Kissinger
had devoted much of his attention to problems in the Middle East, and he was preparing for yet one more round of
visits to Middle Eastern capitals at the time when he
went to Panama. When not occupied with the Arab-Israeli
conflict, Kissinger, as the principal spokesman for Nixon
foreign policy, had been doing the diplomatic work developing a détente with the Soviet Union and China. The
United States was engaged in talks with the Soviet Union
to expand strategic arms limitations and to achieve a
mutual balance force reduction in Europe as well as engaged in the Conference on Security and Cooperation in
Europe. What time remained was devoted to resolving the
growing differences between the United States and its
allies, Japan and the NATO countries. Western Europe was
particularly disturbed with the United States at this
time because of American unilateral actions in support of
Israel during the October War in 1973.
    Latin America had received little attention from
the Nixon Administration and had not been an important
concern of United States foreign policy since the Kennedy Administration. Within this context of neglect of
Latin America and his preoccupation with various other

1

major diplomatic problems, the secretary's visit to one of the smaller Latin American countries was indeed remarkable. Equally significant was that Secretary Kissinger had not flown into one of the several air bases located in the Canal Zone. Before Tocumen was built, all international flights for Panama and the Zone went through Albrook Air Force Base, but by 1974 Panama took considerable pride in having its own international airport, operated independently of the United States in the Canal Zone. If Kissinger had used Albrook, this would have been yet one more reminder to Panamanians that the United States controlled the Zone and that the United States secretary of state had entered Panama from that Zone. Kissinger's task of quieting Panamanian demands for greater participation in the operation of the Canal and administration of the Zone was difficult enough without the symbolic affront of entering Panama from the Canal Zone.

The heavy guard placed on Kissinger also might have seemed unusual, but since feeling in Panama was running high against United States presence in the Canal Zone, the heavy protection was perhaps necessary. The possibility did exist, however, that the heavy guard was designed more to make Kissinger feel that he needed protection in what, in the past, had been a friendly country than to protect him from actual attack.

Also important was that the Kissinger visit produced an agreement between the two governments designed to serve as the basis for a new treaty concerning the status of the United States in the Canal Zone and its operation of the Canal. No such agreement had been possible earlier, even though negotiations between the two countries had been in progress intermittently for nearly ten years.

A special effort to conclude these negotiations began in September 1973, when the United States upgraded the negotiations by appointing the highly regarded and experienced diplomat Ellsworth Bunker as the new negotiator for the United States. Bunker had a reputation for being a trouble shooter, having been involved in a number of sensitive negotiations in Europe, Asia, and Latin America. Bunker first visited Panama in late November and early December 1973 and again in early January 1974. Following these visits, the two governments announced that a list of commitments by the United States had been drawn up, commitments that, for implementation, required unilateral action by the United States. Panama felt that these preliminary concessions were necessary to prove that the United States was seriously searching for a settlement of differences between the two countries. These commitments then led to the agreement, signed during the Kissinger visit.

Significantly, both the list of commitments and the

agreement were signed in Panama. During the decade of
negotiations preceding these agreements, negotiations
had usually taken place in Washington; and even earlier,
when the various agreements that made up the legal basis
for United States presence in Panama were signed, they
were signed in Washington.[1] To the Panamanians, these
1974 agreements were diplomatic victories both because
of the concessions made and because the United States had
sent emissaries to Panama.

While all of this diplomatic activity was a significant milestone in relations between the United States and
Panama, the purpose of this book is to examine the background that created a situation serious enough that the
U.S. secretary of state felt it necessary to visit a nation small both in area and population in the midst of
many other diplomatic problems the United States was
facing.

While much has been written on United States-
Panamanian relations since Panama gained its independence
in 1903, the subject has usually been approached as a
chronology of events or a criticism of policy with alternatives suggested.[2] This study intends to analyze the
problem in terms of linkage politics as it exists among
the various political systems involved.[3]

NATURE OF LINKAGES

Linkage, as a concept, has various meanings in the
social sciences, but when applied to studies of foreign
policy, it refers to any "recurrent sequence of behavior
that originates in one system and is reacted to in
another."[4]

The most obvious linkage in this study is between
the Panamanian and U.S. political systems through the
foreign policies they pursue, this being not only the
most common link established in foreign policy studies
but usually the only link discussed. Linkages are more

FIGURE 1

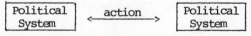

complex, however, than this simple view of one political
system as a unit reacting and relating to another unitary
political system. There are also the domestic demands
within each system producing the various decisions that
make up a nation's foreign policy as well as the bureaucratic conflicts among the various agencies that are responsible for the making of foreign policy. In addition,
reactions to what occurs within one domestic political
system are not confined to that system but are reacted to
within other political systems. Thus, what seems to be

a simple relationship of two nations' foreign policy is
actually a continuum. In this instance, the American
domestic system produces the foreign policy decisions
through its bureaucracy, which in turn are reacted to by
the Panamanian bureaucracy and the Panamanian domestic
system. The process is, of course, reversed for the
Panamanian responses or initiatives that emanate from the
Panamanian system.

FIGURE 2

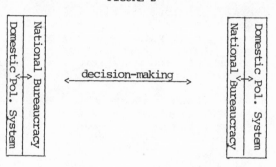

Sometimes, steps in this process are eliminated,
such that events within one domestic system are reacted
to directly by the domestic system or bureaucratic process of another political system. An example was an attack on the United States Embassy in Panama on 23 September 1975 by a mob of 800 Panamanian students. This
demonstration was a reaction to remarks made by Secretary
Kissinger at a Southern Governors' Conference that the
United States had the right to defend the Canal unilaterally and indefinitely. Such responses in Panama to
events in the United States are common.
     A further set of linkages exists between the inter-
national systems and the two primary domestic systems.
In the instance of Panama and the United States, international agencies such as the Organization of American
States and the United Nations have direct linkages with
the conflicts that exist between the two countries.
Through these international political systems, there are
further linkages with the political systems of a number
of other nation-states that have some concern with the
status of the Panama Canal. The conflict over the Canal
developed into a much more complicated pattern of linkages in the early 1970's as Panama sought support among
Latin American and other Third World nations.
     Since linkage politics views political events as a

continuum of activity among several political systems,
both domestic and international, this activity cannot
be compartmentalized validly into the traditional political science fields of foreign policy, international relations or comparative politics. Researchers in these
fields traditionally have worked up to the fringes of the
others' areas of interest but rarely have consciously
attempted to show the fields as continuations of one
another. While in recent years comparative politics has
escaped the confines of descriptions of first one domestic system and then movement on to another, the emphasis
now is to search for patterns of behavior found in all
domestic systems or a category of domestic systems such
as the developing countries. The next logical step would
seem to be to put a greater emphasis on the relationship
of these patterns of behavior to the international system
and the linkages involved between the domestic systems
and their foreign policies. "In some major respects,
governments find it increasingly difficult, or meaningless, to distinguish between foreign policy and domestic
policy."[5]

Scholars in the field of international politics and
foreign policy also have had an artificially imposed
limitation on their areas of investigation that has, to
a great extent, prevented them from looking more closely
at the domestic sources of international behavior by
nations. James Rosenau points out that the field is
"founded on the bedrock of national interest."[6] While
this statement would seem to overgeneralize about the
various approaches employed in studying international
politics, it does make an important point. Studies in
the international field assume that the domestic system
produces the interests that a nation presents within the
international system, but seldom does the investigation
extend to the political process that produced those interests. The application of linkage to the study of the
conflicts between two nations requires investigating
areas of political activity that traditionally fall into
both the comparative and international fields. What will
hopefully emerge will avoid the charge that comparative
studies do not go beyond the boundaries of the domestic
systems being investigated and the charge that international studies do not go into the domestic systems to
discover the sources of the interests nations pursue in
the international system.

DOMESTIC INFLUENCES

In order to accomplish this end, the linkage between
the domestic political systems of the United States and
Panama must be investigated for the sources of the interests and demands each produces as well as the reaction
each displays to the foreign policies of the other. Such

investigation avoids the pitfall of studies of comparative foreign policies that "devote correspondingly little
attention to the peculiarities of individual nation-
states' foreign policies and, by implication, suggest
that insights from the domestic political process of each
country are relatively unimportant."[7] Indeed, it becomes
apparent that if foreign policy is approached as a product of domestic political activity, "the line between
domestic and foreign affairs is blurred if it exists at
all."[8] Linkage politics can allow for both national and
international levels of analysis, particularly when the
conflict at the international level is primarily between
two nations and is concentrated on one particular issue.

    While events at the international level have their
effects at the domestic level, at least as strong an influence moves the other way. A nation's international
behavior is both a product of what occurs in its interaction with other nations and the influences brought to
bear on the foreign policy decision-makers by the domestic system and the bureaucracy of which they are a part.

    Domestic influence in United States foreign policy
has been illustrated numerous times even within the past
few years. A prime example is the U.S. withdrawal from
Vietnam. The withdrawal could hardly be construed as a
military defeat but, rather, as the loss of domestic support for a war that hurried, if was not directly responsible for, the withdrawal. Also, President Nixon's
partial mobilization order during the Yom Kippur War in
October 1973 was questioned as being a means of distrac-
ting the American public away from the president's
domestic problems concerning the Watergate scandals. Indeed, President Nixon's emphasis on foreign policy as a
strength of his administration during his low point of
public support on domestic matters supports the thesis
that domestic activity is a major explanation for a
nation's international behavior.

    In Panama, the equivalent behavior is when General
Torrijos, as head of the military government, used the
Canal issue to rally support for his government. When
the country had economic troubles, he blamed the United
States for economic exploitation of Panama through United
States control of the Canal. The promise of economic
growth was tied to the day when Panama gained what its
leaders regarded as Panama's fair share of the revenues
of the Canal. Other problems in Panama, so the government explained, had to wait until the Canal question was
resolved.

    The use of foreign policy for domestic purposes de-
pends, however, on the circumstances that exist within
the domestic system. Henry Kissinger, writing as a political scientist, viewed the relationship of domestic
activity to foreign activity in this manner:

If domestic structures are reasonably stable,
temptations to use an adventurous foreign policy
to achieve domestic cohesion are at a minimum. In
these conditions, leaders will generally apply the
same criteria and hold similar views about what
constitutes a "reasonable" demand. . . . When the
domestic structures are based on fundamentally
different conceptions of what is just, the conduct
of international affairs grows more complex. Then
it becomes difficult even to define the nature of
disagreement because what seems most obvious to
one side appears most problematic to the other.[9]

Kissinger might have added that when two domestic
systems are as different as are those of the United
States and Panama--with one, the United States, relatively stable, particularly on the Canal issue, and the other
relatively unstable--for both to agree on what constitutes a "reasonable" demand is probably as difficult as
when both systems are unstable. The manner in which the
conflicts between the United States and Panama are viewed
by the domestic systems is so different that reconcilia-
tion of the differences is very difficult. Ultimately,
resolution of the conflict must be acceptable to both
domestic systems.
    Kissinger also makes another point that is particu-
larly applicable to the Canal issue. "At a minimum, [the
domestic structure] determines the amount of total social
effort which can be devoted to foreign policy."[10] Since
the Canal issue is so important to Panama both in its domestic and foreign policies, the "total social effort
which can be devoted to foreign policy" is substantial.
This is particularly the case with Panama, since it is
possible to view the Panamanian position on the Canal as
being the number-one issue of the Panamanian foreign
policy.
    For the United States, the Canal issue is only one
of many issues of concern to its foreign policy decision-
makers. If placed in an order of priorities, the Canal
issue probably would be ranked lower than a number of
other issues perceived as more important. As one U.S.
negotiator with Panama was quoted, "Panama is always sixteenth on any list of the top fifteen issues."[11] In
turn, the Canal issue was not an important issue in U.S.
domestic politics until the presidential primaries in
1976. The "total social effort which can be devoted to
foreign policy" may be substantial in the United States,
but little of this effort was directed toward the Canal
issue.

DOMESTIC-BUREAUCRATIC CONFLICT

    Certainly, one of the most important studies on

linkage politics is Graham Allison's Essence of Decision.
In analyzing the Cuban missile crisis, Allison develops
essentially two models of foreign policy decision-making.
One he labels the Rational Policy Model.[12] This model
assumes that any decision or activity of a nation in its
efforts to implement its foreign policy is the result of
careful, rational choice from among the total number of
alternatives available to the decision-makers. This
model also assumes that the decision-makers, since they
are all rational, arrive at the same decision without
serious dissension. "The nation or government conceived
as a rational, unitary decisionmaker, is the agent. This
actor has one set of specified goals . . . , one set of
perceived options, and a single estimate of the consequences that follow from each alternative."[13] All actions by a government therefore are a matter of rational
choice. This view of foreign policy-making is reinforced
when it is said that "the States announced . . . ," "the
Soviet Union decided . . . ," "France objected . . . ,"
or "Panama declared . . . ." The nation is a single,
unified actor, and whatever domestic or bureaucratic conflict transpired in making the decision is ignored.

This model, though commonly used, is not linkage
politics. Allison's second model (for purposes here, one
model, though actually a combination of Allison's second
and third models), does not commit the error of ignoring
the domestic-conflict level of foreign policy-making.
Even though Allison does not include in his model conflict in the domestic system outside the organizational
and bureaucratic, he does recognize the conflict among
the decision-making units that are responsible for foreign policy. Decisions do not come from a unified group
of decision-makers; nor are the decisions in themselves
necessarily rational in the sense of being the best
choice as the result of careful analysis. Decisions are,
however, a product of working out the differences in the
positions taken by the various units of the bureaucracy.
The product of resolving these differences is the decision or decisions. The decisions thus are a result of
bargaining and may reflect a victory for one or more of
the competing units, or the decision may represent a
negotiated settlement wherein all units win a little and
lose a little. This model of decision-making is the one
used in this study of U.S.-Panamanian diplomacy over the
Canal.

What Allison could have added to his analysis was
that the governmental units that are in conflict over
policy often are, in turn, representative of nongovernmental interests. This act of representation may
or may not be intentional. For example, the members of
Congress who oppose making any concessions to the Panamanian demands are representing the interests of a
majority of the Americans living in the Canal Zone.

Congressmen who support the building of a sea-level canal
are representing the interests of heavy equipment manufacturers that wish a canal to be built for the business
such a project would provide. Whether these congressmen
intend to be representatives of these interests is difficult to determine, but the effect of their actions is
to be representative.

DOMESTIC ADAPTATION TO FOREIGN POLICY

Since the levels of reaction to the Canal issue
have been markedly different in the American and Panamanian systems, the adjustments of the domestic systems
to foreign policy developments--or, as James Rosenau has
labeled such reactions, the "adaptive behavior" of the
two political systems--must be classified differently.
Rosenau sees adaptive behavior as "any foreign political
behavior undertaken by the government of any national
society is conceived as adaptive when it copes with or
stimulates change in the external environment of the
society that contributes to keeping the essential structures of the society within acceptable limits."[14] When
internal change is low and external change high, as
seemed to be the case for the United States until the
1976 presidential primaries in regard to the Canal issue, Rosenau labels this sort of behavior as "deliberative." Deliberative behavior for a nation's decision-
makers is possible when the "absence of new internal
demands on government allows officials to weigh carefully the appropriate course of action to be followed in
meeting the rapidly changing scene abroad."[15] The slowness with which the United States responded to the demands made by Panama makes "deliberative" a most appropriate description.
When both internal and external change is high,
Rosenau calls this sort of adaptive behavior "convulsive"
and characterizes it as operative when

> . . . the top heads of governments must respond
> quickly to societal demand and internal pressures
> that are often contradictory and therefore may
> necessitate erratic, unpredictable, and agitated
> efforts to keep the fluctuating external environ-
> ment in balance with the shifting essential
> structures of their societies. . . . It is . . .
> a primary source of tension in the international
> system.[16]

Panamanian leadership, whether the present military
or the past civilian-elitist governments, has had to
respond to the nationalistic demands of the Panamanian
people on the Canal question in order to stay in office.
The decisions of Panamanian leadership thus often seemed

erratic and unreasonable, at least from the viewpoint of the United States decision-makers. The shifting positions on policy and occasional violence in Panama would certainly place Panama in the category of "convulsive" adaptive behavior.

PENETRATION OF DOMESTIC SYSTEM

There is one additional aspect of linkage politics that applies to this study but is applicable only to Panama and not to the United States. Since both Panama's domestic and foreign policies are dominated by the Canal issue, Panama must be described as a "penetrated" society. Wolfram Hanrieder, in his study of West German foreign policy, develops a concept of penetration that is also descriptive of the situation in Panama. He says that

> . . . external events "penetrated" the domestic political "subsystem" of West Germany to a high degree, making for a fusion of national and international systems patterns. . . . [T]he national society becomes so permeated by its international environment that the traditional analytical distinction between international systems and national systems is imprecise if not untenable.[17]

For Panama, the Canal issue is indistinguishable as to whether it is a foreign or domestic issue and clearly is a major issue at both levels. "[T]he distinction between foreign policy and domestic policy diminishes substantially because few processes of value allocation can remain isolated from external contingencies."[18]
Rosenau also discusses "penetrated" societies, but uses the term in a different manner than does Hanrieder. Rosenau sees a penetrated society as one in which the national decision structure is affected by external decision-making groups such as the administrative and military leadership of the Canal Zone. Certain decisions cannot be made without the acquiescence or consent of the external groups. The Rosenau and the Hanrieder definitions of penetration differ somewhat, but they both are descriptive of the Panamanian situation before the 1977 Canal treaties.

CONCLUSIONS AND ORGANIZATION

This study of United States-Panamanian relations over the Panama Canal thus is approached from the viewpoint of the linkages among the various political systems involved. The events in the domestic and foreign policies of one country are reacted to in the domestic and

foreign policies of the other. The actions of one or
both of the primary political systems involved in the
Canal dispute are reacted to by various international
systems and Third World nations. The manner in which
the domestic political systems adapt to events external
to that system varies according to the level of priority
the system places on the Canal issue.

This study also views the development of a nation's
foreign policy as primarily a product of the domestic
political system, both within the bureaucracy of that
system and otherwise. A heavy emphasis is placed on the
domestic origins of foreign policy, whether the result
is to make the Canal issue the major issue for Panama or
whether the issue had a low priority, as was the case
for the United States for a long period. Because of the
importance attached to the Canal issue by Panama, Panama
is viewed as a penetrated society.

Chapters 2 and 3 develop a number of historical
examples of linkage found in disputes between the United
States and Panama or any of the various other countries
that have been involved in the Canal issue. These chapters discuss the events before negotiations between the
U.S. and Panama were renewed in 1971.

Chapter 4 looks at the Panamanian political system
and probes the intimate relationship between Panama's
domestic politics and the Canal. This chapter also includes the relationship that exists between the residents of the Canal Zone and the Republic of Panama.

Chapter 5 discusses the disputes that make up the
Canal issue, especially the points of conflict between
the United States and Panama.

The search by the United States for an alternative
to the Panama Canal, notably a new sea-level canal, is
the subject of Chapter 6. The political and economic
advisability of a sea-level canal and where to build
such a canal are the principal questions of this chapter.

Chapter 7 develops the efforts of Panama to internationalize the Canal dispute beyond the bilateral
negotiations between the United States and Panama. The
role of the Organization of American States and the
United Nations in this effort will be discussed.

Chapter 8 discusses the longtime negotiations
between Panama and the United States that culminated in
the 1977 treaties.

Chapter 9 studies the domestic reaction to the
Canal question in the United States. Since this reaction, until 1976, was limited mostly to the U.S. Congress, Congress is the focus of much of this chapter.
However, as disputes between the executive branch and
the Congress and within the executive branch itself
developed during 1975, this aspect of domestic conflict
will also be included.

Chapter 10 continues the discussion of U.S. domestic

politics during the ratification of the 1977 treaties.
Conclusions and projections are drawn in Chapter 11.

NOTES

1. The 1955 revision of the 1903 treaty was signed in
Panama, however.
2. As to be expected with such a long-standing dispute, the
literature on the Canal and U.S.-Panamanian relations is extensive
both in English and Spanish. Spanish language publications are
particularly helpful in developing the Panamanian perspective, as
were confidential interviews with Panamanians conducted by the
authors in December 1970 and January 1971. Interviews were also
conducted at that time with Canal and U.S. embassy officials.
3. James N. Rosenau, ed., Linkage Politics: Essays on the
Convergence of National and International Systems (New York: The
Free Press, 1969)
4. Ibid., p. 45.
5. Wolfram F. Hanrieder, "Dissolving International Politics:
Reflections on the Nation-State," American Political Science Review
72 (1978):1280.
6. Rosenau, Linkage Politics, p. 9.
7. Morton H. Halperin and Arnold Kanter, eds., Readings in
American Foreign Policy: A Bureaucratic Perspective (Boston:
Little, Brown and Company, 1973), p. 2.
8. R. Barry Farrell, ed., Approaches to Comparative and
International Politics (Evanston, Ill.: Northwestern University
Press, 1966), p. 169.
9. Henry A. Kissinger, American Foreign Policy (New York:
W. W. Norton and Co., 1969), pp. 11-12.
10. Ibid., p. 13.
11. Thomas M. Franck and Edward Weisband, "Panama Paralysis,"
Foreign Policy 21 (Winter 1975-76):171.
12. Graham T. Allison, "Conceptual Models and the Cuban
Missile Crisis," American Political Science Review 63 (1969):691-93.
13. Ibid., p. 694.
14. James N. Rosenau, "Foreign Policy as Adaptive Behavior:
Some Preliminary Notes for a Theoretical Model," Comparative
Politics 2 (1970):367.
15. Ibid., p. 379.
16. Ibid., p. 381.
17. Wolfram F. Hanrieder, West German Foreign Policy 1949-
1963: International Pressure and Domestic Response (Palo Alto:
Stanford University Press, 1967), p. 228.
18. Ibid.

2
Genesis of the Canal

Relationships between nations are shaped by the number and variety of experiences which they have had with one another. The nature of these experiences often explains the images that the nations have of one another. The importance of past and present images lies in the fact that expectations about future behavior are conditioned by perceptions of past behavior. Thus, hostile or friendly attitudes are the products of events that have occurred in the past. The ability of nations to resolve their current conflicts frequently depends upon their success or failure in resolving past conflicts. Previous patterns of behavior based upon cooperation may inspire mutually trusting attitudes which may permit nations to resolve their differences with less difficulty than if they have had a long history of conflict behavior. Thus, the purpose of this chapter is to describe the historical background of relations between the United States and Panama with the expectation that this description will permit a better understanding of negotiations between the two nations.[1]

This historical background of U.S.-Panamanian relations might be seen as falling into three major periods, the first of which began when the United States developed an interest in the concept of a transisthmian canal and ended when the U.S. government assisted Panamanian rebels in breaking away from Colombia. A second time frame encompasses the relationships between the United States and the fledgling Republic from 1903 through 1936, when the United States gave up its legal authority to intervene in the affairs of Panama. The period from 1936 to the 1964 riots, particularly the breakdown in the relations between the two nations as Panama sought greater autonomy from U.S. influence and greater influence in the operation and defense of the Panama Canal, constitutes a third significant nexus of events. The period from the riots to the takeover of the government by the National Guard in 1968 will be discussed in chapter 3.

THE UNITED STATES AND PANAMA: THE EARLY YEARS

United States interest in a canal across the isthmus
of Panama began to take shape in the early 1800s when the
U.S. shipping industry suffered economic reverses as the
result of the government's efforts to avoid becoming en-
tangled in the Napoleonic Wars then raging in Europe.
U.S. efforts to avoid involvement took the form of an
embargo on trade with Europe. In their search for an
alternative, ship owners found that they could make a
profit in the silk, tea and spice trade of China. Historically, this proved to be a proud era for American
shipping, with giant clipper ships sailing around the
Horn, but the profit-minded New Englanders quickly realized that their profits would be even greater if the
long trip could be shortened by a canal across the
isthmus.
    During this period when a canal was first considered
by U.S. interests, two events occurred that would have
significance for the future construction of a transisthmian canal. First, a majority of the Latin American
nations were able to secure their independence from
Spain as the result of that country's inability to control its colonies during the French occupation of Spain.
Second, the United States put forth the Monroe Doctrine,
which warned European powers to avoid future efforts to
colonize or otherwise become involved in the affairs of
the Western Hemisphere. These two events indicated that
European nations would probably not be involved in the
building of a transisthmian canal and that the United
States would have a large voice in determining who would
construct a canal.
    In 1821, Panama secured its independence from Spain,
but by the following year, it had become a part of the
Republic of New Granada. Joining with New Granada was
to prove an on-again, off-again relationship which would
finally terminate with the revolution in 1903. Shortly
after it became part of New Granada, Panama was the host
for the first Inter-American Conference, held in 1825.
This meeting of leaders from the new Latin American republics was convoked by Simón Bolivar, the famed Latin
American emancipator, and discussed, among other things,
the possibility of constructing a canal across the isthmus. The United States did not take part in the conference, since its delegates failed to arrive until after
the meetings had been adjourned. U.S. domestic politics
probably played a part in the failure of the American
delegates to participate, since some pro-slavery factions feared that the Panamanian Conference might pass
a resolution condemning slavery in the hemisphere.
    Ten years later, there was evidence of continuing
U.S. interest in a transisthmian canal when Alexander
Biddle, president of the Second United States Bank, was

appointed to study possible sites for a canal in Panama
and Nicaragua. However, Biddle's study had little effect on U.S. efforts to build a canal, for he disregar-
ded his instructions and proceeded to Bogota, where he
obtained a private concession to build a Panamanian
canal.

Nothing resulted from Biddle's concession, but in
December 1846, U.S. interests became closely identified
with Panama when the U.S. signed a treaty with the Republic of New Granada to secure and protect a right-of-
way across the isthmus. This treaty was known as the
Bidlack-Mallorino Treaty.[2] The main provisions of the
treaty reflected the needs and the desires of both the
United States and the Republic of New Granada. Article
35 of the Bidlack-Mallorino Treaty guaranteed the United
States the right of passage across the isthmus along
all natural roads and along those railways or canals
which might be built in the future. In exchange, the
United States agreed to guarantee the sovereignty of New
Granada over the province of Panama and to assure the
neutrality of Panama. This reassured the government of
New Granada, which was nervous about the territorial aspirations of Great Britain in Central America. The
neutrality guarantee made President Polk reluctant to
submit the treaty to the Senate despite its other desirable aspects. The need for such a treaty was reinforced
shortly thereafter, however, when the United States
signed the Treaty of Guadalupe Hidalgo, which transferred California from Mexico to U.S. control.[3] Now the
continental United States fronted on both the Atlantic
and the Pacific.

The importance of the Bidlack-Mallorino Treaty cannot be minimized for either the United States or the
Republic of Panama. Wayne D. Bray argues that from the
signing of this treaty "the United States has continu-
ously exercised some attribute of sovereignty over the
isthmus, and conversely the sovereignty of Panama and
its predecessors has been less than absolute."[4] He also
declares that "the threads of contemporary legal controversies over the legitimacy of the enclave lead back to
the same convention."[5]

During the period from 1846 to 1903, the United
States landed troops on the Panamanian isthmus seven
times at the invitation of the government of New Granada
or its successor, Colombia. Each of these landings complied with the provisions of the Treaty of 1846 whereby
the United States had agreed to guarantee the sovereignty of Colombia against other claimants. The duration of
these troop landings varied from a few hours to several
weeks. An eighth landing, the only deviation from the
established pattern, occurred in 1902, when an American
naval officer prevented Colombian troops from traveling
on the Panama railroad to put down an insurrection. His

interference provoked a strong protest from Colombia, and later the United States apologized for the officer's actions.

The year 1849 saw U.S. interest in a transisthmian canal increase sharply as gold was discovered at Sutter's Mill in California. The gold discovery sparked a massive transit of fortune-seekers from the eastern United States to the west coast. The overland trip across the continental United States was both difficult and time-consuming. Many travelers found it much easier to take a ship to the Atlantic side of Panama, then proceed by boat and mule to the Pacific coast, where they could await the arrival of ships that would pick them up and carry them on to the gold fields. The profit potential of this large number of travelers finally resulted in the construction of a railroad across the isthmus. Completed in 1855, the railroad generated fantastic profits for its owners and sparked renewed interest in a canal. About this time, various interest groups in the United States circulated petitions calling upon the Congress to take action to build a transisthmian canal.

Even before the railroad was completed, the United States entered into an agreement with Great Britain whereby the two countries agreed to share equally in the costs and responsibilities for constructing a transisthmian canal. Signed in 1850, this agreement, known as the Clayton-Bulwer Treaty, was clearly contrary to the intent of the Monroe Doctrine, but U.S. reaction to the treaty was limited because of the agitated state of our domestic politics at the time.[6] However, later on, American officials would acknowledge that the signing of the Clayton-Bulwer Treaty was a serious mistake and was the primary reason why the construction of a canal across the isthmus did not begin earlier. It was clearly a diplomatic triumph for the British, who not only blocked the United States from constructing a canal independently but also retained their rights to territory in British Honduras.

The next turbulent decade in U.S. politics saw American interests diverted away from the construction of a canal as the nation fought the Civil War. Following the war, renewed interest in a canal was demonstrated in the suggestion of Secretary of State Seward that the Clayton-Bulwer Treaty be abrogated. About this time, the United States invoked the Monroe Doctrine when it suspected Ferdinand de Lesseps of trying to persuade the government of Colombia to abrogate the Bidlack-Mallorino Treaty, an action which would allow him to build a canal across the isthmus under French auspices.

American interest in constructing a canal waned with the completion of a railroad across the continental United States in 1876. But a new chapter was about to be written in the Panama Canal story as a French adventurer, Lucien Napoleon Bonaparte Wyse, discovered that the U.S. held the concession solely for the construction of a railroad across the isthmus and not for the construction of a canal. He saw the economic advantages of this omission and was able to secure a concession from the government of Colombia to build a canal subject only to his ability to obtain approval from the directors of the Panama Railroad Company. Wyse eventually obtained this approval by buying a majority of the stock in the Panama Railroad at inflated prices. The price of the railroad company shares jumped from a par value of $100 to $250, thereby raising the cost of the railroad to twenty-five million dollars.

Wyse's concession would probably have been worthless if he had not been able to convince Ferdinand de Lesseps, builder of the Suez Canal, that the latter could add to his great fame by constructing a canal across the isthmus. De Lesseps became a central figure in a scheme to build the canal through private funding. The story of the French efforts to build a canal across the isthmus is a combination of heroism, tragedy, stupidity, villainy and greed, a story that is better told elsewhere. Suffice it to say that the French efforts to construct a sea-level canal failed because of disease, insufficient planning, financial problems and declining morale as the French fought the green hell that was Panama. By 1889, the French had essentially given up their plans to build a canal after spending a quarter of a billion dollars.

During this period, American interest in a canal was at a low level and remained so until 1898, when the battleship Oregon made its historic voyage around the tip of South America at the beginning of the Spanish-American War. The warship took 68 days to complete its voyage, and proponents of an inter-oceanic canal used the opportunity that the voyage represented to publicize the need for a trans-isthmian canal. From this time on, there would be more and greater efforts to persuade Congress to take the necessary steps to approve and finance a canal.

While domestic pressure was building on Congress, there was serious debate going on within the executive branch about the legal rights of the United States to build a canal without the participation of the British. Although some U.S. politicians favored ignoring the Clayton-Bulwer Treaty, State Department officials were reluctant to take this drastic step. Despite U.S. efforts, the British resisted changing the treaty until their relations with Germany had deteriorated to a level where they perceived British participation in an isthmian canal as secondary to their need for U.S. support and friendship in the impending crisis. An initial effort to abrogate the Clayton-Bulwer Treaty was

unsuccessful, for the British insisted that the United
States could not have the right to fortify and defend
the canal. The United States Senate was unwilling to
ratify a treaty that did not allow for U.S. defense.
Finally, in 1901, representatives of the two governments
signed a second Hay-Pauncefote Treaty, which simply ignored the question of defending and fortifying the
canal. By implication, now the United States had the
right to construct, operate and defend a Central American canal. The new treaty did contain the concession,
at British insistence, that any canal would be open to
merchantmen and warships of all nations without discrimination in either treatment or tolls.

The ratification of the Hay-Pauncefote Treaty removed an important obstacle to the construction of an
isthmian canal solely by the United States, but it did
not resolve the issue as to where the Canal was to be
built. Proponents of a transisthmian canal were divided as to whether Nicaragua or Panama would furnish the
better construction site. Initially, the supporters of
a Nicaraguan site appeared to have the upper hand, but
while Congress was debating the issue, nature took a
hand. The volcano on the French island of Martinique
exploded, sending clouds of smoke and ash around the
world. One enterprising advocate of the Panama route
rushed out and bought some Nicaraguan stamps picturing
smoking volcanos. These stamps were then pasted on letters to congressmen about to vote on a bill dealing with
alternative canal routes. How successful this ploy was
is not known, but in 1902 Congress passed the Spooner
Act, which authorized the construction of a canal at
Panama utilizing the work already done by the French
Canal Company, if the necessary financial and legal arrangements could be worked out with the company and the
government of Colombia. The provisions of the Spooner
Act provided that President Roosevelt could: (1) buy
all the assets of the French Canal Company for forty
million dollars; (2) negotiate with the Republic of Colombia to acquire the rights and land necessary for the
construction of a transisthmian canal; (3) begin construction of a canal upon the successful conclusion of
the previous steps. If the president could not accomplish the previous steps within "a reasonable time,"
then he was to proceed with the construction of a canal
within Nicaragua.

Although the representatives of the French Canal
Company initially demanded 100 million dollars for their
assets, they eventually agreed to accept the U.S. offer
of forty million dollars. Having accomplished this
step, the U.S. government found it more difficult to
achieve an understanding with Colombia.

In 1902, diplomats from the United States and Colombia signed the Hay-Herran Treaty, which transferred

to the United States the French Canal Company's right to
build a canal. The Hay-Herran Treaty resulted from U.S.
pressure on the Colombian representatives to act quickly
or the United States would turn to the Nicaraguan site
as provided for in the Spooner Act. Despite this pressure, however, the Colombians were able to secure a
treaty more favorable to their interests than the Panamanians would after their successful revolution. Under
the terms of the Hay-Herran Treaty, Colombia retained
sovereignty while the United States was allowed administrative control for the purposes of exercising police
and sanitary functions. Colombia granted the United
States a 100-year lease over a six-mile-wide (ten-kilo-
meter) strip across the isthmus in exchange for an initial ten-million-dollar payment and $250,000 annual
rent. Shortly after receiving the treaty, the United
States Senate ratified it without amendment on 17 March
1903.

The Colombian Senate had not yet ratified the treaty, and domestic pressures were building to reject it.
Colombia grew to feel that it could secure better terms
if ratification were delayed. The French Canal Company's concession was due to lapse shortly, and Colombia
apparently hoped to secure some economic inducements
from the French Company in exchange for Colombian approval of the treaty. Finally, yielding to strong domestic
pressures, the Colombian Senate rejected the treaty by a
vote of twenty-four to nothing, with the three strongest
supporters of a canal abstaining. Representatives from
the Province of Panama were outraged and warned that rebellion was a strong possibility if the treaty were not
approved. The stage was now set for the notorious
little revolution that would give the United States and
President Roosevelt the coveted rights for building a
trans-isthmian canal.

Colombia's failure to ratify the treaty had been
disappointing to several groups: the Americans who had
hoped to build the canal at Panama; the Panamanians, who
saw the possibility of an economic boom if the canal
were built in their country; and the French investors
who had seen a chance to recoup some of their losses.
In the months following the treaty's rejection, these
groups were brought together through the efforts of an
indefatigable Frenchman, Philippe Bunau-Varilla, who represented the French Canal Company. The product of his
efforts was an independent Panama whose leaders would
agree to a treaty giving the United States the right to
build a canal.

A group of Panamanian conspirators sent one of
their members, Dr. Manual Amador, to the United States
to determine what kind of assistance they could obtain
if they were to rebel against Colombia. Dr. Amador was
unsuccessful in his efforts until he met Philippe Bunau-
Varilla, who encouraged the Panamanians to go ahead with

plans for a revolt. Bunau-Varilla's encouragement was extremely important because the conspirators were cautious men, and they were not about to do anything that might put their necks into a noose, even though the potential rewards for success were great. In addition to raising the morale of the conspirators, Bunau-Varilla promised to secure the protection of U.S. warships to prevent the landing of Colombian troops to put down the revolt and promised to pay them $100,000 when the Panamanians notified him that the revolt had been successful. To obtain the money, the Panamanians had to appoint him their Ambassador Extraordinary and Minister Plenipotentiary. Although reluctant to agree to Bunau-Varilla's demands, the Panamanians eventually did so in order to obtain the necessary funds to assure the success of the revolution.

The degree to which there was U.S. involvement in this intrigue is unclear, and the resulting ambiguity has provoked a great deal of controversy over what role the United States played in the revolution. Following the failure of the Colombians to ratify the Hay-Herran Treaty, President Theodore Roosevelt consulted with his advisors, and they agreed that several alternatives were available. First, the United States could forget about building a canal across the isthmus at Panama and construct one in Nicaragua. Second, it could proceed with the construction of a canal in Panama using the provisions of previous treaties as justification. Finally, the United States government could choose to do nothing and await the course of events.

For at least two reasons, the third alternative seemed to have the most to recommend it. In the first place, the relationship between Colombia and its province of Panama had historically been tumultuous, as evidenced by the need to land U.S. troops at least eight times to help the Colombians to put down uprisings in their rebellious province. In the second, Panama was geographically isolated from Bogota and often felt, with some justification, that its interests were ignored by the central government. Several times, Panama had taken advantage of clauses in the Colombian constitution to declare its independence but had always been returned to its subordinate status. Moreover, the drafting of a new Colombian constitution in 1885 had given the government in Bogota even more central authority and had relegated Panama to a secondary provincial status. Thus, it was not unrealistic to expect that a Panamanian nation, independent of Colombia, could come about in a few months, particularly since rumors of a possible revolt were circulating.

Whatever the decisions made by Roosevelt and his advisors, U.S. warships were in Colón Harbor on 3 November 1903 when the revolt broke out. Their orders were to prevent Colombian troops from landing to put down the

uprising. Subsequently, these actions were justified by
citing the Bidlack-Mallorino Treaty, which declared that
the United States was compelled by the terms of that
treaty to prevent any actions which might cut off communications across the isthmus.

The actions of the U.S. navy assured that the revolution would be a success. When Bunau-Varilla was notified that the rebellion had succeeded, he immediately
went to work to draft a treaty that would meet with the
approval of the U.S. government. At first, the United
States hoped to enter into an agreement with the new
government similar to the one negotiated with Colombia.
However, Bunau-Varilla changed the new treaty in several
significant ways in order to steer it past opposition in
the United States Senate. These changes were to shape
the nature of relations between the two nations for the
next seventy-five years.

Although much of the wording of the Hay-Herran
Treaty and the Hay/Bunau-Varilla Treaty was identical,
the latter was significantly more advantageous to the
United States. Article 3 of the Hay/Bunau-Varilla
Treaty granted to the United States "all the rights,
power and authority . . . which the United States would
possess and exercise if it were the sovereign of the
territory . . . to the entire exclusion of the exercise
by the Republic of Panama of any such sovereign rights,
powers, or authority."[7] The United States was granted
a ten-mile-wide strip across the isthmus as opposed to
the six-mile-wide grant in the Hay-Herran Treaty. A-
nother significant difference was that the United States
was granted these rights "in perpetuity," whereas the
lease offered by Colombia was for 100 years.[8]

Secretary of State Hay, who co-signed the treaty,
saw no reason to revise this generosity, and Bunau-
Varilla informed Panama that a canal treaty had been
signed. The Panamanians were shocked and argued that
Bunau-Varilla had acted illegally. Panama later ratified the treaty, nevertheless, when threatened with the
withdrawal of the American fleet if the treaty were not
approved. This threat became even more meaningful when
the Colombians offered significant concessions in a new
treaty if the U.S. would refuse to recognize the new
government.

Colombian efforts to persuade the United States
failed, and the U.S. recognized the new government of
Panama almost immediately after Secretary of State Hay
received a cable from the U.S. vice-consul in Panama
that the revolt had been successful.

U.S.-PANAMANIAN RELATIONS: THE FORMATIVE YEARS, 1903-
1936

During the years from 1903 to 1936, the Republic of
Panama could be characterized as a penetrated system.

James Rosenau has described a penetrated system as "one that has been taken over by another system, a state but not a state, in which non-members of a national society participate directly and authoritatively, through actions taken jointly with the society members, in either the allocation of its values or the mobilization of support on behalf of its goals."[9]

Rosenau's description closely resembles the type of relationship that existed between the United States and Panama during this period. In promoting its own interests, the United States set limits on the decision-making capacity of Panamanian policy-makers. Initially, Panama's leaders accepted the necessity for a subordinate role in the formulation of policy. They rationalized this role as a means whereby other objectives, notably preserving their security by preventing Colombia from re-asserting its hegemony, might be achieved. The result was that although the United States and its representatives allowed the Panamanian government a considerable latitude in formulating domestic policies, the U.S. government reserved an implicit veto over any actions that it considered contrary to its interests. This is not to argue that there were not occasions when there occurred genuine collaboration between the two nations based on a mutuality of interest; but in many policy areas, the leaders of the smaller nations were not permitted to consider alternatives to U.S. policy. As time went by, this dominant-subordinate relationship would produce ever greater conflicts as their respective objectives became more incompatible.

Although he does not explicitly refer to Panama as a "penetrated society," Professor Edwin C. Hoyt provides numerous examples that illustrate the role that the United States played in the affairs of Panama during this time. Hoyt notes that "what it amounted to was that throughout this period the United States was in a position to interpret the law for itself. Politically secure, and vastly stronger than Panama, it assumed a law-giving instead of a law-bargaining role. There were some concessions on economic points, but it was always made clear that these concessions were granted on sufferance, and that the United States retained freedom to end them at will."[10]

The United States was granted the right to intervene in the internal affairs of the Republic of Panama by Article 136 of the 1904 Panamanian Constitution. This article declared that "the government of the United States may intervene in any part of the Republic of Panama to re-establish public peace and constitutional order in the event of their being disturbed, provided that the action shall, by public treaty, assume or have assumed the obligation of guaranteeing the independence and sovereignty of this republic."[11]

Gustavo Mellander, who studied U.S. involvement in

Panama in the years following independence, suggested
that U.S. officials did not want the responsibility
which Article 136 placed upon them.[12] They believed
that they had sufficient authority granted them by the
Hay/Bunau-Varilla Treaty, but ultimately they would use
the article frequently in their dealings with Panama.
Article 136 was probably inserted by the newly installed
and nervous Panamanian leaders who saw the provision as
a means of assuring that Colombia would not regain control of Panama. Presumably, if some Colombian loyalist
were to foment rebellion, it would be the responsibility
of the United States to come to the assistance of Panama. Their haste to gain such assurances led the Panamanian leaders to overlook the future when the majority of
their dealings would be with the United States.

Although U.S. interventions in Panama were the most
overt manifestations of U.S. influence, there were a
number of other areas where the United States forced Panama to accept decisions it disliked.

One problem area concerned the procedures for expropriating territory necessary for the construction,
maintenance, operation, sanitation and protection of the
Canal and the Zone. The 1903 treaty stated that land
outside the Canal Zone could be expropriated if necessary, but it was left unclear how such expropriations
should take place. The Panamanians argued that expropriation was to be a negotiated procedure, while U.S.
officials said that the decision for expropriation was
to be determined by the U.S. alone. In practice, U.S.
officials frequently expropriated land without bothering
to notify Panamanian officials. Another controversy
arose over whether Panama ought to be compensated for
land outside the Canal Zone. The Panamanians wanted
payment for their land, but the U.S. contended that the
$10,000,000 payment the U.S. had made to Panama for the
concession included land outside the Zone. No satisfactory resolution of these issues developed, and the problem periodically arose whenever the United States would
expropriate land. To the Panamanians, these actions
often appeared arbitrary and capricious without any
clear justification for either the expropriation or its
size. The Panamanians protested the taking of 1,160
acres out of 1,410 on the resort island of Tobago. U.S.
officials claimed that this expropriation was necessary
for the defense of the canal, but, eventually, they
bowed to Panamanian protests and settled for 37 acres.

Another dispute developed when the United States
decided to impose tariffs on the importation of goods
into the Canal Zone. This dispute became so heated that
it required a visit by Secretary of War William Howard
Taft to bring about a compromise with Panama over the
imposition of the Dingley Tariff. Other problems resulted from the commercial competition between the U.S.
commissaries in the Zone and merchants in the Republic.

The Panamanian merchants demanded that the commissaries stop selling goods to workers who lived in Panama.
Another source of controversy was U.S. involvement in the economic affairs of the Republic. U.S. policy was to make it extremely difficult for foreign corporations to invest in Panama. When British stockholders established a Panamanian corporation, their action provoked Senator Borah of Idaho to seek an investigation by the State Department. The investigation produced nothing but was an indication of the suspicion which resulted from investment in Panama by other than U.S. corporations. Business in Panama was almost entirely controlled by U.S. interests, and U.S. banks handled the sale of Panamanian securities and investments. The balance of trade between the two countries always proved to be favorable to the United States by a ratio of four or five to one. Not only did the U.S. maintain Panama as a preserve for U.S. business interests, it also objected to the Panamanians undertaking any projects related to the construction of railroads, highways or means of communication without the prior approval of U.S. officials. Panamanians wondered why they could not send telegrams without having to use American installations.

Disagreements over domestic issues were the greatest source of controversy during this period, but American intrusion into the foreign relations of Panama also led to antagonism. Following its independence, Panama assumed Colombian claims to some disputed territory in the Chiriqui region on the Costa Rican frontier. The boundary dispute intensified when two American corporations with competing concessions from the governments of Costa Rica and Panama attempted to reconcile their interests. In 1907, the U.S. State Department informed the Panamanian government that it was important that Panama submit the boundary issue to arbitration. Although the Panamanians objected, they eventually agreed. The State Department recommended that the Chief Justice of the U.S. Supreme Court or some other high American judicial figure be invited to arbitrate. In 1911, Chief Justice Edward T. White agreed to be arbitrator. Unfortunately for Panama, continued non-recognition by Colombia prejudiced its ability to prepare the case for arbitration. Panama could not obtain all of the documents necessary for justifying its position, since many of them were in the Colombian foreign office. Thus, in 1914, the arbitration decision went against Panama. The award provoked the Panamanians to reject the White decision on grounds that the Chief Justice had exceeded his authority. The border dispute threatened to become violent, but the attentions of both parties were diverted as the events of World War I intervened.
Resumption of the dispute developed in 1921 when Costa Rica invaded the disputed territory. The Panamanians notified Washington of the invasion, but American

officials were unwilling to take action for fear that
any policy they developed might be inconsistent with the
policies of the incoming Republicans, who had replaced
the administration of Woodrow Wilson. Eventually, the
United States sent marines into the disputed territory
to force the Panamanians to accept the White decision.
No one is quite sure why the United States was unwilling
to listen to Panamanian arguments, but it was speculated
that the State Department was interested in strengthen-
ing Costa Rican good will as well as diminishing British
influence in the area. Possibly, other pressure was
brought by the implied threat of other Central American
republics that they would go to war on the side of Costa
Rica.

The ability of Panama to resist the dictates of the
United States in both foreign and domestic matters was
compromised by the continuing threat that Colombia might
try to reassert its sovereignty over its former province. This threat was not removed until April 1921,
when the U.S. Senate ratified the Thomson-Urritia Treaty.[13] The treaty had been negotiated in 1914. By approving this treaty, the United States admitted that it
had violated the Treaty of 1846 by signing the Hay/
Bunau-Varilla Treaty with Panama. Although the Senate
refused to accept a treaty provision expressing "sincere
regret" over U.S. actions, it did agree to pay Colombia
twenty-five million dollars for rights which the United
States had improperly acquired. The Senate reduced
Colombia's transit rights but gave free rights of
passage through the Canal for Colombian ships.

The normalization of relations with Colombia allowed Panama to express its dissatisfaction with U.S.
interference in its affairs. This dissatisfaction culminated in 1926 with a request that the unsatisfactory
provisions of the 1903 treaty be revised. At this time,
the government of Panama submitted a list of thirty-two
questions that they wished to negotiate. The product of
these negotiations was the Kellogg-Alfaro Treaty, which
made few concessions to the Panamanians other than regulations on commissary sales to still the protests of
merchants in the Republic. Moreover, the proposed treaty imposed additional obligations upon Panama, including
the requirement that the Republic become involved in any
war in which the United States found itself. The terms
of the proposed treaty outraged Panamanian sensibili-
ties, and public threats were made against any legisla-
tor who favored its passage. In the resulting domestic
furor, no one was surprised when Panama did not ratify
the treaty.

During the controversy over the treaty, the League
of Nations became inadvertently involved when the Panamanian delegate to that organization requested that it
arbitrate the question of Panamanian sovereignty. Two
days later, the United States made a categorical

announcement that there was nothing to arbitrate between the two countries. Furthermore, the United States gave notice that it would allow no external influence whatsoever to interfere with its relations with the Republic of Panama.

Despite this initial failure to revise the terms of the 1903 treaty, relations between the United States and Panama began to change in the early 1930s. Pressures on the government of Panama increased as the Great Depression brought severe economic problems to that country. Also, for the first time, the United States chose not to intervene when the political opposition staged a successful coup d'état. The election that followed brought to power Harmodia Arias, who was determined to alleviate the effects of the depression by strong economic measures. When his efforts failed to bring about the recovery, he took steps to gain a larger share of the benefits from the operation of the Panama Canal. Since Panama's economy depended so heavily on the Canal, it seemed logical to gain a larger share of the benefits derived from the Canal to solve Panama's problems.

In 1933, Arias went to Washington to seek some minor revisions of the 1903 treaty. He received a sympathetic response from President Franklin Delano Roosevelt, who was in the process of formulating the "Good Neighbor" policy in Latin America. Following his meeting with Roosevelt, Arias began separate negotiations with the Departments of War, Navy and State. Secretary of State Cordell Hull was more sympathetic to the Panamanian requests than were the secretaries of the other two departments. Arias' discussions with Hull resulted in a Memorandum of Understanding, which was essentially a victory for the Panamanian position. Hull appointed Sumner Welles, an experienced Caribbean diplomat, to represent the United States in the negotiations.

After an article-by-article examination of the 1903 treaty, the negotiations resulted in four draft treaties, two of which were eventually ratified and two more of which were allowed to rest in the Senate Committee on Foreign Relations until 1947, when they were withdrawn for further consideration. The most important of the four draft treaties was to become known as the Hull-Alfaro Treaty.[14] The important provisions of this treaty were (1) to strike article 1 of the 1903 Treaty, thereby abrogating the right of the United States to intervene in either Panama City or Colón if U.S. officials decided it was necessary; (2) to give Panamanians the right of transit across the Canal Zone; and (3) to remove the right of "eminent domain" over Panamanian territory by Canal administrators. The perpetuity clause remained unchanged. The United States increased Panama's annuity from $250,000 to $430,000 to compensate for the U.S. going off the gold standard.

The treaties were signed in 1936 but were not

ratified until 1939, when the United States actively began to seek allies throughout the Western Hemisphere in
anticipation of U.S. involvement in World War II. The
Hull-Alfaro Treaty was only the first step in the long
process of altering the relationship between the United
States and Panama. One indicator of the changed relationship between the two nations came in 1939 when the
U.S. elevated its diplomatic legation in Panama City to
ambassadorial status. The ratification of the Hull-
Alfaro Treaty plus the need to resist the growing Axis
threat served to delay conflicts between the two countries until after World War II.

U.S.-PANAMANIAN RELATIONS: THE SEARCH FOR CHANGE, 1936-1964

The United States Senate delayed the ratification
of the Hull-Alfaro Treaty until 1939 because of inten-
sive lobbying by the War Department. This lobbying resulted from concern by officials in the War Department
over the abrogation of article 1, which had justified
U.S. intervention in the Republic. They believed that
doing away with article 1 would seriously compromise
their ability to defend the Canal. The State Department
acknowledged the War Department's concern but continued
to support the non-intervention policy affirmed by the
United States at Montevideo in 1933 and reaffirmed at
Buenos Aires in 1936. The State Department believed
that non-intervention was fundamental to the concept of
a Good Neighbor Policy and the improvement of U.S. relations with other countries in the Western Hemisphere.

Eventually, as the ratification process dragged on,
Panama conceded two points to overcome Senate reluctance
to ratify the treaty: first, that the U.S. military
could conduct maneuvers on Panamanian territory and,
second, that the U.S. could take unilateral measures to
defend the Canal if there were insufficient time to consult with Panamanian officials. These concessions resulted in quick ratification by the Senate in July 1939.

The concessions did not resolve another problem
which had emerged from the 1936 treaty and which dealt
with changes in procedures for acquiring defense sites
outside the Canal Zone. Previously, the military had
been able to acquire additional defense sites by citing
article 2 of the 1903 treaty, which granted the United
States the right to territory outside the Canal Zone if
it were necessary to the operation or protection of the
Canal. In practice, the military had simply declared a
need for additional territory and then proceeded to deal
with the private owner for use of the land. Now the
provisions of the 1936 treaty stipulated that additional
territory in the Republic could be acquired only after
negotiations with the government of Panama. This change
frustrated the U.S. military, as they found it necessary

to revise their defense concept for the Panama Canal.
Development of airpower required that the military extend their defense perimeter beyond the Canal Zone to
assure adequate time to respond to enemy aircraft. This
necessitated additional sites in the Republic of Panama.

When the U.S. military requested additional sites
in the Republic, disagreements developed over the length
of the leases and the question of which government would
have jurisdiction over Panamanians employed on the defense sites. Initially, the military asked for 99-year
leases and absolute jurisdiction over the bases. The
Panamanians refused, for they saw this as a prelude to
the establishment of a series of "mini Canal Zones"
throughout the Republic. Negotiations became confused
as President Arnulfo Arias, highly nationalistic, saw
the discussions over the defense sites as an opportunity
to air other issues not directly related to the problem
of defending the Canal. He made the resolution of the
defense sites issue contingent on the consideration of
such issues as the smuggling of goods from the Canal
Zone and the problem of competition between the Canal
Zone commissaries and Panamanian businesses.

Negotiations between the two countries proceeded
slowly until Arias was overthrown late in 1941. In February 1942, the United States signed a Defense Sites Agreement with the new president of Panama, which provided
that the United States occupation of the sites would end
one year following the peace treaty ending World War II.

Controversy between the United States and Panama
broke out shortly after the conclusion of World War II.
The Panamanian foreign minister and his predecessor appeared before Panama's constitutional assembly to give
their interpretation of the 1942 Defense Sites Agreement.
During their appearance, the two officials took the position that the agreement expired on 1 September 1946 and
that the U.S. forces would have to vacate the sites by
that date.

Secretary of State James Byrnes responded to the
Panamanian declaration by announcing that the United
States would abide by the 1942 agreement and would begin
to evacuate the sites. The United States continued to
seek defense sites in the Republic, and negotiations
culminated on 10 December 1947, when representatives for
the two countries signed the Postwar Defense Bases Pact,
which gave the United States a ten-year lease on thirteen bases with an option to renew for an additional
ten-year lease. There was no need for the U.S. Senate
to ratify the agreement, as it was concluded as an executive agreement, but the Panamanian government had to
submit it for legislative ratification. Intense opposition to the agreement developed in Panama, and, bowing
to these pressures, the National Assembly voted fifty-
one to nothing to reject the agreement on 22 December
1947.

Following the rejection of the Defense Sites Agreement, the U.S. military withdrew from all its bases outside the Canal Zone. The evacuation proceeded expeditiously and proved to have a considerable impact on both Panamanian employees who lost their jobs because of the closing of the bases and also on Panamanian businessmen who suffered financial reverses as the flow of dollars from the bases came to a halt.

The overall effect of the U.S. withdrawal was to depress an inherently weak Panamanian economy. Eventually, it appeared that the Panamanian leadership would have to forego their nationalistic aspirations and renegotiate the defense bases issue. This proved difficult, however, because of the unstable political situation that prevailed during the late 1940s and early 1950s. Numerous presidents came and went, including three in one week. Ex-President Arnulfo Arias assumed office for a second time and was ousted for a second time after a bloody shoot-out at the presidential palace in 1951. The only real source of stability in Panama during this period was Jose Antonio Remón, Chief of the Guardia Nacional, or national police, who exercised real power behind the scenes until 1954. At that time, Remón tired of his background role and decided to run for president. Assisted by a broad party coalition and by his own control over the governmental machinery, Remón won on a political platform primarily stressing his anti-communism.

Shortly after coming to office in October 1952, Remón began pushing a foreign policy which called for a revision of the 1903 and 1936 treaties that structured the relations between his country and the United States. To expedite his policy, he appointed two special ambassadors to go to Washington and assist the regular ambassador in securing these revisions. On the occasion of the ambassadors' departure, the new president sought to promote an image of national unity by bringing all of his former opponents together (except Arnulfo Arias) for a mass meeting demonstrating the desire of all Panamanians for a satisfactory resolution of their grievances with the United States.

The U.S. Department of State was reluctant to negotiate any revision of the treaties, and it was not until President Eisenhower invited his Panamanian counterpart to the White House that serious negotiations got underway. Remón personally presented his case to Eisenhower, who directed the State Department to consider all Panamanian demands rather than simply to limit the talks to a consideration of how the 1903 and 1936 treaties were to be interpreted.

Despite Eisenhower's direct intervention, the negotiations proved to be long and difficult. Many of the twenty-one demands submitted by the Panamanians were rejected as non-negotiable by the State Department,

particularly demands dealing with the scope of U.S. control over the Zone and the length of time the U.S. was
to exercise that control. In their turn, the U.S. negotiators presented the Panamanians with an early draft of
a treaty calling upon the latter never again to ask for
revision of the basic treaties. The Panamanians had not
responded to the U.S. demands when Remón was assassinated
at a Panama racetrack on 2 January 1955. Despite Remón's death, the Panamanian foreign minister and the
U.S. ambassador signed a Treaty of Mutual Understanding
and Cooperation, as well as a Memorandum of Understanding, in late January.[15] The Remón-Eisenhower Treaty, as
the 1955 treaty was to be known, did not respond to the
most important of Remón's demands. In retrospect, it
appears that the Panamanians, specifically the commercial elite, accepted a less-than-satisfactory treaty for
the economic benefits that would accrue.

Some of the more important economic benefits which
Panama was to receive from the 1955 treaty and memorandum of understanding were an increase in the annuity
from $430,000 to $1,930,000; an agreement that Panama
could tax all its citizens residing within the Canal
Zone; and an effective end to the hated gold/silver
standard which gave Panamanians a lower wage than their
American counterparts for doing the same job. Now Panamanians would be paid by the same wage standard as U.S.
employees. An equally important part of the treaty was
a promise that the Canal Zone Company would phase out
many of its marginal businesses that shut out Panamanian
commercial interests from a large portion of the Canal
Zone market. In addition to these economic benefits,
the United States agreed to join together the two parts
of the Republic by replacing the ferry across the Canal
with a suspension bridge.

In exchange for these considerations, the U.S. received several concessions, including a fifteen-year
lease on land in the Rio Hato region, which could be
used for a military training base and a maneuver area.
However, the treaty satisfied neither the U.S. nor Panama. The United States did not receive the kind of assurances it wanted if it were to continue to control and
operate the Panama Canal, while the treaty did not effectively respond to the emotional and symbolic issues
that troubled Panamanians. As long as the question of
sovereignty and the perpetuity clause remained unresolved issues, the tensions between the United States and
Panama would remain.

The continuing tensions were demonstrated vividly
by two separate events in the months following the ratification of the treaties. The first was the visit to
Panama of Juan Peron, exiled Argentinean dictator, a
visit that sparked anti-American demonstrations. A second event that revealed the tensions between the two
countries occurred in October 1956, when Egypt's ruler,

Gamel Abdul Nasser, nationalized the Suez Canal. The subsequent conference of twenty-two nations that met to discuss the Suez crisis did not include any representative from Panama despite the fact that ships under its flag were the largest users of the Suez Canal. John Foster Dulles, U.S. secretary of state, was quoted as saying that the U.S. representatives could effectively speak for Panamanian interests. Panamanians were outraged by this affront to their patria, or fatherland.

The potential for further problems between the U.S. and Panama was increased as the U.S. Congress failed to act quickly to implement the main provisions of the 1955 treaty. The delay was reflected in the fact that the Congress did not pass the necessary legislation for building the bridge across the Canal until 1958, shortly before the visit of the president's brother, Milton Eisenhower, to Panama. Congressional delays, along with recurring incidents, negated the positive impact of the economic gains that Panama enjoyed from the treaty. The years following the ratification of the treaties would see Panama experience an economic boom while growing increasingly belligerent about continued U.S. control of the Panama Canal and the Canal Zone.

NOTES

1. When this chapter was written, there was no complete history of U.S.-Panamanian relations. However, in the interim, a diplomatic historian, Walter LaFeber, has written The Panama Canal: The Crisis in Historical Perspective (Oxford University Press: New York, 1978). This book provides a comprehensive, although at times sketchy, view of the main events which have occurred in U.S.-Panamanian relations. Two other works are useful in providing an overall perspective: Thomas Weil et al., Area Handbook for Panama (Washington, D.C.: Government Printing Office, 1972) and U.S., Congress, Senate, Committee on Foreign Relations, A Chronology of Events Relating to the Panama Canal, by the Congressional Research Service (Washington, D.C.: Government Printing Office, 1977).

To review the events dating from the early 1800s to 1968, it was necessary to use a number of sources. For the pre-independence period, the best source is Dwight C. Miner, The Fight for the Panama Canal Route (New York: Octagon Books, Inc., 1940). For the story of the revolt against Colombia and the formation of the Republic of Panama, see David McCullough, The Path Between the Seas (New York: Simon and Schuster, 1977) and G. A. Mellander, The United States in Panamanian Politics: The Intriguing Formative Years (Danville, Ill.: The Interstate Printers and Publishers, Inc., 1971). An admirable work that has not been surpassed for its description of the protectorate period from 1903-1935 is William McCain's book, The United States and the Republic of Panama (Durham, N.C.: Duke University Press, 1937). McCain's description of the contentious relations between the U.S. and Panama is supplemented by two articles by Lester Langley. These are "Negotiating New Treaties with Panama: 1936," Hispanic American Historical Review

48 (May 1968):220-33, and "World Crisis and the Good Neighbor Policy, 1936-41," Americas 24 (October 1967):137-52.

Two books by Lawrence Ealy are useful in understanding more recent U.S.-Panamanian relations. These books have been particularly useful in showing how the Republic of Panama's foreign relations have been inextricably linked with those of the United States. The first book is Ealy's The Republic of Panama in World Affairs: 1903-50 (Philadelphia: University of Pennsylvania Press, 1951). A later book, Yanqui Politics and the Isthmian Canal (Philadelphia: Pensylvania State University Press, 1971) is not up to Ealy's first book, but it is still useful.

The classic work dealing with the Republic of Panama during the 1940s and early 1950s is Larry L. Pippin's The Remon Era: An Analysis of a Decade of Events in Panama, 1947-1957 (Palo Alto: Stanford University Press, 1964). This work is particularly useful for understanding U.S.-Panamanian negotiations that culminated in the 1955 Eisenhower-Remon Treaty. See also another article by Lester Langley, "U.S.-Panamanian Relations Since 1941," Journal of Inter-American Studies 12 (July 1970):339-66.

A useful account of Panamanian politics in the 1950s and 1960s is found in a book by Jules Dubois entitled Danger Over Panama (Indianapolis: The Bobbs-Merrill Company, Inc., 1964). This book contains an excellent description of the 1964 Canal Zone riots and its aftermath.

This chapter owes a heavy debt to many of the above sources in its effort to identify and describe the various linkages which exist between the United States and Panama. The intent was not to provide a comprehensive history of relations between the U.S. and Panama but rather to provide the reader with some contextual background to better understand later chapters of the book.

2. A General Treaty of Peace, Amity, Navigation and Commerce Between the United States of America and the Republic of New Granada, in Charles Bevans, ed., Treaties and Other International Agreements of the United States of America, 1776-1949, 12 vols. (Washington, D.C.: Government Printing Office, 1971), Department of State Publication, vol. 6, no. 8549, pp. 868-81.

3. Treaty of Peace, Friendship, Limits and Settlement between the United States of America and the Mexican Republic, in Charles I. Bevans, ed., Treaties and Other International Agreements, vol. 9, pp. 791-806.

4. Wayne D. Bray, The Common Law Zone in Panama (San Juan: Inter American University of Puerto Rico, 1977), p. 21.

5. Ibid.

6. Convention Between the United States of America and Her Brittannic Majesty, in Charles I. Bevans, ed., Treaties and Other International Agreements, vol. 12, pp. 105-08.

7. Isthmian Canal Convention, Article III, in Charles I. Bevans, ed., Treaties and Other International Agreements, vol. 10, p. 664.

8. Ibid.

9. James N. Rosenau, ed., "Pretheories and Theories of Foreign Policy," in R. Barry Farrell, Approaches to Comparative Politics (Evanston, Ill.: Northwestern University Press, 1966), p. 65.

10. Edwin C. Hoyt, "Law and Politics in the Revision of Treaties Affecting the Panama Canal," Virginia Journal of International Law, vol. 6, no. 2 (April 1966), p. 296.

11. Isthmian Canal Convention, Article III, in Charles I. Bevans, ed., Treaties and Other International Agreements, vol. 10, p. 664.

12. G. A. Mellander, The United States in Panamanian Politics, pp. 52-53.

13. Treaty between the United States of America and the Republic of Colombia for the Settlement of their Differences Arising Out of the Events Which Took Place on the Isthmus of Panama in November 1903, in Charles I. Bevans, ed., Treaties and Other International Agreements, vol. 6, pp. 900-03.

14. Treaty of Friendship and Cooperation, in Charles I. Bevans, ed., Treaties and Other International Agreements, vol. 10, pp. 742-77.

15. U.S., Department of State, United States Treaties and Other International Agreements, vol. 6, pt. 2, Treaty of Mutual Understanding & Cooperation Between the United States of America & the Republic of Panama (Washington, D.C.: Government Printing Office, 1956), pp. 273-367.

3
Riots and Aftermath

The single most traumatic event in the linkage between the United States and Panama over the Canal and, certainly, the one that stimulated the most political change was the riots that broke out in Panama City on 9 January 1964. The rioting spread to the cities on the Atlantic side and lasted until 14 January, when the Panamanian National Guard finally left its barracks and restored the uneasy peace. Four Americans (three soldiers and a civilian) and at least twenty Panamanians lost their lives during the five days of violence, and more than 200 were injured.[1]

For Panama, the riots were a success in that the United States agreed, in April 1964, to negotiate the issues in conflict between the two countries. As Panama interpreted the ensuing negotiations, they included the negotiation of a new treaty to replace the 1903 treaty, although the U.S. denied, at that time, that the negotiations were to be that broad. Later in 1964, the U.S. agreed to negotiate the abrogation of the 1903 treaty. Also, because of the riots, Panama was successful in focusing the attention of the world on the Canal issue and thus expanding linkages to an extent never before achieved. The riots and Panama's position on the Canal question were linked for the first time to the Organization of American States and the United Nations. The American public, for the most part, discovered for the first time that there was a problem in Panama. Also, Panama gained a new national holiday. Nine January largely replaced 3 November, Panamanian Independence Day, as the principal day of national rededication.

The incident that triggered the riots was essentially a symbolic one--whether the Panamanian flag would fly alongside the United States flag at a number of sites in the Canal Zone. But, as is the situation with most symbolic issues, this one represented more significant problems. Panama saw the flag issue as a means of supporting its position that Panama, not the United States, held sovereignty over the Canal Zone.

35

The question of flying the Panamanian flag in the
Zone had been developing for nearly ten years. During
the negotiation of the 1955 revisions of the 1903 treaty, Panama attempted unsuccessfully to include in the
agreement a provision that the Panamanian flag would fly
on all ships passing through the Canal and at certain
sites in the Zone.[2] The first overt act by Panamanians
to find their own solution to the flag question came on
2 May 1958, when Panamanian students engaged in what was
called "Operation Sovereignty" and placed a number of
Panamanian flags in the Zone. These were quickly removed by Canal authorities. The next day, President
Eisenhower, in a news conference, said that the demonstration was "puzzling," since, in 1955, Panama had received modifications to the 1903 treaty which were favorable to Panama. He attributed the demonstrations to
a small group of "extremists."
     The demonstrations marked the beginning of a growing
anti-American campaign on Panamanian radio and in the
newspapers that culminated in widespread demonstrations
on 3 November 1959. As planned, the November demonstrations were to be peaceful, but when the demonstrators
attempted to enter the Zone, violence erupted when there
was contact with the Canal Zone police and, eventually,
the U.S. Army. Among the demonstrators was Aquilino
Boyd, who, under Torrijos, served as Panama's foreign
minister. In retaliation, the demonstrators destroyed
an American flag in front of the United States Embassy
inside Panama City and attacked the U.S. consulate in
Colón. The National Guard did nothing to control the
demonstrators. There were no fatalities, but more than
100 persons were injured.[3]
     Later that month, Deputy Under-Secretary of State
Livingston T. Merchant visited Panama and, while there,
reaffirmed Panama's "titular sovereignty" over the Canal
Zone.[4] This phrase had been the manner in which the
United States had described Panama's status in the Zone
since before the Canal was built; thus, Merchant's
statement did not relieve tensions in Panama. "Titular
sovereignty" was interpreted to mean only that if the
United States left the Zone, that territory would revert
to Panamanian control. Further demonstrations took
place on 28 November but, this time, were controlled by
the Panamanian National Guard.
     In the United States, as a reaction to these events,
on 2 February 1960 the House of Representatives passed,
380 to 12, a resolution rejecting Panama's claim to fly
its flag in the Canal Zone and denying any other changes
in traditional interpretations of the Canal treaties.
The Senate failed to act on the resolution. Earlier, in
July 1958, following demonstrations in May, President
Eisenhower had sent his brother, Milton, to visit Panama,
who, on his return, had recommended to the president that
Panama be allowed to fly its flag in the Zone. But not

until 3 February 1960, the day after the House passed
its resolution, did President Eisenhower state that he
had no objections to flying the Panamanian flag and, after some delay, on 17 September 1960, ordered the Panamanian flag to fly alongside that of the United States
at Shalers Triangle, next to Panama City and just inside
the Zone.[5]
     President Eisenhower's action was well-timed. It
came just after Congress had adjourned to campaign for
the 1960 elections and just before the inauguration on 1
October of the new president of Panama, Roberto Chiari.
In his inaugural speech, President Chiari spoke favorably of Eisenhower's announcement but made clear that
the problems between the two countries were not resolved
by this single act.
     Early in his administration, President Chiari played
down the Canal issue and called on Panamanians not to
become obsessed with the problem.[6] Two developments
other than the announcement that the Panamanian flag
would fly over Shalers Triangle had contributed to the
apparent good relations between Panama and the U.S. In
April 1960, Eisenhower had approved a nine-point program
that increased the wages and fringe benefits of Panamanian employees in the Zone. In addition, the U.S. a-
greed to construct a new water system in Panama City and
to reduce the rate charged for water. A second development came in October 1961 when the U.S. signed an agreement with Panama whereby the U.S. would support Panama's
five-year development plan with funds from the Alliance
for Progress.
     Late in 1961, Chiari sent President Kennedy a letter
in which he asked for the renegotiation of the 1903 treaty. Kennedy refused the request on the grounds that the
time was not right on the U.S. domestic scene and because no decision had yet been made in Washington concerning the construction of a sea-level canal.[7] Kennedy
pointed out that renegotiation of the 1903 treaty would
be unnecessary if a sea-level canal were constructed;
thus, the decision on a new canal was crucial to the
decision to renegotiate. Kennedy also pointed out to
Chiari that there was considerable opposition in the
United States, especially in Congress, to renegotiating
the 1903 treaty. Underlying Chiari's request was a slug-
gish Panamanian economy. He hoped a favorable revision
of the 1903 treaty would help Panamanian economic woes.
Kennedy felt that the Alliance for Progress could accomplish the same end without treaty revision. Both presidents were reacting to domestic concerns about the Canal.
     President Kennedy's observation about congressional
opposition undoubtedly was correct. The year before,
the House Foreign Affairs Committee had issued a report
on United States relations with Panama. This report emphasized the importance of the Canal to the United
States, both economically and strategically. The

committee also pointed out that although Panama received
only $1,930,000 directly from the Canal, one-sixth, in
all, of the GNP of Panama was derived from the Zone;
thus, Panama was receiving its adequate share of the revenue from the Canal. Also, since 1945, the United
States had given Panama $40,000,000 in foreign aid. The
report concluded that whatever Panama's economic problems were they were more likely the result of poor planning by Panamanians than exploitation by the United
States.[8]

In June 1962, President Chiari visited the United
States, renewed his request for renegotiation and, in
turn, received essentially the same arguments Kennedy
had presented earlier as to why the request could not be
granted. The United States did agree, however, to negotiate points of conflict over the 1903 treaty within the
context that the treaty remain in force.

The negotiating teams appointed to carry out this
agreement were, for the United States, Joseph S. Farland, ambassador to Panama, and Major-General Robert J.
Fleming, Jr., governor of the Canal Zone; and, for Panama, Foreign Minister Galileo Soles and former Foreign
Minister Octavio Fabrega. The teams began meeting in
July 1962. Little of substance emerged from the meetings, but they did produce additional wage increases for
employees of the Canal Company, three-fourths of whom
were Panamanian; provided for a bi-national labor relations committee, which dealt successfully with a number
of labor problems; and agreed that, eventually, the Panamanian flag would fly alongside the United States flag
at all civilian sites in the Zone. The talks ended in
July 1963. The Panamanian government considered these
talks far from successful, since there was no agreement
to renegotiate the treaty.

The first location to fly the Panamanian flag after
the original site at Shalers Triangle was the Thatcher
Ferry Bridge. For some time, the United States had refused to build a bridge across the Canal for fear that
a bridge would be sabotaged and block the Canal, but the
United States did, in the 1955 treaty, agree to build a
bridge near the Pacific terminus. This was in response
to the Panamanian view that a bridge would help alleviate the feeling that the Canal cut Panama in half. When
the bridge opened on 12 October 1962, the flags of both
countries were flown over the bridge. There were demonstrations, nevertheless, since some Panamanians felt the
bridge should have been named "Bridge of the Americas."[9]
On 29 October, both flags began flying over the Canal
Zone administration building in Balboa Heights, and on
1 November the policy was applied to the administration
building in Cristobal.

Americans living in the Zone were disturbed by these
concessions, and a group from the Zone filed a court
action to prevent the presence of the Panamanian flag in

the Zone. The case was based on the argument that the United States had sovereignty in the Zone; thus, Panama had no legal claim to fly its flag there. In July 1963, a U.S. District Court ruled that the Panamanian flag could be flown, but the court did not respond to the question of which country held sovereignty over the Zone.[10] Between October and December 1963, the dual-flag policy was applied to the locks and two hospitals in the Zone. By the end of 1963, the dual-flag arrangement applied to ten locations in all.

In addition to the expanding dual-flag policy, Panama also had other successes of a minor nature, and relations between the two countries seemed to improve during the last few months of 1963. Since the United States was considering building a sea-level canal in the Darien Province of eastern Panama, Panama did not wish to press too hard its demands in the Zone for fear such pressure would jeopardize future negotiations on a treaty covering the new canal. Relations, however, did suffer an important setback in August 1963, when Ambassador Farland resigned under pressure from residents of the Zone.

Zonians, who by the 1960s had developed a distrust of the State Department, were generally hostile toward U.S. ambassadors, who resided in the Republic and who were seen as overly sympathetic to the Panamanian position. The Zonians were more attuned to the military position represented by the Department of Defense.

Ambassador Farland had held his post for three years and was highly regarded by the Panamanian government. His reasons for resigning were not clear, but policy differences with other American officials seemed to have been a factor. He disagreed with the manner in which the Alliance for Progress program for Panama was being run and felt that the emphasis on economic development rather than social welfare was an error.[11] The Panamanian government thought Farland had a good understanding of Panama's problems, but the Canal Zone officials and many residents of the Zone saw the ambassador as selling out on the sovereignty question. It was not uncommon even into the 1970s to have prominent Panamanians in and out of government refer to the period of Farland's ambassadorship as the golden opportunity for better relations between the United States and Panama. The rumor, denied by the State Department, circulated in Panama that Ambassador Farland was not debriefed when he returned to Washington, an indication of the disfavor in which he was held by his superiors in the department.

This period of seemingly improved relations was marred further, in October 1963, by a Molotov cocktail attack on the United States Embassy. Further demonstrations were expected but were delayed by the Kennedy assassination in November. Due, probably, to the Alliance for Progress and its popularity in Panama, the country paused and paid the sort of homage to Kennedy

usually reserved for deceased Panamanian heads of state.
President Kennedy has been in the process of appointing
a replacement for Farland at the time of his death, but
the appointment had not yet been submitted to the Senate.
Kennedy's nominee was not acceptable to the Johnson administration, and a new nomination was not made until
April 1964.

After a brief period of mourning for Kennedy, relations between Panama and the United States deteriorated
badly during December and early January 1964. The next
sites at which the dual-flag policy was to be applied
were the schools. This brought intense opposition from
Zone residents, since they were of the view that the
student bodies were overwhelmingly American; therefore,
there was no reason for displaying the Panamanian flag.
Because of this opposition, General Fleming, in an effort to forestall further problems, ordered that if both
flags were not flown then neither would be. This order
was handed down on 30 December 1963, while the students
were on Christmas break.

Upon returning from vacation, students at Balboa
Heights High School, located in the Zone and whose student body was ninety-seven percent U.S. citizenship,
sent a letter to President Johnson protesting Governor
Fleming's action. On 7 January 1964, a group of Canal
Zone Junior College and Balboa Heights High School students carried their protest further by raising the United
States flag on one of the two flagpoles in front of the
high school. School officials took the flag down, but
it was quickly raised again; and students, plus sympathetic parents, surrounded the flagpole to prevent the
flag from being lowered again. The flag flew day and
night through 7 and 8 January under guard of the students, in spite of a request from the governor that the
flag be lowered. Similar demonstrations were carried
out at a number of other locations in the Zone.[12]

On the afternoon of 9 January, a group of between
150 and 200 students from the Instituto Nacional, a
Panamanian high school just outside the Zone in Panama
City, under Canal Zone police escort marched to the Balboa High School and attempted to raise the Panamanian
flag alongside the United States flag. The Canal Zone
police intervened, and in the general melee the Panamanian flag was torn. The Panamanian students were dis-
persed by the police, and as they left the Zone the
Panamanians destroyed property on the way. Needless to
add, the facts surrounding the flag incident continued
in dispute, particularly about when and how the flag was
torn and about the actions of the Zone police.[13]

As stories of attacks on the students and damage to
the Panamanian flag were expanded upon and circulated
through Panama City, crowds formed on the boundaries between the city and the Zone. A call by Zone officials

to the Panamanian National Guard to disperse the crowds
brought no results. Eventually, thousands of Panamanians
penetrated the Zone, damaged the Ancon railway station
and a train, and burned the Ancon laundry. After the
mob was turned back into the City, it commenced to burn
whatever property owned by Americans it could find. Not
only had there been no United States ambassador in Panama since the departure of Farland, but Governor Fleming
had left for vacation during the afternoon of 9 January.
Upon hearing of the events in Panama on his arrival in
Miami, Fleming immediately returned to Panama.

On 10 January, President Chiari broke diplomatic
relations with the United States and charged the United
States with "unprovoked aggression" against Panama.[14]
Also on 10 January, President Johnson sent a delegation
to Panama to investigate the situation. This mission
was headed by Thomas C. Mann, assistant secretary of
state for Inter-American Affairs, who had just taken the
position in 1960-1961. Included in the delegation was
Mann's predecessor, Edwin M. Martin, Secretary of Army
Cyrus Vance, and Ralph Dungan, presidential assistant
for Inter-American Affairs. On the same day, the Security Council of the United Nations met at the request of
Panama to discuss charges of aggression brought against
the United States. Aquilino Boyd, Panama's ambassador
to the United Nations, declared that Panama "is currently the victim of an unprovoked armed attack" committed
by United States forces in the Zone. Ambassador Boyd
also advanced the Panamanian argument that the United
States did not hold sovereignty in the Zone and reviewed
the long list of grievances Panama held against the
United States. Adlai Stevenson, United States ambassador
to the United Nations, categorically denied the charges
of aggression.[15] The Security Council adopted a proposal that the president of the council appeal to the
United States and Panama to bring about a cease-fire but
took no further action.

Also on 10 January, a representative of the Organization of American States told the United Nations that
the OAS would take up the charge of aggression through
the Inter-American Peace Committee. If either the UN or
the OAS was to debate the merits of U.S. actions relative to the riots, the United States appeared to prefer
the forum of the OAS, where the United States had fewer
countries to influence and where United States influence
was relatively greater. But while these diplomatic efforts were taking place at the United Nations and the
OAS, the rioting continued in Panama. Efforts by Panamanians to penetrate the Zone were largely unsuccessful,
since the United States had sufficient armed forces to
hold the boundary lines where Panamanian cities touched
on the Zone. General O'Meara, commander of the U.S.

Army units in Panama, had been ordered by President
Johnson to defend the Zone. U.S. forces did not leave
the Zone, but gunfire between the Zone and the Republic
was common. The most beleagured U.S. position on the
Pacific side was the Tivoli Hotel, a landmark dating
from the construction days and located just inside the
Zone. On the Atlantic side, the boundary between Colón
and Cristobal near the YMCA was hotly contested. Inside
Panama City, damage was even greater. The U.S. Information Agency's office and library, Pan American and Bra-
niff offices and U.S.-owned tire plants were burned.

Secretary Mann and his delegation reported back to
Washington that security in the Zone was such that the
Canal itself was in no danger. But Mann's efforts to
persuade Chiari to call out the National Guard to stop
the riots were unsuccessful. On 15 January, the day
after the riots ended, the Inter-American Peace Committee
announced that Panama and the United States had agreed
to begin discussions thirty days after diplomatic relations were restored "by means of representatives who
will have sufficient powers to discuss without limitations all existing matters of any nature which may affect
the relations" between the two countries.[16] Both Panama
and the United States saw this development as a victory,
but each had its own interpretation of what it meant.
Panama regarded the agreement as a commitment to negotiate a new treaty. The United States saw the talks as
a means of discussing grievances but not the framework
for negotiating a new treaty. At a press conference on
23 January, President Johnson stated that the United
States had resisted aggression rather than committed it,
but, nevertheless, "We have set no preconditions to the
resumption of peaceful discussions. We are bound by no
preconceptions of what they will produce. And we hope
that Panama can take the same approach."[17] Privately,
however, Johnson felt Chiari was attempting to maneuver
the U.S. into new treaty negotiations with the threat of
force.[18]

Since Panama saw this agreement as an opening concession by the United States, Panamanian demands escala-
ted. In Panama, the press and radio demanded that the
United States immediately turn the Zone over to Panama.
On 29 January, Panama asked the Council of the OAS "to
take cognizance of the acts of aggression against Panama."[19] The United States, through its ambassador to the
OAS, Ellsworth Bunker, insisted that there was no basis
to the charge. Panama wanted the council to invoke the
1947 Inter-American Treaty of Reciprocal Assistance (the
Rio Pact) and insisted that the United States declare
its willingness to negotiate a new treaty. When the
Council failed to act on the charge of aggression, Panama threatened to withdraw from the OAS. Panama, after
realizing that the agreement worked out by the Peace
Committee would not lead to the renegotiation of the

1903 treaty, refused to enter into direct talks with the
United States on any of the outstanding issues.

After lengthy discussion, on 4 February the council,
in effect, rejected the charge of aggression by calling
only for the use of the consultative machinery of the
Rio Pact, but agreed to investigate further the situation in Panama. Of the twenty members of the OAS, seventeen felt the United States had used more firepower
than necessary during the riots but refused to find the
United States guilty of aggression. The United States
rejected even this degree of guilt, and Panama and Bolivia withdrew from the discussions before the decision
was handed down. The United States insisted that its
troops had not used live ammunition against the crowds
during the riots but did fire tear gas canisters. The
OAS accomplished little toward bringing the problems
between the United States and Panama to the bargaining
table.

Panama refused to reestablish diplomatic relations
with the United States until the United States agreed to
renegotiate the 1903 treaty. President Johnson's reply
to this demand was that "We are not going to make any
precommitments, before we sit down, on what we are going
to do in the way of rewriting new treaties with a nation
that we do not have diplomatic relations with."[20]

On 3 April 1964, the chairman of the General Committee of the OAS Council announced that Panama and the
United States had agreed to reestablish diplomatic relations and that special ambassadors would be appointed
"with sufficient powers to seek the prompt elimination
of the causes of the conflict between the two countries,
without limitations or preconditions of any kind."[21]
Again, Panama argued that this agreement covered the renegotiation of the 1903 treaty, an interpretation again
rejected by the United States. Also on 3 April, the
United States announced the nomination of Jack H. Vaughn
to the long-vacant post of ambassador to Panama.

Another effort by Panama to gain outside support
for its charges of aggression came to an end when, on 9
June 1964, the International Commission of Jurists handed
down its decision stemming from charges brought earlier
by the Panama Bar Association that the United States had
violated various articles of the Universal Declaration
of Human Rights.[22] The commission found that both governments had to bear the blame for the riots and the
course they had run. The commission found the United
States innocent of the most serious charges brought by
the bar association but did point out that actions by
United States forces during the riots were, on occasion,
unnecessarily harsh. The commission said that the Canal
Zone police had fired into crowds when other measures of
crowd dispersal could have been employed and criticized
the use of marksmen in returning sniper fire from the
Republic. The commission pointed out that the Zonians

had done little to get along with the Panamanians and
criticized the United States government for not encouraging more contact between the Zone and the Republic.
The Panamanian government was criticized for failing to
control the mobs and for not using the National Guard
until near the end of the riots.[23]
      The negotiations that had been announced in April
1964 commenced in May with former Secretary of Treasury
Robert B. Anderson as the United States representative
and Jorge Illueca, editor of El Panama American and a
former delegate to the United Nations, as his Panamanian
counterpart. Even though the talks did not go well in
that the old question as to whether a new treaty was to
be negotiated overshadowed whatever else was discussed,
they did mark the beginning of on-and-off negotiations
that proceeded until 1977.
      In Panama, the Canal issue was set aside temporarily
for the presidential elections held in May, with the new
president to take office in October 1964. President
Chiari was prevented by the Panamanian constitution from
seeking a second term. The Canal was not an issue in
the campaign, since all seven candidates were in agreement that the 1903 treaty should be replaced. The principal election issues were domestic problems such as tax
reform and charges of fraud committed by government officials. The two main candidates were Arnulfo Arias and
Marco Robles, with Arias taking a more tolerant view
toward the United States than did Robles or the other
candidates. Arias had twice before been president, but
neither time had he completed his term of office. In
1941, he was removed from office through a coup because
of what were regarded as his pro-Axis leanings, and in
1951 he was impeached by the National Assembly. Arias'
World War II reputation was revived during the campaign,
and Robles won.[24] In June, the president-elect visited
the United States, followed by a state visit by President
Chiari later in the month. These visits, plus careful
control by the National Guard of demonstrators on the
Fourth of July, one of the days when Panamanians traditionally show their hostility toward the United States,
indicated a short period of improvement in relations
between the two countries.[25]
      When Robles took office on 1 October, Panama had
serious economic problems. Considerable capital had
left the country following the riots, and unemployment
was nearly twenty percent of the work force. Panama
still showed the physical scars of the riots. For the
time being, Robles was occupied with these problems and,
unlike many of his predecessors, did not stir up anti-
United States feelings to distract Panamanians from their
domestic plight. Although the negotiations that began
in May still had produced little, the fact that they were
going on was important in holding down anti-United States
moves by Panama. The one continuing effort by Panama

that was a disturbing element, first under Chiari and
now under Robles, was a search for financial support to
build a canal without United States backing. The search
was mainly among other Latin American countries and was
unsuccessful.

　　After years of U.S. refusal to negotiate a new treaty with Panama, on 18 December 1964, Johnson, following
consultation with former Presidents Truman and Eisenhower, made the surprising announcement that the United
States was now willing to negotiate "an entirely new
treaty on the existing Panama Canal." In the United
States, the announcement went largely unnoticed by all
but the few in Congress who kept a watchful eye on Panamanian affairs; they felt the announcement was tragic.
The Panamanian government was astonished and delighted.
While Panama had long pushed for a new treaty, it had
not pushed the issue since the nature of the current
negotiations had been settled in May. President Johnson
also announced that the United States was launching a
search for a route for a new sea-level canal.[26]

　　Panamanian leadership praised the United States for
its commitment to a new treaty. President Robles and
his foreign minister, Fernando Eleta, proclaimed a new
era of good feelings between the two countries. Temporarily, anti-United States propaganda from both the
government and left-wing Panamanians stopped. Clearly,
Panama did not anticipate a long period of negotiation.
The negotiations commenced in January 1965.

　　In April 1965, Ambassador Vaughn was replaced by
Charles W. Adair, Jr. Adair had served in Mexico and
Argentina, thus was an experienced Latin American diplomat. Vaughn had failed to gain the popularity enjoyed
by Farland; therefore, the change did not bring forth
the protests that had occurred when Farland resigned.
When President Johnson announced the Adair appointment,
he also announced the appointment of John N. Irwin II,
a New York lawyer, to assist Anderson in the negotiations. Both Irwin and Anderson carried the rank of ambassador. Irwin would be the principal working negotiator for the United States during the talks.

　　In September 1965, Presidents Johnson and Robles
simultaneously issued statements as to what the new
treaty would contain. There were to be, in fact, three
new treaties to replace the old treaty. The presidents'
announcement included the following objectives:

(1) The 1903 treaty would be abrogated.
(2) The new treaty would effectively recognize
　　Panama's sovereignty over the area of the
　　present Canal Zone.
(3) The new treaty would terminate after a speci-
　　fied number of years or on about the date of
　　the opening of the sea-level canal, whichever
　　occurred first.

(4) A primary objective of the new treaty would be
to provide for an appropriate political, economic and social integration of the area used
in the canal operation with the rest of the
Republic of Panama. Both countries recognized
that there was a need for an orderly transition
to avoid abrupt and possibly harmful disloca-
tions. It was also recognized that certain
changes should be made over a period of time.
The new canal administration would be empowered
to make such changes in accordance with the
guidelines in the new treaty.

(5) Both governments recognized the important responsibility they had to be fair and helpful
to the employees of all nationalities who were
serving so efficiently and well in the operation of this very important canal. Appropriate
arrangements would be made to insure that the
rights and interests of these employees were
safeguarded.[27]

The day before the announcement was made by the
presidents, the United States presented Panama with a
draft of a defense treaty for the Zone, one of the three
treaties contemplated; and on 14 January 1966, the United States offered the other two treaties. These treaties covered (1) United States operations of the Canal
and governing of the Canal Zone, and (2) the conditions
under which the United States would construct a sea-
level canal and the period during which the United States
would control the new canal. The Panamanian government
responded on 17 June 1966 with its objectives for the
new treaties and its objections to what had been proposed
by the United States. Late in June, the negotiation
teams went to work to resolve the differences. The
negotiations were held in secret by joint agreement.

By June 1967, in spite of the secrecy provision,
rumors began to circulate that the new treaties were
nearing a final draft. Finally, on 26 June, the two
governments announced that three draft treaties had been
agreed to. The draft treaties did not accompany the
announcement, and except for general statements as to
their contents, the treaties remained secret. In both
Panama and the United States, this secrecy aroused suspicions. In the U.S. Congress, the treaties were sharply
criticized by Panama watchers on the basis of rumors
as to their contents.[28]

The first public revelation of the content of the
treaties in the United States came in July when the
Chicago Tribune ran copies of the draft treaties from
sources in Panama, where copies had been made available
unofficially. The Tribune's version of the draft treaties was then placed in the Congressional Record on 17,
21, 27 July.[29] The Chicago Tribune's reaction to the

treaties and the reaction of Canal watchers in Congress was that they were a "sell-out" of American interests. The press in the United States in general, however, viewed the treaties favorably.[30]

In Panama, the treaties were off to a bad start. The treaties had arrived with only an English version available. Panamanian sensitivities once more were offended, since a Spanish version had not yet been agreed to. Reaction to the contents of the treaties, however, was initially favorable, although this support eroded rapidly. The treaties were complicated, thus subject to a variety of interpretations. Overall, the opposition in both Panama and the United States saw their respective governments as granting too much. The ability for both domestic systems to adapt to the new treaties was weak. The treaties clearly contained a number of significant changes compared to the 1903 treaty and 1936 and 1955 revisions, however.

The most important of the three treaties was the one related to the operation of the Canal and administration of the Canal Zone. This treaty abrogated the 1903 treaty as well as the 1936 and the 1955 revisions. A joint administration was to be set up to operate the Canal. This administration was to take over the operation of the Canal in not less than six months or more than two years after the treaty went into effect. The governing body of the joint administration would consist of nine members, five appointed by the president of the United States and four appointed by the president of Panama. The joint administration would operate and maintain the Canal, administer the Canal Zone, and administer and collect tolls. Also, it would have the power to establish employment policies, maintain and operate a water system, the railroad in the Zone, and a postal service. Educational and health facilities in the Zone would also be under the control of the administration. Employment policies would recognize that the Canal was the principal source of employment for Panamanians and that there would be equality of treatment for all employees without regard to nationality. The postal service would use the same postal rate as the Republic and would issue only Panamanian stamps. The wide variety of other activities carried on by the Canal government would continue, but under the control of the joint administration. The joint administration would discontinue within five years "the operation of food stores, department stores, milk products, plants, bakeries, pastry shops, cafeterias, luncheonettes, theaters, bowling alleys, and recreational facilities for which a charge is payable, optical shops, hotels, laundries, dry cleaning plants, printing plants, automobile repair services, tire recapping services, and gasoline stations that are operated for the public." The joint administration was to arrange for the private operation of these services and facilities in the Zone.

Also, the joint administration would have the responsibility to relinquish to Panama land or other property no longer needed for the operation of the Canal. The laws of Panama would apply in the Zone with certain exceptions spelled out in the treaty. The administration would set up a court to handle cases arising in the Zone. Panama would receive a substantially larger share of the tolls from the Canal. In the first year after the treaty went into effect, Panama would receive seventeen cents per long ton of cargo, with one cent per ton added each year until the maximum of twenty-two cents was reached. The estimate in 1967 was that Panama would receive about $17,000,000 the first year (compared to less than $2,000,000 under the 1955 treaty) and a maximum of $22,000,000.

The treaty would remain in force until the end of 1999. If a sea-level canal were opened to traffic before 1999, the treaty would expire one year after the opening of the new canal. If the United States had commenced construction of a sea-level canal in Panama but had not completed the project by 1999, the treaty would expire one year after the completion of the new canal or at the end of 2009, whichever came first. When the treaty did expire, full control of the lock canal would go to Panama.

The second treaty was concerned with the construction of a sea-level canal. The treaty allowed the United States to construct such a canal, but the lands and waters needed for the canal would be under Panamanian sovereignty. If nuclear excavation methods were used for construction, Panama would have to agree and to approve of the safety measures employed. The United States would finance the canal, and it would be run by an authority known as the Panama Interoceanic Canal Commission, made up of four Panamanians and five Americans. The powers of this commission would be similar to those of the joint administration for the lock canal. The treaty would remain in force for sixty years from the date the canal opened to traffic, provided that that period did not go beyond the year 2067. The treaty would terminate if the United States did not notify Panama within twenty years of its intention to construct a new canal and if the United States did not begin construction within five years of notification. The treaty also would terminate if the United States did not complete construction within fifteen years of the start of construction.

The defense treaty called for joint action by Panama and the United States for defense of both canals. Panama was obligated to provide areas for the stationing of United States armed forces. Such areas would be under Panamanian sovereignty, and Panamanian laws would be enforced there. The United States would have no jurisdiction over Panamanian citizens. Panama would have the "primary right to exercise jurisdiction" in all

violations of the law by United States citizens except
when the offense was solely against the property or security of the United States, against the person or property of another member of the United States armed forces or a member of the United States civilian component
or their dependents, or when the offense "arises out of
any act or omission done in the performance of official
duty." These provisions were similar to those found in
the status of forces treaties the United States had negotiated with the various countries where United States
armed forces were stationed. The defense treaty would
expire five years after the expiration of the new treaty
for the lock canal or when the United States was no
longer responsible for defending a new canal, whichever
came later.

In both Panama and the United States, it was assumed
that President Robles was willing and politically able
to act on the new treaties before his term of office was
up in October 1968. On 26 June in a press conference,
President Robles strongly supported the treaties.

> I will call the Foreign Relations Council [an
> advisory group to the president] for a meeting
> . . . to present them with copies of each of these
> documents. I will also invite all former presi-
> dents of the Republic to a meeting . . . to obtain
> their viewpoint on the issue. I will prepare an
> extensive information campaign throughout the
> nation so that the people will know the exact texts
> of these three documents . . . . Once this is done,
> and if deemed favorable by the different organiza-
> tions and persons--including our own government--
> to the national interests, as I personally consider
> it, then I will authorize its approval; and, final-
> ly, they will be sent to the National Assembly for
> ratification.[31]

In order to expedite matters, Robles said he would
call a special session of the National Assembly. When
ratification was completed, "the documents will be
signed by us without delay." In response to whether he
was satisfied with the treaties, Robles said, "If I were
not satisfied, I would have never called this press conference, for I would have flatly rejected the documents."[32] Although Robles did not give a specific date
as to when the treaties would be signed, he estimated
that the process he had outlined would take about three
or four weeks.

The first Panamanian attack on the treaties came
from the leftist United Front. It charged that the new
treaties were merely a revision of the 1903 treaty and
did not obtain "the total abolition of the 1903 treaty
which is what the people want and demand." The Front
also was critical because the treaties were "drafted and

negotiated exclusively in English." This group felt
that "the original language of the English text will
predominate over any later translation into another
language."[33]

Attacks on the treaties quickly spread beyond the
Panamanian left, however. Among the critics was Gustavo
Tepada Mora, who had been on the negotiating team in the
early stages of negotiation. He commented that he considered that the "U.S. negotiators have in truth created
a masterpiece in defense of their nation's interest."[34]
A second former negotiator for Panama, Eloy Benedetti,
claimed that under the new treaties the "canal area could
be regarded as a new microstate with territory, a population, its clearly defined jurisdictional, administrative, police and legislative authorities and its own
legal system guaranteed by international law and inde-
pendent--in principle--from Panama and the United
States."[35] Benedetti called for the renegotiation of the
treaties. Charges were also made by various members of
the National Assembly that the treaties were being presented by Robles with a bias favorable to the treaties
and that parts of the treaties violated the Panamanian
constitution.

One of the principal problems for the treaties in
the early stages of consideration was that the texts of
the treaties had not been released officially. In early
July, opposition groups demonstrated outside the National Assembly building claiming that the treaties were
treasonous even though what was known of the contents of
the treaties were as yet only rumors. Foreign Minister
Fernando Elata refused to release the treaties to a committee of the National Assembly on the grounds that the
treaties had been agreed to only in principle and would
be released when final details were worked out. The demand for the treaties had come from the Permanent Legislative Council, an interim body that carried on the work
of the National Assembly when the Assembly was not in
session.[36]

The Council of Foreign Relations, which consisted
of former presidents, former foreign ministers and other
persons deemed competent in the field of foreign relations, was the first to review the treaties; and questions it raised suggested that the treaties would need
further negotiation before they were acceptable to the
Council. The president of the Council, Octavio Fabrega,
seemed, nevertheless, to be pushing for approval of the
treaties. Robles could, under the constitution, bypass
the Council and his cabinet and sign the treaties, but
such an action probably would have increased opposition
in the National Assembly.

Little action on the treaties took place during
July. There was talk of a special session of the National Assembly to be called in August, but nothing came
of it.[37] As a result of the questions being raised

about the treaties, on 9 August Robles announced a shift
in his position. "I forcefully assert that--and this I
want you to render as textually as possible--the treaty
drafts do not contain all that the country wants nor
that the government expects. Personally, I am not satisfied with what has been obtained."[38] However, despite this broad hint that the Panamanians wished to
reopen regotiations, the United States refused to go
back to the bargaining table.[39]

The objections coming from the Council of Foreign
Relations were numerous. The council felt that the
powers granted to the joint administration were too
broad. There also was objection to the five-to-four majority for the United States on the governing board.
The option granted to the United States for the construction of a sea-level canal was considered to be for
too long a period. The defense treaty was objected to
in that it allowed the United States to maintain and
operate bases in Panama for a period to be determined by
the United States.[40] On 2 September, Robles announced
that when the council concluded its deliberations all of
its recommendations would be noted and the Panamanian
negotiating team sent back to the United States.[41]

In spite of mounting opposition, Foreign Minister
Eleta stated on 7 September that he was still optimistic
that the treaties would be approved. He now described
the treaties as rough drafts and, therefore, subject to
further negotiations.[42]By this time, the only defenders
of the treaties other than the foreign minister were the
negotiating team for Panama, Diogenes de la Rosa, Roberto Aleman, and Guillermo Chapman. Their defense, presented in various public addresses throughout Panama,
was that the treaties, while not an ideal solution to
Panama's problems, were a reasonable compromise and the
best Panama could obtain. Robles clearly had withdrawn
as a defender of the treaties.[43]

Presidential elections were scheduled in Panama for
May 1968, with the new president to take office in October. By November 1967, the selection of candidates by
the nineteen political parties had begun, and the treaties became secondary. Robles endorsed David Samudio,
Robles' campaign manager in 1964, but the coalition of
parties that brought Robles into office split, with four
of the parties and a faction of the fifth supporting
Arnulfo Arias.[44] It had been five months since the
draft treaties had been announced, and there was little
prospect that they would be approved before the May elections. Arias' candidacy was given a substantial boost
when twenty-six members of the forty-two-member National
Assembly endorsed Arias for president.[45]

An additional problem arose that indirectly had an
effect on the treaties. Generally, Latin American countries supported the Panamanian claim to greater participation in running the Canal. Colombia, which under the

1903 treaty was granted free passage for its naval vessels, did not oppose the draft treaties but did state
that it would not give up these rights even if the treaties were agreed to by the United States and Panama.[46]
An important source of opposition in Panama to the
treaties was the high school and university students.
Student organizations held a number of demonstrations
opposing the treaties, and on 11 December a national
students' congress was held, in which one of the major
topics discussed was the new treaties. Not only had
students been involved in the initial incident that triggered the January 1964 riots, but, as in many Latin American countries, were deeply involved in Panama's political life. Student opposition to the draft treaties was
encouraged by virtue of the students' success in preventing an earlier treaty with the United States that they
did not want. In 1947, the Filos-Hines Treaty on defense
areas outside the Zone, including what the United States
regarded as an important base at Rio Hato, was rejected
by Panama following demonstrations against the treaty by
students.
On 14 December, the Panama Bar Association came out
in opposition to the draft treaties. Its list of objections is noteworthy both because of the number of objections and because it provides an overall summary of the
objections being voiced in Panama.

(1)   The draft treaties use an obscure and unneces-
       sarily complicated terminology. There are too
       many clauses liable to different interpreta-
       tions. This entails a serious risk for Panama,
       because in our relations with the United States
       we have sufficient experience with the country's
       onesided approach as the strongest nation.
(2)   The draft treaties contain provisions that
       breach various provisions of our constitution.
(3)   Our government branches lack the power to trans-
       fer to any other authority the exercise of pub-
       lic power granted by the constitution, as the
       draft treaty on the sea-level canal would.
(4)   The abrogation of the existing treaties is sim-
       ply a formality and not effective since many of
       its provisions are incorporated in the new
       draft treaties. Hence, the situations which
       were the cause of conflicts between both coun-
       tries are maintained.
(5)   The international juridical body created for
       the present Canal Zone prevents reaffirmation
       of our sovereign rights in the Canal Zone.
(6)   The international juridical body created for
       the future sea-level canal controvenes Panama's
       rights over its territory and the constitution.
(7)   The canal defense and neutrality draft treaty
       provides for a military occupation of any

territory of the Republic for U.S. armed forces.

(8) The date of termination of the aforementioned draft treaty is indefinite and virtually subjected to the will of the United States and could be extended to perpetuity.

(9) This same draft treaty would legalize the presence of the U.S. armed forces in the present Canal Zone and the rest of the nation in the future, in open opposition to one of the basic aspirations of the republic.

(10) The sea-level canal draft treaty creates a new area of conflict between Panama and the United States. It imposes definite obligations on Panama without establishing the benefits to be received nor the way to solve the disruption that this new canal would cause in the nation in its economic, social and political order.

(11) The draft treaties would lead to the perpetuation of the colonialism which exists in the Canal Zone and grants new concessions to the United States to the detriment of the Panamanian nation's sovereignty and territorial integrity.[47]

On 16 December, Arnulfo Arias became the presidential candidate of the National Union, a coalition of five political parties, including his own Panameñista Party. In his address on the occasion of his nomination, Arias spoke at length about the draft treaties. He denounced the 1903 treaty as "maliciously concocted behind the backs of the Panamanian people" and described the treaty as "very damaging to the country's dignity and the Panamanian people's pride." He supported the construction of a sea-level canal in Panama but felt the new treaties must be "objective, strong and fair" and must be written "with pristine clarity and be the result of respectful regard for the Republic of Panama and the Panamanian people's dignity, interests and fair demands."[48] This statement and others made by Arias led observers to conclude that Arias, if he became president, would approve the new treaties without major revisions.

Any hope that might have remained that President Robles could complete the ratification of the treaties before the elections was dashed in February, when a move developed in the National Assembly to impeach Robles. Robles was charged both with supporting a presidential candidate, David Samudio, which was in violation of the constitution, and with using government resources to support Samudio's candidacy, also in violation of the constitution. Robles, in an effort to stop the impeachment move, agreed to the demands of both the Christian Democratic Party (whose candidate, Antonio Gonzales, was the third major candidate in the race) and the National

Union--demands that he appoint a new "non-political" cabinet.[49] An impasse developed, however, when Robles would not name a new cabinet until the National Assembly dropped the impeachment proceedings and the National Assembly would not drop the proceedings until a new cabinet was named. On 15 March, the National Assembly impeached Robles and set his trial for 24 March. Robles stated that he would not recognize any attempt to remove him from office.[50] The National Assembly found Robles guilty of the charges, and Robles refused to accept the verdict but did appeal the decision to the Supreme Court. On 5 April, the Court overturned Robles' conviction by an eight-to-one vote.[51] The decision saved Robles, but only when the National Guard announced that it was willing to go along with the decision.

During the campaign, the Canal and the new treaties were hardly an issue, since all three candidates supported the view that Panama was entitled to a new arrangement with the United States. Of the three candidates, Arias was considered to be the most favorably disposed toward the treaties, even though Arias announced on 13 March that the treaties would have to be renegotiated. He did not make clear the extent of the changes he wanted.[52]

The elections went off as scheduled on 12 May, even though Arias accused Robles of trying to postpone or cancel the elections unless it was apparent that Samudio would be elected. There were numerous charges of vote fraud and interference by the government in the voting. A number of violent incidents took place on election day, and sporadic violence continued for the next week. Results of the election were not known for some time, and Arias was not declared the winner until 30 May.[53] Samudio claimed that Arias' victory was a fraud resulting from the intervention of the United States and the Panamanian National Guard.[54] Robles claimed that the CIA had manipulated the election so Arias would win.[55]

Arias was inaugurated on 1 October. Robles left Panama for retirement in the United States early on the morning of Aria's inaugural day. In his inaugural speech Arias made no direct reference to the Canal treaties. One of the first moves expected of the new president was that he would, in order to neutralize the National Guard as a political force, replace the head of the National Guard, Gen. Bolivar Vallarino. Before he could do so, on 11 October, the National Guard overthrew Arias. A military government was established under the leadership of Lt. Col. Omar Torrijos and Major Boris Martinez. Arias fled to the Canal Zone.

The State Department saw the coup as removing a president who was likely to support the draft treaties, if they were revised, and placing in power a government of unknown quality and concern for the treaties. The United States, lamenting the overthrow of a

constitutionally elected government, broke diplomatic
relations with Panama. Arias lingered in the Zone for
a few days, hoping to rally support in the Republic,
which did not materialize. He then came to the United
States, first to Washington but eventually settling in
Miami. On 13 November, after the National Guard had
prevented any major anti-U.S. demonstrations on Panamanian Independence Day (3 November), the United States
restored relations with Panama.

Arias' overthrow by the National Guard was not related to the treaties except in the sense that the controversy over the draft treaties contributed to the destabilization of the political system. The immediate cause
for the coup was clearly the anticipation that Arias was
going to move against the National Guard in order to
consolidate his regime, and the National Guard simply
moved first. The coup had the immediate effect of delaying any further consideration of the draft treaties.
The Torrijos government for a time called for renegotiation of the treaties, but eventually Torrijos felt even
renegotiation would not satisfy the domestic opposition,
and in September 1970 he rejected the treaties outright.

The period in Panamanian-United States relations
from the build-up of emotion that led to the 1964 riots
to the rejection of the 1967 draft treaties by Panama
produced essentially no progress in resolving conflict
over the Canal.

Neither the domestic system in Panama nor the United
States was prepared to approve the draft treaties. The
"adaptive behavior" of the Panamanian political system
was not up to accepting what the diplomats had delivered.
Robles apparently had felt, in the early stages of the
debate on the treaties, that the necessary approval
could be obtained within the Panamanian political system.
But as the debate proceeded within Panama, eventually
only the diplomats who negotiated the treaties were defending them.

The Canal issue had, since independence, been prominent on the Panamanian political scene, but the 1964
riots represented such opposition to U.S. presence in
the Zone that the Panamanian political system could not
accept the 1967 agreements. Neither the elected Robles
government nor the Torrijos military government could
risk supporting the treaties in such a politically hostile atmosphere. Economic conditions in Panama, although
depressed following the riots, were not yet serious
enough to force a negotiated settlement with the United
States.

The controversy over the draft treaties illustrated
once more the extent to which the Canal issue had penetrated the Panamanian political system. The Panamanian
political system again showed that no distinction between domestic and foreign policy was made when it came
to the future of the Canal.

The "adaptive behavior" of the U.S. domestic political system was not tested over the draft treaties, which
were never put in final form and thus could not be submitted to the U.S. Senate. A full-blown public debate
never took place. The possibility that the draft treaties might have been turned down by the Senate if they
had been submitted was a real one, however. The future
of the Canal had not yet become a high-priority issue a-
mong U.S. domestic and foreign policy decision-makers.

NOTES

1. Estimates of Panamanian dead vary from eighteen to
twenty-two. Some Panamanians died in the violence of the rioting
and were not killed through direct U.S. action.
2. Lester D. Langley, "U.S.-Panamanian Relations Since 1941,"
Journal of Inter-American Studies 12 (July 1970):349.
3. New York Times, 4 November 1959, p. 1.
4. Panama: Canal Issues and Treaty Talks (Center for
Strategic Studies, 1967), pp. 15-16; U.S., Department of State,
Department of State Bulletin, 14 December 1959, p. 859.
5. U.S., Congress, Senate, Committee on Foreign Relations,
Background Documents Relating to the Panama Canal, 95th Cong., 1st
sess., 1977, pp. 1049, 1058; Langley, "U.S.-Panamanian Relations,"
p. 353; Sheldon B. Liss, The Canal: Aspects of United States-
Panamanian Relations (South Bend, In: University of Notre Dame
Press, 1967), p. 66.
6. Liss, The Canal, p. 117; Canal Issues, p. 16.
7. U.S. Department of State, Department of State Bulletin,
4 December 1961, pp. 932-33.
8. U.S., Congress, House, House Committee on Foreign Affairs,
Report on United States Relations with Panama, H.R. #2218, 86th
Cong., 2d sess., 1960.
9. Liss, The Canal, p. 119.
10. Ibid., p. 120.
11. Ibid., p. 122.
12. Langley, "U.S.-Panamanian Relations," p. 357.
13. Background Documents, pp. 1110-15. Perhaps the best
account of the day-to-day events of the riots is found in Jules
Dubois, Danger Over Panama (New York: Bobbs-Merrill Co., 1964).
14. U.S. Department of State, Department of State Bulletin,
22 April 1974, p. 442.
15. Ibid.
16. Ibid., p. 443.
17. Ibid.
18. LaFeber, The Panama Canal, p. 141.
19. U.S., Department of State, Department of State Bulletin,
22 April 1974, p. 443; Background Documents, p. 1079.
20. U.S., Department of State, Department of State Bulletin,
22 April 1974, p. 443.
21. Ibid.
22. Report on Events in Panama, 9-12 January 1964, International Commission of Jurists, Investigating Committee (Geneva,
1974), in Background Documents, pp. 1099-1145.

23. Langley, "U.S.-Panamanian Relations," p. 360; Liss, The Canal, p. 150; "Panama," Hispanic American Report (August 1964), p. 509.

24. Liss, The Canal, p. 155.

25. Ibid., pp. 157-58.

26. See chapter 5 for Panamanian reaction to the second part of Johnson's announcement and the implications of the search, which included sites outside of Panama. See U.S., Department of State, "Developments in U.S. Relations with Panama, 1903-Present," Department of State Bulletin, 22 April 1974, p. 444.

27. U.S. Department of State, Department of State Bulletin, 18 October 1965, p. 625.

28. The 1967 draft treaties were released by the State Department in January 1977 during the debate on the 1977 treaties.

29. Congressional Record, 17 July 1967, pp. S9709-16.

30. Langley, "U.S.-Panamanian Relations," p. 363.

31. FBIS, 27 June 1967, p. RRRR1, Press Conference on Televisora Nacional, 26 June 1967.

Foreign Broadcast Information Service (FBIS) is published five times a week and covers both electronic and print media. Until March 1974, the FBIS White Paper had worldwide coverage. After that date, coverage was broken down on a regional basis; thus, quotes in this manuscript after March 1974 are from the FBIS regional publication for Latin America. FBIS is compiled by the U.S. Department of Commerce.

32. Ibid., p. RRRR2.

33. FBIS, 30 June 1967, p. RRRR1, Radio Union, 28 June 1967.

34. FBIS, 26 July 1967, p. RRRR4, Radio Libre, 25 July 1967.

35. FBIS, 2 August 1967, p. RRRR8, Radio Mil Cien, 31 July 1967.

36. New York Times, 7 July 1967, p. 9.

37. FBIS, 9 August 1967, p. RRRR6, Radio Aeropuerto, 8 August 1967.

38. FBIS, 10 August 1967, p. RRRR1, Critica, 9 August 1967.

39. LaFeber, The Panama Canal, p. 148.

40. FBIS, 16 August 1967, p. RRRR1, Radio Mia, 14 August 1967.

41. FBIS, 7 September 1967, p. RRRR1, Radio Panama City, 2 September 1967; New York Times, 4 September 1967, p. 15.

42. New York Times, 8 September 1967, p. 2.

43. New York Times, 14 September 1967, p. 12.

44. New York Times, 2 December 1967, p. 29.

45. FBIS, 1 December 1967, p. RRRR1, Panama American, 30 November 1967.

46. FBIS, 12 December 1967, p. RRRR1, Star and Herald, 7 December 1967.

47. FBIS, 15 December 1967, p. RRRR4, Televisora Nacional, 14 December 1967.

48. FBIS, 18 December 1967, p. RRRR6-7, Radio National Union, 16 December 1967.

49. New York Times, 5 March 1968, p. 18.

50. New York Times, 15 March 1968, p. 22; 16 March 1968, p. 11.

51. New York Times, 5 April 1968, p. 2.

52. New York Times, 14 March 1968, p. 12.
53. New York Times, 13 May 1968, p. 16; 14 May 1968, pp. 1,
3; 20 May 1968, p. 7; 31 May 1968, pp. 1, 6.
54. New York Times, 31 May 1968, p. 6.
55. LaFeber, The Panama Canal, pp. 156-57.

4
The Two Panamas

The linkages discussed thus far have dealt mainly
with the linkages existing between the United States and
Panamanian domestic and foreign policy-making systems.
The bilateral linkages reviewed have been those developed
primarily through traditional diplomatic means, such as
between ambassadors, heads of state, special envoys and
various levels of officials from the U.S. Department of
State and the Panamanian foreign ministry.

A second linkage between the United States and Panama, often more direct and, certainly, geographically
closer, was that between the U.S.-controlled Canal Zone
and the Republic of Panama. The development of the Zone
after 1903, with its own government and economy, parallel to and separate from the development of similar
functions and institutions in Panama, was a source of
both conflict and contrast. The Americans in the Zone
were seen by Panamanians as existing in a colonial enclave in Panama, living a different sort of life and
culture. In Panama, the reality of the United States
was just across the fence in the Zone. The linkage of
these two Panamas was an important part of the conflict
between Panama and the United States.

There are at least two reasons for examining the
social and political regimes that have evolved since
1903 in both the Republic of Panama and the Panama Canal
Zone. The first reason is to better understand the
attitudinal set of inhabitants on both sides of the
boundary separating the Canal Zone from the rest of Panama, for it is these attitudes that complicated and delayed the efforts to negotiate a new Canal treaty. An
exploration of the similarities as well as the differences between the two Panamas may explain the longstanding
hostility and aloofness each has felt toward the other.
Paradoxically, it would appear that it is the similarities rather than the more overt differences that have
the greater power to explain the relationship existing
between the people of Panama and the people of the Zone.

A second reason for examining the two political systems is the presence of several issues raised during the ratification process in 1977 and 1978 in the United States Senate. These issues were the product of questions about the political regime that ruled Panama and included concerns about human rights violations, restrictions on the press and the media, the degree of regime involvement in drug traffic from Latin America to the United States, and the nature of Panama's ties to the Cuban regime of Fidel Castro. However, the most critical issue centered on the ability of the military regime to secure approval for the new treaties after they were signed: how could a military regime that came to power by overthrowing an elected government give legitimacy to its subsequent actions?

Unlike the development of other Latin American nations, the history of Panama is not typified by frequent intrusions of the military into the political sphere. The assumption of power by a military regime in October 1968, therefore, was something of an anomaly. Equally unusual was its enigmatic leader, Gen. Omar Torrijos, whose highly personalized, ten-year rule reflected the ambiguities of the man himself. An account of the militarization of Panama, from its beginnings to its culmination in the Torrijos regime, will shed some light on the linkages between the Republic and the Canal Zone. But the similarities and differences forming the two peoples' sense of "we" and "they" can best be traced by first examining the more general history of the evolution of the two Panamas. Ironically, it is especially the underlying similarities of the two regimes that have contributed most to the increasing gulf between the Zonians and Panamanians.

THE DEVELOPMENT OF THE PANAMA CANAL ZONE

Many of the institutions and attitudes of the recent Canal Zone government can be traced to the early years when the Panama Canal was under construction. According to the provisions of the Hay/Bunau-Varilla Treaty, the United States was given the right to govern, as if sovereign, a ten-mile-wide strip across the isthmus of Panama. One of the immediate tasks facing the U.S. government following the mutual ratification of the treaty was to establish authority patterns and regime structures for the governance of the territory that came to be known as the Canal Zone.[1] The regime would gradually evolve over the eight-year period between 1904 and 1912, and the nature of that regime would result from President Theodore Roosevelt's increasing frustration with the apparent inability of the Isthmian Canal Commission, relatively decentralized in its political structure, to proceed speedily with the construction of a canal. Roosevelt's solution was to eventually concentrate all power in the hands of a single individual, Colonel G. W. Goethals; and the final form of the Canal Zone government largely reflected the personalities of both men.

Initially, the responsibility for governing and administering the Canal Zone rested with the Isthmian Canal Commission, created by the Spooner Act of 1902. The ICC was made up of seven members of equal authority who reported directly to the president. To the growing frustration of Roosevelt, the performance record of the Commission provided empirical support for the old generalization that "you cannot govern by committee." Eventually, Roosevelt asked Congress to amend the Spooner Act to resolve this problem of fragmented authority. When Congress refused to act, the president moved to reform the ICC by executive order. He transferred control of the commission to the Secretary of War and created a three-man executive committee within the commission to handle day-to-day administrative tasks. Authority was to be divided among a chairman, who would remain in Washington, D.C., to secure necessary supplies and to provide governmental liaison; a chief engineer, who would supervise the construction of the Canal; and a governor, who would be the political administrator with the responsibility for overseeing such tasks as health and sanitation.

Roosevelt's initial efforts at reform did not produce the desired results, and so he listened carefully when ICC Chairman Theodore Shont began calling for a "clear-cut organization with centralized power."[2] To accomplish this objective, the president proceeded again to reorganize the ICC by abolishing the three-man executive committee and placing full authority in the hands of the chairman, who reported directly to the Secretary of War, William Howard Taft. When a clash of personalities frustrated Roosevelt's efforts to expedite construction, he decided to go all the way and turn the task over to the army, who would be used to taking orders and would stay out of politics. Using his executive authority, the president consolidated the positions of chairman and chief engineer. The man he chose to fill this powerful new position was Army Lt. Colonel George W. Goethals. Henceforth, Goethals would exercise supreme authority over all facets of the Canal project based on executive orders drafted by the president.

Goethals took his charge seriously and exercised his powers in an arbitrary fashion.[3] He was determined to complete the Canal with as little delay as possible. To accomplish this, he allowed no job actions of any type. If a strike were threatened, he published the names of the strikers and passed the word that they were to be dismissed. Since only those individuals involved in the construction of the Canal could remain in the Zone, this effectively meant that all undesirables would be deported. This practice continued through the period of U.S. rule in the Zone.

Goethals had a propensity for personalistic rule and implemented this by means of audiences with Canal Zone employees every Sunday morning, at which time he handed down judgments in various and sundry disputes brought before him. Although individuals might object to this kind of despotic rule, they had no appeal from it except to the president of the United States. Eventually, critics of Goethals were to note that "By gradual encroachment . . . all the power legislative, executive and even judicial, within the Canal Zone has been transferred to and absorbed by the Chairman and Chief Engineer of the Canal Commission."[4]

In 1912, Congress finally got around to approving the governmental structure that had evolved through executive orders promulgated by the president and through practices developed by Goethals. In August of that year, the Panama Canal Act was passed. The provisions of this act did away with the ICC and established the office of Canal Zone governor. It also established the principle that civil government in the Zone was to be subordinated to the primary task of operating and maintaining the Canal. Goethals assumed the new position and continued to rule as he previously had ruled, despite the objections of his critics against his type of despotism.[5] His successors were to continue to govern in the same manner established by Goethals.

The provisions of the 1912 Act were not to be modified until 1950, when Congress passed legislation that made the Canal Zone government an equal concern with the operational aspects of the Canal.[6] To reflect this changed philosophy, two separate organizations were established. One, the Panama Canal Company, was to assume responsibility for operating both the Canal and the transisthmian railroad. The second organization was to be a Canal Zone government headed by a governor. However, the centralized authority established by earlier legislation and practice was to continue, since the Canal Zone governor would also be the president, ex-officio, of the Board of Directors for the Panama Canal Company. Thus, in practice, one individual continued to exercise absolute authority within the Canal Zone. This individual would be, as in previous practice, a general officer appointed from the U.S. Army Corps of Engineers.

The only qualification to this absolute authority was the division of responsibility for defending the Canal Zone. This responsibility was to be shared with the commander in chief of the U.S. Southern Command. If a threat to the Canal should arise, under statutory authority, CINSOUTH would prevail, subject to appeal to the president of the United States.[7]

Even as the governmental structure can be traced back to the initial years of Canal construction, so can many of the antecedents for the later social structure and attitudes. One obvious characteristic of the old

Canal Zone is the determination by the ICC to provide
for the entirety of needs of all employees with particular attention to the interests of white employees.[8]
Their justification for this policy was that it would
facilitate their ability to recruit and retain American
employees for the duration of the Canal's construction.
To accomplish this policy, they established commissary
stores stocked with American products, built low-cost
housing, provided free medical care, constructed libraries and organized voluntary associations. All of these
efforts were made with the purpose of transplanting a
small part of the United States to the isthmus. The
distinctive U.S. culture that resulted was not allowed
to assume foreign characteristics, for another decision
was made not to allow any private land ownership in the
Zone. In December 1912, the Canal Zone implemented a
depopulation policy designed to remove all Colombians
and Panamanians from the Canal Zone.[9] The result of
these two policies would be an homogenized American society, one consequence of which was to create a social
as well as a physical separation between Panamanians and
residents of the Zone. There is evidence that efforts
to separate the two groups were deliberate. One early
observer relates an incident that supports this conclusion:

   In 1913, Goethals was called upon to testify before
the House Committee on Appropriations. In his budget,
Goethals had requested $52,000 to build a clubhouse.
The Committee reflected surprise at this request and
questioned him about it. The colonel reaffirmed his
position, saying, "Yes, sir. We need a good clubhouse
because we should give them [American employees] some
amusement and keep them out of Panama.[10] [Italics
added.]

   The distance between Zonians, as they came to be
known, and Panamanians was marked by hostile attitudes
on both sides. The former made little effort to conceal
their contempt for the latter, whom they indiscriminate-
ly characterized as "spiggoty" (a term coined from
"speak-da English"), the connotations of which were
small size, lack of education, and a high proportion of
Negro blood.[11] The Panamanians responded in kind by
using the term "gringo" to reflect their own malice and
suppressed wrath over Zonian attitudes.[12] The distance
between the groups was intensified by Americans who
could never understand why the Panamanians did not emulate what the former perceived to be the clearly superior institutions of the Zone.

   In the years following the construction period of
the Panama Canal, successive generations of Americans
continued to reside in the Zone to oversee its operation
and maintenance. These subsequent generations less and
less frequently interacted with the Panamanians. They
lived in the privileged luxury of Southern Comfort, the

military's term for duty in the Canal Zone. In exchange
for their favored status, they were required to live in
a controlled and regimented regime. They lived in a
place where time stood still, or at least moved very
slowly; for the concern of all was to resist change and
to maintain the status quo. Until the early 1970s when
it was torn down, the old Hotel Tivoli, built for the
visit of President Theodore Roosevelt, represented this
commitment to the past.

To be sure, the Zonians were not without complaints,
but these were not about their lack of opportunity to
participate in the decisions that affected their lives
but were, rather, against those things that threatened
their privileges.[13] Thus, they were irate when only one
spouse or the other could have a twenty-five percent al-
lowance if both were employed by the Canal Company; and
they objected strenuously to congressional supporters
when they were required to pay income taxes on their
earnings. They continually complained about the fact
that they could only rent, rather than own, their homes
and were bitterly antagonistic about the fact that they
were required to leave the Zone when they either quit or
retired from its employment. But their most bitter com-
plaint, which grew over the years, was that their government did not appreciate what they were doing and the
kind of sacrifices they had made to serve their country.
The result was a kind of Zonian nationalism that railed
against the American embassy, located in the Republic,
as an institution that did little or cared little for
the interests of residents of the Zone.

A visitor to the Zone would become aware of these
recurring complaints only as time went by. Initially,
he would be struck by the relative affluence and poverty
that distinguish the Canal Zone from the Republic. If
the visitor were from the United States, he or she was
likely to accept the affluence gap as the result of
Americans' propensity for hard work and technological
modernization. Most Latin American visitors were likely
to view the gap in another way and to explain the difference as the product of a colonialist relationship in
which one nation (the United States) had exploited the
people and resources of a weaker country (Panama) for
its own benefit.

REPUBLIC OF PANAMA: A PENETRATED SOCIETY

In 1964, Ronald Hilton introduced Larry Pippin's
book on the Remón era by observing that domestic politics
in Panama had not been extensively studied because it
was more interesting to focus on the Panama Canal and
its international dimension.[14] This observation can be
applied equally to both U.S. and Panamanian scholars.
One explanation for this lack is the fact that it is
virtually impossible, in many instances, to separate

Panama's domestic politics from the issues fomented by
the Panama Canal and the Canal Zone. The intrusive
presence of a foreign nation in its geographic center
has had a dominant impact on Panama's social structure,
internal integration, economy, and politics.

Although its territory and population are much larger than that of the adjacent Canal Zone, the Republic's
status vis-a-vis the Zone is clearly subordinate. Despite its limited size and population, the Canal Zone is
an extension of the overwhelmingly greater economic and
political power possessed by the United States. It is
this power exercised by the Yanqui Colossus that is so
important for explaining how Panama has developed both
economically and politically.

Earlier, in chapter 2, it was noted that after the
1903 Revolution the United States had assumed a role as
both protector and administrator for the new nation.
This role was legitimized, in part, by both the Hay/
Bunau-Varilla Treaty and article 136 of the 1904 Constitution of Panama.[15] Prior to the initiation of the Good
Neighbor policy of the 1930s, when the U.S. affirmed its
willingness to abide by the principle of non-intervention
in Latin America, Panama, in many ways, had the characteristics and coloration of a protectorate.

This protectoral relationship was compatible with
the interests of both the military regime that governed
in the Canal Zone and the entrepreneurial elite that
ruled Panama.[16] This common interest was political stability. The Zonian military was primarily concerned
with having a stable and friendly regime in the Republic
that did not represent a threat to the Canal, while Panama's elite wanted stability in order to control the
national economy for their own economic benefit. Thus,
on several occasions, the United States would intervene
in the Republic at the invitation of Panama's governing
regime.[17] Although the most typical reason for U.S.
intervention was to help monitor Panamanian elections,
in 1925 600 marines would be called upon to cross into
the Republic and to confront those lower-class Panamanians who were protesting the excessive rents charged by
the nation's economic elite. Ultimately, the decision
by U.S. officials not to come to the aid of a venal and
corrupt president of the Republic in 1932 would consti-
tute a kind of intervention.[18]

Even after the Hull-Alfaro Treaty incorporated the
principle of non-intervention, the United States military was concerned about its ability to intervene if events
in the Republic constituted a threat to the Canal. Article 10 of the revised treaty simply allowed joint action by Panama and the United States after consultation.[19] This was not satisfactory to American military
leaders, and they used their legislative clout to block
approval of the treaties until the chairman of the
Senate Foreign Relations Committee was able to reassure

them that Panamanian leaders were willing to interpret
article 10 liberally so that the United States could intervene unilaterally if need be. This continuing concern of the military was reflected also in the abortive
1967 draft treaties, which contained an article that
gave the U.S. the right to deploy troops and armament
anywhere in the Republic.

In addition to collaborating with the Panamanian
elite to maintain political stability, the Canal Zone
government provided a number of services for the Republic, such as water, garbage collection, and certain
health services (e.g., mosquito control).[20] The result
was that Panama was and is one of the healthiest nations
in the Western Hemisphere.

However, the influence of the Canal Zone went far
beyond the formal agreements to assure political stability and to provide various services to Panama. One
of the most important consequences was to restrict Panama's level of national integration and its economic development. The majority of Panama's population was concentrated in the narrow transit zone that lay alongside
the Canal Zone between Panama City and Colón. The
reason for this concentration was Panama's extreme dependence upon the Canal Zone for jobs and markets.[21]
The most important part of Panama's economy was the provision of goods and services for the Canal Zone. Agri-
culture and other areas of the economy were neglected in
favor of producing light consumer products such as beer,
the brewing of which represented Panama's largest industry. Even illicit sectors of the economy, such as pros-
titution, depended upon the Zone and its military bases
for their primary source of income.

Panama's close ties with the Zone resulted in both
advantages and disadvantages. One disadvantage was reflected in the health of the economy. If the Canal Zone
cut back on hiring or on the purchase of goods and services, Panama would suffer a recession.

Recessions occurred not only as a result of Panama's
dependence on the Zone but also from a reluctance by
Panamanian entrepreneurs to develop a capacity to produce
goods for international markets. Panama's legal monopoly of the Canal Zone market rendered it incapable of
competing in the international marketplace. Its reluctance to share this captive market also made it unwilling to join the Central American Common Market, because
it might have had to share its monopoly with other
members.[22]

Panama's response to its economic problems was not
to increase its ability to compete nor to join in cooperative ventures like the CACM but, rather, to demand
an even larger share of the Zone markets or to call for
additional restrictions on the smuggling of goods from
Zone commissaries to the Republic.

Despite its inability or unwillingness to deal with
its economic problems outside the Canal Zone markets,
Panama enjoyed one outstanding advantage from its close
economic ties with the United States. The use of the
American dollar as its own currency gave the Panamanian
balboa a degree of stability which currencies of Panama's
neighbors did not have because exchange rates were often
allowed to fluctuate for political purposes. This stable
currency was attractive to foreign bankers and investors.

The traditional democratic process by which Panama
was governed was closely linked to these economic ties
between the two countries. An article written in 1952
describing the Panamanian political process declared
that its main function was to enable a small group of
powerholders to distribute available resources among
themselves.[23] These powerholders included a few extended
families in the urban centers and some large landholders
in the interior. The resources they divided among themselves resulted from the profits they derived from the
sales of goods and services to the Canal and the Canal
Zone. Thus, the immediate concern of the powerholders
was to control the supply of these to the Canal Zone.
They perceived the Canal and the Canal Zone as primarily
an economic issue that became a political issue only
when the commissary system or the illicit smuggling of
goods threatened their monopoly of trade. This largely
explains why, in both 1936 and 1955, the powerholders
were willing to accept additional economic concession in
lieu of negotiating the symbolic political issues of
sovereignty and perpetuity. The elites' willingness to
depend exclusively on the Zone for its markets frustrated
any efforts to improve Panama's position in the international marketplace or to develop effectively that part
of Panama removed from the Canal Zone.

The result of this type of political system was to
deny the majority of Panama's population, including the
urban and rural poor, any share in the available resources. The small middle class was weak and was dependent
primarily upon government jobs as their means of livelihood. These jobs frequently were botellas: political
jobs that were awarded in exchange for political service
and that required no large amount of work.

The structure of governing authority was centralized
in the president of the Republic, whose power was tolera-
ted because he was needed to resolve disputes among the
ruling group. The National Assembly and the judiciary
clearly were subordinate to the executive. However, the
form of government was not as important as the personal
characteristics and style of the political leader, because the system was heavily reliant upon personal, rather than rule-oriented, relationships. The elections
that took place every four years occasioned struggles
among several contenders who formed personalistic

political parties for the purpose of gaining political
power and enhancing their economic self-interest. Politicians used the Canal treaties as an issue to gain political support.

The personalistic nature of Panamanian politics was
exacerbated by the absence of institutionalized interest
groups in the Republic. Aside from the labor unions,
whose concerns were primarily linked to the Canal Zone
and efforts to obtain greater economic benefits for Canal
Zone employees, the only groups capable of challenging
the elite were the students and the military.

The majority of student political activity was intermittent and often focused on the issue of American
control of the Zone and the Canal.[24] These students
were drawn from both the university and the secondary
schools located along the boundaries of the Zone. Highly nationalistic, they constituted an available group
which could be mobilized readily by radical professors
or aspirant politicians alike. On such occasions, as
they went into the streets to demonstrate or riot, they
were likely to clash with the National Guard that would
be called upon to control them. These clashes produced
a longstanding enmity between the military and students
that carried forward into the period when the military
ruled Panama.

THE MILITARIZATION OF PANAMANIAN POLITICS

During the last ten years of the Panama Canal negotiations, Panama was ruled by a military government.
Historically, this period of military rule differed from
a typical pattern in Panamanian politics that had seen
little of the militarism that has impacted so adversely
on many other nations in Central and South America.[25]
The successful conclusion of the Canal negotiations may
be due, in part, to the presence of the military regime
and the popularity of its leader, Omar Torrijos.

Modern involvement of the Panamanian military in
the political arena might be said to have begun in 1904,
when the new Republic of Panama faced its first constitutional crisis and General Huertas, who had come over
to the side of the conspirators during the 1903 Revolution, brought pressure to bear upon President Amador to
get rid of two of his conservative ministers.[26] The
president appealed to his U.S. counterpart, Theodore
Roosevelt, for assistance. As a result of his appeal,
the U.S. envoy warned the general that if he persisted
in his plans, the United States would use those powers
granted it under both article 136 of the Panamanian constitution and article 4 of the Hay/Bunau-Varilla Treaty.
After the general backed down, the new government's
leaders seized the opportunity to reduce the size of
the army to its statutory minimum of seven officers and

twenty men. Shortly thereafter, the military was abolished completely and replaced by a 700-man police force.
This action was seen as compatible with the interests of both the United States and Panama. The Panamanian leaders saw it as a chance to rid themselves of a
political threat and, at the same time, to avoid the
burden of an expensive military organization that was
superfluous, since U.S. marines were available in the
Zone for providing external defense and maintaining internal order. On the other hand, the Americans saw this
action as removing a potential Panamanian military
threat while substituting a police organization more
suitable for protecting American lives and property.
Panama would remain without a military for a period
of fifty years. It would have a police force that would
spend most of its time putting down demonstrations and
dealing with the periodic crime waves that struck the
Republic. A low-prestige, nonprofessional organization,
it seemed to function primarily as a goon squad to inti-
midate voters during election years.[27] It is not surprising that during election years the police force
would swell to twice its normal size, as the government
hired its supporters in an effort to maintain power.
Attempts to change this image began in the 1940s,
when Colonel Jose Remón took command of the police organization. He set out to professionalize the police
and, at the same time, to provide them with a degree of
status they had previously lacked. His efforts to give
the police more prestige coincided with his desire for
an organization that would support his climb to the top
of the Panamanian hierarchy. In the latter stages of
this endeavor, he was assisted by the new U.S. military
assistance program, which provided him with a justification for militarizing the police and thereby becoming
eligible for U.S. funds and equipment. In addition, the
change in status allowed the Panamanians to use training
facilities in the Canal Zone and gave them exposure to
foreign military training.[28] One result of this exposure was to change the military's perception of its role
in Panama's political process. This may have been the
product of a U.S. military doctrine that saw the role of
the military not so much as an instrument for external
defense but more as an instrument of development.
Even after Remón's assassination in 1955, the
Guardia Nacional continued to grow in power and prestige,
as a result of which it became much easier to recruit
talented young Panamanians into the organization. At
about this time, other events intervened to also
strengthen the Guard, such as an abortive invasion by
Cuban-supported guerrillas and a student uprising, which
was put down.
U.S. officials reacted to these events as they
usually did when they perceived the possibility that

instability might occur in the Republic and threaten
the security of the Canal. Military assistance programs
were used to increase the number of guardsmen. Initially, the Americans anticipated providing extra funding to
add five public order companies to the overall strength
of the Guard. These plans were modified later when the
Guardia took a neutral position during the 1964 Canal
Zone riots.[29]

During this period, however, the military chose not
to become directly involved in national politics. One
observer believes that this choice was made by Remon's
successor, General Bolivar Vallarino, who was perceived
to have close ties with the rabiblancos, the ruling
plutocracy of Panama. After 1955, the Guardia Nacional
"would support the reestablishment of a power structure
operating to preserve the status quo and did not appear
to have a definable, independent political position except for its permanent, unspoken demand for the continuation of its perquisites."[30]

The role of the military would change dramatically,
however, in the events leading up to the 1968 elections
in Panama.[31] President Marco Robles had won election
in 1964 by developing a fragile electoral coalition of
eight political parties. But Robles' efforts to hand-
pick his successor caused the unstable party alliance to
fragment, and the dissident parties joined with the man
they had worked against in 1964, Arnulfo Arias, to create
a new electoral coalition.

The break-up of the president's electoral coalition
also created other problems for him, since it destroyed
his legislative majority in the National Assembly. His
former supporters, now in the opposition, accused him of
violating the constitution by using his office to further
the candidacy of David Samudio. After heated debate, a
majority of the Assembly voted to impeach the president
and to replace him with the first vice-president. This
action was frustrated, however, when Robles refused to
accept the act of impeachment or to leave office. His
opposition was furious and appealed to the National
Guard to support the impeachment. But the Guard supported the president indirectly by refusing to act until
the Panamanian Supreme Court had an opportunity to review the impeachment. After returning from their recess,
the justices of the Supreme Court threw out the impeachment on the basis of technical factors. The leaders of
the Guard chose to accept the decision of the court as
final, and Robles was permitted to remain in office for
the rest of his term.

On 12 May 1968, Panama held elections for a new
president. During the interim between the impeachment
crisis and the elections, the attitude of the Guard had
changed from its previous support for the president.
Implicit support for the opposition coalition was given

when it indicated that it would uphold the decision of
the national electoral board that reviewed the ballots
and then declared the winner of the presidential contest.
Since a majority of the electoral board were known to be
supporters of Arnulfo Arias, this was tantamount to
throwing military support behind the opposition candidate.

Following his election, Arias proceeded to pack the
National Assembly with his supporters, possibly in anticipation of the need for a large majority to bring about
the ratification of the 1967 draft treaties that had
been negotiated by the Robles regime. Because events
would intrude to deny him this opportunity, it is difficult to ascertain whether Arias would have submitted the
draft treaties to the National Assembly for ratification.

Although the Guard had given Arias its implicit support during the election, on the whole the military felt
a basic mistrust for the new president-elect, and on two
previous occasions (in 1941 and 1951), it had acted to
remove Arias from the presidency. To complicate matters,
prior to the inauguration, rumors began to spread that
Arias would force the retirement of several officers,
including Colonel Omar Torrijos, executive secretary of
the Guard. However, the basic conflict resulted from a
desire by the new administration to appoint Guard com-
manders of its own choosing, which went against the interests of ranking Guard officers, who wished to protect
their positions. The growing tension between the administration and the military appeared to be reduced as the
result of some behind-the-scenes maneuvering; but on 11
October 1968, when General Vallarino retired, his
second-in-command, who had been expected to succeed him,
was retired also. Arias' appointment of the number-three
officer in the chain of command was not expected by the
threatened officers, and they launched a coup. As a
result, Arias was forced to flee to the Canal Zone after
having held office only ten days.

Following the military take over, the United States
suspended diplomatic relations with Panama on 15 October.
Less than a month later, on 13 November, State Department
officials decided to resume relations after receiving
assurances from the military junta that it intended "to
hold elections, to return to constitutional government,
to respect human rights and to observe Panama's international obligations." U.S. officials may have been willing to accept these assurances at face value because, in
their estimation, the junta appeared to represent the
best chance for controlling high school and university
students who were felt to be the greatest obstacle to
Panamanian approval of the 1967 draft treaties.

Even if self-preservation were the motive for the
coup, from the beginning the take over by the Panamanian
military did not appear to be a typical Latin American

coup d'état. Rather, it seemed to reflect a set of attitudes held by some National Guard officers, including
Torrijos, who "rejected the legitimacy of the traditional
'democratic' process and, with it, the right of the Panamanian oligarchy to dictate national policy."[32] Their
attitudes may have been inspired by earlier events in
Peru that had seen the ouster of a civilian government
and its replacement by a highly nationalistic populist
military regime. Some Panamanian officers had trained
in Peru and were familiar with the policies and programs
of the new Peruvian regime.[33]

Several months after it had taken over, the military
junta appointed two civilians, Demetrio Lakas and Arturo
Sucre, to be the president and vice-president, respectively. Despite the appointment of the civilians, it
soon became apparent that the military leaders had no intention of returning power immediately to a civilian
government. Their true intent was clearly revealed when
the junta took steps to do away with two mechanisms that
could have been used to restore civilian rule by dissolving the national legislative assembly and by abolishing
all political parties.

The structure of the new regime did not become apparent in the months following the coup. As business
confidence in the government decreased, the junta responded by declaring that, although it was revolutionary,
it was not communist and that it had no intention of
expropriating land or interfering in private business.
At the same time, it moved to still domestic criticism
by closing the university and by banning the sale of
both The Miami Herald and The New York Times.

Although the nature of the regime was still ambigu-
ous, it soon became clear that the real power in Panama
rested with Colonel Torrijos, although, on at least two
occasions, he had to withstand challenges to his position from both leftist and rightist factions within the
National Guard. The first challenger was Colonel Boris
Martinez, who, in March 1969, apparently attempted to
radicalize the Revolution by appealing overtly to anti-
American sentiments. Martinez appeared on national television, along with other members of the National Guard
staff, and announced that the Guard would not try to
prevent nationalistic demonstrations. This statement
was seen as threatening to the United States, since it
was reminiscent of the passive stance the Guard had taken
during the 1964 student demonstrations. Martinez's
challenge failed, and he was shipped off to Miami. Torrijos' decision to oust Martinez appeared to be based on
his realization that he could ill afford to alienate
either U.S. economic aid or business support if he hoped
to carry out his proposed reforms.[34]

The second challenge to Torrijos came in December
1969, when, during a visit by Torrijos to Mexico, two
colonels in the junta took over. Their take over seems

to have been provoked by Torrijos' call for a New Panama
Movement that would appear to take the form of the Mexican one-party system, an idea that may have struck conservative members of the Guard as radical. The two colonels, Sanjur and Silvera, promised a rapid return to
civilian rule. However, this never came about. Torrijos flew back to Panama in a small plane, launched a
counter-coup, and staged a triumphal tour to Panama City
as Guard officers quickly rallied to his support.

Following his successful counter-coup, Torrijos assumed a more overt role in the government and directed
his efforts toward implementing his social and agrarian
reform programs. These reforms were integral aspects of
an ambitious, long-run development program previously
announced by the military regime. Ideally, this plan
would achieve two primary objectives. First, it would
reduce Panama's dependency on the Canal and the Canal
Zone by developing other parts of Panama outside the
transit zone and by exploiting other resources, such as
the Cerro Colorado copper deposits, reputedly among the
world's richest. Initially, however, the resources for
this development program would have to come from increased revenues from the Canal and increased control
over land adjacent to the Canal, which would allow for
the expansion of Panamanian industry and the Colón Free
Trade Zone.

A second objective of the plan was to integrate Panama's rural population into the national political and
social system. Previously, a large part of the rural
population had little political power or influence, as
authority flowed from Panama City to the rural towns and
villages.[35] Torrijos set out to change this. He em-
barked on an ambitious program of land reform and made
frequent trips to rural areas to demonstrate his interest
and concern with the problems of the campesinos. At
such times, he might personally present a tractor to an
agricultural cooperative or make a gift of a trip to
Panama City to the graduating class of a small rural
school.

Such flamboyant gestures undoubtedly increased Torrijos' popularity with the rural sector and, in the long
run, may also have increased his ability to negotiate
the Canal treaties and eventually secure their ratification. For the first time, the campesinos saw themselves
as being linked with the government in Panama City.
Previously, they had had no concern with foreign policy
issues generally or, in particular, with the issue over
the relationship of the Canal to Panama.[36] Their lack
of concern sharply contrasted to urban Panamanians, who
were constantly aware of U.S. control of the Canal and
who constituted an attentive public that considered the
Canal issue the most important political issue. Now,
with a mobilized rural population, Torrijos could count
on the support of both groups in his efforts to change

the status quo.

Despite his own personal popularity, Torrijos was troubled by both domestic and international criticisms of his regime. Some charges resulted from the failure of the regime to hold elections as promised. Others came from international organizations such as the Inter-American Press Association, which censured the regime's efforts to suppress criticism by controlling the mass media. The most intense criticisms, however, resulted from the disappearance of Father Hector Gallegos, who vanished after threatening some vested rural interests (including one of Torrijos' cousins) by initiating an active rural cooperative movement.[37] The priest's disappearance provoked the disapproval of the Roman Catholic Church within Panama and expressions of concern by human rights groups abroad.

In the face of such criticism of his regime, early in March 1972 Torrijos announced the appointment of a Constitutional Reform Commission. The task of its twenty-five members and twenty-five alternates was to revise the 1946 Panamanian Constitution and present it to a new National Assembly after its members had been elected in August 1972.

On 6 August, Panamanian voters went to the polls in record numbers to cast their ballots for their representatives to this new body, which was to be known as the National Assembly of Corregimientos (Municipal Representatives). This unusually large turnout, estimated to be between eighty and ninety percent of the eligible electorate, can be explained by the severe penalties that Panamanians faced if they did not vote. Before the election, the government had announced that it wanted a vote larger than the 300,000 ballots that had been cast in the most recent presidential election in 1968. To assure this larger turnout, the government penalized nonvoters in a number of ways, such as denying them the necessary papers to leave the country or the ability to transact business with the government.

Despite this, Torrijos declared that he felt "proud" of the turnout and viewed it as a reaffirmation of the people's trust in him and in his government. In his words, "We took the power away from the oligarchy by force four years ago and today it has been buried under half a million votes."[38]

The election had all the overt features of a democratic election, and the National Guard scrupulously stayed away from the polling places. In actuality, however, the process was far from democratic. The military regime had orchestrated the election to legitimize Torrijos as the chief of government, and candidates for the office of corregimiento were sponsored by the political arm of the military regime, the New Panama Movement. No other political parties were allowed to sponsor candidates. In addition, several candidates were

government employees or were clearly dependent upon the
government for their livelihood or position.

The new Panamanian constitution came into force on
11 October 1972, but its implementation did not produce
significant changes in the political structure or diminish the absolute power exercised by Torrijos and the
military regime. A review of the 1972 constitution will
show that the real constitutional process differed significantly from the institutions and procedures described
in the written document.[39] As one observer of the Latin
American constitutional process has noted, Latin American constitutions are one of two main types: nominal or
real.[40] Most Latin American constitutions are nominal
in that they do not actually describe the real distribution of authority or the actual workings of government.
Panama's constitution is of this type insofar as the
written document differs greatly from the actual process
in which decisions are made and implemented.

The document that the Corregimientos ratified in
August 1972 was largely a statement of programs and
ideals rather than a description of reality. A majority
of its forty-five pages were used to discuss nonconsti-
tutional matters, such as the role of the family in Panamanian life, the need to defend and preserve the
national culture, the approved method for organizing the
personnel system, and the relationship of the agrarian
system to the nation.

Superficially, the constitution appeared to describe
a political system based on principles for the "separation of powers," with provisions for executive, legislative, and judicial branches of government. Although the
government would seem to be made up of three separate,
co-ordinate, and equal branches, in reality the polity
was dominated by a centralized executive in the person
of Omar Torrijos.

From its first meeting, the National Assembly of
Corregimientos was clearly subordinate to the executive.
Two days after their formal election, the new representatives met to ratify the constitution and to select a
"jefe maximo," or supreme leader. They clearly understood that they were to ratify, without change, the revised 1946 constitution and that they were to choose
General Omar Torrijos as the chief of government. In
addition, they were to approve the handpicked candidates
selected by Torrijos to be president and vice-president.
At this opening session, only one assembly member spoke
against the selection of Torrijos as supreme leader.

The domination of the legislative branch by the executive came about in several ways. One such was a constitutional limitation on the length of time that the
National Assembly could meet. Its sessions were limited
to one month each year, from 11 October to 11 November.
This limitation effectively restricted its ability to
study and pass policy matters even if its members had

chosen to do so. This choice was not likely to occur, since the military regime had structured the representative districts to overrepresent constituents from rural areas where Torrijos was most popular and had the greatest support. The resulting electoral distribution allowed forty-five percent of the population to elect ninety percent of the Assembly that effectively served as a rubber stamp for Torrijos and his policies. The judicial branch, which was headed up by a Supreme Court of Justice, was also subordinated to the executive and had little power to limit actions of the latter.

The executive article (article 6) describes its structure and indicates that it was headed by a president and a vice-president elected by the National Assembly for six-year terms. But, as already indicated, these officials were simply the handpicked choices of Torrijos. The president exercised no real power but served primarily to perform the ceremonial functions that Torrijos disliked intensely. Article 6 is explicit also in identifying the various governmental officials within the executive branch as well as the governmental councils that met to make decisions.

To conclude the discussion of Panama's constitutional arrangements, it is necessary to note that the 1972 Constitution is composed of 277 articles. The first 276, however, are all subordinate to the last article, which is reproduced in full below because it actually describes how power is centralized within the Panamanian political system. Article 277 clearly shows that the constitutional facade that represents Panama as "unitary, republican, democratic and representative" is underlaid by the real power structure, where all authority was concentrated in a personalistic military regime headed by General Omar Torrijos.

Article 277. Brigadier General Omar Torrijos Herrera, Commander in Chief of the National Guard, is recognized as Maximum Leader of the Panamanian Revolution. Consequently, and to ensure the fulfillment of the objectives of the revolutionary process, he is authorized to exercise the following powers for a period of six years: to coordinate all work of the public administration; to appoint and remove freely the Ministers of State and members of the Legislative Commission; to appoint the Controller General and DeputyController General of the Republic, the General Directors of autonomous and semiautonomous entities, and the Magistrate of the Electoral Court to be appointed by the Executive, as provided in this Constitution and the law; to appoint the chiefs and officers of the Public Forces in accordance with this Constitution, the law and the Military Register; to appoint, with the approval of the Cabinet Council, the Magistrates of

the Supreme Court of Justice, the Attorney General
of the Republic, the Solicitor General, and their
respective alternates; to approve the execution of
contracts and the negotiation of loans; and to direct foreign relations.

In addition, General Omar Torrijos Herrera
shall be empowered to attend meetings of the
Cabinet Council and the National Legislative Council with voice and vote, and to participate with
voice in the deliberations of the National Assembly
of Municipal Representatives, the Provincial Coor-
dinating Councils and the Community Boards.
Done in Panama City, October 11, 1972.[41]

Article 277 represented a constitutional "catch-22"
which legitimized the personalistic rule of Omar Torrijos. The absolute grant of power ultimately made the
government of Panama and the person of Torrijos one and
the same. Thus, to better understand the confusing aspect of Panamanian politics, it is necessary to consider
the enigma that was Omar Torrijos.

Omar Torrijos Herrera was one of twelve children
born to middle-class parents. After attending a military academy in El Salvador, Torrijos joined the Panamanian police force shortly before Jose Remón transformed
it into a military type of organization, the Guardia
Nacional. Torrijos rose rapidly through the ranks, in
part because of his anti-guerrilla training in the Canal
Zone at the School of the Americas. During the 1960s,
he used his training to confront anti-government guerrillas, and, by the time the coup occurred in 1968, Torrijos
was one of the ranking officers in the Guard. Torrijos
did not come to the forefront immediately; but, shortly
after a joint military-civilian junta dissolved, it became apparent that the young officer was the actual
leader of the new military regime.

Many questions were raised about Torrijos during
the time he ruled Panama.[42] Some of his critics felt
that Torrijos simply was another typical Latin American
caudillo, abusing his power to enrich himself and his
family. Others have been more generous and have wondered
if he were one of the new breed of Latin American military reformers exercising power through populist appeals
to the urban and rural poor. Rightists, quizzical about
Torrijos' meetings with Fidel Castro on several occasions, have asked whether or not he was actually a
Marxist in disguise. Leftist critics were prone to
question his nationalist credentials whenever multinational banks came to his rescue with large loans to
temporarily bail Panama out of its increasing financial
difficulties. Unfortunately for those who want to cate-
gorize Torrijos, the answers usually have been less than
satisfactory; for they reflect, in part, the colonel's
volatile nature. However, the answers also indicate

Torrijos' position as the leader of a small nation dependent upon the economic largesse of the Canal Zone as
well as a man determined to secure his place in Panama's
history by achieving an honorable resolution to the problem of the Canal and the Zone.

In addition, Torrijos was subject to pressures from
both the left and the right, pressures that caused him
to become a political chameleon, able to assume the appropriate coloration necessary to satisfy differing constituencies at various times. Although these frequent
shifts made Torrijos difficult to understand, they allowed him to maintain power despite opposition. It was
this complex man whom the United States was called upon
to deal with during the 1970s, when the momentum of the
treaty negotiations picked up.

THE TWO PANAMAS: SOME CONCLUSIONS

It was observed earlier that underlying similarities
appeared to explain better the relationship between the
residents of the Zone and the people of Panama than more
overt differences, such as language, religion, culture,
or income level. These similarities are primarily attitudinal, but they are important because of the way
they affected the negotiating environment as diplomats
from both the United States and Panama undertook efforts
to modify the historical relationship between the two
nations.

It is ironic that the political regimes that evolved
in both Panamas would greatly resemble each other by the
1970s. Both would be ruled by military regimes headed
by single individuals with virtually unlimited power.
The Zonian regime had come about early in the Zone's
history as the result of political and administrative
decisions giving Goethals the authority to construct
those governmental structures necessary to expedite the
building of the Panama Canal. None of his successors
had any desire or saw any need to modify the centralized hierarchical system established by the original
military governor. Within the Republic, military control had occurred later in its history as first the Panamanian police and later the Guardia Nacional moved to
fill the political vacuum which had resulted when the
United States chose not to maintain its heavy-handed involvement in Panama's affairs. This incremental movement
toward military rule was then culminated when Torrijos
and his cohorts staged their military takeover in 1968.

Perhaps, surprisingly, the obvious similarity of
these two military governments would appear to be less
important to understanding the negotiations between the
United States and Panama than several other characteristics shared by the two Panamas. These similarities were
reflected mostly in a set of attitudes and behavioral
predispositions which combined to make up an environment

wherein negotiators found it difficult to take the initiatives which would allow them to achieve effective closure
on the outstanding issues between the two nations.
One attitude shared by a majority of both Panamanians and Zonians was a sense of political powerlessness.
This feeling was realistic and resulted from the ability
of elites within both Panamas to deny a majority of their
populations effective access to the political process.
The resulting lack of political activity in the Zone was
observed and described by the Biesanzes when they wrote,

> Politics is of little importance to the Zonian, who
> has no vote in national elections or much voice in
> local government; he may find expression for his
> public spirit in civic councils, or put pressure on
> Congress through his affiliation with labor unions,
> but he is a member of a regimented community and
> things are decided for him.[43]

As a contrast to the lack of political activity in
the Zone, the Biesanzes compared it to the intense level
of politics which occurred in the Republic.[44] However,
in reality, the differences they described were differences more of style than of substance. Prior to 1968,
Panamanians participated frenetically in a political
ballet which was choreographed to give the impression of
significant and meaningful involvement in the political
process. But Panamanians' participation in campaigns
and elections counted for little as the traditional
elites, utilizing fraud and corruption, were able to
maintain their power and privileges. After their takeover in 1968, the military continued the practice of li-
miting the majority of Panamanians' effective participation in the national political system. Although the new
regime created a facade of constitutional and electoral
mechanisms which gave the impression of widespread political involvement, it was unwilling to grant the majority
any real power that might challenge the regime's ability
to rule for as long as it chose to do so.
Because they were denied effective participation in
the political decisions that daily affected them, it is
understandable why a large percentage of both Zonians
and Panamanians felt alienated from their governments.
Zonians were hostile toward the Department of State,
which they perceived as having no interest in representing their needs but as actually working against them by
continuing to negotiate for a satisfactory resolution of
Panamanian grievances. Zonians were much more favorably
disposed toward the Department of Defense and toward U.
S. politicians like Daniel Flood, who made a career of
denouncing any attempts by Panamanians to gain greater
control over the Zone and the Canal.
Panamanians were also hostile toward their leaders,
who, aside from Arnulfo Arias, were perceived as having

collaborated with Zone officials to maintain U.S. control over a vital part of Panama. Their frustration was
forcefully vented on occasions when they went into the
streets to demonstrate or riot against the continued U.
S. presence in the Zone.
Alienation from their respective governments merged
with the mutual paranoia of Zonians and Panamanians.
The former constantly were afraid of a repetition of the
1964 Canal Zone riots, while they also feared negotiations as a threat to their privileged status and comfor-
table life style. The fears of the Panamanians centered
around their awareness of the large number of U.S.
troops in the Zone and their concern that the United
States might decide to use them to restore the protectorate status that existed prior to the non-intervention
pledge of 1935.
On both sides of the Fourth of July Avenue, also
known as Avenue of the Martyrs or John F. Kennedy Avenue,
growing suspicion and fear produced societies unnaturally
imbued by an extreme nationalism which took the form of
super-patriotism. Frederick Wiseman's notable film
essay, Canal Zone, effectively illustrates the great emphasis that Zonians placed on patriotic symbols and
ceremony. Panamanians also practiced a fervid nationalism which set aside the day of 9 January each year to
honor the martyrs who had given their lives for La
Patria in the 1964 riots.
Thus, similar attitudes within both Panamas served
increasingly to restrict any meaningful relations between
Zonians and Panamanians. This insularity was noted by
one prominent Panamanian banker, who blamed it on the
Zonians' increasing sense of insecurity. He noted that
the split between Zone and Republic extended even to
U.S. residents living in the Zone and in the Republic.
The banker's observations were echoed by a young USIA
official, who lamented the difficulty of initiating contacts between Zonians and Panamanians.

NOTES

1. Harry N. Howard, Military Government in the Panama Canal
Zone (Norman: University of Oklahoma Press, 1931).
2. David McCullough, The Path between the Seas (New York:
Simon and Schuster, 1977), p. 491. Shont's view was supported by
the chief engineer, John J. Stevens, in a letter to Roosevelt where
he argued "that the commission constituted in whatever way it may
be . . . must resolve itself into what will amount to a one-man
proposition."
3. Wayne D. Bray, The Common Law Zone in Panama (San Juan:
Inter-American University of Puerto Rico, 1977), pp. 62-64.
4. William P. Borland, "The Permanent Government of the
Canal Zone," Yale Law Journal 21 (1912):578.
5. Ibid.

6. Richard R. Baxter and Doris Carroll, The Panama Canal: Background Papers and Proceedings of the Sixth Hammarskjold Forum (Dobbs Ferry, N.Y.: Oceana Publications, Inc., 1965), p. 19.

7. Jack Hood Vaughn, "A Latin American Vietnam," The Washington Monthly (October 1973):30-34.

8. See chapter 20 of McCullough, in which he describes the benefits enjoyed by non-Panamanian employees.

9. Bray, p. 66.

10. Willis J. Abbot, Panama and the Canal in Picture and Prose (New York: Syndicate Publishing Co., 1913), p. 144.

11. Abbot, p. 234.

12. Ibid.

13. John B. Biesanz and Mavis Biesanz, The People of Panama (New York: Columbia University Press, 1955), p. 77.

14. Larry L. Pippin, The Remón Era (Stanford: Institute of Hispanic American and Luso-Brazilian Studies, Stanford University Press, 1964), preface.

15. G. A. Mellander, The United States in Panamanian Politics (Dannville, Ky.: The Interstate Printers and Publishers, Inc., 1971), pp. 50-54.

16. Steve C. Ropp, "Panama's Domestic Power Structure and the Canal: History and Future," in Latin American Politics and Development, ed. Howard J. Wiarda and Harvey F. Kline (Boston: Houghton Mifflin Co.), p. 485.

17. E. S. Costrell, "U.S. Policy towards Panama, 1903-Present," Department of State Bulletin 70 (April 22, 1974):438-40.

18. Ibid., p. 440.

19. Lester B. Langley, "The World Crisis and the Good Neighbor Policy in Panama, 1936-1941," Americas 24 (October 1967): 142.

20. Sheldon Liss, The Canal: Aspects of United States-Panamanian Relations (South Bend, In.: University of Notre Dame Press, 1967), p. 55.

21. James D. Cochrane, "Costa Rica, Panama and Central American Economic Integration," Journal of Inter-American Studies and World Affairs 7 (July 1967):331-44.

22. Ibid.

23. John B. Biesanz and Luke M. Smith, "Panamanian Politics," Journal of Politics 14 (August 1952):386.

24. Daniel Goldrich, Sons of the Establishment: Elite Youth in Panama and Costa Rica (Chicago: Rand McNally & Co., 1966), p. 88.

25. Jose Enrique Miguens, "The New Latin American Military Coup," Studies in Comparative International Development 6 (1970-71): 3-15.

26. Mellander, pp. 64-65.

27. Steve C. Ropp, "Military Reformism in Panama: New Directions or Old Inclinations?" Caribbean Studies 12 (October 1972):48.

28. Ibid., pp. 50-51.

29. John W. Mallett, "Group Conflict in the Panamanian Coup d'Etat of 1968" (M.A. essay, University of Texas at Austin, 1972), pp. 89-90.

82

30. Daniel Goldrich, "Panama," in Political Systems of Latin America, ed. Martin C. Needler (New York: Van Nostrand Reinhold Co., 1970), p. 157.

31. Ropp, "Military Reformism," p. 57.

32. Ibid.

33. Ruben Darin Sousa, cited by Mallett, p. 56, from an article in The New Times of Moscow, 30 September 1970.

34. Ropp, "Military Reformism," pp. 58-59.

35. Stephen Gudeman, Relationships, Residence and the Individual: A Rural Panamanian Community (Minneapolis: University of Minnesota Press, 1976), p. 25.

36. Ibid., p. 18.

37. Stephen Kinzer, "The New Panama," The New Republic (February 10, 1979):21-23.

38. Miami Herald, 9 August 1972.

39. Constitution of Panama, 1972 (Washington, D.C.: Organization of American States, 1974).

40. J. Floyd Mecham, "Latin American Constitutions: Nominal or Real," Journal of Politics 21 (May 1959):258-75.

41. Constitution of Panama, 1972, p. 44.

42. Despite his rural background, Torrijos was very complex. This is reflected in several efforts to analyze Torrijos as a man and as a political leader. See Kinzer, pp. 22-24; Martin C. Needler, "Omar Torrijos, the Panamanian Enigma," Intellect (February 1977); and Graham Greene, "The Country with Five Frontiers," New York Review of Books (17 February 1977). Kinzer is positive, Needler is critical, and Greene is an advocate, as shown by the quote, "General Torrijos in seven years has given Panama a national pride. It would be a tragedy if he fell a victim to the impatience of the left or the chicanery of the right" (p. 13).

43. Biesanz and Biesanz, p. 137.

44. Ibid., p. 138.

5
Points of Conflict

Within the linkage theory of politics, there are two principal sources of conflict for a nation's foreign policy. The first is the conflict that develops within the domestic system during the process of making the decisions that ultimately add up to a nation's foreign policy. Although events outside the system form an important consideration in this process, the development of foreign policy is essentially a domestic affair. Conflict of this nature will be discussed in a later chapter. The second area of conflict, and the main thrust of this chapter, is the linkage between the foreign policies of two or more nations, in this case between the United States and Panama.

The foreign policies of any two nations are never so similar that some conflict does not exist. Since the foreign policies of various nations represent different domestic interests, differences in the respective foreign policies are not only expected but unavoidable. On the other hand, the foreign policies of any two nations probably are never so different that the nations will not find areas of agreement. Thus, given such linkage, one may expect some conflict between the most friendly of nations and some areas of agreement between countries that regard themselves as enemies. Somewhere on this continuum of cooperation and conflict, the foreign policy conflicts of any two nations can be placed. The purpose of this chapter is to examine the foreign policies of the United States and Panama relative to the Canal, identify their points of conflict, and evaluate the intensity of conflict between the two nations.

Virtually all the differences that have contributed to conflict between the United States and Panama relate in some manner to control of the Panama Canal and the adjacent Canal Zone by the United States. This issue system is complex and dominates the Panamanian political system. The environment in which this conflict takes place is shaped by the ways the two countries perceive themselves and each other.

Previous to the 1977 treaties, Panama saw itself as an exploited nation. The country had not produced significant mineral wealth, but it did have the very important geographic features of being a narrow country, fifty miles wide at its narrowest waist, and separating two continents. Panama regarded these features as its most valuable natural resource, but it was a resource controlled by a major foreign power that failed to give Panama a just share of the benefits extracted from it.

Such exploitation of a modernizing nation by a powerful, already-modern nation is perhaps the most common manifestation of imperialism. In Panama's view, other imperialistic situations also stemmed from United States control of the Canal. This was especially emphasized by the military government of General Omar Torrijos, which considered the previous civilian governments of Panama as puppets of the United States. The presence of United States troops in Panama for purposes that the Panamanian government did not approve also was regarded as evidence of an imperialistic relationship. Panama further viewed as imperialism any relationship in which a small nation is so dominated economically by a major power that the weaker nation feels that it has little control over its own destiny.

The United States justified its presence in the Canal Zone and its continued possession of the Canal by treaty with and by payment to both Panama and Colombia. In addition, the United States purchased all the land from the individual Panamanian landowners. This has prompted the claim by a number of United States congressmen that the U.S. not only owned the Canal Zone but that it had purchased it twice. The costs of land acquisition and extensive additional investments in the Zone were not included in the Canal construction costs of $387 million. In all, the U.S. spent $993.1 million for the Canal, land, titles, structures, equipment, support facilities, schools, hospitals, and other facilities.[1] The cost of defense installations were still an additional expense. The United States claimed that revenue from the Canal covered only the expense of operation and interest on the outstanding debt for canal construction, while only occasionally showing a profit. In fiscal year 1972, a deficit of $1.3 million was reported. In 1976, the last year before the new treaties were concluded, the deficit had grown to $15 million. One of the highest estimates of overall U.S. investment in the Canal and the Zone, an estimate made by John McClellan (D. AR) was $5.7 billion. The Panama Canal Company's estimate for replacement cost of the Canal, its facilities, and defense facilities was $9.8 billion.[2]

Thus, the position of the United States was that, far from exploiting Panama, the U.S. had made considerable investment in the country. In addition, the Canal provided jobs for thousands of Panamanians at wages

considerably higher than those received in the Republic.
In 1976, the Panama Canal Company payroll for non-U.S.
citizens was $81.6 million. Also, the United States
paid an annuity of more than $2 million to Panama in
addition to the $10 million paid Panama at the construc-
tion stage of the Canal and $25 million to Colombia. In
addition, the U.S. averaged about $15 million annually
in economic aid to Panama. In all, the United States
claimed that the Canal operation pumped from $160 to
$170 million dollars a year into the Panamanian Gross
National Product.[3]

The Panamanian response to the economic input argument was that the Canal made so little money or had deficits because tolls were deliberately kept low in order
to subsidize United States and world shipping at Panama's
expense. The jobs available to Panamanians would still
be available if Panama controlled the Zone and shared in
the operation of the Canal. The economic aid Panama received was essentially a bribe to keep Panama silent and
was only a fraction of what was financially due. Panama
felt that the investment argument differed little from
arguments presented in other colonial relationships. In
the Panamanian case, an investment had been made in the
past that was used as justification for future exploitation until the investment was returned--an investment
that could never be returned as long as the tolls were
kept low by the U.S.

An important part of the environment surrounding
the conflicts between the United States and Panama was
that if change did not take place in the Canal arrangement, the interests of the United States would best be
served. The pressures Panama put on the United States
through bilateral negotiations and international forums
such as the Organization of American States and the United Nations made a successful defense of the status quo
unlikely. The United States therefore attempted to minimize change and, at the same time, hoped to reduce Panamanian demands. Rather than regarding itself as an
imperialist power, the United States held that it had a
legal right under the 1903 treaty to be in Panama and
that it was helping a weaker country by being there.

The degree of change the United States was willing
to accept was difficult to fix because of disagreement
within the U.S. domestic system. The State Department
leaned toward greater compromise with Panama than did
Congress, especially the House of Representatives. The
Defense Department position seemed to be somewhere between the State Department and congressional positions.
Change was accepted by all, except for a few congressional militants, but there was no agreement on the extent and kind of change acceptable.

Although the United States often has been accused
of being imperialistic, the charge usually results from
other than direct United States control in another

country. Ordinarily, the charge relates to activities
of American corporations, as during the Allende regime
in Chile, or to United States support of a country that
still maintained control over a colony. In the latter
case, an example was the United States supplying military equipment to its NATO ally, Portugal, which used the
equipment to retain control over its colonies in Africa.
On other occasions, the charge of imperialism came when
the United States supported a friendly government (for
example, the Thieu regime in South Vietnam) that did not
have the general support of its people. But in the instance of the Panama Canal, the United States had direct
control over part of the country and over activities
challenged as being imperialistic. This was a situation
with which the United States had had little experience.
        The discomfort of the United States with its posi-
tion--that is, with its ·preference for the status quo in
the Canal Zone--coupled with the low priority of Latin
American problems in U.S. foreign policy since the early
1960s could account for the slow progress of negotiations between the United States and Panama since 1964.
The Panamanian government had long seen the negotiations
as only a delaying tactic by the United States, which
had no real intention of finding a solution to the Canal
issue. Panama recognized that Congress and the State
Department were divided on how much the United States
could give up, but Panama felt even the more generous
State Department position fell short of what Panama
could afford to accept. Negotiators for the United
States realized, however, that the United States Senate,
and perhaps the House, had to be satisfied before a new
treaty could be concluded. Thus, from the viewpoint of
American negotiators, any new agreement had to satisfy
both Panama and Congress, whose positions were far apart.
        The United States consistently saw the Panamanian
demands as too great but also recognized that Panama
used these demands to rally domestic support to a military government unsure of its support. There was strong
U.S. sentiment, too, that the military government used
the Canal issue to distract domestic attention away from
the various domestic failures of the Torrijos government.
Thus, both the United States and Panama had strong domestic linkages that related to negotiating a settlement
of their wide range of differences.

THE ISSUES

        Considering the highly charged environment of Uni-
ted States-Panamanian relations, almost any difference
of opinion could develop into an issue between the two
countries. Undoubtedly, some issues were advanced by
Panama to harass the United States and to give Panama
room to bargain. Others, however, were fundamental

issues with deep meaning to Panamanians.

Without question, the most emotional and fundamental issue was the one of sovereignty over the Canal Zone, an area which encompassed 558 square miles of territory and water. The 1903 treaty gave the United States the right to operate a canal and to administer and defend a canal and canal zone "as if it were the sovereign of the territory . . . to the entire exclusion of the exercise by the Republic of Panama of such sovereign rights, powers or authority." Further, these rights of sovereignty were granted to the United States "in perpetuity." Even though alterations in the 1903 treaty were negotiated in 1936 and 1955, the sovereignty and perpetuity clauses remained as originally written. The Panamanian government claimed that these clauses were no longer enforceable since the United States had exceeded the rights it was given in the 1903 treaty.

Although Panamanians, like other Latin Americans, are fond of defending their position with principles of international law, the issue of sovereignty over the Zone was not simply a debate over a principle of law. The sovereignty question had such day-to-day meaning that the Panamanians usually thought of the issue not as a legal abstraction but in terms of specific conflicts, such as legal jurisdiction in the Zone, political asylum, water rights, and the use of Panamanian territory for military purposes.

Long before the 1964 riots, various Panamanian regimes argued that Panamanian laws should be applied in the Zone just as they were in the rest of the Republic. Even Panamanians friendly toward the United States noted that the two countries did not have a Status of Forces agreement, although the U.S. had such agreements with several other countries in which it had substantial numbers of troops stationed. A status of forces agreement allows local courts to try American military personnel for violations of the law unless the violations occur in the line of duty. In Panama, the United States expected military personnel who violated the law in the Republic to be turned over to the U.S. authorities in the Zone. Panama felt that it was entitled to a Status of Forces agreement since the U.S. forces were stationed on territory over which Panama should have legal jurisdiction. In the absence of an agreement, Panama felt it was being treated as a subordinate to United States law.

In the Zone, American law exclusively prevailed for civilians and military, whether United States citizens or non-citizens. The United States Congress made the laws for the Zone, United States courts administered them, and the president of the United States appointed the military governor of the Zone. If a U.S. citizen broke the law in the Zone and was sentenced to a prison term, he usually was sent to the United States to serve his sentence. If a Panamanian citizen broke the law in the Zone, he was arrested by the Zone police, was tried in an American court, and served any sentence in a U.S. prison located in the Zone. The penitentiary located in the Zone thus had almost exclusively Panamanian inmates. Panama believed that since the Zone was part of Panama, all lawbreakers should be tried under Panamanian law and in Panamanian courts and should serve their sentences in Panamanian jails.

Some recent incidents illustrate the problem of legal jurisdiction between the Republic and the United States. In February 1971, U.S. authorities arrested a Panamanian charged with possession and sale of narcotics. The accused was the former international transit chief at the Tocumen International Airport near Panama City and located in the Republic. He was charged with smuggling $1 million worth of heroin to Dallas, Texas. Arrested while attending a baseball game in the Zone, he then was flown to Dallas for trial and received a five-year sentence. Panama claimed that the accused was tricked into entering the Zone and that, if he were guilty of a crime, the crime had been committed in the Republic and the Panamanian government should have jurisdiction. Further, Panama claimed that investigation of the case had been carried out in the Republic by agents of the U.S. Bureau of Narcotics and Dangerous Drugs without knowledge of the Panamanian government. El Panama America questioned the trial by calling it "a court of justice composed of Texan 'vigilantes' and cowboys."[4] Panamanian Foreign Minister Juan Tack filed a strong protest with the United States over the whole affair.[5]

In July 1974, two Panamanian students were arrested in the Zone for being in an area off-limits to Panamanians. The students had entered a commissary which was barred to anyone not working or living in the Zone. The U.S. ambassador felt the incident was blown out of proportion, but the Panamanian press argued the Panamanians had a right to go where they wished since the Zone was a part of Panama. The students were convicted and given a light fine, which closed the incident.

Another incident involving both jurisdiction and political asylum occurred in May 1971 when three American soldiers escaped from a military stockade in the Zone and fled to the Republic. Although the crimes with which they were charged were not political, the escapees sought and received political asylum from the Panamanian government. In the past, Panamanian authorities would have turned the soldiers over to American military authorities. Following the escape, Panama claimed that the chief of the Gamboa penitentiary in the Zone and a military policeman had entered the Republic in an attempt to kidnap the escapees and return them to the Zone. Foreign Minister Tack protested to the United States embassy that this unsuccessful effort violated

the sovereignty of Panama. Tack also stated that the
escaped soldiers were under the protection of Panama and
could not be extradited since the Zone was a sovereign
part of Panama. The Panamanian government suggested
that the escapees had fled because of racial discrimination against blacks in the United States and because
they were opposed to the war in Vietnam.[6]
Although this incident was a question of political
asylum for American citizens fleeing to the Republic,
most disputes regarding asylum involve individuals going
the other way. International law grants the United
States the right to provide political asylum at the United States embassy in Panama City. The embassy is inside the Republic, and an individual seeking political
asylum there could become a prisoner inside the embassy
if the Panamanian government refused him exit from the
country. Because of its long boundary line with the
Republic, the Canal Zone is more accessible than the embassy and has the added advantage of air transport out
of the Zone from several United States air bases. Since
the Panamanian government does not recognize the Zone as
American territory, disputes developed whenever the
United States offered asylum to Panamanians who fled to
the Zone.
Several instances of the political asylum problem
have occurred in recent years. When General Torrijos
carried out the coup that overthrew the eleven-day-old
government of President Arnulfo Arias in October 1968,
Arias fled to the Canal Zone. For several days, Arias
remained in the Zone and appealed to Panamanians to
overthrow Torrijos. The new government strongly protested the use of the Zone for this purpose, and, eventually, Arias went into exile in the United States.[7]
What was perhaps the most serious dispute over political asylum began in December 1969. While General
Torrijos was attending a horse race in Mexico, his first
trip outside the country since coming to power, Colonels
Ramiro Silvera and Amado Sanjur took over the government.
Torrijos immediately flew back to Panama and, within two
days, was solidly back in power. The two colonels were
arrested, but fifteen others, including the families of
the colonels, fled to the Zone. Since no major figures
in the group were connected with the coup, the Panamanian government did not make an issue of the fugitives.
However, in June 1970, Silvera and Sanjur escaped to the
Zone, along with a captain who reportedly helped them
escape. The Panamanian government filed a strong protest and demanded the return of the three men. At the
time, Tack was in Washington for an OAS meeting and personally delivered the protest to the State Department.
The United States did not return the men.[8]
On still another occasion, the leader of an urban
guerrilla movement in Panama City sought and found asylum
in the Zone after his followers had been killed by the

Panamanian National Guard. A similar case occurred in
September 1976, when an opponent of the Torrijos government fled to the Zone during demonstrations by leftists
against the government. He was transported out of Panama
and later appeared in Venezuela, where he published
anti-Torrijos tracts. Again, Panama protested the
granting of asylum. Since political refugees, by definition, are in disagreement with the government in power,
the use of the Zone, with its dubious legal status as a
sanctuary, frequently contributed to the poor relationship between the United States and Panama.

Another activity that Panama considered a serious
impingement upon its sovereignty was the manner in which
the United States interpreted its responsibility to defend the Canal. The 1903 treaty gave the United States
authority to station troops in the Zone for defense of
the Canal, but Panama argued that the armed forces in
the Zone, both in composition and training programs, went
beyond the rights granted by the treaty. Because of
this illegal use of armed force, Panama claimed the entire treaty to be invalid.

Panamanian authorities saw the mission of the American military as defending the Canal from attack by a non-
hemispheric power but regarded the composition of United
States forces in the Zone as more like that of an occu-
pying army. They claimed that the forces far exceeded
the number necessary for Zone defense and that the best
defense was not from the Zone but from bases at a distance from the Zone and outside Panama.

From 1973 to 1977, the United States reduced, as it
did in other parts of the world, the size of its forces
in Panama from 12,000 to about 9,000. Only four combat
aircraft were stationed there in 1973. Many of the forces were not combat forces, but there was a full brigade
of infantry, the 193d Infantry Brigade, totaling about
4,000.[9] Panamanian authorities regarded the force as
about the size necessary, not to provide protection from
outside attack, but to defend against the 6,000 to 7,000-
man Panamanian National Guard and to protect the Canal
from sabotage.

The Panamanians also charged that the United States
used the Zone for military purposes that had little to do
with defense of the Canal. For instance, the United
States had used the Zone as a training site for the
Green Berets and as a location for jungle survival
school. Another military program not related to Canal
defense was the training, particularly in counter-
insurgency, of military personnel from a number of Latin
American countries. In addition, the United States operated a Latin American air academy in the Zone.

Although the Panamanian government protested these
activities, many members of Panama's National Guard--in-
cluding nearly all of its officers--attended some of
these schools. Before General Torrijos came to power,

he attended four courses in the Zone, including a two-
week counter-insurgency course and a forty-two-week
course in military administration.[10] Panamanians who
opposed the military government were quick to point out
that the tough, well-trained National Guard received most
of its advanced training in the Zone. Between 1969 and
1973, 170 officers and 412 enlisted men attended schools
in the Zone.[11]

The United States Southern Command, which covers the
Caribbean area in addition to the Zone, had its headquarters at Quarry Heights in the Zone. Panama felt that
this activity also exceeded the 1903 treaty provisions.
Torrijos described the Southern Command as "a command of
repression," because he saw its principal purpose as
protecting the Canal from Panamanians. Early in 1971,
the Southern Command reportedly was to be incorporated
into the Atlantic Command at Norfolk, Virginia, as part
of a simplification of command structure.[12] This change
was not carried out, however. The official Panamanian
explanation was that the State Department, which wanted
the change, was overruled by the Defense Department.[13]

Perhaps the most serious charge Panama made was
that the United States stored nuclear and bacteriologi-
cal weapons in the Zone. To this charge, an American
military spokesman said, "No, no, hell no, a thousand
times no, of course not."[14] Since the United States did
not have in the Zone aircraft capable of delivering such
weapons, the denial would appear to be valid.

Related to the dispute over defense needs for the
Canal was the issue which developed over the return to
Panama of the United States base at Rio Hato. This
33,000-acre site, located outside the Zone, was used by
the United States during World War II and until 1947,
when demonstrations in Panama led to the ousting of the
United States from the base. Despite further protests
in 1955, the United States again was authorized by Panama to use the base, this time for a fifteen-year period
with the provision that the authorization could be renewed. When the lease period expired in August 1970,
Panama notified the United States that its request for
renewal was denied. The Panamanian press hailed the action as a great victory for Panamanian nationalism and a
step toward the restoration of Panamanian sovereignty
over all of Panama. In December 1972, the press and
officials in Panama gave considerable coverage to the
twenty-fifth anniversary of the 1947 ouster.[15]

The regulation of air space over the Zone also
caused difficulty. The United States required that all
Panamanian aircraft fly above a minimum altitude over
the Zone and be regulated by air controllers in the Zone.
Panama protested such regulations over territory that it
considered part of Panama. In addition, Panama objected
that air control over the Zone was conducted in English
and not in Spanish.[16]

Panama also complained that U.S. aircraft often
violated Panamanian air space. One of the more serious
examples came in July 1976, when Panama protested that
two low-flying U.S. aircraft not only violated Panamanian air space but also fired on Panamanian troops. U.S.
Ambassador Jorden said that the aircraft were making a
landing approach to an air field in the Zone and that
the Panamanian government had given permission for the
flight pattern that went over Panamanian territory.
What was taken for gunfire was actually the popping of
the aircrafts' engines.[17]

A dispute also existed over landing rights. Panama
claimed that its national airline, Air Panama, should
have landing rights at all the international airports
in the United States, since United States airlines had
full access to the single international airport in Panama. But as matters stood, because Panama had only the
one international airport, Air Panama had landing rights
only in Miami. In Panama's view, it was a simple matter
of reciprocity.

A number of other issues were also interpreted by
the Panamanians as impinging on their sovereignty. The
United States operated its own postal system in the
Canal Zone with rates that were less than those in the
Republic. The Zone administration also issued its own
distinctive license plates, which cost only about one-
tenth that of plates in the Republic.

Also, there was a continuing conflict over the control of the water used to operate Canal locks and the
water systems in the Zone, Panama City, and Colón. The
United States had water rights to the rivers that feed
into Gatun Lake, the major source of water in the Zone.
The passage of each vessel through the Canal requires
about fifty-two million gallons of water, approximately
the amount used daily in an American city of about
250,000 population. The water is dumped into the oceans
after use in the locks; thus, an enormous volume of Panamanian water was used by the United States without any
control by Panama. Panama charged that this use of water
was as much an exploitation of a natural resource as
would be similar use of mineral wealth. As for the water
systems in and near the Zone, the United States treated
and purified the water before it was fed into the systems in the Zone, Panama City, and Colón. The Panamanians objected to the United States charging them for
the cost of water treatment, since they contended that
the water belonged to Panama in the first place and that
the United States did not pay them for water used in the
Zone. The United States furnished Agency for International Development funds to modernize the water distribution system in Panama City, but the protests continued.

In addition to these specific charges of violation
of Panamanian sovereignty, Panama was sensitive to the
question of how the United States interpreted the "as

if sovereign" clause of the 1903 treaty. Any effort to
suggest that the 1903 treaty granted the U.S. sovereignty in the Zone would invariably bring protests from Panama. Protests often greeted statements from those members of Congress who felt the U.S. had full sovereignty
in the Zone. Officially, the United States considered
Panama, from 1903 on, to have "titular sovereignty," but
not actual control in the Zone.

Closely related to the sovereignty question was the
one of perpetuity. Panama wanted a date set for transfer of the Canal and restoration of the Zone to Panama.
Panamanians often referred to the nationalization of the
Suez Canal by Egypt in 1956 and suggested such a prospect for the Panama Canal if the United States did not
agree to a withdrawal date. The Panamanian government
was aware that its situation was somewhat different from
Egypt's when the Suez Canal was nationalized, but it
nevertheless made good political use of the precedent.
One major difference was that British troops had been
withdrawn from the Suez Canal in 1954, two years before
the Canal was seized. Also, Egypt had jurisdiction over
all but the operation of the Canal, whereas Panama had
neither of these advantages. Too, Panama was more dis-
advantaged than was Egypt, when one compares factors
such as size and population, geographic position relative to receiving outside help from a major power, and
military capacity.

When the Panamanian government announced in September 1970 that the 1967 draft treaties were unacceptable,
it explained its position relative to the perpetuity
clause as follows:

> Every stipulation as to perpetuity carries, in
> international law, the seed of its own inefficacy
> because of the universally accepted principle rebus
> sic standibus which voids a stipulation when the
> circumstances which prevailed when it was adopted
> have changed.[18]

Panama argued that since the 1903 treaty, which was
to apply in perpetuity, was modified in 1936 and 1955,
the granting of perpetuity could be challenged. These
changes served as a recognition by both the United States
and Panama that the circumstances under which the original 1903 treaty was negotiated had changed; therefore,
perpetuity became legally questionable.

The manner in which Panama worded its objections to
the 1967 draft treaties could lead to the conclusion
that in those treaties the United States insisted on
perpetuity in the new treaties, but such was not the
case. When President Johnson announced in December 1964
that new treaties were to be negotiated with Panama, he
also said that the United States was willing to give up
its rights in perpetuity to the Canal and Zone. The

draft treaties scheduled the United States to relinquish
the Canal and Zone to Panama no later than 2007. If a
sea-level canal were built, the United States would
withdraw sixty years after completion, and under no circumstances later than 2067. Panama felt that these time
periods were too long--so long, in fact, that changes in
technology might make the canals worthless by the time
they became Panamanian property. For Panama, then, the
provisions of the new treaties differed little from the
perpetuity of the 1903 treaty. The 1977 treaties provided for a shorter period of U.S. control.

The scope of conflict between the United States and
Panama does not end with the questions of sovereignty
and perpetuity, however. Another major problem was the
tolls charged by the United States for use of the Canal
and the related problem of the amount the United States
paid Panama annually.

While the United States argued that the Canal was
not profitable--witness that $312 million of the $387
million cost to build the Canal was still to be amortized
and deficits for Canal operations remained after 1973--
Panama claimed that the United States deliberately had
kept tolls at a break-even rate as a subsidy for the
United States and other major shipping nations. Panama
pointed out that the toll structure for the Canal had
remained virtually unchanged since the Canal opened in
1914 except for two increases in tolls that did not take
place until 1974 and 1976.[19] Despite the increases,
with the inflationary changes in the world's economy
over a sixty-year period since the Canal opened, the
rates in effect were substantially lower in the late
1970s than they were in 1914.

Revenue from tolls in 1976 was $135 million with
about 13,000 ships passing through the Canal, or about
thirty-five ships a day with an average toll of $10,000
a ship. The pre-1974 rates were $.90 a ton laden and
$.72 in ballast; the 1974 rates were $1.08 and $.86,
respectively; and 1976 rates were $1.29 and $1.03. A
ton is figured as 100 cubic feet of below-deck cargo
space, both for laden ships and those in ballast. Panamanians considered the increases very modest and called
for increases that would as much as triple the old rates.
Also, Panama denounced the 1976 increase as a unilateral
decision by the United States but did not oppose the
increase in tolls.[20]

In its demand for toll increases, Panama was supported by a report on the Canal made by the United Nations Economic Commission for Latin America. The report
estimated that during the decade of the 1960s, if rates
had been slightly more than tripled, traffic would have
been reduced by only fourteen percent, but an additional
$1.845 billion in tolls would have been collected. This
estimate was based on continued increases in Canal traffic and did not take into account a decline in traffic

which took place after 1974. "To sum up," the report
stated, "the Canal Company's rate policy amounts to an
implied and substantial subsidy of international traffic,
a sizable proportion of which accrues to the United
States economy, since it is the major user of its services."[21] The report also claimed that users of the
Canal saved $5.4 billion between 1960 and 1970 by not
having to use alternate routes. This was about seven
times the amount of tolls collected during that period.
Panama, of course, did not argue that a substantial increase in tolls was justified so that the United States
would make greater profits. Panama wanted to show that
tolls were deliberately held low to subsidize shipping
and that, in this way, Panama was being exploited by the
United States.

The United States justified the rather modest rate
increases on the grounds of deficits after 1972, increased costs, failure of the Canal to receive its share
of shipping because supertankers could not go through
the Canal and new automated ships could profitably go
around Cape Horn. There was also speculation that the
increase was intended to help cover larger payments to
Panama if new treaties were signed. Although the United
States regarded the Canal as a marginal operation at
best, Panama pointed out that from 1960 to 1970 the Canal
produced "$450 million which was used to cover interests
payable to the U.S. government, to finance many of the
Canal Zone Government's expenses and increase the company's reserves."[22] For these reasons, Panama felt that
even at the old rates the Canal, in fact, had shown a
substantial profit.

Panama also pointed to a number of hidden profits
and advantages for the United States in the operation of
the Canal. During World War II, about 5,300 warships and
8,500 vessels transporting troops and war supplies went
through the Canal. During the Korean and Vietnam wars,
the Canal again was used extensively to support those
war efforts. During peacetime, the Canal was of strategic value to the United States in moving naval vessels
and materials from one ocean to the other. Panama noted
that these savings did not appear in the Canal Company's
balance sheet.

Despite conflict over profitability of the Canal,
Panama received none of the tolls. The United States
annually gave Panama a fixed payment that was not affected by Canal revenues. From 1912 to 1939, the United
States paid Panama $250,000 annually; from 1939 to 1957,
$430,000; from 1957, $1.93 million; and in 1973, $2.1
million, increased to $2.3 million in 1974. The 1939
and 1957 increases resulted from the respective 1936 and
1955 changes in the 1903 treaty. The increases were
made primarily to compensate for the declining buying
power of the dollar. However, Foreign Minister Tack
claimed the $1.5 million increase in 1957 was not an

increase at all. The agreement which raised the U.S.
payment forbade Panama to levy various taxes on persons
living in the Zone. The resultant revenue loss was about
$1.5 million, thus offsetting the increase in the annui-
ty.
    As a gesture to protest the amount paid Panama, in
September 1972 the Panamanian Assembly of Corregimientos
recommended the annuity be refused, and in October 1972
Gen. Torrijos announced that "we reject the annuity" and
refused to accept further payments from the United States
until new treaties were completed.[23] This proved to be
a very popular move among Panamanians.
    Torrijos' gesture meant little, however. The an-
nuity had, for some years, been used as a guarantee of
payment on interest and amortization of bonds to refi-
nance Panama's foreign debt. The Panamanian government
had instructed the U.S. to send the annuity directly to
the National City Bank and the Chase Manhattan Bank in
New York City, which were acting as fiscal agents for
the loans. The arrangement was not changed.
    The 1967 draft treaties allowed $17 million to be
paid Panama the first year, with increases over a four-
year period until the annual payment totaled $22 million.
In rejecting the treaties, Panama argued that the new
payment schedule was still too low, considering the
benefits the United States derived from the Canal:

    . . . The value of these payments turns out to be
    doubtful because the constant depreciation of the
    buying power of the American dollar has not been
    taken into account, with the added aggravation that
    Panama does not participate in the fixing of toll
    rates. Moreover, the maximum duration of the new
    Panama Canal . . . would be until the year 2007,
    but it would expire before if the Sea Level Canal
    is constructed before that year, without any stipu-
    lation . . . as to the advantages or benefits which
    would be ascribed to Panama upon the expiration of
    the new treaty . . . .[24]

    A problem of a different sort is the enclave psy-
chology of the administration and residents of the Canal
Zone. Although it is hardly possible to negotiate into
a treaty a new set of attitudes for the Zonians toward
the Panamanians, the sharp contrast in lifestyles and
standards of living between the two groups was a long-
standing source of irritation. The Zone was thoroughly
Americanized and resembled a cross between a Southern
community and a military base. Contrasts between the
Republic and the Zone were accentuated by the Zone's
abutment on some of the poorest housing in Panama City.
    The enclave feeling held by the Zonians was further
aggravated by little interaction between the groups.
Interaction was never extensive, especially outside the

ruling elite of Panama, but after the 1964 riots many U.
S. citizens were afraid to leave the Zone or could find
no reason to visit the Republic. Many Zonians did not
learn to speak Spanish even after many years residence
in the Zone. The schools in the Zone were conducted in
English. In 1964, at Balboa High School, where the flag
incident took place, only three percent of its students
were non-U.S. citizens. The Zone exhibited little evidence of Spanish culture, and Zonians made little effort
to become acquainted with the nearby Spanish culture.
Zonians therefore had little understanding of life in
the Republic or of the Panamanian position concerning the
Canal. When the 1967 draft treaties were announced,
Zonians perceived them as a threat to their way of life,
for if the treaties were approved, insularity of the
Zone would no longer exist. Subsequent negotiations for
a new set of draft treaties were received similarly.

The Zonians also were upset over the prospect of a
treaty permitting construction of a sea-level canal.
About eleven thousand civilians are required to operate
and maintain the lock canal and other facilities in the
Zone. The Canal is indeed an engineering marvel, but it
requires considerable maintenance. The proposed sea-
level canal would require far less maintenance, requiring possibly as few as one thousand employees. Since
about eight thousand of the eleven thousand employees
are Panamanians, most of the layoffs would occur among
that group, but many U.S. citizens also would lose their
positions.

A sea-level canal provided a threat to Zonians in
another way as well. Appointed by President Johnson and
granted a $24-million appropriation by Congress to search
for a sea-level canal route, the Interoceanic Commission
reported to the president in December 1970. After investigating routes from Mexico to Colombia, the commission recommended a route parallel to and ten miles west
of the present canal. The proposed canal would require
a treaty between the United States and Panama before it
could be built; such a treaty was among the draft treaties that Panama rejected in September 1970. Even if a
treaty acceptable to both countries were negotiated, any
new canal zone doubtless would not be a U.S. colonial
domain like the old Zone. Consequently, many Zonians
believed that the new canal should not be built, but,
rather, the old canal should be modernized. Zonians
pushed for modernization of the lock canal as being more
economical than a new canal, but their motives appeared
to be to preserve their way of life in the old Zone.

Another area of dispute involved Panamanians who
worked in the Zone for the American military, the Canal
Company, or other U.S. agencies. Before 1955, employees
in the Zone were paid according to the gold standard for
the Americans and the considerably lower silver standard
for Panamanians. These pay differentials were officially

abolished in the 1955 treaty, but Panama pointed out
that U.S. citizens continued to dominate the higher-
paying administrative and skilled positions, and Panamanians, the lower-paying, semiskilled positions.

In 1976, the twenty-seven percent of the Canal Company work force that held U.S. citizenship received
forty-eight percent of the payroll ($76.5 million), and
the Panamanians, fifty-two percent ($81.6 million). The
percentage relationship between the two groups was consistent throughout the 1970s. In sum, the pay structure
appeared highly discriminatory against Panamanians.

The ethnic composition of Panamanians employed in
the Zone provided a further complication. When the Canal was built, nearly all the manual labor was provided
by forty thousand men imported from the West Indies,
notably Barbados. Since the workers came mainly from a
British possession, their first language was English.
Further, they were black and their culture was non-Latin.
After the Canal was completed, many laborers did not return home but stayed on and furnished the bulk of the
labor required to maintain and operate the Canal. This
aroused resentment among Latin Panamanians, and during
the 1930s the Panamanian government attempted unsuccessfully to deport these people to the West Indies. The
administration of President de la Guardia (1952-1956)
launched an official campaign to stamp out the long-
standing prejudice in Panama against West Indians. The
campaign had only limited success.

Preference for West Indians to fill jobs in the
Zone seemed to stem from two factors. The first was
that since West Indians helped build the Canal, West Indians were sought when positions opened up to operate
the Canal. Since that time, working for the Canal Company had become a family tradition for many. A second
factor was that the West Indians had English as a first
language, and U.S. citizens found them easier to work
with than Spanish-speaking Panamanians. Even though the
United States agreed to hire more Latin Panamanians, in
1977 approximately half of the non-U.S. employees in the
Zone were of West Indian ancestry--considerably higher
than the percentage of Panama's population that was West
Indian. As a result, Panama continued to claim that Latin Panamanians were discriminated against in the Zone
and that West Indians generally occupied the better-
paying positions available to Panamanians.

An unusual incident that reflects the conflicts between Panamanian nationalism and the economic well-being
of Panamanians employed in the Zone occurred in November
and December 1972. A number of Panamanian drivers for
the privately owned, Delaware-chartered Canal Zone Bus
Company hijacked seventeen buses to the Republic. This
was done to force the company owner to sell the bus company to Corporación Única de Transporte (CUT), a privately owned Panamanian corporation operating under

government regulation. The Panamanian government intervened and supported the sale on the grounds that the bus
company thus would be brought under the laws and jurisdiction of the Republic. About three-fourths of the
drivers, realizing that they would come under the Panamanian $.50 hourly minimum wage law rather than the U.S.
minimum wage that was then $1.60, opposed the sale. The
company owner then negotiated a new contract, including
a promise to pay Panamanian social security, and the
company remained American-owned.[25] The buses were returned, but the Panamanian press claimed that the drivers
either were forced into their statement of preferring
American ownership or were lackeys of the Americans.

A more serious dispute regarding American-owned
property developed earlier in 1972 when the Panamanian
government, on June 1, announced that it was "temporarily" seizing the Panamanian Power and Light Company (Com-
pania Panama de Fuerza y Luz), a subsidiary of the Boise
Cascade Corporation of Boise, Idaho. The Panamanian
government justified the seizure that eventually resulted in Panama's nationalizing the company on the grounds
that the company was not increasing its investment, that
it owed $2 million in back fuel bills, that it was for-
getting about the "social welfare it must satisfy," and
that it had "halted the pace of development of the country."[26]

The Panamanian government apparently had been preparing for this action for some time. Three years earlier, it had reduced the margin of profit allowed the
company until the company had become a marginal operation. The company attempted to curtail some of its un-
profitable operations but ran into labor difficulties
from employees who thought they could lose their jobs,
and encountered opposition from the Panamanian government to any relief from governmental restrictions. The
company, long criticized in Panama for its inefficien-
cies, was an ideal target for expropriation, since it
had few Panamanian supporters. Panama went ahead with
nationalization but had little success in making the
company more efficient.[27]

The State Department took a hands-off attitude, preferring that the company and the Panamanian government
negotiate a settlement for compensation. However, Congressman John Murphy, Democrat from New York and chairman of the House Subcommittee on the Panama Canal, held
hearings on the seizure and sharply criticized Panama's
action. John Hennessy, assistant secretary of the Treasury, announced that if the negotiations for a settlement were not successful, the United States would suspend $22 million in aid projects for fiscal 1973. The
United States also would vote against World Bank and
Inter-American Development Bank loan applications from
Panama.[28] Such actions were not taken, however.

Another major dispute came to light after

Congressman Murphy charged that high Panamanian officials
were involved in smuggling narcotics to the United
States. In July 1971, Rafael Richard, son of the Panamanian ambassador to Taiwan, and his uncle, Guillermo
Gonzalez, had been arrested in the United States for
smuggling narcotics and sentenced to seven years in prison. On 8 March 1973, Congressman Murphy released a report entitled "Overview of the Narcotics Problem in Panama," in which the foreign minister, Juan Tack, and
Gen. Torrijos' brother and Panamanian ambassador to
Spain, Moise Torrijos, were accused of involvement in
smuggling narcotics to the United States. Murphy said
he based his report on briefings by the Bureau of Narcotics and Dangerous Drugs (BNDD). Tack was furious and
denied all charges. He retaliated by expelling three
BNDD agents operating in Panama.[29] These charges sur-
faced again during the debate in 1977 and 1978 over the
new treaties.
Besides these problems in United States-Panamanian
relations, other incidents and disputes have constituted
additional nagging problems. In aggregate, they have
accounted for considerable ill feeling between the two
countries.
Before December 1971, persons landing at Tocumen
Airport in the Republic who were bound for the Canal
Zone did not have their luggage inspected by Panamanian
custom officials but, rather, by customs officials from
the Zone. In December, Panama started inspection, justifying its action by referring to United States accusations of Panamanian laxity on narcotics control.[30] Inspection apparently was intended as a mild form of
harassment for people going to the Zone, as evidenced
by the simultaneous imposition of an airport tax on anyone arriving at Tocumen and destined for the Zone.[31]
During World War II, the United States built the
Boyd-Roosevelt Highway that runs from Colón on the Atlantic to Panama City on the Pacific. Under an agreement with Panama, the United States agreed to maintain
the highway even though it is almost entirely outside
the Zone. The highway had been in poor condition for
some time, and the Panamanian government often complained
to the United States about the level of maintenance.
The United States defended its apparent neglect of the
highway by pointing out that it was built under wartime
standards and was not intended to last over a long period
of time. Therefore, normal maintenance would not suffice to put the road in good condition; it must be re-
built. Since funds for additional work on the highway
repeatedly were cut by the Defense Department, prospects
for putting the highway into good repair were not prom-
ising. Also, the United States argued that it could do
little about the highway as long as there were no controls over traffic or load limits.
Bad feelings also resulted from restrictions on

commercial activity by Panamanian merchants in the Zone.
Although Panamanians were no longer barred from the Zone
(several years before, two Panamanian salesmen had been
arrested in a Zone commissary for trying to sell their
products to the commissary), Panamanian merchants still
felt that they were the subtle target of discrimination.
Panamanian businessmen were allowed to bid for contracts
with Zone commissaries, but they were at a relative disadvantage to American businessmen, since all goods purchased by the Canal Company were F.O.B. New Orleans.
Panamanians regarded as senseless the basing of the cost
of their products on cost plus shipping from New Orleans.
In addition, the commissaries did not usually buy Panamanian products, for, as the president of one of the two
major breweries in Panama pointed out, U.S. citizens
would import Danish beer before they would buy Panamanian
beer.

Two programs the United States operated in the Republic that caused tension were not directly related to
the problems of the Canal: the Peace Corps and A.I.D.
The Peace Corps began operations in Panama in 1962 and
at its peak had two hundred volunteers in Panama. In
late 1970, the Panamanian government started a Peace
Corps-style program of its own and sent young Panamanians
to carry out projects similar to those being done by the
United States Peace Corps. These projects were of short
duration, usually lasting no more than a few weeks, but
clearly were intended to demonstrate that Panamanians
could do the same things the U.S. Peace Corps was doing.
Half the cost of this domestic program was paid for by
A.I.D. funds. In February 1971, Foreign Minister Tack
announced that the U.S. Peace Corps no longer was needed
in Panama since "we can enlist Panamanians and international volunteers to do the same things that the Peace
Corps is doing." He gave the Peace Corps--which, at the
time, had one hundred-twenty volunteers--ninety days to
complete its operations.[32] Panama was the first Latin
American country to expel the Peace Corps, but, consistent with its established policy in other parts of the
world, the United States made no protest. The American
embassy took the view that if Panama could handle the
projects, the program had been a success, since the purpose was to help countries to deal with their own problems.

In one sense, the expulsion of the Peace Corps was
mystifying, since the volunteers deliberately avoided
close associations with the Zone and visits to estab-
lishments ordinarily frequented by U.S. citizens in the
Republic. Many volunteers were critical of United
States policy toward Panama and in Vietnam. On the
other hand, the volunteers also were critical of the military government in Panama and its neglect of the problems of the poor. The volunteers were U.S. citizens, and
the Peace Corps was the one aspect of United States

policy in Panama that could be thrown out by Panamanian
initiative; thus, the Peace Corps became the victim of
anti-American feelings in the government.

The A.I.D. program in Panama, as in Latin America
generally, assumed a low profile beginning early in the
Nixon administration. A.I.D. provided Panama with economic assistance averaging about $15 million a year.
From 1961 to 1971, the United States authorized $157
million to be spent in Panama, but about one-half ($83
million) was not spent during that time period. Some of
these funds eventually were spent, but the reasons for
the delay were twofold. First, the Panamanian government had no general development plan, although many individual projects were underway, and the United States
delayed releasing some funds until such a plan was received. A second reason was the failure of Panama to
allocate some $80 million in counterpart funds for the
financing of certain projects.

The Panamanian government took the view that this
economic aid was somewhat like blackmail, designed to
keep Panama from complaining about the status of the
United States in the Zone. If, indeed, that was the
purpose, the aid programs were not very successful. Panama received the highest per capita aid of any Latin
American country, but the Panamanian government said it
could do without the aid if it received its fair share
of Canal revenue.

Both the symbolic and the legal basis of the conflicts between the United States and Panama was the 1903
Hay/Bunau-Varilla Treaty. Panama used the treaty as the
symbol of the discrimination and imperialism Panama
claimed to suffer. It was this treaty that split Panama
into two parts by allowing the Canal Zone to bisect the
country and thus restrict travel and commerce between
the two parts. To make matters worse, to Panamanians,
the treaty was imposed on Panama by intrigue and deceit;
only by abrogating this treaty could U.S.-Panamanian relations be significantly improved.

NOTES

1. U.S., Department of State, Panama Canal Treaty Information (Washington, D.C.: Government Printing Office, September
1977). (No pagination.)
2. Ibid.
3. This estimate was the one commonly used by the State
Department in the early 1970s.
4. FBIS, 16 February 1971, p. M1, El Panama America, 13
February 1971, p. 4.
5. Ibid., and FBIS, 12 February 1971, p. M4, Televisora
Nacional, 11 February 1971.
6. FBIS, 12 May 1971, p. M2, La Estrella de Panama, 11 May
1971, p. 1; FBIS, 13 May 1971, pp. M1-3; El Panama America, pp. 1,
4; and Matutino, 12 May 1971, p. 4.

7. New York Times, 16 October 1968, p. 12.
8. New York Times, 16 December 1969, pp. 1, 8; 18 December 1969, p. 3; 29 June 1970, p. 8.
9. New York Times, 15 March 1973, p. 16.
10. New York Times, 16 October 1968, p. 12.
11. New York Times, 16 March 1973, p. 16.
12. New York Times, 14 February 1971, p. 7; 22 April 1971, p. 15; 15 March 1973, p. 16.
13. FBIS, 15 July 1971, pp. 4-8, La Estrella de Panama, 13 July 1971, pp. 1, 25.
14. New York Times, 15 March 1973, p. 16.
15. FBIS, 13 December 1972, pp. M1-12, Televisora Nacional, 12 December 1972, Radio Libertad, 13 December 1972; FBIS, 14 December 1972, Radio Libertad, 14 December 1972.
16. FBIS, 17 December 1970, p. M7; Star and Herald, 17 December 1970, p. 1; FBIS, 18 December 1970, p. M3, Televisora Nacional, 17 December 1970.
17. FBIS, 19 July 1976, p. N1, ACAN, 16 July 1976.
18. Panamanian Foreign Ministry, Bases of the Position of the Panamanian Chancellory in Regard to the Rejection by Panama of the Three Draft Treaties, September 1970, p. 4.
19. The manner in which tolls were calculated was changed in 1937, but the change essentially did not alter the amount charged.
20. New York Times, 22 December 1973, p. 33.
21. United Nations, Economic Commission for Latin America, 23rd session, 15 September 1972, The Economy of Panama and the Canal Zone (designated S/10900 by Security Council, 9 March 1974), pp. 48-55.
22. FBIS, 21 March 1973, p. A31, Domestic Service, 20 March 1973.
23. FBIS, 27 June 1974, p. N1, La Estrella de Panama, 24 June 1974, p. 2; FBIS, 22 October 1972, p. M1, La Estrella de Panama, 17 October 1972, p. 1.
24. Bases of . . . Rejection, pp. 21-22.
25. FBIS, 27 November 1972, pp. M3-4, Televisora Nacional, 20 November 1972; FBIS, 1 December 1972, pp. M2-3, Radio Libertad, 29 November 1972.
26. FBIS, 2 June 1972, pp. M1-2, Radio Mia, 1 June 1972.
27. Miami Herald, 22 June 1972.
28. New York Times, 11 August 1972, p. 43.
29. FBIS, 17 December 1971, pp. M1-2, La Estrella de Panama, 12 December 1971 (no page number given); New York Times, 28 January 1973, sec. 3, p. 50; Miami Herald, 16, 17 and 18 March 1972.
30. Miami Herald, 23 December 1972.
31. FBIS, 12 January 1971, p. M4, El Panama America, 11 January 1971, pp. 1, 8.
32. New York Times, 25 April 1971, p. 17.

6
Search for an Alternative

When a nation has a serious conflict with another nation, presumably its decision-makers will review a number of possible actions. Even though all alternatives may not be given equal consideration and the search for alternatives is not necessarily exhaustive, perhaps the simplest strategy is to select an alternative that renders the conflict moot. This seems to have been U.S. strategy when, in December 1964, President Johnson announced the beginning of a search for a route for a sea-level canal--a route that would not necessarily be in Panama. The president also announced the appointment of a commission to conduct the search and requested an appropriation from Congress to finance the search. Congress quickly complied with the request.[1]

Along with the announcement of the search, the United States also stated its willingness to negotiate a new treaty concerning control of the lock canal and defense and control of the Canal Zone. Panama received the joint announcement with mixed reaction. Panamanians were delighted that the United States at long last was willing to negotiate a new treaty, but the search for a new canal route troubled them. If a route were found outside Panama, or even if a route were recommended that was in the sparsely populated eastern portion of Panama, the present canal and other facilities located near the terminal cities of Panama and Colón would be obsolete. These terminal cities had become the major cities of Panama because they were on the Canal and would suffer serious economic decline if a sea-level canal were built some distance away.

Although Panama before 1974 received only $1.93 million annuity direct payment from the United States, some thirty percent of Panama's foreign exchange came from the Canal by indirect economic benefits, and about twenty-eight percent of Panama's GNP was derived directly or indirectly from the Canal.[2] Even if the canal were to be built near the present canal so that present facilities would still be utilized, a new canal would

result in loss of jobs for about ten thousand Panamanians
employed by the Canal Company and the Canal Zone Government.[3] A sea-level canal would require far less maintenance than the lock canal, and only a thousand or so individuals would be needed to run it. If the new canal
were some distance away, so that defense facilities the
United States maintained in the Zone were no longer
needed, then an additional four thousand Panamanians employed by the American military also would be out of
work.[4] Only if a sea-level canal were reasonably close
to the present canal would Panama's losses be minimized.
     The argument for building a sea-level canal was a
strong one, particularly if the position were accepted
that the United States had an obligation to support
world commerce by guaranteeing quick and economical passage through the isthmus. The United States noted such
an obligation in the legislation authorizing the original lock canal and has reiterated it many times since.
More directly in the interests of the United States,
however, is that the U.S. was, in 1964, the largest single user, accounting for about one-sixth of all tonnage
through the Canal.[5] Of even greater significance,
though, is that seventy percent of all Canal cargoes
either originate in or are destined for the United
States, regardless of the registry of the vessels.[6]
Thus, when the United States defended its position of
guaranteeing access to the Canal for all shipping at
reasonable tolls, the United States was the chief bene-
factor of this policy. If, as President Johnson stated
in his December 1964 statement, "the Canal is growing
old," and a new sea-level canal was necessary, then the
United States was the country most concerned.
     Projections of traffic through the lock canal have
been made frequently. Such studies were conducted as
early as 1927, followed by others in 1944, 1947, 1958,
1964, and 1967.[7] The study, started by the Canal Commission in 1964 and completed in 1970, projected that
the lock canal would reach its capacity by the end of
this century. The projected maximum capacity of the Canal is 26,800 passages per year, but when traffic
reached that level, the waiting time to enter the Canal
would increase considerably over the normal eight hours.
The Panama Canal Company considered more than 20,900
transits a year as requiring a substantial increase in
the waiting period.[8] Traffic in 1970 was over 15,000
transits, or about forty per day.[9] The projection for a
single-lane, sea-level canal with wider areas for passing is about 35,000 transits a year. This number would
be sufficient for the foreseeable future. If the sea-
level canal were to be widened to two-lane traffic
throughout its length, its capacity would be about
60,000 transits annually.
     In addition to traffic limitations, the present
canal has serious limitations as to the size of vessel

that can pass through. Fully laden ships of about 55,000 tons are the maximum size that can go through. Larger vessels, up to 65,000 tons, can pass through with less than a full load or unladen. Since the locks have a draft of about 41 feet, a width of 110 feet, and length of 1,000 feet, any ship exceeding these dimensions is unable to use the lock canal, regardless of tonnage. This included 1,300 super tankers and other vessels a-float in 1970; 1,750 such vessels were projected for the future.

The limits on the size of vessels had national se-curity implications, as well. For many years, United States naval vessels were built so that they could use the Canal. The largest of the battleships built by the United States, the Missouri class, could go through the Canal with only inches to spare, but the larger, slant or angle-deck aircraft carriers exceed the Canal's capa-city. A sea-level canal could accommodate these car-riers plus all but the largest of the supertankers.

Another national security problem is that the lock canal is particularly susceptible to sabotage. If one of the locks were destroyed by either sabotage or the explosion of a ship in a lock, the Canal could be closed for months. If damage were extensive enough to cause substantial loss of water from Gatun Lake, since the locks act as dams for the lake, the Canal could be in-operative for up to two years. Also, dams that create Gatun Lake could be destroyed with the same effect.

During World War II, the Korean War, and the war in Vietnam, many troop ships, warships, and supply ships passed through the Canal. During the 1962 Cuban missile crisis, the Canal played an important role in the pas-sage of Pacific-fleet naval vessels headed for the blockade. To have the Canal closed in a time of crisis could be a serious problem for the United States. A sea-level canal, of course, would not be vulnerable to attacks on locks or dams. Even if a vessel were sunk in the channel, it could be removed quickly with explosives. If a sea-level canal were subject to nuclear attack, it could be closed; however, such an event doubtless would mean a general nuclear war, which would confront the United States with far more serious problems than a threat to the Canal. Short of nuclear war, however, a sea-level canal would be much easier to defend than a lock canal, and, thus, a sea-level canal would be better for the national security of the United States.

ALTERNATE ROUTES

From the time of Balboa, men pondered the possibili-ty of constructing a sea-level canal across the Isthmus of Panama. The original effort by the French Canal Com-pany to build a canal was at sea level and, when the United States took over the effort, the original U.S.

design was for a sea-level canal. Only after American
engineers realized that a sea-level canal would be more
expensive and difficult was the lock canal constructed.[10]
The dream of a sea-level canal was not lost with completion of the lock canal, however, and during the past
forty years several study commissions have examined possible routes. Before 1964, the most comprehensive study
was conducted in 1947 by the Panama Canal Company at the
direction of Congress. In all, thirty routes were identified. These extended from Route 1, between the Bay of
Campeche and the Gulf of Tehuantepec at the narrow waist
of Mexico, southeast to the last possible route, Route
30, in western Colombia. However, when President Johnson
requested a new commission in 1964, he identified only
four of the thirty routes for intense investigation.
These were Route 8, along the Nicaraguan-Costa Rican
frontier; Route 14, which called for the conversion of
the present lock canal to sea-level; Route 17, in Panama
but about 110 miles east of the present canal; and Route
25, near the Panamanian border, but located wholly in
Colombia. Curiously, the route the commission eventually recommended in 1970 was not one of these.

The Atlantic-Pacific Interoceanic Canal Study Commission, the formal title of the study group, reported
to President Nixon on 1 December 1970. The commission
was to have completed its work by mid-1968, but delays
resulted in the commission requesting an eighteen-month
extension. In all, the commission spent $24 million to
conduct the study.

When the commission began its work, the single question seemed to be where to build a sea-level canal, but
as the investigation progressed another question became
equally important: How should the canal be constructed?

While the commission's report was hundreds of pages
long and included appendices devoted to foreign policy
and economic considerations as well as to the engineering problems of building a sea-level canal, the essence
of the report was simple. First, the commission reported that the canal could and should be built. Second,
the commission recommended that the canal be built by
conventional rather than nuclear means. Finally, the
commission recommended that the canal be built in Panama
along Route 10, a route considered only in the last
weeks of the commission's work and located about ten
miles west of the present canal.

The commission found no engineering difficulties
that could not be overcome in the construction of a sea-
level canal. In addition, the report noted that there
were sound reasons for building a canal, the most com-
pelling being that the present canal would be unable to
handle projected traffic by the end of the century.
Even if various improvements were made in the lock canal
as recommended by the Panama Canal Company, the present
canal would still have a more limited capacity than

would a sea-level canal.

The commission also pointed out the problems faced in the future with giant tankers and bulk carriers. The commission argued that improvements in the present canal would not resolve the problem of the lock canal's vulnerability to sabotage and guerilla attacks. The commission stated that if capacity beyond the present canal were not developed to allow for larger ships and increased number of transits, several consequences were likely. World shipping routes could be changed to avoid the Canal, transisthmian pipelines could be constructed so that supertankers could be loaded and unloaded at either end of the Canal, and air and rail transport could be used to avoid the inconvenience of a limited-use canal. Finally, the commission also pointed out that the United States, as a hemispheric power, had the responsibility to provide an adequate canal, since such a canal was important to the United States and other world shippers.

The commission estimated the cost of a sea-level canal along Route 10 to be $2.88 billion. This estimate was for construction only and did not include the cost of relocation of port facilities and military bases. The commission pointed out, however, that since Route 10 was near the bases along the present canal, little relocation of military facilities would be necessary.

When the commission began its consideration of alternative routes, it operated under the assumption that the new canal would be built, at least in part, with the use of nuclear devices. Why this assumption was made is difficult to understand, since the Nuclear Test Ban Treaty was already in force and had been signed by the United States. The Test Ban Treaty allows nuclear detonations only if they are underground. An exception to the treaty can be negotiated, but an exception requires the consent of a majority of the signatories to the treaty, and of all three of the major signatories (the United States, Great Britain, and the U.S.S.R.). The possibility of obtaining an exception would be doubtful under the best of circumstances but extremely unlikely at the present level of technology, which cannot guarantee that radioactivity produced by nuclear excavation of a canal would not cross into other countries. Panama also comes under the Latin American Nuclear Free Zone Treaty, but this treaty specifically allows for the use of nuclear explosions for peaceful purposes.

Two of the four routes mentioned by President Johnson in his December 1964 statement depended on some nuclear excavation to keep the cost of a sea-level canal at an acceptable level. These were Route 17, which crosses the isthmus in the sparsely populated Darien area of eastern Panama, and Route 25 in western Colombia. The commission eventually added additional routes to the four the president had mentioned, and one of these,

Route 23, in both Panama and Colombia, would also be excavated in part by nuclear devices. The commission speculated that Route 8 on the Nicaraguan-Costa Rican border could be constructed by either conventional or nuclear means.

The commission devoted considerable attention to Route 25 in Colombia and ultimately found it to be the one best suited for nuclear excavation. This route would require that a minimum of population (about forty-three thousand people) be removed. Since those evacuated would have to be gone for as much as two years, a remote site with little population was essential. Heavy concentrations of people ruled out the use of nuclear devices for excavation along some of the routes considered by the commission. Besides being in a sparsely populated area, Route 25 had another advantage: The portion to be excavated by conventional means was in the low-lying floodplain of the Atrato River.

Since the commission looked at the routes over which nuclear excavation could be used first--routes necessarily in remote areas and, in the case of Route 25, outside Panama--the commission action supported the argument of a number of Panamanians and United States congressmen who opposed a new canal that the commission's real purpose was to bring the Panamanian government in line to negotiate a more lenient treaty with the United States. Why was the commission looking at routes requiring extensive nuclear excavation when such excavation was unlikely, if not for the purpose of pressuring Panama by threatening to build a canal in another country?

Whatever the reasons, the idea of nuclear excavation was ruled out in July 1970, when the Atomic Energy Commission, then conducting experiments on nuclear excavation, notified the Canal Commission that it had "not been able to do all the experiments which would be required to make a determination for the feasibility or infeasibility of using nuclear explosions for the excavation of the canals under study. . . ."[11] The AEC therefore concluded that "any decision to construct a sea-level canal in the near future must be made without being able to rely on nuclear excavation."

The AEC for several years had been engaged in the Plowshare program that was to develop nuclear excavation for the construction of a canal. Six to eight nuclear tests were considered the minimum necessary to develop the technology. Although these tests were to be completed by June 1968, only three underground tests had been carried out by July 1970. As the Canal Commission stated the problem, "Political and budgetary constraints caused the planned Plowshare . . . program to move slowly"--so slowly that the necessary technology could not be developed by the time the Canal Commission was to have made its report.[12]

Faced with these problems, the commission then

focused its attention on the routes where conventional means of excavation were economically feasible. The two most likely routes were 10 and 14, both in Panama. Two other routes, in Nicaragua and Costa Rica (Route 8 and a variation on 8, Route 5) were found by the commission to have "disadvantages of sufficient magnitude to eliminate them from consideration as alternatives to other routes."[13] Engineering studies on Route 14 were unnecessary, since this route was essentially the conversion of the present canal to a sea-level channel, and several studies already had been made of such a project. Route 10, just ten miles west of the present canal, was the last canal location to be given serious consideration, and the engineering studies for that route came so late in the investigation that the commission had to hire an outside engineering firm in order to complete the study in time. (The Army Corps of Engineers had conducted the other studies.) Route 10 was then examined as quickly as possible to meet the December deadline set for the commission report.

The commission found several reasons for recommending Route 10 rather than Route 14. From an engineering standpoint, the construction of Route 10 presented no apparent problems and would be less expensive than converting the present canal. The selected route had the advantage of not disrupting traffic, as would be the case if the present canal were converted. The commission was concerned about the hardship on world shipping, should the lock canal be closed for several months during conversion; also, there was concern that shipping routes bypassing the Canal would develop, resulting in permanent loss of some Canal traffic. Such a development would, of course, affect future revenues.

Furthermore, the commission was concerned about the hostility of Panamanians if a construction site were chosen outside Panama. The lock canal, so susceptible to damage, might be a target of Panamanians angry over the selection of a remote site. Thus, the selection of a route in Panama and close to population centers hopefully would reduce the likelihood of sabotage of the lock Canal during the construction period.

The question of the cost of installations to defend a sea-level canal was a major consideration in the selection of a site. Route 17, as well as Routes 10 and 14, was considered to be so close to present installations that new construction would not be required. If the route in Colombia had been chosen, the commission assumed that the defense of a canal constructed there would be provided by the Colombian military. It should be pointed out once more, however, that estimates made by the commission for each route, including Route 10, were for actual canal construction; such costs as new defense facilities (if needed), harbor facilities, purchase of land from Panamanian owners, resettlement of

people if nuclear excavation were used, and the payment
for a concession to Panama or Colombia were not included.

Several disadvantages also had to be considered if
Route 10 were to be chosen. The land along Route 10 was
more heavily populated than that along routes east of
the present canal, and the cost of purchasing the land
along the route would make it more expensive. The commission did note, however, that much land along Route 10
was undeveloped, particularly in the interior, which
would reduce its cost.

Another problem with Route 10, especially when compared with Route 14, was that the route lay outside the
present Canal Zone, except for short portions that went
through arms of Gatun Lake. Thus, this route would require a new treaty with Panama to provide for the operation of the new canal. A treaty concerning a sea-level
canal was one of the three 1967 draft treaties and was
rejected by the Panamanian government just three months
before the commission released its report. The draft
treaty concerning a sea-level canal mentioned no specific site but was to apply wherever a sea-level canal was
built in Panama.

With the release of the commission's report on 1
December 1970, Panama was secure in the knowledge that
if a sea-level canal were to be built, it would be built
in Panama and near Panama's major population centers.
A second development earlier in 1970 also contributed to
Panama's confidence that the United States would find it
difficult in the future to threaten to build a new canal
elsewhere if negotiations with Panama became deadlocked.

In 1916, the United States had negotiated the
Bryan-Chamarro Treaty with Nicaragua. This treaty paid
Nicaragua $3,000,000 in exchange for the United States
having the exclusive right to build a canal in Nicaragua.
Panama had long seen this treaty as a means of keeping
Panama in line since it had been negotiated two years
after the Panama Canal was completed. In 1970, the Uni-
ted States negotiated the abrogation of the treaty.

Panama was delighted with this development for two
reasons. The first was that the United States no longer
had the necessary diplomatic prerequisite for building a
canal in Nicaragua. This, plus the commission's findings of geological problems with the Nicaraguan routes
helped to further rule out a sea-level or lock canal in
Nicaragua. The second reason Panama found the treaty
abrogation encouraging was the feeling that if the United States was willing to give up its treaty rights in
Nicaragua, the 1903 treaty with Panama might be more
easily abrogated as well. While the United States was
already committed to abrogating the 1903 treaty eventually, the rejection by Panama of the 1967 draft treaties indicated that long-term negotiations would be necessary before the 1903 treaty would be replaced. The
abrogation of the Bryan-Chamarro Treaty was an

encouraging development for Panama in forcing the new
negotiations.

Secure in their knowledge that a sea-level canal
would be built in Panama, when negotiations resumed between the United States and Panama in June 1971 following
Panama's rejection of the draft treaties in September
1970, the Panamanians no longer were interested in a
treaty on a sea-level canal. The emphasis of the negotiations turned to control of the present canal and the
Canal Zone and to the defense of both. Whatever advantage the United States had when the site of a sea-level
canal was unknown and Nicaragua or Colombia could provide
alternative sites had now been lost. Considering the
difficult negotiations that followed, one easily could
surmise that Panama would drive a hard bargain over the
arrangements for a new canal when Panama was ready to
talk about such a treaty.

The announcement made during Secretary Kissinger's
visit to Panama in February 1974 made only indirect reference to a sea-level canal as a point of negotiation.
The treaties completed in August 1977 essentially postponed the question of a sea-level canal to future negotiations. The treaty on operation of the lock canal
stated that a sea-level canal, if dug, would be in Panama, but would be dug only after agreement between the
U.S. and Panama. They also agreed to study the need for
a new waterway, and the U.S. agreed to not negotiate with
a third state to construct a canal outside Panama without Panama's permission during the duration of the treaty. Panama did grant the U.S. the right to construct "a
third lane of locks to the existing Panama Canal."[14]
The U.S. also agreed that without Panama's permission
it would not use nuclear excavations in any construction
undertaken on a new canal.

REACTION TO CANAL COMMISSION REPORTS

After the commission's recommendations became known,
reaction in the United States generally was negative,
particularly in Congress. The administrators of the Panama Canal Company and the Canal Zone also expressed
strong opposition, although these sources of opposition
differed in their reasoning. Some congressional opponents charged that the United States never intended to
build a new canal but conducted the search only for negotiating purposes.

Regardless of where the commission recommended
building a sea-level canal, Panama's negotiating position
would be affected. The commission reasoned that Panama's fear of losing the advantage of its most valuable
resource, the narrow isthmus, would make Panama less demanding, especially if it felt the United States were
likely to build a sea-level canal in another country.
On the other hand, if the commission decided to build a

new canal in Panama, Panama would be easier to deal with, since the prospect of an economic gain would ease the negotiation of new treaties.

Opponents of a sea-level canal charged that the commission always had intended to support the building of a sea-level canal and to build it along Route 10. They also claimed that the only reason for the lengthy studies of other possible routes was to provide time to negotiate new treaties. When Panama rejected the draft treaties in 1970, there was no further reason to delay the commission's report.

This conspiratorial view of the commission's investigations can neither be confirmed nor refuted with the evidence at hand. However, if this had been the intent of the United States, the strategy failed. Panama was now secure in the knowledge that if a sea-level canal were to be built, it would be built in Panama, and if the purpose of the studies were to gain time for negotiations, then time ran out when the commission's report was made public.

Other congressional opponents based their opposition on grounds other than the alleged conspiracy. They believed that any new treaties negotiated with Panama to allow for the operation of a sea-level canal would not allow for the same strict United States control possible at the present lock canal. They argued that security for a new canal would be difficult unless the United States had strict control. They also regarded joint control of canal operations with Panama as less efficient than the present arrangement. Basically, these opponents preferred the present relationship between the two countries, which allowed the United States virtually unrestricted control of the Canal and the Zone.

Opposition to a sea-level canal was also strong among United States citizens in the Zone, particularly among administrators of the Panama Canal Company. They did not dispute the commission's findings that the present canal would be obsolete by the end of the century, but they preferred either one of two proposals which would improve the present canal. They believed these proposals would be less expensive than a new canal and would be sufficient for increased needs during this century. They also had some congressional support for these alternative plans.

The less expensive of the two proposals would cost $92 million (1970 estimate) and would make improvements in the Canal necessary for the immediate future. If traffic increased as projected, then a combination of the Third Locks Plan and the Terminal Lake Plan should be implemented.

This latter set of improvements would eliminate the separation of the locks on the Pacific side at Miraflores and Pedro Miguel and place the locks at one location. In addition, a third set of locks would be constructed.

The new set of locks would be 200 feet longer, 30 feet
wider, and about 10 feet deeper than the old ones and
would allow for passage of ships up to 110,000 tons.
These changes in the present canal were estimated to cost
$1.53 billion, about half the estimated cost of a sea-
level canal. This set of locks would increase the capacity of the canal from its present capacity to that of a
sea-level canal. The proponents of this plan felt that
the Terminal Lake-Third Locks Plan had the major political advantage in that it could be built under the provisions of the 1903 treaty.

A third set of locks had been planned once before,
and construction began in 1939. After $75 million was
spent, construction was stopped in 1942 owing to wartime
shortages of materials and the realization that the
locks could not be completed in time to aid the war effort. After the war, Congress was not interested in resuming the project.

The Inter-Oceanic Canal Commission rejected the
Terminal Lake-Third Locks Plan for several reasons. One
was that Gatun Lake lacked sufficient water for additional locks unless sea water was used or water from Gatun Lake was recirculated. Either alternative would be
costly. Also, this plan would increase the need for
skilled employees and management personnel, rather than
reducing these needs, as would the sea-level canal. The
commission also pointed out that this plan did not solve
the problem of the tankers and bulk carriers; nor did it
resolve the question of the vulnerability of a lock canal to sabotage or military attack. Also, if the projected increase in traffic through the Canal were correct, these improvements would not be enough, and, in
the long run, a sea-level canal would be necessary.

A very different source of opposition to a sea-
level canal, by the late 1970s still poorly organized,
was those who were concerned with the ecological effects
of having a direct water link between the Atlantic and
Pacific Oceans. Owing to the greater extremes of tides
on the Pacific side as compared with the Atlantic, a
sea-level canal would have a tidal flow that would change
twice a day. The flow in either direction would not
last long enough for a complete flow-through of water to
either ocean, but there "would be a gradual net transport of water from the Pacific to the Atlantic because
of the slightly higher mean sea level of the Pacific."[15]
This would mean that a sea-level canal would allow marine life to pass through the Canal, especially from the
Pacific to the Atlantic. The effects of the interchange
are, for the most part, unknown.

Many of the same species are found in both oceans,
but they have been separated from one another for an
estimated three million years and have undergone slightly different changes and adjustments to their environ-
ments. One often-cited example is the relationship

between the red snapper, found in both oceans, and the
poisonous sea snake, found only in the Pacific. The Pacific red snapper and the sea snake are not enemies and
ignore each other. Experiments placing the Atlantic red
snapper in tanks with the sea snake result in the red
snapper killing the sea snake. The long-term interaction of the sea snake with its new enemy, if the sea
snake moved through a sea-level canal, is unknown. However, one fear that has been expressed is that if the
sea snake moved to the Atlantic it would jeopardize the
tourist attraction of the Caribbean beaches.

Since the lock canal opened, some sea life has gone
from one ocean to the other in ballast tanks and attached
to the hulls of ships, with little apparent effect. The
effects of a more substantial interchange of sea life
are still an open question, however.

Observing that marine biologists are not in agreement on what an interchange would mean and that predic-
tions range from "disaster to possible beneficial results,"[16] the commission contracted with the Battelle
Memorial Institute in association with the Institute of
Marine Sciences of the University of Miami to investigate the problem. The report given the commission did
not yield any evidence of serious threat if an interchange took place. This led the commission to conclude
that the "risk of adverse ecological consequences stemming from construction and operation of a sea-level isthmian canal appears to be acceptable."[17] The commission and the institute admitted, however, that the investigation was not extensive because of the limited
time for tests. Marine biologists have conducted additional tests, the results of which suggest that the
exchange of sea life would have more effect than the
commission indicated in its report. To the commission's
credit, it requested that the National Academy of Science
conduct long-term studies of this problem. It is perhaps important to note that the ecological issue is
voiced primarily by U.S. citizens, and Panamanians have
said little. Panamanians are more concerned with a new
canal zone under U.S. control splitting their country a
second time and with its consequences for the movement
of goods and people.

Domestic Panamanian reaction to a sea-level canal
through Panama has undergone change over the years. Until 1971, Panamanians for the most part were in favor of
a sea-level canal, but only if a suitable agreement
could be worked out with the United States. (This assessment of Panamanian reaction to a sea-level canal is
based on a number of interviews the authors conducted
among prominent Panamanians in early 1971.) The general
feeling among those in leadership positions shortly after release of the commission report was one of relief
that the canal was to be built in Panama and of enthusiasm for the economic boom that the construction period

would bring. But even during this period of enthusiasm, opposition was voiced. Some expressed disappointment that the canal was not to be constructed in the Darien area. Such a move would help to open up this almost undeveloped part of Panama. A second source of opposition, little heard in 1971 but a common view later in the 1970s, was that although the construction period would be a period of economic boom for Panama, the subsequent substantial layoffs, plus the dismissal of thousands of Panamanians by the Canal Company when the new canal opened, could spell economic disaster for Panama.

If the United States started the investigation in 1964 to put Panama off balance and thus alter the linkages between Panama and the United States, time ran out on that strategy when the Canal Commission report was issued. Panama has played down a sea-level canal in its press and in the negotiations since 1971. The country's attention turned to the negotiation of a new treaty with the United States for the old canal. In June 1975, Carlos Lopez Guevara, a member of the Panamanian negotiating team, stated that Panama had no interest in a sea-level canal. He also said that the U.S. was not pushing as hard for a new canal as it once had. All of this apparently came as a result of decline in annual transits by nearly 2,000 following the reopening of the Suez Canal in 1975.[18] Even though traffic increased in 1980, after the treaties went into effect in 1978, an interest in a sea-level canal has not been revived.

NOTES

1. The Atlantic-Pacific Interoceanic Canal Study Commission, comprised of Robert B. Anderson (chairman), Robert G. Storey, Raymond A. Hill, Milton S. Eisenhower, and Kenneth E. Fields, was announced by President Johnson on 18 April 1965. The commission was authorized by Public Law 88-609. The commission had an initial appropriation of $17 million.

2. FBIS, 12 June 1974, p. M3, Jornal Do Brasil, 10 June 1974, p. 2. (Interview with Foreign Minister Tack.)

3. Immanuel J. Klette, From Atlantic to Pacific: A New Interocean Canal (New York: Harper & Row, 1967), p. 65.

4. Ibid.

5. Interoceanic Canal Studies, 1970, Report of Atlantic-Pacific Interoceanic Canal Study Commission, p. 15.

6. Ibid., p. 6.

7. Ibid., p. 17.

8. Klette, From Atlantic to Pacific, p. 30.

9. Traffic through the canal in 1976 dropped to about 34 daily transits following the reopening of the Suez Canal in 1975. A number of ocean routes through the Panama Canal were economically feasible when the Suez Canal was closed but were no longer used after the canal was reopened. Traffic increased again in 1980 to levels well above the 1970 level, however.

10. David McCullough, The Path Between the Seas: The

118

Creation of the Panama Canal, 1870-1914 (New York: Simon and Schuster, 1977), pp. 483-88.

11. Canal Studies, p. 127.
12. Ibid., p. 35.
13. Ibid., p. 45.
14. Article 12, part 2 of the Neutrality Treaty.
15. Canal Studies, p. 60.
16. Ibid., pp. 60-61.
17. Ibid., p. 62.
18. FBIS, 13 June 1975, La Estrella de Panama, 10 June 1975, p. 2.

7
Internationalizing the Conflict

A generalization that holds reasonably well in international politics is: the fewer political systems or linkages between systems involved in a conflict, the easier it is to arrive at a solution. The minimum number of systems necessary to have an international conflict is, of course, two. With the addition of each new national system, an additional set of interests, both domestic and international, must be satisfied. A solution to the conflict becomes more difficult, and the linkages between political systems more complex.

Exceptions to this generalization are (1) when the opponents are deadlocked and the intervention of outside parties is needed to offer new alternatives, or (2) when one of the two nations is negotiating from a position of weakness and needs outside support to bolster its position. The dominant nation may be more willing to compromise if it sees its opponent gaining support, and the weaker nation may feel more secure and willing to negotiate if it can do so as more nearly equal. Even though these exceptions may result in resolution of the conflict, one aspect of the generalization--that the introduction of new parties makes the linkages more complicated--remains valid. The subject of this chapter is the manner in which this generalization and its exceptions apply to the efforts of Panama to internationalize the Canal issue beyond bilateral negotiations between the United States and Panama.

Virtually from the time the 1903 treaty was negotiated, Panama had pressed for changes; but until the 1970s, any attempts had, with only minor exceptions, been conducted on a bilateral basis. Other nations or international organizations made no serious efforts to interfere, and the United States did not attempt to bring in third parties. Throughout this period, Panama negotiated from a position of weakness; consequently, the United States was happy to keep the relationship bilateral, since any concessions to Panama were at the discretion of the United States.

Occasionally, however, United States presence in
Panama would create such opposition in Panama that the
United States agreed to changes. Concessions, such as
those made in the treaties negotiated in 1936 and 1955,
were incremental and fell short of altering the basic
status of United States control in the Zone. The Panamanian military government saw the 1967 draft treaties
in the same light: the new treaties did not significantly alter the traditional relationship between the
United States and Panama; consequently, these treaties
were rejected in 1970.[1]

Negotiations between Panama and the United States
were renewed in June 1971, but in Panama's view they
failed to produce the kind of U.S. concessions that
would significantly change control of the Canal Zone.
Panama consequently made the decision to internationalize
the negotiations beyond the bilateral level and attempt
to gain outside support for its position.

Panama faced one important risk in internationalizing the Canal question. From time to time, various nations had suggested that control of the Canal should be
internationalized as a means of settling the conflict
between the United States and Panama. But neither Panama nor the United States had ever favored such a move.
Whether the Canal was controlled by the United States or
by an international body made little difference to Panama; under either circumstance, Panama did not control its
most vital resource. The United States wanted neither
Panama nor an international body to control the Canal
but, instead, wished to maintain its historical position.
In internationalizing the Canal issue, Panama wished to
avoid even the discussion of international control.

Internationalization of the Canal issue--as distinct
from internationalizing control of the Canal--offered
Panama several favorable diplomatic opportunities. In
the past, Panama had not attempted to identify strongly
with the large and growing number of Third World nations.
This was especially the case before the military takeover in 1968, when the Panamanian government was controlled by the monied aristocracy. This elitist government, while often critical of the United States, maintained overall cordial relations with the United States.
With the advent of the military government, anti-American
statements of an official nature were more frequent,
but even then little was done to associate Panama with
other developing nations. The economic advantages Panama enjoyed from the Canal, even with the United States
in control, set Panama apart from the typical problems
found in the Third World nations. For example, Panama
had remained aloof from the Central American Common Market on the grounds that the standard of living in Panama
was substantially higher than those of the members of the
Common Market. If Panama were to join, participation
might do damage to the Panamanian economy.

If Panama were to internationalize the Canal question, especially if this were done through the United Nations, Panama had to identify with the Third World nations, since they comprised about three-fourths of the U.N. membership. The Third World's position both in and out of the United Nations was anti-colonial and anti-racist, and it demanded economic development and control over its own natural resources. All these positions could easily be adapted to the Canal question by Panama.

Within the United Nations, the Security Council rather than the General Assembly offered the better forum for Panama because of its smaller membership. Also, resolutions passed by the Security Council carried more impact than those passed by the General Assembly. Panama's opportunity came when it was elected to the Security Council for a two-year term commencing in January 1972.

With the enlargement of the Security Council to fifteen members in 1965, it, as well as the General Assembly, was dominated numerically by Third World votes. Other than the five veto-bearing nations--the United States, the United Kingdom, France, the Soviet Union, and China--the nonpermanent members in 1973, in addition to Panama, were Australia, Austria, Guinea, India, Indonesia, Kenya, Peru, Sudan, and Yugoslavia. Panama could count on at least seven votes if the Third World nations of Africa, Asia, and Latin America voted with Panama; and if China and the Soviet Union supported Panama, Panama would have the necessary constitutional majority of nine in support of its position.

In January 1972, the Council met in Addis Ababa, Ethiopia, on African questions. Thus, a precedent was set for holding Security Council meetings outside New York. If Security council meetings on Latin American problems were to be held in Panama, this would provide a unique opportunity for Panama to bring world attention to the Canal question. Panama had long felt that the world press as well as the American press paid far too little attention to the Canal issue, and Security Council meetings in Panama, which undoubtedly would have worldwide news attention, would help rectify this neglect. Ideally, from Panama's perspective, the meetings should be held in Panama in March 1973, because Panama's representative then was to serve as president of the Security Council. (The presidency rotates on a monthly basis in the alphabetical order of membership.)

Council meetings in Panama with a Panamanian presiding would be an ideal forum. Panama could appeal to the Third World through the anti-colonial argument so long applied by Panama to the Canal issue, gain support for the Panamanian position, cast the United States as an imperialist power, and focus world attention on Panama. All this made an attractive package to encourage Panama to break out of the bilateral negotiations that characterized Panama's relations with the United States.

The Torrijos government also saw domestic advantages
in going international with the Canal issue. As a developing nation, Panama's economic problems had not been
solved by Torrijos. Under his leadership Panama's in-
debtedness had doubled, and in 1973 stood at
$324,000,000. Servicing this debt accounted for 30 per-
cent of the national budget. Panama was now importing
rice, whereas in the past it had been an exporter of rice.
In addition, Panama had experienced little industrial
growth under Torrijos. The Canal issue had long been
used by the government to distract the people away from
domestic economic problems, and Security Council meetings
on the Canal would serve as a further distraction.[2]
Also, such a major international event would be an important boost to national pride.

For the United States, the prospect of Security
Council meetings in Panama offered little. U.S. policy
during the Nixon administration placed Latin America low
in its foreign policy priorities. In this light, Security Council meetings in Panama would be embarrassing and,
certainly, detrimental to the policy the United States
was pursuing in bilateral negotiations with Panama. An
unstated advantage for the United States in the bilateral
negotiations was that as long as the conflict continued
unresolved, the United States held and operated the Canal under the 1903 treaty--undoubtedly a situation more
advantageous to the United States than would exist under
a new treaty. The United States had suffered little
damage in world opinion, since the Canal issue had not
gained worldwide attention; meetings in Panama would
change this, at least temporarily. The United States
wanted a minimum of public discussion of the Canal issue
and argued that the bilateral talks were far from deadlocked; therefore, there was no need for council meetings
on the subject.[3]

Also, the United States was fully aware that the
Canal issue was not the only issue that could place it
on the defensive. The status of Puerto Rico, the dispute
over a definition of territorial water and fishing
rights on the west coast of South America, and the economic boycott of Cuba might also be aired.

DEVELOPING INTERNATIONALIZATION

Even though Panama's efforts to internationalize
the Canal issue climaxed with attempts to have Security
Council meetings in Panama, on earlier occasions Panama
had taken recourse to international organizations as
well. Even as far back as 1926, Panama had attempted to
have the Canal issue debated before the League of Nations. But a more concerted effort was made following
the 1964 riots, when Panama filed charges of aggression
against the United States in the OAS and in the General
Assembly of the United Nations. In the OAS, the charge

was not dealt with directly. The organization avoided
supporting either country by recommending that the United States and Panama enter into direct negotiations to
settle their differences. The OAS thus refused to take
the Canal issue out of the bilateral relationship and
make it a regional, multilateral issue.

The same charge before the United Nations was not
forced by Panama, and the General Assembly took no action, although Panama did not withdraw the charge. This
inaction continued the general policy of the United Nations in regard to Latin American problems: to leave
action to the OAS as the regional organization. Even
though Panama did not press for United Nations action,
in subsequent years Panama would occasionally threaten
to push those charges in an effort to obtain concessions
from the United States.

In deciding to internationalize the Canal issue,
Panama's choices were limited essentially to the OAS and
the United Nations. Panama had been critical of the OAS
even before the military government came to power, and
criticism increased after the take over. In 1968, Panama presented a Panamanian, Eduardo Aislan Ritter, as a
candidate for secretary-general of the OAS to replace
José A. Mora, who was retiring after fifteen years.
When Galo Plaza Lasso of Ecuador was elected, Panama
charged that its candidate had lost because the United
States pressured other Latin American countries to vote
for Plaza. Galo Plaza was considered pro-United States,
even though he had strongly opposed the actions of the
U.S. in the 1965 Dominican Republic crisis. The election
was one of the incidents that led Panama to promote the
argument that the Organization of American States was
too heavily influenced by the United States. In 1969,
Panama began to call for changes in the OAS structure to
reduce the big power dominance of the organization by
the United States.

The depth of Panamanian feelings about the OAS was
revealed in April 1973, when Foreign Minister Tack introduced reforms for the structure of the OAS. At the
Third General Assembly of the OAS, Tack noted that the
organization was growing weaker. Without mentioning the
United States, he said that the OAS permanent council
was "subservient" and the "developed countries are under
obligation to cooperate with the efforts of the less
developed ones."[4] Tack expressed Panama's opposition to
the OAS policy of economic and diplomatic isolation of
Cuba and vowed that Panama would "support without reservation any resolution aimed at radically changing the
structure of the organization, which is publicly in agony
and for which a resounding and moving requiem has been
said at this meeting." He called for "an overall re-
structuring" of the OAS and stipulated that meetings for
changes should take place in Latin America and that no
member of the Secretariat of the OAS should participate

in the work. Tack wished to remove any discussion of
reforms from Washington and conduct them outside what he
considered a U.S.-dominated secretariat. Given Panama's
conviction that the OAS was U.S.-dominated and therefore
helpless to act favorably toward a Latin country, the
choice of the United Nations as the forum to internationalize the Canal question appeared obvious. Also important in the choice was the possibility of Security
Council meetings in Panama, whereas probably the best
Panama could hope for from the OAS would be a foreign
ministers' conference. A foreign ministers' meeting
would not draw the publicity Security Council meetings
would, nor would it have the broad Third World representation found in the United Nations.

After the charge of aggression following the 1964
riots, the first suggestion that Panama might internationalize the Canal issue in the U.N. came in a speech
by Foreign Minister Tack, before the General Assembly on
6 October 1971. Reaffirming Panama's confidence in bilateral negotiations, Tack warned that if negotiations
did not result in a satisfactory treaty, Panama would
bring the issue before the United Nations. Tack also
presented Secretary-General U Thant with a document out-
lining the background of the Canal issue and Panama's
position. Tack, however, did not call for the United
Nations to make the Canal an agenda item.[5]

A further indication that Panama might take the Canal issue to the United Nations arose when Panama took
its seat on the Security Council in January 1972. Both
Tack and Aquilino Boyd, Panama's ambassador to the United
Nations, made statements that the Canal issue would go
to the United Nations only as a last resort but that
this action had not been ruled out. Boyd said that "we
recognize that the current U.S. administration is making
efforts to reach a satisfactory solution, but Panama's
position has not changed a bit from what has been announced by our leaders. . . . Should the bilateral negotiations fail we shall not hesitate to resort to the U.
N. Security Council, taking advantage of the possibilities provided by this organization for the solution of
this type of problem." Boyd also criticized U.S. news
media and said that the "world public should be better
informed on the nature of the problem existing between
the United States and Panama.[6]

The new round of talks between the United States
and Panama that began in Washington in June 1971 had
not been going well. In December 1971, Panamanian negotiators carried a treaty offer back to Panama. From Panama's perspective the talks had made little progress
and the treaty offer was unacceptable, and in January
1972, Gen. Torrijos warned the United States that he
would make public the details of the deadlocked talks
unless the United States made further concessions.[7] The
United States said that such a move would violate the

agreement between the two countries that the talks were
to be conducted in secret.[8]

Panama made further threats to internationalize the
Canal issue in late January 1972, at the Security Council
meeting in Addis Ababa. Boyd compared colonialism in
Africa, which was the overall topic of the meetings, to
American occupation of the Canal Zone. He said that
"the danger of a violent confrontation between Panamanians and North Americans grows every day."[9] George
Bush, the United States ambassador to the U.N., argued
that the situations were not analogous, since colonialism in Africa was based on racism. Bush also said that
the meetings were not an appropriate place to bring up
the Canal issue, since the agenda was limited to African
questions. Even though the exchange between the two ambassadors was sharp, no resolution was introduced concerning the Canal, and the African states did not attempt
to include the issue in their attacks on colonialism.

Panama made no further moves toward internationalization of the Canal issue until November 1972, when Boyd
made informal inquiries of the Security Council membership to see if a majority favored meetings in Panama.
The result of Boyd's survey was that the Security Council would accept an invitation if one were extended.[10]
On departing for a visit to Panama, Boyd stated that unless talks between the United States and Panama resumed--
they had been suspended since the U.S. treaty offer in
December 1971--and some progress was likely he would return to New York with a formal invitation for the Security Council to meet in Panama. In December 1972, Panama
formally rejected the U.S. treaty offer. A result of
this rejection seems to have been the decision by the
Panamanian government to continue with its efforts to
internationalize the Canal issue at the United Nations.[11]

On his return to New York, Boyd issued a formal invitation and began Panama's campaign to have the meetings
in Panama approved by the Security Council. While Panama clearly wished to discuss the Canal issue at the
meetings, the appeal was on the broader scope that Latin
America had a number of problems that needed airing.
Even before a formal vote was taken by the Security
Council approving the meetings in Panama, the Panamanian
government, certain that the meetings would be approved,
heralded the pending decision as a "victory," and "triumph" for Panama, and a "setback for the United States."
On 16 January 1973, the Security Council approved the
meetings in principle and on 26 January formally approved
and scheduled the meetings for 15-21 March 1973. Panama
had won few victories in its diplomatic experience with
the United States, and this initial success at the United
Nations in internationalizing the Canal issue resulted
in enthusiastic approval in the Panamanian news media.

When interviewed on Panamanian radio after the
meetings had been approved in principle, but before

formal approval, Tack said, "The truth is that we deem
the problem of Panamanian-U.S. relations stemming from
the Canal as no longer being a bilateral problem."[12]
Even though the Canal issue had not been put on the a-
genda, Tack said that "it is logical that the problem of
Panamanian-U.S. relations resulting from the Canal in
our territory is a problem that concerns world peace and
security and that, in one way or another, it will have
to be discussed during this meeting."[13]

When the resolution to hold meetings in Panama was
approved by the Security Council, no negative votes were
cast, although the United States and Great Britain abstained. The agenda adopted for the meetings read, "Review of the steps to maintain and strengthen peace and
international security in Latin America, in accordance
with the provisions and principles of the Charter."
Specific items or disputes were not mentioned. Tack
stated that this general statement was "sufficiently
flexible to permit the consideration of the problem we
consider to be the most important."[14]

The United States had actively opposed meetings in
Panama, but could hardly use the arguments that the
meetings might embarrass the U.S. or that internationalization of the Canal question would strengthen the Panamanian negotiating position. Instead, George Bush used
a variety of other arguments. Bush said that the call
for meetings to review Latin American problems came only
from Panama and that such meetings should be requested
by the Organization of American States; the meetings in
Addis Ababa had been requested by the Organization of
African Unity. In response, Panama pointed out that the
United Nations Charter allows for any member state of
the United Nations to call for any of the bodies of the
United Nations to meet, and this was what Panama had
done. Further, Panama pointed out that in 1972 the United States had supported the Security Council meeting in
Addis Ababa and found it curious that the United States
did not now want similar meetings in Latin America on
Latin American questions.

Bush also argued that Africa had before the United
Nations a number of serious problems, such as apartheid,
the Portuguese colonies, the status of South West Africa,
and various guerrilla movements, but that Latin America
did not have any serious problems that called for Security Council action. Panama responded that the charge of
aggression against the United States filed by Panama on
10 January 1964 was still pending and noted "the explo-
sive situation existing in [Panama] because of the colonialist enclave called the Panama Canal Zone."

The argument the United States pushed hardest was
the cost of meetings in Panama. Bush pointed out that
the United Nations was in serious financial trouble and
was undergoing cutbacks in personnel and programs through
the efforts of the new secretary-general, Kurt Waldheim.

To hold meetings in Panama would be an added expense and one the United Nations could ill afford. Panama saw the cost of the meetings as minor and substantially less than the cost of the meetings in the more-distant Addis Ababa. Panama argued that the United Nations would pay only the transportation costs of United Nations personnel and that Panama would assume costs incurred by the Security Council while in Panama. The Security Council had approved a budget of $93,800 for the meetings--$75,500 for travel and per diem for 151 United Nations officials, $12,000 for communications, and $6,300 for supplies and other services. The Panamanian Foreign Ministry compared this expenditure to a figure of $137 billion that it said the Vietnam War had cost the United States, while "with a bare $229 million annual budget the Panamanian Revolutionary Government is carrying out a true process of recovery for the people. Could an expenditure of less than $100,000 be excessive when an attempt is made to avert possible conflict of unforeseeable consequences?"[15]

Still another argument used by the United States was that if the meetings were held in Panama the Canal Zone was certain to become an issue before the Security Council. This issue was being negotiated bilaterally, and the negotiations were not deadlocked; therefore, Security Council discussion was unnecessary. Security Council meetings in Panama would create a heated atmosphere that would make bilateral negotiations more difficult to conclude successfully.[16]

Two additional comments made by Christopher H. Phillips, member of the United States delegation, were that the agenda for the meetings was so "general that it opened the door to the sort of debate that was the function of the General Assembly, not the Security Council," and that in New York communications for the Security Council were excellent. If an international emergency should arise, communications in Panama would not be nearly so good and the records needed by the Council would be in New York.[17]

During the debate over holding meetings in Panama, the proceedings were considered of such importance that some sessions were broadcast live over Panamanian radio. From the time the Security Council approved Panama's request until the meetings actually were held, the Panamanian news media was ecstatic and heaped praise on the Torrijos government. Panamanian nationalism was perhaps never at a higher nonviolent level. Awareness that victory lay in internationalizing the Canal issue over United States objections was expressed typically in the somewhat conservative La Estrella de Panama.

> Once the Security Council is installed at the Justo Arosemena Palace, together with our flag will be flown those of the 131 members of the United

Nations. Panama will never again be alone in the
long and painful battle in which it has been engaged
since 18 November 1903. People everywhere are always fair and freedom-loving. The people of the
world will be with us next March. . . .
There are problems in the region, however, not
due to differences or controversies involving the
Latin American nations, but due to their relations
with foreign powers. . . . The most serious problem
is that which Panama confronts in its relations
with the United States concerning the occupation
and arbitrary use of its sovereign territory through
which the Canal was built, and the entity known as
the Canal Zone was established.[18]

Immediately after the meetings were approved, the
Panamanian government began a campaign to explain to the
Panamian people the reasons the Security Council meetings
would benefit Panama and to give an extended explanation
once more of the Panamanian position on the Canal issue.
There also was a call for national unity to maximize the
force with which Panama would present its case before
the Security Council. Foreign Minister Tack and his
chief foreign policy adviser, Jorge Illueca, delivered
the principal addresses in this effort. The Panamanian
government clearly wanted no domestic opposition to the
meetings or internal debate over the position Panama
would take during the meetings.
Shortly before the meetings, Tack visited Peru and,
on returning, announced, "Never again will we say that
Panama is alone. Now we have Peru to accompany us in
our struggle."[19] Peru was the other Latin American
country on the Security Council and had a military government similar to Panama's.
A number of organized groups sent resolutions to
the government expressing their support for the meetings.
One statement came from the influential National Council
of Private Enterprises (CONEP), the Panamanian equivalent of the United States Chamber of Commerce. Statements of support also came from the Federation of Trade
Unions of Panama (FSTRP) and the National Federation of
Democratic Women (FENAMUDE).
In anticipation of the meetings, the United States
announced on 14 February that the fence separating the
City of Panama from the Zone was being removed. The
fence had been constructed following the 1964 riots.
The Panamanian press had mixed feelings about the development. On the one hand, it was hailed as an initial
beneficial product of having the Security Council meetings in Panama. However, having the fence there during
the meetings would help the Panamanian government drama-
tize the enclave environment of the Canal Zone. Panamanian Televisora Nacional remarked that "this fence was
built by the U.S. Government without consulting Panama

and at present is also being taken down without consultation, within a few days of the Security Council meeting in this capital."[20]

After the meetings were approved, the press in the United States barely mentioned them until they opened. Even the New York Times, with its extensive coverage of international events, carried no major stories on the Security Council meetings during February and early March. The Miami Herald, which carries considerable coverage of Latin America, printed little about the meetings during this interim period. If one of Panama's objectives in requesting the meetings was to obtain attention from the U.S. news media, little had been achieved up to the opening of the meetings.

After sustained attacks on the United States throughout February and early March, the Panamanian press and government officials moderated their comments shortly before the meetings began. What was a conciliatory statement for Torrijos came shortly before the meetings opened: "I want the moral backing of the world, and especially, I want the people of the United States to know how we feel about the Canal. The Americans are very decent people, and when they realize what is happening here, they will feel a sense of shame, just as they did during the Vietnam War."[21]

When the Security Council held its opening session on 15 March, it met in familiar surroundings. The Panamanian government had remodeled a portion of the Justo Arosemena Palace so that the council met in a replica of its meeting room in the New York headquarters.

Just in case the Panamanian government had not made its point earlier concerning Panama's concern for having the Security Council meetings in Panama, a giant billboard greeted the delegates across from the palace. In all five official United Nations languages, the following message was available to the delegates:

> Let the Ambassadors of the friendly republics and the members of the foreign press here present answer: What nation of the world can withstand the humiliation of a foreign flag piercing its own heart? Brig. Gen. Omar Torrijos.[22]

SECURITY COUNCIL MEETINGS 15-21 MARCH 1973

The opening address was delivered by Gen. Torrijos, presumably as a welcoming address, but he devoted most of his speech to an attack on colonialism. While Torrijos did not mention the United States by name, the target of his remarks was obvious.

> Panama understands very well the struggle of the people who suffer the humiliation of colonialism, of the people who suffer the same restrictions and

servitude we do, of the people who resist acceptance
of the control of the strong over the weak as a
norm of coexistence, of the countries which are prepared for any sacrifice in order not to be subjected to the more powerful, of the person who does
not accept the exercise of political power by a
foreign government over the territory in which he
was born, of the generations who struggle and will
continue to struggle to eliminate from their fatherland the presence of troops without the consent of
the occupied country, of the natives who struggle
to exploit their own resources for their own benefits and not to subsidize the economy of an over-
powering country, of the countries which do not accept being exporters of cheap labor, of the unre-
deemed masses who pay with their blood for the
elimination of misery, injustice, and inequality to
which the powerful at home and abroad have subjected them, because oligarchy has no nationality.[23]

Torrijos also charged that the economic aid Panama received was used by the sender to control rather than
benefit Panama. Torrijos did not mention any Latin
American problem other than the Canal Zone. During the
meetings, nearly every speaker mentioned the Canal issue
in some manner, although not necessarily with the strong
emphasis of Torrijos' speech.
Torrijos was followed by other speakers from Latin
American countries. The first was the Peruvian foreign
minister, General Miguel Angel de la Flor Valle, who also
made a strong anti-colonial address. He placed at the
top of his agenda the "so-called Canal Zone," although
he also made critical references to the Pell and Hickenlooper amendments and briefly defended the Peruvian
claim to 200-mile territorial waters.[24]
Following the two Latin American members of the Security Council, representatives from various other Latin
American countries spoke. The Mexican and Colombian
delegates emphasized the need for bilateral negotiations.
The Mexican delegate stated, "We believe that if the two
parties directly concerned with this problem, which obviously has aspects which also interest all of the international community, make efforts to adapt their respective positions to the UN Charter, it would not be
difficult to reach a mutual and generally acceptable a-
greement."[25] This position, giving a little to both the
United States and Panama, was typical of statements to
follow except for those from the few countries that took
an adamant anti-United States stand. The Colombian delegate described the Canal issue as a "bilateral problem
between the Republic of Panama and the United States
which must first decide about a revision of the Hay/
Bunau-Varilla Treaty of 18 November 1903." He also
pointed out the special consideration that Colombia had

been granted which allowed for the free passage of Colombian ships through the Canal and argued that Colombia
should retain this right under a new treaty.[26] Later in
the meetings, Panama chastised Colombia for taking a
narrow self interest view of the Canal issue when the
broader question of colonialism was much more important.

Through these early speakers, criticism of the United States was by implication but not by name. When the
United States was named, the comments were, at worst,
only mildly critical. Under these circumstances, the
United States had no basis to ask for a right of reply,
which is allowed under Security Council rules of procedure when a country is attacked by name. But on the
evening of the first day, the Cuban foreign minister,
Paul Roa, delivered an hour-long, blistering attack on
United States policy toward Cuba and Latin America in
general. He reviewed, from the Cuban viewpoint, the
history of United States imperialism, including OAS actions taken against Cuba, the overthrow of the Arbenz
government in Guatemala in 1954, the Bay of Pigs, and the
crisis in the Dominican Republic in 1965. Roa then
turned to the Canal question and devoted the last part
of his address to defending Panama against what he labeled United States imperialism in the Canal Zone. His
references to the United States were by name and done in
a most undiplomatic and critical tone.

John Scali, who replaced George Bush as ambassador
less than a month before the meetings, asked for and was
granted the right of reply. Scali denied the Cuban
charges but said that the United States would give its
version of the Canal issue later in the meetings. At
this time and in response to other attacks by other
speakers, the United States took a rather tolerant view
of the charges made against it and made no effort to
challenge specific charges.

The Latin American speakers who followed took more
the tone of the Mexican and Colombian delegates than that
of the Peruvian and Cuban delegates. The Guyanese delegate supported bilateral negotiations with Security
Council support, and the Ecuadoran delegate made general
comments about the Canal and suggested vaguely that any
solution should be based on the United Nations Charter
and international law.

The Chilean delegate spent most of his speech defending the Allende regime and attacking United States
corporations operating in Chile, but stated near the end
of his address that bilateral negotiations were not
finding a solution to the Canal question because of the
"intransigence of the great power." He also expressed
support for a "sister country because of the existence
of a colonialist enclave to its territory which the U.S.
Government insists on holding."[27]

The Salvadoran representative supported bilateral
negotiations but said that regional or United Nations

participation would be necessary if negotiations should
fail. He did offer El Salvador's "full support to the
Panamanian demands over the Canal Zone."[28] Argentina
mentioned the Canal Zone only briefly and only in terms
calling for a revision of the perpetuity clause of the
1903 treaty. Jamaica encouraged the continuation of bilateral negotiations and said that Jamaica could "understand the vigorous viewpoints that the two parties maintain, mainly concerned with the Canal Zone."[29] Venezuela, Uruguay, and Costa Rica took similarly moderate positions on the Canal question. Costa Rica did not renew
the suggestion made by President Figueres the month before that the Canal should be under the international
control of the OAS. Bolivia and Trinidad-Tobago encouraged renewed efforts on the bilateral level.

Delegates outside the Americas began speaking on
the third day of the meetings. A number of African
countries spoke and, as expected, attacked colonialism,
but were somewhat moderate on the Canal question. Zam-
bia mentioned the Canal Zone as the major issue for Latin America and called for the Security Council to "take
effective measures to make the Panamanian people's
aspirations come true."[30] Tanzania did not delve into
the Canal issue but did attack colonialism. Kenya stated
that "my delegation feels that the matter of the Panama
Canal is to be solved between the Republic of Panama and
the United States of North America."[31] Guinea, Algeria,
and Zaire all delivered addresses supporting Panama in
its aspirations, but, generally, they called for continued bilateral negotiations. None of the African countries opposed action by the Security Council.

Speakers from the communist countries were less
moderate. Despite the progress of détente since early
1972, the communist countries sensed the vulnerability
of the United States on the Canal issue and took advantage of it.

The address by the Chinese ambassador, Huang Hua,
was what had become, for China, a typical attack on United States imperialism. China indicated its full support
of Panama in its aspirations for the Zone and advised
that Panamanians would succeed if they "strengthen their
unity and persist in their struggle."[32] Overall, the
Chinese ambassador fit the Canal question into a broader
attack on United States imperialism.

The Soviet delegate delivered a similar address.
In reference to the Canal, he said that the USSR "consi-
ders it necessary to favor a solution in which Panama's
sovereignty is respected, gives it full jurisdiction
over the Canal Zone and guarantees freedom of navigation
through the Canal." The Yugoslav delegate expressed his
country's "complete support for Panama's indisputable
right to completely establish its effective sovereignty
over every inch of its territory."[33]

The speech by the Indonesian delegate deserves special mention since he was one of the few speakers from
the developing and Communist countries who recognized
that the United States had already indicated that it was
"willing to give up the concept of perpetual authority
over the Canal Zone. We also know that there is a basic
agreement on Panama's sovereign rights over the territory."[34]

The delegates from France and Australia, countries
which the United States looked to for support, called
for continued bilateral negotiations but did not oppose
Security Council action. Other than the United States,
only the United Kingdom expressed opposition to the Security Council entering into the Canal issue.

Although Gen. Torrijos had used the opportunity of
the welcoming address to launch the initial attack on the
United States, the formal address for Panama was delivered in two parts by the Panamanian ambassador to the
United Nations, Aquilino Boyd, who also was serving as
president of the Security Council. Boyd's initial remarks followed a report by the president of the Special
Committee on Apartheid. This report was given to com-
memorate International Day for the Elimination of Racial
Discrimination. After expressing support for the black
African countries' struggle against discriminatory policies of the white minority governments in Africa, Boyd
characterized the United States presence in the Canal
Zone as racial discrimination:

> Panama feels it can speak with authority about
> colonialism. In a very small portion of its terri-
> tory, the richest country with the greatest resour-
> ces in the world divided our country in two and
> established its own government. . . . As you know,
> all territories subjected to colonialism or to a
> colonialist situation, no matter in what form, are
> always plagued by a characteristic ailment--that of
> discrimination. These forms of discrimination in
> the Zone especially concern the following aspects:
> First, discrimination with regard to jobs and
> wages; second, racial segregation in the Canal Zone;
> third, discrimination with regard to housing.[35]

Concerning job discrimination, Boyd said that high-
level positions were "reserved . . . for North Americans," thus discriminating against Panamanians. Using
1972 figures, he pointed out 3,581 North Americans received $67.8 million in wages while 10,436 non-North
Americans (Panamanians, West Indians, Central Americans,
and other Indo-American nationalities) received $62.5
million in wages. Thus, "one-fourth of the Canal Zone
employees receive collectively more than the remaining
three-fourths, solely because of their nationality, that

is, their race." Boyd said that this discrimination is
because "North Americans receive salaries equal to those
paid for similar jobs in the United States, non-North
Americans receive salaries based on an arbitrary proportion related to the minimum salaries paid in the Republic of Panama."[36] Although Boyd had an unusual way of
defining race by equating it with nationality, his explanation of the manner in which salaries for North Americans and non-North Americans were set was essentially
accurate.

Boyd also accused the United States of segregating
blacks in several communities within the Zone. In education, Boyd claimed, the facilities were superior for
the North Americans. "Nationals of the colonizing state
are offered the best education systems as well as the
best physical conditions in school buildings." There
are "two educational systems based on nationality, and
especially the fact that these systems benefit U.S. citizens more than those who are not U.S. citizens, is
clear proof of discrimination in education in the Canal
Zone."[37]

The second address by Boyd was devoted almost exclusively to the Canal issue, but dealt with the problem
in a broader perspective than racial discrimination.
After giving what had become a routine, general statement
of anti-colonialism and support for Latin Americal soli-
darity, Boyd delivered the Panamanian version of the
history of Panamanian-United States relations. The
principal theme was that Panama, for seventy years, had
been a victim of United States imperialism, and he summarized the present situation as follows:

Among the causes of conflict that still persist, the most injurious to Panamanian interests
are: The perpetuity of the canal concession; the
unilateral interpretation by the United States of
present treaty articles and the imposition of those
interpretations on Panama; the exercise of jurisdiction by the United States in the Canal Zone
which characterized it as a colonialist enclave;
the situation and installation of military bases
for purposes other than the protection of the canal;
and the insufficient and unfair benefits Panama de-
rives from the interoceanic waterway.[38]

Boyd said that even though the United States had
agreed to a new treaty granting Panama sovereignty over
the Zone, a new treaty had not been possible because the
"United States is proposing a very long period for the
new treaty to put an end to the perpetuity clause of the
canal concession, whereas Panama advocates a short
term."[39]

In the single reference to a sea-level canal made
during the meetings, Boyd said that another obstacle to

the new treaty was the intent by the United States "to modernize the present locks canal or to construct a sea-level canal." Boyd stated that "the U.S. also insisted on establishing--as a prior condition for the conclusion of a new treaty--that the two countries reach a package agreement, including the matters pertaining to the locks canal, the expansion of said canal or the construction of a sea-level canal. They also propose--as a part of the package deal--to legalize the U.S. military presence in Panama through a defense treaty including a status of forces agreement."[40] In the past, Panama had complained because there was no status of forces agreement, but no longer. Panama now saw such an agreement as recognition that the United States had a legal right to have troops in the Canal Zone.

Shortly after Boyd's second speech, the Security Council voted on a resolution concerning the Panama Canal issue. The resolution took note of the efforts already made by the United States and Panama to conclude a new treaty, but it urged them to conclude "without delay" a new "just and fair treaty" that "would fulfill Panama's legitimate aspirations and guarantee full respect for Panama's effective sovereignty over its territory."[41] The vote on the resolution was thirteen in favor, one abstention (the United Kingdom), and one opposed (the United States). The United States vote, was, of course, a veto; thus, the resolution failed. (A veto occurs when a constitutional majority of nine or more supports a resolution but one or more of the veto-bearing nations votes against it.) The United States had hoped Australia, France, and the United Kingdom would oppose the resolution, but they did not.[42] While these countries provided no reason for not supporting the United States, a likely explanation was that they did not wish to be identified with the colonial side of what had become a colonial/anti-colonial issue. In the case of the United Kingdom and France, as veto-bearing members, their negative votes would have been redundant in the sense that the United States vote vetoed the resolution, and additional negative votes were not necessary. Generally speaking, vetoes in the Security Council have been by a single country, since only one negative vote from a veto-bearing power is necessary to kill a resolution.

Immediately following the announcement of the vote by Foreign Minister Tack, who was serving as head of the Panamanian delegation as well as president of the Council, John Scali requested and was given the floor. He gave the U.S. version of the history of United States-Panamanian relations, countering the earlier attacks from Panama. He pointed out that the 1903 treaty was not forced upon Panama since, after the treaty was signed in Washington, it was sent to Panama and ratified by the Panamanian government. The treaty was then

overwhelmingly approved by local municipal councils
throughout Panama by unanimous votes.
Scali agreed that circumstances had changed since
the treaty was negotiated in 1903 but said that the United States was as aware of this as Panama. A new treaty
was called for, and the United States had long ago agreed
to negotiate one. He said that the United States veto
of the resolution "should not have surprised our host,
the Republic of Panama, in view of the repeated exchanges
of viewpoints that we have held regarding this meeting
and how it would conclude. . . ."[43] He also accused Panama of not keeping its word: "Up to the moment of our
departure for Panama, we continued to receive reassuran-
ces that everything would be done to maintain an atmosphere of moderation and care. I regret to say . . . it
has not been true in regard to some declarations made
here."[44] Scali said that the United States was willing
to give up the perpetuity clause and agree to a fixed
term in a new treaty. He objected to the use of the Security Council to bring pressure on the United States
when bilateral negotiations were continuing. He concluded by saying that "the present resolution which had been
drafted by Panama refers to the matter of interest for
Panama but ignores those legitimate interests that are
important for the United States. The Panama Canal is not
the result of nature, nor a work of nature, or as some
have tried to say, a natural resource."[45] At the conclusion of Scali's address, Tack, as presiding officer,
did not deliver the customary "thank you."
Initially, the Panamanian press and government officials expressed anger over the veto, but shortly after
the meetings adjourned, anger turned to a celebration of
the diplomatic victory they felt Panama had achieved.
The United States had been made to stand alone, and the
veto symbolized the loneliness of the United States position. The United States had not even received the support of its traditional allies. If the United States
had not vetoed the resolution, the effect of the resolution on the bilateral negotiations would likely have been
minor, but now Panama could point to the widespread international support it received in spite of United States
opposition. A resolution passed with both United States
and Panamanian support would have been a hollow victory.
Panama had successfully sold the Canal situation as colonialist and had internationalized the issue. The
month following the meetings, Gen. Torrijos spent much
of his time touring the rural areas of Panama and delivering victory speeches in the lesser cities of Panama
such as David, Los Santos, La Palma, and Colón. It was
in these areas that he received his greatest support
from the Panamanian people.
The United States could do little but explain its
reason for casting its third veto and take its diplomatic
"lumps."[46] Following the argument set forth in Scali's

address in Panama, a United States diplomat described
the resolution as "unbalanced and incomplete and therefore subject to serious misinterpretation."[47]   Scali
said that it was regrettable that the United States had
been forced to veto the resolution "because there is so
much in it with which we agree," but it contained such
"sweeping generalities when we know that the real difficulties lie in the application of these generalities."[48]

In an appearance before a joint hearing of the
House Subcommittees on Inter-American Affairs, International Organizations and Movements and the Panama Canal,
on 3 April 1973, Scali said that Tack had accepted the
U.S. version of the resolution several hours before the
Security Council voted. Tack then switched and supported the final resolution. Scali concluded that Tack did
this because it would force a U.S. veto.[49]

Following the meetings, Boyd threatened to present
a resolution to the General Assembly similar to the one
vetoed, but did not do so. This threat was somewhat
ironic, since the United States had stated before the
Security Council meetings that if the Canal issue were
taken up by the United Nations at all, it should come
before the General Assembly. Boyd blamed the veto on
pressure brought on the president and the State Department by the Pentagon.

The next opportunity for Panama to further internationalize the Canal issue came with the meeting of foreign ministers from Latin America and the United States
to be held in Mexico City from 18 to 24 February 1974.
The agenda for that meeting was set in a conference held
in Bogota in November 1973, but the United States was
unable to keep the Canal issue off the agenda. At Bogota, one of the principles agreed upon stated that "the
other Latin American countries, reaffirming their soli-
darity with the Republic of Panama, state that settlement of [the Panama Canal] question is a matter of common interest and high priority for Latin America and express hope that the already delayed negotiating process
may reach a settlement which will satisfy the just aspirations of the Republic of Panama." The prospects
were that the United States again would find itself facing a united Latin America in support of Panama. Ellsworth Bunker arrived in Panama about two weeks after the
Bogota conference and began negotiations that in January
1974 resulted in a statement of actions the United States
would take to relax tensions with Panama. Secretary of
State Kissinger then visited Panama on 7 February 1974,
and the Kissinger-Tack Agreement that was to serve as
the basis for a new treaty was signed.

By the time the Mexico City conference began on 18
February, the United States had also successfully removed
two other issues from the agenda that might be used to
embarrass the United States. An agreement with Mexico
was reached on the salinity of the Colorado River, and

the U.S. had worked out an arrangement by which American
businessmen would be compensated for property nationalized by the Peruvian government. In an additional move
to protect the United States at these meetings, Kissinger
insisted that the Latin American foreign ministers work
out a single position on disputes they had with the United States before the conference began. In this manner,
the United States would have to respond to only a single
list of charges and not a shotgun spray of accusations
from the many Latin American countries.[50] At the end of
the conference, the foreign ministers issued what was
called the Declaration of Tlatelolco, which included a
statement welcoming "the agreement reached . . . on 7
February 1974."[51] "The conference holds that [this]
agreement is a significant step forward on the road to
a definitive solution. . . ."[52] Also at the conference,
Kissinger announced that bilateral negotiations between
the United States and Panama, which had been in recess,
would resume in Panama in May 1974.[53] Panama had asked
for a resumption of the talks in July 1973.[54]

    The foreign ministers' conference continued its de-
liberations in April and "reiterated [its] confidence
that the bilateral negotiation presently in progress
. . . would continue in a positive tone and conclude as
soon as possible. . . ."[55] This conference was held in
Washington, D.C. The question continued to be discussed
in a similar vein when the Fourth OAS General Assembly
met in Atlanta, Georgia, from 19 April to 1 May. The
Fifth General Assembly of the OAS, held in Washington in
May 1975, adopted a resolution that "expressed the hope
that a prompt and successful conclusion will be reached
in the negotiations."[56]

    U.S. efforts to forestall Panamanian attempts to
further internationalize the Canal issue were effective
only temporarily, however. In May 1974, at a conference
of banana-producing countries, Torrijos spoke at length
about the Canal question.[57] Later the same month, Panama, at the 17th Congress of the Universal Postal Union,
attacked the U.S. postal service in the Zone.[58]

    In August 1975, Panama was accepted as a member of
the non-aligned nations that were then meeting in Lima.
The conference fully supported Panama's demand for
sovereignty over the Zone, and at the fifth meeting of
the non-aligned nations, held in Sri Lanka during August
1976, Panama pushed for and obtained a statement from
the conference supporting Panama's position on the Canal
issue.[59] On his way home from the conference, Torrijos
made various stops in Europe, looking for further support. When he made his report to the Panamanian people
on the conference of non-aligned, Torrijos said how
proud he was "to see our flag waving [among the flags
of the 87 nations present] so far from home and not be
able to see it wave in the heart of our fatherland
[sic]."[60] His statement, although inaccurate inasmuch

as the Panamanian flag had been flying in the Zone since
the flag-dispute days, was made in the context of the
support Panama was now receiving from the non-aligned
nations of the world.

In June 1976, at the sixth General Assembly of the
OAS, Panama was successful in obtaining a statement from
the Latin American foreign ministers calling for a new
Canal treaty in 1976. Panama continued to push its campaign of internationalization virtually up to the announcement that the new treaties were ready for signature.
In June 1977, at the conclusion of the seventh OAS General Assembly held in Grenada, Panamanian Foreign Minister Nicolas Gonzalez Revilla refused to sign a joint
communique on the Canal, as had been done for several
years. The Panamanian delegate said that the only thing
Panama would sign was a new treaty.[61] "After thirteen
years of negotiation that have produced no definite a-
greements the Panamanian people are no longer in condition to accept another communique, statement, or joint
document."[62] New disagreements in the negotiations between the United States and Panama prompted the foreign
minister's lack of cooperation.

After five years of effort, the Panamanian government had successfully broken out of the confines of discussing the Canal issue as a bilateral question between
the U.S. and Panama. Panama now had widespread support
in Latin America, including Cuba.[63] The non-aligned nations in Asia and Africa also were supportive. The Canal had become an issue before both the U.N. and the OAS
on a recurring basis. The Panama Canal was now an international question, and the linkages between systems
went well beyond the simple bilateral ones of a few
years earlier.

NOTES

1. Panamanian Foreign Ministry, Bases of the Position of
the Panamanian Chancellory in Regard to the Rejection by Panama of
the Three Draft Treaties, September 1970.
  2. Cf., LaFeber, The Panama Canal, p. 182.
  3. New York Times, 15 March 1973, p. 16.
  4. FBIS, 10 April 1973, p. M4, Radio Libertad, 9 April 1973.
  5. New York Times, 7 October 1971, p. 15.
  6. FBIS, 14 January 1972, p. M4, Prensa Latina (Havana),
13 January 1972.
  7. U.S., Congress, Senate, Committee on Foreign Relations,
Background Documents Relating to the Panama Canal. 95th Cong.,
1st sess., 1977, p. 1482.
  8. New York Times, 24 January 1972, p. 11.
  9. New York Times, 1 February 1972, p. 3.
  10. New York Times, 12 November 1972, p. 18.
  11. New York Times, 24 December 1972, sec. 4, p. 3.
  12. FBIS, 18 January 1973, p. M1, Radio Libertad, 17 January
1973.

13. Ibid., p. M2.
14. FBIS, 31 January 1973, p. M1, Matutino, 30 January 1973, pp. 1, 10.
15. Ibid.
16. U.S., Department of State, Department of State Bulletin 26 February 1973, pp. 242-43.
17. New York Times, 27 January 1973, p. 4.
18. FBIS, 1 February 1973, pp. M1, M3, La Estrella de Panama, 31 January 1973, pp. 1, 32.
19. FBIS, 12 March 1973, p. M1, Dominical, 11 March 1973, pp. 1-2.
20. FBIS, 15 February 1973, p. M4, Televisora Nacional, 14 February 1973.
21. New York Times, 15 March 1973, p. 16.
22. New York Times, 6 January 1974, sec. 6, p. 12.
23. FBIS, 16 March 1973, p. A1, Domestic Service, 15 March 1973.
24. Ibid., p. A5.
25. Ibid., p. A11.
26. Ibid., p. A14.
27. FBIS, 19 March 1973, p. A10, Domestic Service, 16 March 1973.
28. Ibid., p. A12.
29. Ibid., p. A18.
30. FBIS, 20 March 1973, p. A3, Domestic Service, 19 March 1973.
31. Ibid., p. A20.
32. Ibid., p. A6.
33. Ibid., p. A11.
34. Ibid., p. A9.
35. FBIS, 22 March 1973, p. A3, Domestic Service, 21 March 1973.
36. Ibid., p. A4.
37. Ibid., p. A5.
38. Ibid., p. A13.
39. Ibid., p. A14.
40. Ibid.
41. Ibid., pp. A16-18.
42. LaFeber, The Panama Canal, pp. 182-83; Richard P. Stebbins and Elaine P. Adams, eds., American Foreign Relations, 1973: A Documentary Record (New York: 1976), pp. 134-39.
43. FBIS, 22 March 1973, p. A17, Domestic Service, 22 March 1973.
44. Ibid.
45. Ibid., p. A18.
46. The United States had not cast a veto vote in the Security Council until 1970, but cast vetoes with greater frequency after 1973.
47. New York Times, 22 March 1973, p. 1.
48. Ibid.
49. Background Documents, p. 1464.
50. New York Times, 21 February 1974, p. 14.
51. Background Documents, p. 1486.
52. New York Times, 25 February 1974, p. 3.

53. New York Times, 22 February 1974, p. 10.

54. New York Times, 4 July 1973, p. 3.

55. Background Documents, p. 1487.

56. Chronology of Events, p. 11.

57. FBIS, 1 May 1974, pp. N1-3, Radio Libertad, 30 April 1974.

58. FBIS, 22 May 1974, pp. N1-2, Matutino, 20 May 1974, p. 1.

59. FBIS, 26 August 1976, p. N1, ACAN, 24 August 76; El Panama America, 23 August 1976, pp. 1, 6.

60. FBIS, 1 September 1976, p. N2, Matutino, 31 August 1976, pp. 1, 2.

61. FBIS, 16 June 1977, pp. N1-2, Domestic Service, 15 June 1977.

62. Chronology of Events, p. 30.

63. General Torrijos had visited Cuba in January 1976. At that time, Torrijos was careful, however, to in no way suggest support for Cuba's activities in Angola.

8
Efforts Toward Settlement

In December 1964, when President Johnson announced that the U.S. was willing to abrogate the 1903 treaty, he appointed Robert Anderson, former secretary of the treasury, to the dual role of heading the commission to search for a new canal route and of serving as chief U.S. negotiator of new treaties with Panama.

Anderson's appointment as head negotiator marked the beginning of negotiations that lasted for nearly thirteen years before the 1977 treaties were agreed to. During these prolonged negotiations, the primary linkages were between the negotiating teams of each country, but on several occasions events within a domestic system were linked to responses by the other's domestic system or government. For the most part, this sort of linkage was between events in the U.S. domestic system responded to with demonstrations in Panama or threats made by Panamanian officials, usually General Torrijos.

The 1977 treaties were negotiated mainly following the February 1974 Kissinger-Tack Agreement. Negotiations before 1974, however, served as a foundation for the negotiations that produced the 1977 treaties. The events leading up to the Kissinger-Tack Agreement briefly were as follows:

In September 1965, President Johnson announced that three treaties were being negotiated: one to replace the 1903 treaty for operation of the Canal and the Zone, another for defense of the Canal, and a third that was concerned with the provisions under which a sea-level canal would be constructed. In June 1967, three draft treaties were announced. Marco Robles was still in office, but his political position was so weak domestically that he chose to leave approval of the treaties to the next president, who would be elected in May 1968 and take office in October. Arnulfo Arias, the new president, was in office only ten days before the military took over. A top Panamanian diplomat under the Robles and the short-lived Arias administrations speculated that with only minor changes in the draft treaties Arias

143

would have pushed for their ratification. In September
1970, after an extensive campaign against the draft
treaties, the military government formally rejected them.
In June 1971, negotiations began once more. Anderson was still head of the U.S. team but, as had been the
situation with the earlier negotiations, was not the
working negotiator. The earlier treaties had been negotiated by John Irwin, a New York attorney, who was later
replaced with John Mundt. In 1973, Mundt was followed
by David H. Ward.

In December 1971, the United States made a proposal
designed to serve as the basis of new treaties. General
Torrijos, unhappy with the proposal, in January 1972
made public the negotiating positions. The United States
protested that this violated the understanding that the
negotiations were to be private and confidential.[1] Despite this difficulty, the negotiations got underway
again in March 1972 but were adjourned in May. The United States rejected a Panamanian counterproposal in
February 1973. The United Nations Security Council met
in Panama in March 1973 while the bilateral talks were
in recess. The Security Council meetings gave worldwide
publicity to the Canal issue, most of which was critical
of the United States.

In September 1973, perhaps as a result of the bad
press the United States had been receiving, President
Nixon upgraded the negotiations by appointing the highly
regarded and experienced diplomat, Ellsworth Bunker, to
replace Robert Anderson. (Anderson had resigned in
July.) Unlike Anderson, Bunker directly participated as
chief negotiator. Bunker's experience prepared him well
for his assignment. He had served as U.S. ambassador to
Argentina in 1951, during the time the United States had
strained relations with that country; as ambassador to
Italy in 1952, during the period of negotiation to settle
the Trieste dispute; as U.N. mediator in 1962, to settle
the West Irian conflict between the Netherlands and Indonesia; as U.N. mediator, to get Nasser's troops out of
Yemen in 1963; as U.S. ambassador to the OAS from 1964
to 1966, during the Dominican Republic crisis in 1965;
and as ambassador to South Vietnam, 1967 to 1972. Bunker was clearly a top diplomatic trouble-shooter.[2]
Bunker's appointment was welcomed by the Panamanians,
who saw his appointment as a symbol that the U.S. was
finally taking them seriously.

Following visits by Bunker to Panama in late November and early December and again in early January 1974,
both governments announced that a preliminary agreement
had been concluded. The agreement contained seven promises made by the United States, two of which President
Nixon announced could be carried out immediately. One
was the return of Old and New France Fields to Panama.
These old military airfields were no longer used by the
United States. The airfields adjoined one of Panama's

most successful economic efforts, the Free Zone, a ware-
house area designated for the storage of imported goods
destined for reshipment to markets outside Panama. This
enterprise had been hampered by the lack of territory in
which to expand. Panama had been pressing for return of
the airfields for some time, but the United States took
the position during the negotiations that it would settle
only for an overall agreement and would not grant piece-
meal concessions.

The other provision immediately adoptable was that
the United States would allow Panamanian national lottery
tickets to be sold legally in the Zone. Panama's national lottery vendors, who are numerous in downtown Panama City and along the area next to the Zone, had been
restricted from selling tickets in the Zone. To sell
the tickets legally in the Zone would have necessitated
the application of Panamanian law in the Zone. On December 28, President Nixon announced his intention to
submit legislation to Congress permitting these changes.

Other guarantees made by the United States in this
preliminary agreement were (1) elimination of the Canal
Zone mail system, (2) elimination of auto license plates
issued by the Zone, (3) the "possible" application of
Panamanian traffic laws in the Zone, meaning that the
laws might be enforced by Panamanian rather than Canal
Zone police, (4) "possible" authorization for Panama to
use port installations not being used in the Zone (this
request along with that for Old France Field had been
pending throughout the negotiations), and (5) the "possible" ceding to Panama of territorial jurisdiction over
the area that would be occupied by the planned Arraijan-
Chorrera-Tocumen highway. This highway would run across
the Zone on the Pacific side of the Canal. Among the
port installations mentioned in the agreement was a dry-
dock used by the United States during World War II to
repair submarines; this could be converted to a ship repair facility. The operation would employ eight hundred
to one thousand Panamanians.[3]

All these promises were concessions by the United
States and required no compensating actions by Panama.
Panama saw the agreement as a show of good faith on the
part of the United States and as evidence of serious U.S.
interest in settling its differences with Panama.

A more comprehensive, but less specific, agreement
was announced after a few hours' visit to Panama by
Secretary of State Henry Kissinger on 7 February 1974.
If the January agreement between Tack and Bunker were a
a show of good faith, this second agreement, negotiated
between Foreign Minister Tack and Kissinger, was to
serve as the basis for a new treaty between the two
countries. Although devoid of specifics, the Kissinger-
Tack Agreement did clarify a number of points. A new
treaty would abrogate the 1903 treaty and eliminate perpetuity. A fixed date would be established as to when

the Canal would be turned over to Panama. No date was
mentioned, however. Both concessions had been made by
the United States in the 1967 draft treaties and had
been valid during the negotiations after June 1971.
The agreement also called for the "termination of
United States jurisdiction over Panamanian territory,"
which would take place "promptly in accordance with terms
specified in the new treaty." A qualification on this
turnover of jurisdiction was an interestingly worded
clause that would allow the United States to remain in
the Zone on a limited basis:

> The Panamanian territory in which the canal is
> situated shall be returned to the jurisdiction of
> the Republic of Panama. The Republic of Panama, in
> its capacity as territorial sovereign, shall grant
> to the United States of America, for the duration
> of the new interoceanic canal treaty and in accor-
> dance with what that treaty states, the right to
> use the lands, waters, and airspace which may be
> necessary for the operation, maintenance, protec-
> tion and defense of the canal and the transit of
> ships.[4]

Again, this sort of arrangement either had been included
in the 1967 treaties or subsequently had been negotiated.
The agreement also stated that Panama would "have a
just and equitable share of the benefits derived from
the operation of the canal" and "recognized that the
geographic position of its territory constitutes the
principal resource of the Republic of Panama." Panama
was to share in the operations and defense of the Canal
until the time this responsibility became wholly Panamanian. "The Republic of Panama shall participate in the
administration of the canal, in accordance with the procedure to be agreed upon in the treaty" and "the Republic
of Panama shall participate in the protection and defense
of the canal in accordance with what is agreed upon in
the new treaty." The agreement closed with a provision
affirming agreement on new projects "which shall enlarge
canal capacity." Other than this general reference, no
mention was made of a new sea-level canal.
The Panamanian government hailed the Kissinger-Tack
Agreement as a great diplomatic victory. The Zonians
were reported to have mixed feelings but generally opposed it. In the United States Senate, a resolution
jointly sponsored by Senators Strom Thurmond and John
McClellan opposed giving sovereignty of the Zone to Panama. Thirty-eight senators signed the resolution, a
sufficient number to prevent any treaty negotiated along
the lines of the agreement from receiving the two-thirds
vote necessary for ratification.[5] The State Department
said the agreement "clarified the parameters of the
negotiations."[6] But, the agreement did not contain any

basic commitments that had not been agreed upon in principle months and even years earlier.

Perhaps the major development introduced by this new agreement was the enthusiasm Panama displayed for it, despite the lack of any new concessions. Throughout the negotiations, the United States had stated its position on the time periods necessary before various functions would be turned over to Panama. The United States agreed to turn the Canal over in fifty years. If a new set of locks were built, the turnover would be in eighty-five years, and if a sea-level canal were built, the lock canal would be turned over in ninety years. Jurisdiction in the Zone would be granted to Panama in fifteen years.[7] Panama wanted the Canal by the year 2000, although reports in 1974 indicated that it might be willing to settle for 2005 or 2010. Panama wanted legal jurisdiction in the Zone in five to eight years. The Kissinger-Tack Agreement reflected no change in these rather substantial differences in position.

In 1973, Gen. Torrijos had said that a treaty was not urgent and that Panama could wait until pressure on the United States gave Panama what it wanted. By early 1974, however, Torrijos felt that the need for a new treaty was immediate.[8] Perhaps the explanation for Torrijos' shift in position was the domestic problems he was having. Speculation had long been that Torrijos needed the Canal issue in order to distract the Panamanian people away from other problems. But by late 1973, Torrijos was getting opposition from both the political left and right. The left felt that he had already given away too much in the Canal negotiations; prolonging the negotiations would alienate the left even further. The conservatives were disgusted with his fiscal policies. In 1973, inflation had been ten percent, which then was considered to be high. In October 1973, Torrijos had frozen rents and ordered all banks to set aside one-half of domestic savings for low-interest-rate housing loans. Conservatives organized against this move and formed the National Civic Movement, made up of thirty-four business, professional, and civic groups, including the Panamanian Chamber of Commerce, the Lions Club of Panama, the National Medical Association, and the Association of Housewives.[9]

Whatever the motivation, the Panamanian government now called for a conclusion to the negotiations and ceased the diplomatic offensive against the United States that had been in progress since before the rejection of the 1967 draft treaties in September 1970. Secretary of State Kissinger announced that the United States hoped to complete the negotiations on the new treaty by the end of 1974.

If the Panamanian motivation to compromise were linked to domestic difficulties, the United States was anxious to reach an agreement because of the criticism it had received during and following the Security Council meetings in Panama. Any future international conference where the United States and Panama were present could prove to be equally embarrassing if a treaty were not forthcoming. The Kissinger-Tack Agreement would only temporarily alleviate such embarrassments.

Just before Bunker returned to Panama in early April for a new round of talks, Morey Bell, U.S. deputy chief negotiator, optimistically stated that "the most critical period in the negotiations . . . has been passed."[10] On arriving in Panama, Bunker left immediately for Contadora Island, where the new talks were to be held. Much of the negotiation of the 1977 treaties took place on Contadora. Also in early April, the U.S. appointed a new ambassador to Panama, William Jorden. His appointment was favorably received by the Panamanian press.

Panama was well aware of the opposition by some members of Congress to the negotiations in general and, specifically, the Kissinger-Tack Agreement as the basis of the negotiations. Reacting to the claim by Senators Thurmond and McClellan that Panama was too unstable to be a party to a new treaty, one Panamanian newspaper speculated that if there were any doubts in the U.S. about Panama's stability, then the C.I.A. must have a plan to destabilize Panama.[11]

A more rational Panamanian explanation for opposition in the U.S. was expressed by Tack in a press interview in which he said that "in the United States the public power structure is made up of various levels of consultations and decisions, and it is natural that there should be a divergence of opinion between the administration and the representatives."[12] Tack also returned to the long-standing position of the Panamanian government: the length of the negotiations was not important, but results were.

On June 26, Bunker arrived in Panama for the second round of negotiations under the Kissinger-Tack Agreement. Tack announced excellent progress and predicted that a draft treaty could be ready by the end of 1974.

During July and August, the Panamanian press grew increasingly alarmed over the Watergate crisis in the U.S. They saw Nixon and Kissinger as supporters of a new treaty and their unknown replacements as possible opponents. When Nixon resigned, the Panamanian press was shocked. La Estrella de Panama, however, understood the U.S. political system well enough to observe that the senators who supported Nixon during the crisis also were opposed to a new treaty.[13]

In October, a new member of the Panamanian negotiating team, Carlos Lopez Guevara, in a speech to the Panama Council of U.S. Navy League, outlined the status of the negotiations. He described neutrality and defense of the Canal as the "knottiest" problems. He said there was agreement that the Canal Zone would be abolished immediately on conclusion of a new treaty. Also, the Canal would be administered by a board with a U.S. majority with an eventual increase in Panamanian membership until they became a majority.[14] Tack, in November, added to the list of U.S. concessions. He said the new treaty would give Panama full control over the Canal. He also said the U.S. had agreed to remove the Southern Command and reduce the number of U.S. military units in Panama. Tack observed that since Kissinger's visit, Panama had "noticed a new U.S. spirit regarding the Canal and [Panama's] rights over the territory."[15]

In January 1975, Bunker came again to Panama, this time for thirteen days, a longer-than-usual negotiating session. Following this session, Torrijos, on several occasions, reiterated Tack's earlier comment that the length of time necessary to obtain a new treaty was unimportant, but a just treaty was. He did, however, starting in early 1975, say that 1977 was now his deadline for a new treaty. He also implied that if the deadline were not met, Panama would have to pursue an alternative other than negotiation. The only other possible alternative, as Torrijos saw the situation, was violence. In spite of this extended deadline, rumors began circulating in Panama in February 1975 that a treaty would be signed within ten weeks.

On 1 March 1975, Kissinger delivered a speech in Houston that greatly upset the Panamanians. In that speech, he mentioned fifty years as the proper term of a new defense arrangement. Panama saw that time limit as far too long.[16]

On 6 March, Bunker again came to Panama. Immediately following this visit, the U.S. turned Old France Field (216 hectares, or 534 acres) over to Panama. This move received widespread support from the Panamanian press. Also in March, Major General Harold R. Parfitt became governor of the Zone, replacing General Parker. Since Panama did not consider the post as legitimate because it involved a U.S. general governing Panamanian territory, the transfer of command received little attention.

A series of events took place late in March and April which Panama felt might leave some impact on the negotiations. On 27 March, Colombia, Costa Rica, Venezuela, and Panama issued the Panama Declaration, which was strongly supportive of Panama's position on the Canal, and "expressed their deep concern over the slow progress of the negotiations."[17] On 25 April, the Cuban embassy in Panama was reopened, and Panama was well aware what congressional reaction to this move would be. The fall of South Vietnam, also in April, was of particular interest to Panama. In one sense, Panama was delighted to see its powerful opponent suffer a defeat. But Panama was also concerned that a defeat in Southeast Asia would harden the U.S. position on withdrawal from Panama.

In early May, Tack reported that the negotiations
had reached an impasse, largely as a result of pressure
from the Pentagon and the U.S. Senate. This report came
out of Madrid and did not appear in the Panamanian
press.[18]

One of Torrijos' recurring problems was explaining
to the Panamanian people why the negotiations were held
in secret even though leaks about the negotiations as
well as public statements by Panamanian negotiators were
frequent. Similar sources of information in the U.S.
were rare. In spite of loosely guarded secrecy in Panama, Torrijos was attacked for not revealing more about
the negotiations.

On 13 June, Carlos Lopez Guevara spoke before the
Lions Club of Panama. His report on the negotiations
indicated that among the unsettled issues were how long
a period before Panama would gain full control over the
Canal and its defense. He also indicated that economic
questions, including Panama's share of the tolls, were
far from resolution.[19] In July, Jorge Illueva, another
Panamanian negotiator, in a speech before the Assembly
of Corregimientos, said that Panama wanted full control
by the end of the century, but the U.S. wanted control
of the Canal for fifty years.

In June 1975, Tack, who had been foreign minister
since Torrijos had become head of state in 1968, was
granted a leave of absence in order to devote full time
to the Canal negotiations. This unrequested leave was
undoubtedly a demotion for Tack, since he had long been
both the chief negotiator and foreign minister.

By September, the talks were again stalemated. In
an apparent effort to revitalize the negotiations, a top-
level team arrived from the U.S. on 3 September. The
meeting on Contadora included General George Brown,
chairman of the Joint Chiefs of Staff, William Clements,
deputy secretary of defense, and William D. Rogers, assistant secretary of state for Inter-American Affairs.
Panama's President Lakas also attended, as well as National Guard representatives. The composition of the
respective delegations indicated that future defense of
the Canal was the principal item of discussion. Bunker
joined the talks on 8 September. He had not been in
Panama since May.

Later in September, Kissinger, in a speech to the
Southern Governors' Conference, said that the U.S. would
retain the right to defend the Canal for an indetermi-
nate period. In response to a question asked by Governor George Wallace, he said that "the United States must
maintain the right, unilaterally, to defend the canal
for an indefinite future, or for a long future." The
use of the words "unilaterally" and "indefinite" were
immediately protested by Panama. This produced yet another demonstration outside the U.S. embassy. On 17
September, Bunker, while in Panama, said that Kissinger's

remarks had been "distorted" and "misinterpreted." He
said that he was sure Kissinger "meant to say that our
country could not renounce our right to defend the canal
from foreign enemies. . . ."[20]

The Kissinger speech apparently irritated Torrijos
to the point that he released a report on the status of
the negotiations on 20 September. Torrijos said that
under the new treaty there would be no Canal Zone government, no U.S. police laws, courts, or judges; and fire-
fighting, auto license issuance, and postal service
would be Panamanian. The Panama Canal Company would be
abolished, and a new entity representing both countries
created. Panamanian workers would be promoted, with Panamanians placed in administrative positions.

Agreement had been reached on these points, but
many other issues remained. Defense would be carried
out jointly during the life of the treaty, and no nuclear
arms would be placed in Panama; but Panama wanted a
twenty-five-year limit for both the treaty to operate
the Canal and the defense treaty. The U.S. wanted a
fifty-year limit on the defense treaty but had backed
off from an equally long period for operating the Canal.
The United States also wanted to retain all of its bases,
and Panama wanted a cut to a total of three. Panama
wanted only ten percent of the present Zone used for Canal operation while the treaty was in effect, but the
U.S. wanted eighty-five percent. Panama wanted control
of the harbors at Balboa and Cristobal, but the U.S.
wanted them controlled by the new administrative entity.
The U.S. wanted an annuity to Panama of $35 million.
Panama wanted to discuss economic matters later. The
U.S. wanted the right to expand Canal facilities unilaterally, but Panama wanted bilateral decisions on new
facilities.[21] The relative positions of the two countries were still far apart.

Torrijos said the status of the negotiations was
made public in response to the charge that the Panamanian people had been uninformed about the negotiations.
Press reaction in Panama was mixed but seemed to be more
critical than supportive of what was seen as too many
Panamanian concessions.

On 23 September, about 800 students of the Federation of Revolutionary Students (FSR) demonstrated
outside the U.S. embassy, apparently in response to the
Torrijos report. They demanded that the Canal be nationalized, neutralized, and demilitarized. The State
Department regarded the demonstration as the most serious since the 1964 riots. The U.S. ambassador strongly
protested the slowness with which the National Guard responded to the incident. The next day, Panama apologized
for the demonstration.

On 30 September, a new round of talks began. Bunker was not present. The U.S. was represented by Morey
Bell, deputy director for Central American Affairs

and director of Panamanian Affairs in the State Department. Bunker did not return to Panama until 19 November.
With him then was Lieutenant General Welborn Dolvin.
They departed on 26 November. The Panamanian press approved of Dolvin's visit since it indicated that military matters were being discussed. No agreement was
near, however, as was indicated in Torrijos' remarks to
Bunker on his departure on 1 December, that the U.S.
delegation need not return until the U.S. was prepared
to make new concessions.

Early in February 1976, William Rogers visited Panama and announced that progress was being made in the
talks. Bunker arrived on the 10th for two weeks of negotiation. This round apparently produced no progress.
On 14 February, Panama's ambassador to the OAS Council
delivered a blistering attack on U.S. policy while this
round of talks was in progress. Secretary Kissinger,
during a week-long visit through Latin America, attempted to improve U.S. relations with Latin America by committing the U.S. "to negotiate on the basis of parity
and dignity" with Panama.

Juan Tack resigned, apparently under pressure from
Torrijos, on 1 April, from both his positions as chief
negotiator and foreign minister. He was replaced by
Aquilino Boyd, Panamanian ambassador to the U.N., in
both positions. Jorge Illueca replaced Boyd as ambassador to the U.N. Boyd had been at the U.N. for fourteen
years. Tack was appointed as ambassador to Switzerland
and, in effect, became a political exile. Tack had on
several occasions advised patience with the talks. Although Torrijos had often taken a similar position, he
may have thought Tack was too patient with the U.S.

Several incidents in early 1976 indicated that the
talks were deadlocked. In January, Torrijos visited
Cuba and received Castro's full support on the Canal.
In February, the Panamanian ambassador to the U.N. delivered a strong attack on the U.S. In March, Torrijos
warned that Panama would have to "resort to the violent
stage" if a new treaty was not concluded.

Late in March, Torrijos suffered a setback. A conference of Latin Americans scheduled to meet in Panama
in June was cancelled. The conference was intended to
produce support for Panama. Concern about Cuba's involvement in Angola was reported to be the basis for the
cancellation.

In April 1976, the House Subcommittee on the Panama
Canal held hearings on the negotiations.[22] Bunker and
Parfitt were among the witnesses and were subject to some
criticism in the Panamanian press for their comments.
In closed sessions, Bunker was reported to have said
that there was no immediate prospect of a new treaty.
But the principal targets of attack in the Panamanian
press were Leonor V. Sullivan (D., Mo.) and John Murphy
(D., N.Y.). Both representatives were outspoken in

their opposition to the negotiation of a new treaty.
Yet another round of talks began with Bunker's return to Panama on 7 May. Again, little progress was
made. In June, however, Nicolas Barletta, a member of
the Panamanian delegation, said that a treaty would be
forthcoming in 1977 and that the election campaign in the
U.S., then just completing its primaries, had not delayed
the negotiations. Also in June, Torrijos, in a press
conference, again said his patience would run out in
1977. He also claimed that the Canal had 500 vulnerable
spots and could not be defended.[23]
     Due to the U.S. presidential primaries, Bunker did
not return to Panama during the summer. The Canal had
become an issue in the presidential race during the
Florida primary. During April and May, Reagan frequently attacked Ford for his support of the negotiations.
Until the Republican nomination was settled, further
negotiations were pointless.
     The deadlock on defense arrangements existed not
only between Panama and the U.S., but also between the
State Department and the Defense Department, since they
differed on how long the U.S. should be responsible for
defense of the Canal. Bunker refused to go back to Panama until the U.S. position was resolved. (See chapter
9 for discussion of the conflicts between the State and
Defense Departments during the summer of 1976.) Torrijos indicated his understanding of bureaucratic conflict
in the United States when he said that he was "now also
negotiating with the Pentagon because there are no elections in the Pentagon."[24]
     On 18 August, President Ford received the Republi-
can nomination. In the struggle between Ronald Reagan
and Ford for the nomination, Panama had strongly supported Ford. Panama had been disturbed with Reagan's comments about the Canal since the Florida presidential
primary in February. Reagan's campaign statement that
"we bought it, we paid for it, and it is ours" particularly offended Panama.
     Following Ford's nomination, Boyd pushed for the
resumption of the recessed talks. He also said he
wanted a treaty concluded before elections in the U.S.
on 2 November. Even though the Canal issue had become a
part of the campaign, the campaign in turn had distracted the U.S. from returning to the negotiations. As is
typically the case, U.S. foreign policy was inactive
during national elections.
     Panama was suddenly presented with its own internal
problems when riots broke out in mid-September and continued for nearly three weeks. Leftist students were
protesting the price of milk and rice. Panama attempted,
however, to blame the riots on the U.S. In a protest
sent to Ambassador Jorden on 17 September, Boyd said
that the "riots are a product of a destabilization plan,

hatched in the zone, involving U.S. intelligence agencies."[25] During the riots, three U.S. soldiers had been arrested by Panama. Boyd said that they had organized the riots and that U.S. Armed Services Radio in the Zone had been encouraging the rioters.

Boyd's efforts to shift blame to the U.S. failed. On 4 October, Geraldo Gonzales, vice president of Panama, admitted that the Panama economy was in trouble. Unemployment of 1974 was five percent but had risen to nine percent in 1976. "It is true that the Panamanian Government is struggling."[26] On 10 October, the occasion of the eighth anniversary of his takeover, Torrijos said that Panama was now fighting on two fronts--imperialism and inflation.[27]

As the presidential campaign in the U.S. progressed, Panama watched closely. Following the televised Carter-Ford foreign policy debate, Torrijos responded to comments made by both candidates. Torrijos said, "President Ford prides himself that no young person of the United States is fighting in any part of the world, but in Panama 20,000 [sic] soldiers of the Southern Command sleep lightly . . . waiting for Latin America to reclaim the sovereign rights of Panama which are denied it in the negotiations." Also, he strongly objected to Carter's use of "never" in Carter's response to whether the U.S. should give up complete control of the Canal.[28] A few days after his attack on the debate comments, Torrijos claimed both Ford and Carter had apologized to him for their remarks during the debate.[29]

Following a conference in Washington between Boyd and Kissinger, Panama's demands that the negotiations resume before the election were finally met. On 20 October, Bunker arrived in Panama. He departed on the 27th. Little was accomplished other than satisfying the Panamanian demand that the meetings be held. Bunker presented the territorial needs for operating the Canal under a new treaty, but Boyd said that the U.S. refused to discuss the duration of a new treaty in the latest round.

Following Carter's election, Boyd commented on future relations between the U.S. and Panama, now that Ford would soon be out of the presidency. He said he was confused by Carter's television comments about never giving up the Canal but was encouraged because Carter was a Democrat. As a Democrat, he would have more influence in the Democratic-controlled Senate. He also felt that Carter would be a stronger leader than Ford. He mentioned that when the OAS met in Atlanta during Carter's tenure as Georgia governor, Carter had delivered part of his welcoming address in Spanish.[30] Press reaction to Carter's election was favorable and tended to dismiss his Canal comments as campaign rhetoric.

No negotiations were planned during the interim

between the election and Carter's inauguration, but Panama pressed for immediate talks. A new round was held
13 to 18 December, but accomplished nothing. On 21 December Boyd described the Ford administration as "extremely indifferent" to negotiation now that it was
leaving office. When Cyrus Vance was selected as Carter's nominee to be secretary of state, the Panamanian
press was supportive.

A further strain on U.S.-Panamanian relations developed after there were at least three bombings in the
Zone. The first incident was on 31 October. Initially,
the Panamanian government blamed U.S. youth in the Zone
for the bombings. Adding to the tensions, late in December, Torrijos released a letter he had written to
Jorden. Torrijos demanded that Jorden produce the proof
that Jorden claimed to have that the National Guard was
behind the bombings. Torrijos denied that Panama had
anything to do with the bombings. Torrijos said that
his reason for making public this private correspondence
was that Jack Anderson, the American columnist, had revealed the contents of Jorden's letter in one of his
columns. The incident quickly died down, however. The
U.S. did file a protest over demonstrations in the Zone
by Panamanians on 9 January 1977, the thirteenth anniversary of the 1964 riots, but the bombing incidents
were not discussed further.

In November 1976, shortly after the election, President Ford approved a nineteen percent increase in Canal
tolls, only the second increase in the Canal's history.
The increase had been recommended by the Panama Canal
Company in October. Panama protested the increase, not
because of its opposition to higher tolls, but because
the U.S. had made the decision without consultation with
Panama. The OAS Special Committee for Consultation and
Negotiation opposed the toll increase, but on the basis
of the impact an increase would have on Canal traffic.
Tolls had also been increased in 1974, but the Canal had
run a $36 million deficit between July 1975 and Septem-
ber 1976. This deficit was attributed mainly to the de-
crease in traffic resulting from the reopening of the
Suez Canal.

On 31 January, following a meeting in Washington
between Secretary Vance and Foreign Minister Boyd, it was
announced that negotiations would continue on the principles established under the Kissinger-Tack Agreement of
February 1974. Vance said that the major unresolved
issues were duration of a new treaty, the question of
defense, and U.S. access to the Canal after the U.S.
turned the Canal over to Panama. Boyd said that 2000
was still Panama's date for full control of the Canal to
be relinquished to Panama. He expressed satisfaction
with the talks.[31]

In early February 1977, twelve U.S. senators visited
Panama. Since a majority of the delegation was favorably

disposed toward a new treaty, the visit generally had
favorable press response. A joint statement by Senators
John Sparkman and Clifford Case at the conclusion of the
visit urged "a successful conclusion [to the negotia-
tions] at the earliest possible date."
     On 8 February, Torrijos announced that negotiations
would resume before 20 February. He also announced a
reorganization of the Panamanian delegation. Henceforth,
there would be no "frontline men," and there would be
different teams for different issues. Upon hearing of
the new arrangement, Boyd resigned. He said he had not
been notified of the change--he had learned of it from
Panamanian television--and he did not agree with the new
method. Nicolas Gonzalez Revilla, ambassador to the U.
S., replaced Boyd as foreign minister. Dr. Escobar
Bethancourt, a member of the negotiating team under Boyd,
was appointed chief negotiator under the new arrangement.[32] The U.S. negotiating team arrived on 13 February
and departed on 23 February. On departure, the U.S.
team announced that "During the negotiation . . . we
were able to make a little progress. But the main problems are still unresolved." The feeling on both sides
seemed to be that the talks were stalemated again.
     A second congressional delegation, mainly from the
House Appropriations Committee, visited Panama in February, but unlike the earlier senate delegation was not
as favorably disposed toward a new treaty. On their departure, a majority of the congressmen described the
Torrijos government as a dictatorship and making unreasonable demands.
     On 9 March, in a speech to CONEP (the Panamanian
Chamber of Commerce), the new foreign minister reported
on the talks. He voiced his approval of not having
"frontline men." He said both countries during the latest round agreed to continue confidentiality on unresolved points. He also mentioned that under the new
treaty, Panama would have complete control, including
control of all military bases, by 2000. Jurisdiction in
the Zone would revert to Panama three years after the
ratification of a new treaty. The next day, the Panamanian newspaper, La Estrella de Panama, expanded on these
comments and said that there was to be a gradual reduction of U.S. troops and no nuclear arms in the Zone;
economic issues were still unresolved. The negotiation
teams did, in this latest round, uphold the Thompson-
Urritia Treaty that allowed free transit of the Canal
for Costa Rican and Colombian warships.[33]
     The U.S. negotiating team now included Sol Linowitz
as co-negotiator with Bunker. Carter had retained Bunker, originally appointed by Nixon, but Linowitz was
Carter's appointee. Linowitz, an attorney, and, like
Bunker, a former U.S. ambassador to the OAS, had recently
headed the privately funded United States-Latin American
Relations Commission, a bipartisan study group. This

group, in its report in December 1977, described the Canal question as the "most important issue" in U.S.-Latin
American relations and urged the upcoming Carter administration to "promptly negotiate a new Canal treaty
with Panama . . ." and to "make clear to the American
public why a new and equitable treaty with Panama is not
only desirable but urgently required." Clearly, Linowitz strongly endorsed the negotiations he was now a
part of. In a more general sense, the commission recommended a fresh approach to Latin America, particularly
in U.S. economic policy.

On 18 March, Torrijos responded to statements made
in the U.S. by Linowitz and Gov. Parfitt before the
House Merchant Marine and Fisheries Committee. Torrijos
criticized Linowitz for saying that the U.S. would remain in the Canal Zone "in perpetuity." Linowitz apparently had reference to the right of the U.S. to intervene to maintain the neutrality of the Canal, but
Torrijos saw the statement as indicating a permanent U.S.
presence. Parfitt had released a fifteen-point guarantee to Canal Zone workers. Torrijos said that neither
Linowitz's or Parfitt's statements indicated negotiating
points, but were merely U.S. aspirations.[34] Linowitz
denied that he had told the committee that the U.S. intended to stay in the Zone indefinitely. On 18 March,
Torrijos said that the Carter negotiating team was
making new demands but did not specify what these were.

During his testimony, Linowitz informed the committee that he had resigned as director of the Marine
Midland Bank of New York. Earlier, Linowitz had been
accused by Senator Helms of a conflict of interests,
since the bank had outstanding loans to Panama. Linowitz said that his resignation should remove any question
about his abilities as an ambassador.

The first significant talks under the Carter administration began on 9 May and adjourned on 1 June.
This round was held in Washington. Shortly before the
talks began, Carter, speaking before the OAS Council,
stated that he was "firmly committed to negotiating in
as timely a fashion as possible a new treaty which will
take into account Panama's legitimate needs as a sovereign nation and our interests and the efficient operation
of a neutral canal . . . ."[35]

After the talks ended, Panamanian leadership reported that the negotiators were near agreement. The
Panamanian team unexpectedly returned to Washington on
8 June, and talks resumed on 23 June. This round was to
discuss economic matters. These talks were recessed on
5 July but resumed on 15 July. The negotiations had
reached a critical stage, particularly on economic
issues. Defense arrangements were reported to be settled. On 5 July, Escobar said that on economic issues
the negotiating positions "are significantly different."

While the talks from May to July were going on, each
of the countries made gestures designed to influence
them. Shortly after the talks began in May, Panama carried out a military operation called "Oh, What Fear."
Only about 1,000 men were involved in the maneuvers, but
Torrijos said the operation proved that Panama could defend the Canal.

In mid-May, the U.S. announced that in June Major
General William Richardson, commander of the 193d Infantry Brigade, would be replaced with Brigadier General
Richard W. Allen. Panama saw this as a conciliatory
gesture, since Richardson was not well liked in the Republic.

Also in May, Panama was partially distracted from
the negotiations by another foreign policy issue. Torrijos made a statement supporting independence for Belize; and Guatemala, which claimed Belize, strongly protested. The two countries broke diplomatic relations.

On the Fourth of July, as occurs in many U.S. em-
bassies all over the world, a reception was held at the
U.S. embassy in Panama. For three years, only the Panamanian foreign minister had attended the reception, a
gesture which was diplomatically proper but nothing
more. On this Fourth, a number of Panamanian officials
attended. During July, major newspapers in the U.S.
and Panama carried stories speculating that two treaties
were near completion. The details of the treaties were
not consistent from one country to the other, but clearly there was disagreement over a lump-sum payment to Panama. Panama was demanding $1 billion, a figure already
scaled down considerably. On 29 July, Vance confirmed
that economics was the remaining obstacle.

President Carter, on 29 July, called both U.S. and
Panamanian negotiators to the White House to urge them
to complete the new treaties. Panama claimed that it
was now asking only $460 million in an initial lump-sum
payment.

Between 7 and 10 August, rumors in the Panamanian
press were common that the new treaties were near at
hand. Also, there was renewed pressure from the Panamanian Bar Association that the government reveal details
of the negotiations. The association further asked that
the U.N. be made responsible for the Canal's neutrality.
Panama had long objected to a role for the U.N. in the
Zone.

Late on 10 August, the announcement came in Panama
that two new treaties had been completed in principle.
The actual text of the treaties still remained to be negotiated. The announcement was made jointly by the U.S.
chief negotiators, Linowitz and Bunker, and their Panamanian counterparts, Escobar and Aristides Royo.[36] In
spite of the prohibition that Panama would have no
"frontline men," Escobar and Royo had indeed become

such in the latter stages of the negotiations.

On 12 August, President Carter announced the major provisions of the treaties: the U.S. would operate and defend the Canal until the end of the century. Panama would, shortly after the treaties were approved, have legal jurisdiction in the Zone. Those portions of the Zone not needed for the operation of the Canal would be turned over to Panama. Panama would receive $50 to $70 million a year from Canal revenues. The U.S. would arrange loans and credits for Panama up to $345 million. No lump-sum payment would be made to Panama. Under the neutrality treaty, the U.S. would have the right to guarantee the neutrality of the Canal indefinitely.

For a time following the announcement, it was reported in Panama that Carter was coming to Panama for their signing.[37] Such was not to be, but the new treaties were generally greeted with enthusiasm in Panama. Torrijos called for a special meeting of the Assembly of Corregimientos to review the treaties on 19 August.

When the assembly met, speeches were delivered by Revilla, Escobar, Royo, Planning Minister Barletta, Labor Minister Ahumada, and Edwin Fabrega, as well as Torrijos. All had been involved in the late stages of the negotiation of the treaties.

The speeches were less emotional than were typical of addresses delivered by Panamanian officials in the past, but the intent was different on this occasion. Past speeches on the Canal had been intended to rally support from the Panamanian people for the Panamanian position or to chastize the United States for not making more concessions. Now that Panama had the treaties, the task was to sell them to the Panamanian public, including the assembly and various government and National Guard officials present. Emotional appeals were for the opposition to the treaties; the negotiators were before the assembly to present the treaties as factually and favorably as possible.[38] From the U.S. perspective, the presentation outlined how Panama interpreted the treaties. For that reason, when the Senate Foreign Relations Committee hearings were held on the treaties, these speeches were frequently referred to.

The task was divided among the speakers, with each explaining different aspects of the treaties. Foreign Minister Revilla gave a short address in which he emphasized Panama's "proud and constant struggle." He said that if the treaties were not ratified, Panama would "be committed to continue [its] struggle under unpredictable conditions." Escobar, in the first of two addresses, spoke of the campaign "to force the United States to sit at the negotiating table." While past governments had also attempted to negotiate with the United States, their error had been to make the attempt on a bilateral basis. General Torrijos, Escobar said, "understood that a struggle for national liberation

carried out at only a bilateral level was a struggle
without a future, for the simple reason that it was a
struggle of a very small country against the major power
of the world." Escobar then reviewed the Panamanian efforts to internationalize the Canal issue and the long
negotiating process. He also warned that if the U.S.
Congress did not approve the treaties, Panama "will take
a course of violence."

Planning and Economic Policy Minister Barletta then
spoke to the assembly on the economic aspects of the new
treaties. This speech was particularly important since
the economic arrangement was one of the last points to
be negotiated and there had been little opportunity for
discussion of the arrangement. Barletta said that Panama would receive an average income of $80 million a year
for a total of $1.8 billion over the 23-year duration of
the treaty. The income the first year would be about
$65 million. By the end of the treaty period, the in-
come would rise to $100 million a year. Barletta also
explained the clause providing Panama with an additional
$10 million a year if the money was available; but if
not available, the money would be paid from subsequent
profits of the Canal. He mentioned the additional benefit to Panama of $82 million worth of buildings and
other facilities that would be turned over to Panama
immediately. All of the dollar figures used by Barletta
were Panamanian projections and did not necessarily agree
with those made later by U.S. officials.

Panama, Barletta said, would receive an economic
package of $345 million within the next five years. In-
cluded would be loans totaling $200 million from the
Export-Import Bank, housing loans totaling $75 million
guaranteed by AID, $20 million guaranteed by OPIC for
Cofina, Panama's development bank, and other loans (prin-
cipally for military equipment) amounting to $50 million
over a ten-year period. These loans plus revenue from
the Canal would provide Panama with a total of $2.262
billion by 1999. Barletta compared this figure to the
amount Panama would receive under the 1903 arrangement
as amended, which would be "the ridiculous amount of $52
million."

In 1999, Barletta pointed out, Panama would receive
facilities valued in 1977 at $3 billion. In addition,
Panama would receive $10 million each year until 1999,
with inflationary correction, to cover the cost of public
services in the former Zone area. All of these benefits
would provide nineteen percent of the government's budget, twenty-five percent of operational expenses of the
current budget, and fifteen percent of investments in
the public sector. In sum, Barletta described the treaties as of enormous economic benefit to Panama.

When Labor and Social Welfare Minister Adolfo Ahumada spoke, he discussed the new status of forces agreement included in the new treaties and the arrangement

for defending the Canal. He emphasized that the new
treaties immediately would reduce both the number of U.S.
troops and bases in Panama and that, henceforth, defense
of the Canal would be a joint U.S., Panamanian operation.
Of the fourteen U.S. bases, only four would remain, and
these would gradually disappear by 1999. He said that
"we are not going to make four small zones out of the
Canal Zone," but "Panamanian law will apply there also."
Panamanian law would apply in the defense zones to the
extent that Panamanians who broke the law in the new
zones would be tried in Panamanian courts. Only U.S.
soldiers who broke the law in the zones would be tried
by U.S. military courts. If a U.S. soldier broke the
law outside the zones, Panamanian law would apply. Ahumada explained that the limited application of U.S. law
in the zones was not a concession, in that Panamanian
soldiers stationed in the Middle East had the same pro-
tections. (There was a Panamanian contingent in the U.N.
Emergency Force in the Middle East.) The U.S. flag
would fly only inside the defense zones.

Education Minister Aristides Royo stated that the
new treaties "clearly establish the principle of nonin-
tervention" in the domestic affairs of Panama. There
would no longer be a U.S. governor in the Zone, and the
Panama Canal Company would disappear. The Canal would
now be run by a commission, which would eventually be
controlled by a Panamanian majority. Although there was
to be no expulsion of U.S. employees, within five years
there would be a twenty-percent reduction in the foreign
work force. Royo also mentioned the flag issue but said
that the U.S. flag would fly only over the new Canal
commission facility. He did not mention the flying of
U.S. flags over the defense zones.

Edwin Fabrega, a negotiator, talked of the land Panama would recover under the new treaties. Fabrega mentioned the installations around and including the Port
of Balboa, half of Fort Amador, Albrook Field, and most
of Ancon Hill on the Pacific side. Also, within three
years Curundu Heights would be returned to Panama. The
railroad would be turned over to Panama immediately, as
would the port of Cristobal and its installation, as well
as Rainbow City, on the Atlantic side.

Up to this point in the discussion, the interpretations placed on the treaties did not differ significantly from how the United States interpreted them. Certainly, the intended audience was Panamanian (the speeches
were broadcast live), and the objective was to present
the treaties as favorably as possible. The listening
audience could not be exclusively Panamanian, however,
and during Escobar's second address, he made a number of
comments that caused considerable concern in the U.S.
Congress, which was also gearing up for consideration of
the treaties.

Escobar, who discussed the neutrality treaty, said that during the negotiations the United States insisted on a military pact with Panama and that the Canal be neutral. He said Panama opposed a military pact for two reasons, the first of which was the U.S. military presence in Panama after the expiration of the new treaty. "Second, as a great power, the United States is often involved in wars in other parts of the world, and we did not want a situation in which, on the basis of a military pact, our country's future generations would be required to fight in U.S. wars under the pretext that they were fighting because the war was being waged to defend the Panama Canal." He said this was the Panamanian position until the U.S. "stopped insisting on the military pact and discussions began only regarding the neutrality pact."

Under the neutrality agreement, the U.S. wanted "preferential transit" for its warships. This, Escobar said, was pursued by the U.S. negotiators "to please their Pentagon" and in order to have something to show for having constructed the Canal. Escobar said Panama denied the U.S. the right of preferential transit on the grounds that to do so would violate the neutrality agreement itself. Escobar never stated what was meant by the phrase "expeditious passage" that was in the neutrality treaty, but, certainly, he felt it did not mean "preferential transit."

As to the right of the U.S. to intervene to maintain the neutrality of the Canal after 1999, Escobar said, the "big powers intervene whenever they damn well please with or without a pact . . . . A country like the United States can land its troops in Panama whenever it pleases after 2000 with or without a neutrality pact." He said the U.S. wanted the neutrality pact because it feared that Panama would "become Socialist and will turn into their enemy." Also, the U.S. negotiators wanted the neutrality treaty, Escobar said, "to show to their Congress; in order to be able to tell their Congress, 'look, we are turning the Canal over to the Panamanians, but we still have the right to watch over them so they behave' . . . . They are solving an internal problem regarding a Congress that is largely opposed to [these] negotiations . . . ."

Opposition to the treaties in Panama concentrated on two issues: the first, the right of the U.S. to intervene after 1999 to maintain a neutral Canal, and the second, the option granted the U.S. to build a sea-level canal in Panama. Escobar said that a sea-level canal received very little attention during the negotiations. He said that if a sea-level canal became necessary and both countries agreed to such, "then Panama and the U.S. would negotiate its construction in the terms agreed on by both countries." On this issue he concluded, "As you can see, it is not even an option to build a sea-level canal. It is an option to promise to study the viability of it." Gen. Torrijos concluded the speeches and delivered the only emotional speech of the day. His was a direct appeal to Panamanian nationalism.

Escobar's interpretations of the neutrality treaty became perhaps the single most discussed subject of the hearings before the Senate Foreign Relations Committee, which began on 26 September. The issues raised by Escobar arose with many of the witnesses before the committee. (See chapter 10 for discussion of the hearings.)

On 7 September, the day the treaties were signed in the OAS headquarters in Washington, students in Panama demonstrated against the treaties. On 13 September, Torrijos announced that a plebiscite on the treaties would be held on 23 October. He also sent an invitation to the secretary-general of the U.N., Kurt Waldheim, inviting him or his representative to observe the plebiscite.

Leftist students proved to be the most ardent of the opponents in Panama. Torrijos took no overt action to restrict their activities. Panama did, in fact, experience more political freedom during the period leading up to the plebiscite than it had since Torrijos took over in 1968. On 15 September, students asked the government for, and received, a daily page in the newspapers, an hour a day on radio, and an hour a week on television. During the course of the plebiscite campaign, the students took the opportunity of greater freedom to demand the return of political exiles and the return of democratic freedoms.

On 14 September, the government released the rules that would govern the plebiscite. All citizens who were eighteen years of age or older and those who had indicated their intentions to become citizens could vote. There were to be two ballots of different colors, one color for "no" and one for "yes." Each ballot carried the same statement:

> I am in agreement with the new Panama Canal treaty, the treaty of permanent neutrality of the canal and the operation of the canal, the appended agreements and annexes signed between the governments of Panama and the United States on 7 September 1977.[39]

The negotiation of new treaties between the U.S. and Panama passed through many critical phases: the 1964 riots, the 1967 draft treaties, the 1970 Panamanian rejection of those treaties, intermittent negotiations until the Kissinger-Tack Agreement, months of negotiation with no progress, and, finally, the 1977 treaties. The phases of the negotiations provided numerous examples of linkages between U.S. domestic activities and reactions by the Panamanian political system. Reactions between the systems became even more intense as the U.S. domestic system became more aware of the Canal issue,

beginning with the 1976 presidential campaign: 1) Panamanian reaction to congressional opposition became more
vocal as the negotiations advanced; 2) speeches primarily for domestic consumption by U.S. national leaders
were strongly reacted to in Panama; 3) controversy during
the Republican primaries and the general presidential
election caused further problems in Panama; and 4) policy
conflicts between the Defense and State departments--all
served as illustrations of linkages from the U.S. domestic system to the Panamanian. These developments also
contributed to delays in the negotiations.

    Although the more typical reaction was for events in
the U.S. domestic system being reacted to in Panama, the
reverse occurred with the August meeting of the Corregimientos to explain the treaties. The U.S. Senate, in
particular, paid close attention to how the Panamanian
leadership, speaking essentially for domestic consumption, interpreted the treaties. Panama was now receiving
the sort of attention it long had sought from the Congress, but some of this attention eventually proved embarrassing to Panama during the Senate's deliberations
over the treaties.

    But why were treaties possible now, when such agree-
ments had not been possible for over thirteen years of
negotiation? One explanation certainly could be that
the U.S. finally had made the concessions necessary
for Panama to conclude new agreements. If, however, one
concludes that the 1977 treaties were not significantly
more advantageous to Panama than were the 1967 draft
treaties, then why did Torrijos accept these new agreements? Economic conditions in Panama had deteriorated
over the last ten years. Unemployment was up, as was
inflation, but more serious for the Torrijos government,
internal development had not gone well, while Panama's
foreign debt had increased substantially. Torrijos
needed funds to service this debt and to provide money
for economic development. This, coupled with a growing
impatience with Torrijos by the Panamanian people for not
gaining an agreement, could provide an explanation for
treaties in 1977. Torrijos had promised the Panamanian
people a 1977 deadline for concluding the negotiations.
Torrijos met his own deadline. His next problem was to
adapt the Panamanian domestic system to the new agreements. The meeting of the Corregimientos was the first
step by Torrijos to carry out the selling of the
treaties.

    The Carter administration had a no less difficult
problem of adaptive behavior. The 1976 presidential race
made the Canal a national domestic issue. No longer was
this issue domestically limited to Congress and the administration. Congressional opposition to the treaties
was substantial; and a majority of the public, if polls
were correct, opposed the new treaties. Carter now had

to sell the treaties to the Senate, a Senate in which
thirty-eight members had already sponsored a resolution
in opposition to the new treaties. Both the United
States and Panama had major domestic considerations to
deal with before the new treaties could go into effect.

NOTES

1. New York Times, 24 January 1972, p. 11.
2. Mary Patricia Chapman and Richardson Dougall, United
States Chiefs of Mission 1778-1973, Department of State, Bureau of
Public Affairs, Historical Office (Washington, D.C.: Government
Printing Office, 1973), p. 206.
3. FBIS, 18 January 1974, p. M1, LATIN (Buenos Aires), 17
January 1974; New York Times, 11 January 1974, p. 3.
4. U.S., Congress, Senate, Committee on Foreign Relations,
Background Documents Relating to the Panama Canal, prepared for the
Committee on Foreign Relations by Congressional Research Service,
95th Cong., 1st sess., November 1977, pp. 1478-79; New York Times,
8 February 1974, p. 2
5. New York Times, 30 March 1974, p. 3; 7 May 1974, p. 45.
6. New York Times, 6 February 1974, p. 3.
7. New York Times, 15 March 1973, p. 16.
8. New York Times, 6 January 1974, sec. 6, p. 12.
9. New York Times, 6 February 1974, p. 3.
10. FBIS, 30 March 1974, p. N1, El Panama America, 28 March
1974, p. 3.
11. FBIS, 15 April 1974, p. N1, El Panama America, 10 April
1974, p. 4.
12. FBIS, 12 June 1974, pp. N1-2, Journal do Brasil, 10 June
1974, p. 2.
13. FBIS, 12 August 1974, p. N2, La Estrella de Panama, 11
August 1974, p. 1.
14. FBIS, 10 October 1974, p. N1, Star and Herald, 9 October
1974, pp. 1, 8.
15. FBIS, 11 November 1974, p. V2, Paris AFP (from Quito),
8 November 1974.
16. FBIS, 4 March 1975, p. N1, Critica, 3 March 1975, p. 4.
17. U.S., Congress, Senate, Committee on Foreign Relations,
A Chronology of Events Relating to Panama Canal, by Congressional
Research Service, Library of Congress, 19th Cong., 1st sess., 1977,
p. 11.
18. FBIS, 7 May 1975, p. N1, EFE (Madrid), 6 May 1975.
19. FBIS, 16 June 1975, pp. N1-6, La Estrella de Panama, 13
June 1975, p. 2.
20. Chronology, p. 13.
21. FBIS, 22 September 1975, pp. N1-5, Star and Herald, 20
September 1975, pp. 1, 7.
22. U.S., Congress, House, Committee on Merchant Marines and
Fisheries, Panama Canal Finances. Hearings before the Subcommittee
on Panama Canal of the Committee on Merchant Marines and Fisheries,
House Resolution 12641, 94th Cong., 2d sess., 6, 7, 8 April 1976.
23. FBIS, 24 June 1976, p. N1, ACAN, 23 June 1976.
24. FBIS, 4 August 1976, p. N1, ACAN, 2 August 1976.

166

25. FBIS, 20 September 1976, pp. N4-6, Domestic Service, 17 September 1976.
26. FBIS, 4 October 1976, p. N3, Domestic Service, 4 October 1976.
27. FBIS, 12 October 1976, p. N5, Domestic Service, 11 October 1976.
28. FBIS, 7 October 1976, p. N1, Matutino, 7 October 1976, pp. 1, 6.
29. FBIS, 12 October 1976, p. N7, Domestic Service, 11 October 1976.
30. FBIS, 4 November 1976, p. N1, Domestic Servide, 5 November 1976.
31. Chronology, p. 25.
32. FBIS, 10 February 1977, pp. N1-2, Televisora Nacional, 8 and 9 February 1977.
33. FBIS, 11 March 1977, pp. N1-4, La Estrella de Panama, 10 March 1977, pp. 1, 4; FBIS, 10 March 1977, p. N1, Radio Exitosa, 9 March 1977.
34. FBIS, 18 March 1977, pp. N1-2, Televisora Nacional, 18 March 1977.
35. Chronology, p. 27.
36. FBIS, 11 August 1977, p. N1, Domestic Service, 10 August 1977.
37. FBIS, 12 August 1977, p. N1, Televisora Nacional, 11 August 1977.
38. The speeches delivered before the Assembly of Corregimientos are found in FBIS, 22 August 1977, pp. N1-18, Domestic Service, 19 August 1977.
39. FBIS, 16 September 1977, pp. N9-13, La Estrella de Panama, 14 September 1977, pp. 1, 25.

9
The Canal and U.S. Domestic Politics

Earlier discussions of domestic linkage in the
United States to the Canal issue have made three points.
One was that until the 1976 presidential primaries, the
American public paid little attention to the Canal dispute, and any number of other foreign policy questions
were given a higher priority by U.S. decision-makers.
Second, perhaps as a result of its low priority, the
press in the United States devoted little attention to
the Canal question except when there were major developments such as the January 1964 riots or the 1967 announcement that draft treaties had been negotiated with
Panama. Third, domestic opposition to new treaties was,
at least until 1976, limited substantially to a few members of Congress.

To state that the United States placed a low priority on the negotiations with Panama is not to imply that
the problem was ignored. From 1964 on, the United States
carried on negotiations with Panama, and even though the
negotiations often were recessed, they never were officially broken off. The Office of International Security
Affairs in the Defense Department and the Office of
Inter-American Affairs in the State Department were always in close touch with the problem.

Until the last months of the negotiations, U.S. policy was to not push for a settlement of the Canal dispute. The hope seemed to be that if the situation were
allowed to drift and if too much pressure did not develop
from Panama, the day would come when a less nationalistic and more moderate leader would come to power in Panama.
A new treaty could then be negotiated that would be acceptable to both Panama and the congressional opposition.

The commission to search for a sea-level canal
route was generally viewed as a means of keeping Panama
in line by use of the threat to build a canal other than
in Panama. Another effort to quiet Panamanian demands
came in the form of economic aid. Panama received the
highest amount of aid on a per-capita basis of any Latin
American country. These moves resulted in no reduction

in pressure by Panama for a new treaty, however. General
Torrijos remained in power and even survived several do-
mestic crises, especially over economic conditions in
Panama.

The prospect of building a new canal had greatly
diminished by 1973, and even if one were to be built,
the recommendation from the Canal Commission was that it
be built in Panama. The March 1973 meetings of the United Nations Security Council in Panama marked the failure
of the United States to keep the Canal question on a bilateral basis. Thus, after the administrations of two
presidents, Johnson and Nixon, it was clear that the
United States policy of delay had failed.[1]

As is often the pattern in Congress, concern with
an issue that is not yet of high priority is left to the
appropriate committees or subcommittees. Since no major
Canal legislation or treaties came before either house
after 1964, until the 1977 treaties, the issue of the
Panama Canal took no specific form except for that group
of a dozen or so legislators that expressed periodic
concern that the United States was making too many concessions to Panama in the negotiations.

Congress, even though it had no direct connection
with the negotiations, through its committee structure
periodically reviewed what was going on in the Canal
Zone and in Panamanian-United States relations. The
Canal was run on the revenues the Panama Canal Company
received from tolls, but the budget for the Canal Company
was reviewed annually by Congress. While this annual
budget review in the form of hearings before a subcommittee of the House Appropriations Committee had little
effect on United States policy toward Panama, it did
serve to provide Congress with up-to-date information on
Panama.

A more direct means of expressing congressional
concern over the negotiations was hearings held by the
Merchant Marine and Fisheries Committee and the Foreign
Affairs Committee in the House. In turn, each of these
committees had a subcommittee, the Subcommittee on the
Panama Canal and the Subcommittee on Inter-American
Affairs, respectively, that kept an eye on the Canal issue. These committees and subcommittees held several
sets of hearings on United States-Panamanian relations,
hearings generally critical of negotiating with Panama
for a new treaty.

Critics in Congress of a new treaty reflected two
basic attitudes, attitudes often found in Congress on
foreign policy issues. First, since the negotiations
were conducted in secret, Congress had difficulty in
finding out just what was going on. Thus, they tended
to suspect the worst. Congress felt the State Department
made little effort to keep the appropriate committees of
Congress informed even as to the general nature of the
negotiations.

In the absence of information from the executive branch, a major source of information for Congress was Panama. In spite of the agreement that the negotiations be secret, Panama often attempted to break deadlocks by making the negotiating positions public. In January 1972, Torrijos threatened to release and eventually did release the status of the negotiations.[2] In June 1975, following approval by the House of the Snyder Amendment to the State Department appropriation that would have denied any further money for negotiations with Panama, a document was circulated in Panama that was purported to be a statement of the status of the negotiations. This document was inserted into the Congressional Record on 1 August 1975.[3] On still a third occasion, following a statement by Secretary Kissinger on 16 September 1975, at a Southern Governors' Conference, that the United States had the unilateral right to defend the Canal, General Torrijos released what he claimed was a full account of the negotiations.

Torrijos apparently released the status of the negotiations to show that the United States was not, in his view, negotiating seriously and was not making significant concessions, as the United States claimed. To Congress, however, the position of the United States revealed in these public disclosures went far beyond what the congressional critics were prepared to accept. While the public disclosures by Panama were designed to embarrass the United States, congressional critics saw the negotiations as being held in secret because the State Department did not want Congress to know just how extensive the concessions had been. The critics felt that if a draft treaty were handed to Congress without prior knowledge of its content on Congress' part, such a treaty might be approved by the Senate without its full implications being known.

The United States, on the other hand, strictly adhered to the secrecy agreement on the negotiations. The result of all this, as summarized by Franck and Weisband, was that

> Most of what Congress knew about the negotiations—some of it inaccurate—was learned from published versions of interviews given by Foreign Minister Tack or official leaks in the Panamanian press. On September 24, [1975] Ambassador Gonzalez-Revilla, the deputy Panamanian negotiator, in an off-the-record discussion at the Council on Foreign Relations (which promptly found its way into Washington Post and New York Times news stories), detailed what had and what had not been agreed to date. Inevitably, these leaks put the direction of the talks in a light most favorable to Panama, thereby further arousing the concern of Congress.[4]

A second attitude that influenced Congress toward being anti-treaty was the feeling that the State Department was negotiating for, not with, a foreign power. The reasoning behind this attitude was the charge that the State Department had already decided to give Panama essentially what it was demanding, and therefore the only serious obstacle remaining was to overcome congressional opposition to a treaty containing such concessions. Rep. Larry McDonald reflected this attitude when he said, "Apparently, some of our public officials will stoop to anything in their efforts to weaken the United States. As for Mr. Bunker, someone should remind him that he represents the United States of America and that his proper posture, particularly when confronting a country ruled by a Marxist oriented military strongman, is proudly erect, not cringing on his belly."[5] Congressional critics felt that the only means of preventing such a development was for Congress to be vigilant.

Before the 1977 treaties were submitted to the Senate, nearly all of the committee activity and many of the critics of a new treaty were found in the House. Since, constitutionally, treaties are acted upon only by the Senate, the question arose as to the role the House would have if a new treaty were presented to the Senate. House critics argued that any new treaty would involve the disposition of United States-owned property. Under the provisions of article 4, section 3, clause 2, of the Constitution, U.S.-owned property cannot be disposed of without the consent of both houses of Congress. The House argument was that even if the Senate alone acted on a treaty, the House should be involved in any enabling legislation involving the disposition of U.S. property.

ACTIVITY IN CONGRESS

The first important activity on the part of Congress following the riots in 1964 was to approve an appropriation for the Atlantic-Pacific Interoceanic Canal Study Commission. As described earlier, the responsibility of the commission was to recommend a route for a sea-level canal. There was little opposition to this action, since Congress saw an opportunity to be rid of the problems with Panama if a new canal were constructed in a country other than Panama. The only critics of the study for a new route were a few congressmen who felt that improvement of the present canal was preferable to a sea-level canal; therefore, a search for a new route was unnecessary.

When the United States and Panama announced in July 1967 that three new draft treaties had been agreed to, Congress came to life. The announcement did not include release of the treaties themselves. Copies of what were purported to be the treaties appeared on the streets in Panama City, and, shortly after, the Chicago Tribune

published the treaties. (Copies of the treaties were
not officially released by the State Department until
January 1977). A howl of protest immediately arose from
Congress that the treaties gave away too much. The
House Foreign Affairs Committee held hearings on the
treaties even though the treaties had not been submitted
to the Congress. These hearings were held in executive
session and were not subsequently made public, but staff
members of the committee described them as being generally critical of the treaties. A member of the committee
described the hearings as "comprehensive and generally
in opposition to the treaties."

Criticism of the draft treaties continued until
September 1970, when Gen. Torrijos announced that the
treaties were unacceptable to Panama. A high-ranking
Defense Department official expressed the sentiments of
many in Congress when he pointed out that "Panamanian
rejection of the draft treaties bailed out the United
States. The opposition in the House and Senate was too
great for the treaties to pass." In the House, over 150
members had introduced resolutions opposing the treaties
and supporting continued United States control of the
Canal and the Zone.

In September 1971, after negotiations between Panama and the United States resumed in June, the Subcommittee on Inter-American Affairs held two days of
hearings on forty-two House resolutions designed "to express the sense of the House of Representatives that the
United States maintain its sovereignty and jurisdiction
over the Panama Canal Zone."[6] These hearings did not
result in the House passing any of the resolutions and
probably were not intended to. The hearings did remind
the negotiators that the House was watching and that many
representatives opposed any change in the status the
United States held in the Zone.

These hearings are noteworthy because they set out
the arguments of those opposing a new treaty. In all,
thirty-four members of the House testified or submitted
statements, all in support of continued United States
control of the Canal and the Zone. The only support for
a new treaty came from Senator Alan Cranston (D., CA).
At that time, Senator Cranston stood virtually alone in
either house in support of a new treaty. Over half of
the representatives involved in the hearings were from
southern or border states, and all could be considered
to be within the conservative segment of the House.

The first representative to testify was Daniel J.
Flood (D., PA). His testimony is worthy of special attention since he was regarded as the most involved member of Congress with the Canal issue and the most ada-
ment in his opposition to a new treaty.[7] He supported
abrogating the 1936 and 1955 treaties that modified the
original treaty, thus returning the 1903 treaty to its
pristine form. Although the residents of the Canal Zone

do not elect a representative to Congress, Flood was
viewed as their unofficial representative, since he wanted no change in their status within Panama.
Representative Flood's arguments in opposition to a
new treaty were wide-ranging. He argued that the United
States had under the 1903 treaty exclusive control and
sovereignty in perpetuity. In addition to full sovereign
rights, the United States purchased "all privately owned
land and property in the territory from individual property owners, making the Canal Zone the most costly territorial acquisition in the history of the United
States."[8] He felt that the Hull-Alfaro Treaty of 1936
began "our great give-away program," and the Eisenhower-
Remón treaty of 1955 further weakened our position in
Panama. Such concessions as agreeing in 1960 to fly the
Panamanian flag over parts of the Canal Zone encouraged
rather than quieted the radicals in Panama. Representative Flood was particularly critical of the Eisenhowers,
the president, and his brother, Milton. (Milton Eisenhower served on the Anderson Commission that investigated
routes for a sea-level canal.) He felt that Milton
Eisenhower exerted pressure on President Eisenhower to
make concessions to Panama. Flood also described President Johnson as giving in to radical Panamanian pressure
when he agreed to negotiate new treaties with Panama
following the 1964 riots. He claimed that the reason
President Johnson did not release the text of the 1967
draft treaties was because Johnson hoped a delayed release of the treaties would result in the treaties being
ratified by the Senate without adequate debate.
Representative Flood opposed a sea-level canal and
wanted the present canal improved, including a third set
of locks. He felt the government of Panama was so unstable that it could not be relied upon to run the Canal.
In addition, there was a grave danger that a communist
government would take over Panama, and the Canal would
be denied to the United States. He also was a strong
advocate of United States control of the Canal for defense and trade purposes.
Representative Flood's intense interest certainly
could not be explained by the nature of his constituency,
which included Wilkes-Barre. He had had a life-long interest in Panama, and his father was a friend of Teddy
Roosevelt. But whatever the causes of his interest, he
was undoubtedly the strongest advocate in the House for
the United States making no changes in its status in the
Canal Zone.
The Subcommittee on the Panama Canal held one day
of hearings on 20 November 1969, the stated purpose of
which was "to receive the State Department's views with
respect to the problem of Panama versus the United States
both as to the treaties and the future of treaty negotiations, as well as with respect to the interim report
that was made earlier that year by the Interoceanic Canal

Commission concerning plans for a sea-level canal site."[9]
Intermittently, from 29 November 1971 to 10 August 1972,
the subcommittee held further hearings on the Panama Canal negotiations. Similar hearings also were held before the subcommittee on 20 February 1973 and 3 April
1973. The February hearings, held the month before the
Security Council met in Panama, resulted in the recommendation that the United States retain "undiluted sovereignty" in the Zone. On 13 April 1973, the Merchant
Marine and Fisheries Committee held hearings on the status of the negotiations. All of these hearings were
critical of the direction of the negotiations.

Occasionally, a delegation from the Subcommittee on
the Panama Canal visited Panama. Such a delegation
visited Panama in January 1970 and again in December
1971. The head of the delegation on the first visit was
Representative Leonor K. Sullivan (D., MO), chairwoman
of the subcommittee until 1971 and then chairwoman of the
parent committee, the Merchant Marine and Fisheries Committee. She, like Flood, had a long-time interest in
Panama, which she said began when she started taking va-
cations in Panama during the 1930s. She, too, was a
critic of the manner in which negotiations had gone.
Rep. Sullivan, as chairwoman of the committee that would
have to approve any enabling legislation for a new treaty, was quoted as saying she would sit on such legislation "forever" and that "the House of Representatives
will never enact a law to give away the Zone. . . . If
the Hay/Bunau-Varilla Treaty isn't honored no treaty is
worth anything. They'll be renegotiating the Louisiana
Purchase next."[10] On the second visit, the new chairman
of the subcommittee, John M. Murphy (D., NY), headed the
delegation. Hearings held in Panama during this visit
created a storm of protest from Panama, both as to the
nature of the testimony and the fact that a U.S. congressional committee was holding hearings on Panamanian
territory.

After his return from Panama, Murphy received more
criticism in the Panamanian press when he held hearings
on the seizure of the U.S.-owned electric company in Panama. Murphy again received bad press in Panama in 1972
when he accused Foreign Minister Tack and Moise Torrijos,
Gen. Omar Torrijos' brother, of being involved in drug
traffic between Panama and the United States.[11] After
the hearings in early 1973, Congress did little on the
Canal question during the last half of 1973 but revived
its interest in the issue after Ellsworth Bunker was appointed as chief negotiator late in the year. This tem-
porary lack of attention by Congress to the Canal issue
was undoubtedly prompted by its preoccupation with the
Watergate scandals rather than any decline in the degree
of opposition to a new treaty. As the negotiations led
by Bunker indicated promise and resulted in the Kissinger-Tack Agreement in February 1974, congressional

opposition came to life once more and in greater force
than ever before. The first major response to the Kissinger-Tack Agreement came from Senator Thurmond (R.,
SC), who introduced a resolution, sponsored by thirty-
eight senators, that opposed any treaty that did not
provide "undiluted sovereignty" for the U.S.

Congressional opposition, by early 1974, consolidated around several arguments. The first was very simply
that the Canal and the Zone belonged to the United States
and that there was no reason for the United States to
give up its control; certainly, Panama's threats of violence need not be taken seriously, since Panama could
not successfully threaten our position in Panama. The
U.S. was on firm legal grounds in that it controlled the
Canal Zone by treaty and had paid Colombia, Panama, and
the individual landowners for the property. A second
argument was that Panama was politically unstable; therefore, Panama could not be relied upon to run the Canal
or to defend it. The technique used to make this point
was to cite the lengthy list of heads of state Panama had
had since independence and the large number of coups,
revolutions, and riots that had occurred in Panama. A-
nother argument was that Panama lacked both the technical
skills and the work ethic to make the Canal function.[12]
Still another argument was that Panama had a leftist military government that was both undemocratic and in danger of evolving into a communist government. Panama and
the Canal were far too strategic assets for the U.S. to
run the risk of an unfriendly government in Panama controlling the Canal or the Soviet Union gaining control
of the Canal through a communist government in Panama.
These arguments changed little after the new treaties
were made public in September 1977.

There were two additional points often made by members of Congress. While not arguments directed at Panama, they did support the positions of the opposition to
a new treaty. The first was the argument that the Canal
was "an engineering marvel" and one the United States
designed and built. To turn over the Canal to Panama,
was, in effect, to give away a part of our national heri-
tage. Some of the remarks made by the opposition were
strongly nostalgic of the era when Panama was guided to
independence by the United States and the United States
wielded the "big stick" in international politics. To
turn the Canal over to Panama or to share control of the
Canal with Panama was to admit that that era was over;
the Canal was a symbol of United States imperialism at
its best.

A second point that worked against a treaty was the
reaction in Congress to our withdrawal from and the subsequent collapse of South Vietnam. The United States
lost South Vietnam, but why should the United States
give away the Canal when it possessed it? As one adviser to a Senate committee observed, "Coming on the heels

of Vietnam, there's a certain tendency in some quarters
to say: don't give up an inch of American territory!"[13]
Congressional opponents neither felt that there was the
threat of a Vietnam-type war in Panama nor that Panama's
threats to launch such a war were meaningful.

The thirty-eight cosponsors of the Thurmond Resolution were a large enough body, assuming that they would
all vote against a new treaty, to prevent such a treaty
from gaining the necessary two-thirds of the Senate for
approval. This coalition of opposition was not thought
to be without its possible defectors, however. A congressional aide said, "The Senate list is weak. There's
quite a difference between co-sponsoring a resolution
and voting on a major treaty."[14] The proponents of a new
treaty, led by Senators Gale McGee (D., WY), Hubert
Humphrey (D., MN), Alan Cranston (D., CA) and Edward
Kennedy (D., MA), were thought to include about sixty
senators. At this stage, neither coalition, of course,
had seen a new treaty, but by the end of 1975 the lines
were generally drawn in the Senate.

As indicated by the Legislative Reorganization Act
of 1946, all treaties must be presented to the Senate
Committee on Foreign Relations for consideration. This
committee had not displayed the hostility toward a new
treaty shown by various House committees and subcommittees. Committee action by Foreign Relations would probably not be a problem for the treaty, but approval by
the full Senate was clearly marginal.

A tradition that worked in favor of the treaty was
the rarity of a treaty being rejected by the Senate.
The Senate had not rejected a major treaty since the
Treaty of Versailles. Treaties that run into difficulty
in the Committee on Foreign Relations or appear to be
facing trouble in the full Senate are either "pigeon-
holed" in the committee indefinitely, withdrawn by the
executive, or sent back to the executive at the request
of the committee. The record for holding a treaty in
the committee is held by the Genocide Convention, which
has been awaiting committee action since 1949. (The
treaty was still in committee in 1983.) Major treaties
ordinarily are not delayed. If the Senate followed the
pattern of its past behavior, a new treaty on the Canal
would be taken up by the committee and the full Senate
within a reasonable time after being submitted by the
executive. The unknown factor, however, was the degree
to which the Senate would continue its struggle with the
executive over foreign policy in the post-Vietnam era.
Such actions as cutting off military aid to Turkey and
Angola and the War Powers Act were not within the traditional pattern of behavior of the Senate either.

No action was taken in the Senate on the Thurmond
Resolution, which read in part, "The government of the
United States should maintain and protect its sovereign
rights and jurisdiction over the Canal and Zone, and

should in no way cede, dilute, forfeit, negotiate, or transfer any of these sovereign rights. . . ."[15] Over 100 members of the House of Representatives had introduced similar resolutions. No action was taken on the House resolutions either.

The only actual vote taken by either house by the close of 1975 was by the House and pertained to the Snyder Amendment. This amendment introduced by M. Gene Snyder (R., KY), a member of the Subcommittee on the Panama Canal, passed 264 to 168. The Snyder Amendment was attached to the State Department appropriation for fiscal 1976 on 26 June 1975 and read, "None of the funds appropriated in this title shall be used for the purposes of negotiating the surrender or relinquishment of any U.S. rights in the Panama Canal Zone."[16]

The House had made a similar effort to control executive activities in Panama in 1960. As an aftermath to riots in Panama on 3 November 1959, Panama's independence day, the United States announced that it recognized Panama's titular sovereignty over the Zone. As a recognition of this sovereignty, Panama wanted the United States to fly the Panamanian flag over various points in the Zone. Following this request, on 2 February 1960, the House of Representatives passed a concurrent resolution by a vote of 382 to 12 opposing the formal display of the Panamanian flag in the Zone. The Senate failed to act on the resolution. On 9 February, the House adopted an amendment to the 1961 Department of Commerce appropriation prohibiting the use of any funds for the formal display of the Panamanian flag in the Zone. The Senate accepted the amendment. President Eisenhower subsequently ordered the Panamanian flag to be flown over a limited number of points. Congress made no effort to overturn the presidential order, although there was some talk that the president's defiance of a congressional act was grounds for impeachment.

The 1975 effort to restrict funds differed in that the Senate refused to accept the Snyder Amendment, and the State Department appropriation went to conference committee. In conference committee, a compromise was worked out and read, "It is the sense of the Congress that any new Panama Canal treaty or agreement must protect the vital interests of the United States in the operation, maintenance, property and defense of the Panama Canal."[17] The compromise prompted a lengthy debate on the floor of the House.

When the House voted on the compromise statement, the vote was 197 for and 203 against; thus, the disagreement with the Senate remained. On 7 October 1975, the matter came before the House for a third vote. By now, the conference committee had inserted the words "in the Canal Zone" into the compromise statement. This revision was accepted 212 to 201. On 29 October, Representative Flood rose on the House floor and sharply criticized

the compromise and characterized the insertion of "in the
Canal Zone" as worthless. Congress had, in his view,
once more come close to a meaningful act on the Canal and
then had backed off by adopting a shallow compromise.[18]
     The votes for the compromise could hardly be inter-
preted as an indicator of the strength treaty-enabling
legislation might receive in the House. A number of the
representatives who voted for the compromise expressed
their opposition to any treaty that would result in Panama's eventually gaining control of the Canal, but
stated that the reason for their vote was to not interfere with the president's right to negotiate treaties.
It would be equally misleading to state that the members
who refused to accept the compromise would also have refused to support enabling legislation. The vote did
give a good indication, however, of the intensity of
feeling in the House on the issue and indicated the absence of strong House support for any new treaty along
the lines being negotiated at the time.
     The membership of the two House committees most
concerned with the issue voted as follows: the Foreign
Affairs Committee voted twenty votes for the compromise,
ten votes against, and four not voting; the Merchant
Marine and Fisheries Committee voted fourteen for the
compromise and twenty-five against, with no abstentions.
If the vote were any indication, this latter committee
remained the hotbed of opposition to a new treaty. This
contention was also supported by the amount of participation during the debate by the members of the Merchant
Marine and Fisheries Committee, most of whom were in
opposition to backing off from the original Snyder Amendment. While the chairwoman of this committee, Mrs.
Sullivan, did participate (in opposition) in the debate,
Representative Thomas E. Morgan (D., PA), chairman of
the Foreign Affairs Committee, did not. This factor
could have affected the behavior of each committee's
membership.
     While the situation in the Senate was not parallel
to that in the House, since no roll call votes had been
taken in the Senate, the Thurmond Resolution had only
one cosponsor, Senator Stuart Symington (D., MO), who
was also a member of the Foreign Relations Committee,
the crucial committee for a new treaty in the Senate.
     The tone of the debate on the Snyder Amendment,
while clearly anti-treaty, was also anti-State Department. The antagonist of the anti-treaty people was as
much the State Department as it was Panama. The president was not directly attacked in the debate, and the
Defense Department was generally described as being an
ally of the anti-treaty coalition.
     In June 1976, when the State Department Authoriza-
tion Act was under consideration in the House, Rep.
Snyder made a second effort. This time, his amendment
would prohibit the use of funds "for the purpose of

negotiating the surrender or relinquishment of the Canal
Zone or the Panama Canal."[19]   A compromise was introduced by Rep. John H. Buchanan, Jr. (R., AL), similar to
the 1975 compromise. Snyder's attempts to strengthen
the Buchanan substitute failed, while Buchanan's compromise passed 229-130. When the Foreign Relations Authorization came before the House in May 1977, Rep. Robert K.
Dornan (R., CA) attempted to amend it with a Snyder-like
restriction on the negotiations. Again, Rep. Buchanan
introduced a compromise, which passed 220-182.   In June
1977, Rep. Snyder failed in an attempt to attach a similar amendment to the State Department appropriation bill.
        During the time of the controversy over the origi-
nal Snyder Amendment, from June to September 1975, a major bureaucratic conflict had developed within the executive between the State Department and the Defense Department over provisions of a treaty with Panama.   The
debates in the House on the Snyder Amendment undoubtedly
were intended to influence the outcome of the conflict
within the executive.   The conflict in the executive had
brought the negotiations with Panama to a halt, and
Ambassador Bunker refused to return to Panama until decisions were made as to what the negotiating position of
the United States was to be.

CONFLICT WITHIN THE EXECUTIVE

        Like the conflict between the executive and Congress
over the Canal question, the conflict between the State
Department and the Defense Department did not develop
any intensity until the Kissinger-Tack Agreement in
February 1974, when it seemed that a new treaty was imminent. During the period of negotiations prior to 1974,
the Defense Department and the State Department developed
no apparent differences concerning the negotiating position of the United States; at least when differences a-
rose, they were handled quietly. The Defense Department
did, however, during the pre-1974 period make it clear
that defense of the Zone was the responsibility of the
Defense Department and that the position of the United
States in that regard must be preserved. The announcement in 1971 that the headquarters of the Southern Command was to be moved out of the Canal Zone appeared to
weaken this position, but the proposed move did not take
place.
        Among the residents of the Zone, an interesting
transposition as to who were friends and enemies of the
Zonians took place. Over the years, the Congress had
been seen as the institution that failed to appropriate
the money to carry out such projects as a third set of
locks or the rebuilding of the Roosevelt-Boyd Highway.
The State Department was viewed as friendly to the Zonians, since it was primarily responsible for maintaining
good relations with Panama and thus securing the

position of the United States in the Zone. Except for
the riots in 1964, United States relations with the Panamanian government were generally stable until Gen. Torrijos came to power in 1968. With the 1967 draft treaties, which the Zonians saw as seriously eroding the
United States position, the Zonians now saw the State
Department as the enemy in Washington. Zonians felt the
State Department, through its negotiators, was giving
away too much. The negotiating position the U.S. assumed
after the 1967 draft treaties were rejected by Panama
was seen by the Zonians as even more favorable to Panama
than were the draft treaties, thus giving the Zonians no
reason to revise their view of the State Department.

Congress, on the other hand, became the friend of
the Zonians, since the hard-line option toward Panama
was often heard in Congress. The Defense Department
gradually gained the same status, as that agency challenged the State Department's actions. Thus, by 1974
Congress and the Defense Department were seen as the
protectors of the Zonians and the State Department as
the source of government efforts to undermine the status
of Americans living in the Zone.

Another major element that contributed to the conflict in Washington over concessions to Panama was a
change in policy toward Latin America overall. Neglect
of Latin America by the United States was commonplace by
1974 after two administrations had contributed little of
their efforts toward that part of the world. After the
embarrassments of the Security Council meetings in Panama in March 1973 and the growing attacks upon the United
States within the OAS and the United Nations, Secretary
Kissinger turned to the major outstanding problems the
United States had in Latin America. The principal reason for this change in policy was the unanimity of opinion among the Latin American countries on the Canal issue. This unity was expressed by the unprecedented
election of Panama to the Security Council in 1975. The
tradition was to pass the two Latin American seats around
among the twenty-six countries in the region, but Panama
was returned after only a two-year lapse since its last
term. This second term was intended to give Panama an
opportunity to continue to promote its position on the
Canal. The first move in this renewed interest in Latin
America came with the appointment of Ambassador Bunker
as U.S. negotiator. In the Fall of 1974, Kissinger appointed his own man as assistant secretary of state for
Inter-American Affairs, William D. Rogers. Both men
were identified with a conciliatory position toward
Panama.

The problems the United States had with Allende
ended with the coup in Chile in September 1973. The
United States also settled the longstanding dispute
with Mexico over the salinity of the Colorado River.
Peru and the United States settled their differences

over nationalization of American property and fishing
rights. The isolation of Cuba by the OAS was softened.
These actions, coupled with the renewed diplomatic efforts by the United States in regard to the Canal, marked
a major effort on the part of Kissinger to improve relations with Latin America. While these efforts had little
of the broad, high-minded appeal of the Alliance for
Progress, the efforts were substantial. Few issues in
the history of regional diplomacy had shown the unity of
the Latin American countries such as did the Canal issue.
This issue had to be dealt with effectively, and soon,
if the United States was to be successful in Latin America.

The announcement of the Kissinger-Tack Agreement
marked a major initial success for the new Kissinger Latin American policy, but it also raised the danger signal
for those in Washington who opposed a conciliatory policy toward Panama. The Snyder Amendment was a result in
the Congress. Following the passage of even the compromise in the House, Kissinger felt it necessary to write
Gen. Torrijos a letter to calm Panamanian fears.[20]

The specific dispute between the State Department
and the Defense Department pertained to defense of the
Canal under a new treaty. The United States had offered
to end its jurisdiction over the Zone three years after
a treaty was approved by both countries; and after
twenty-five years, at about the end of the century, operation of the Canal would be turned over to Panama. In
regard to defense matters, there was to be a reduction
in the number of United States bases in Panama from the
present fourteen. The number of bases was still to be
determined, but Panama wanted no more than three. These
bases would be operated under a lease arrangement and
status-of-forces agreements similar to the arrangements
for other United States overseas bases. The duration of
the lease arrangement for the bases was still to be negotiated with Panama, but Panama wanted the U.S. to
withdraw militarily from Panama at the same time the
operation of the Canal was turned over to Panama.

The provisions for defense were unacceptable to the
Defense Department, and from March to September 1975,
State and Defense were deadlocked. The Defense Department insisted on a fifty-year defense agreement, but the
State Department argued for a shorter period. Secretary
of Defense James Schlesinger was outspoken in his opposition to an agreement of shorter duration. There was,
however, disagreement reported within the Defense Department. Deputy Secretary of Defense William D. Clement
and Assistant Secretary of Defense of International Security Affairs Robert F. Ellsworth disagreed with their
secretary and supported a shorter period.[21]

Another opponent of the proposed defense agreement
was Howard Callaway, secretary of the army until June
1975 and then campaign manager for President Ford.

President Ford, for a time, seemed reluctant to intervene in the dispute, but in July and August the National Security Council arrived at a new set of instructions for the negotiators, and these were approved by the president. On 4 September, the chairman of the Joint Chiefs of Staff, General George S. Brown, Deputy Secretary of Defense William P. Clements, Jr., and Assistant Secretary of State William D. Rogers visited Panama. They represented the conflicting factions in Washington, and their mission was to assure Gen. Torrijos that they all supported new treaties with Panama.[22]

The decision in the National Security Council appeared to be a State Department victory, or at least was so heralded by the press. Kissinger and his assistants had argued for a treaty of twenty-five years' duration before the United States withdrew entirely, as opposed to the fifty years the Defense Department wanted. The State Department's victory was better described as a compromise, since the Defense Department was successful in dividing the issue so that operation of the Canal was separated from the defense provisions. Under the compromise, defense of the Canal would continue for forty years rather than fifty years, even if the Canal was turned over to Panama in twenty-five years. Bunker then returned to Panama on 7 September 1975, and the negotiations resumed.

Panama, like the press in the U.S., initially thought the State Department had won, but soon learned that such was not the case. The United States was not only asking for a defense treaty for up to forty years but also claiming the right to defend the Canal indefinitely beyond the expiration of the treaty by asking that the defense treaty include renewal provisions.[23] Anything less than total withdrawal at the time the Canal was turned over to Panama was unacceptable to Panama. The negotiations in Panama broke off on 17 September, and even though negotiations resumed early in January 1976, no progress was made.[24]

The lack of progress in negotiations fulfilled the prophecies of both the supporters and opponents of a new treaty. The State Department argued that to make demands for a long-term defense arrangement undermined the negotiations and agitated radicals in Panama. Kissinger, Bunker, Rogers, and Deputy Secretary of State Robert S. Ingersoll all supported this position.[25] The disappointment of the Panamanians and the breakdown in the negotiations verified the hazards of the compromise.

The opponents of a new treaty had warned that to make concessions to the Panamanian government would only raise false hopes. The demands of Panama could not be met and at the same time hope that the resulting treaty would be approved by Congress. To raise Panama's expectations and then dash them would only worsen the situation between the United States and Panama.[26] Thus,

the compromise of separating the operation of the Canal
from defense of the Canal did not meet with enthusiasm
in either Panama or Congress. Previous to its conflict
with the Pentagon, the State Department supported the
position that it would be an error to solicit congressional support for a new treaty until either a draft was
ready or at least the basic agreements had been made.
To solicit support, the State Department felt, would only
attract publicity and damage the possibilities of a successful conclusion to the negotiations.[27] "The likely
length of the negotiations, their undertain outcome, and
the embarrassment of having to conceal--or worse, dis-
close--differences between State and Defense all fed into
the decision [to negotiate in secrecy]."[28]

The result of this choice of tactics was to give
the opponents of a treaty time to organize and say what
they wished about the treaty without any countering
statement from the State Department. But as a consequence of growing congressional opposition to a new
treaty, the State Department was forced to abandon its
secrecy decision; and in May 1975 Ambassador Bunker began to make public statements in support of the State
Department's position of conciliation with Panama. When
the Pentagon openly lobbied for support of its position
in Congress, the State Department did the same. In July
1975, supporters of a new treaty, Senators Humphrey and
McGee, surveyed the Senate and found over sixty senators
ready to vote against an anti-treaty resolution prepared
by Harry F. Byrd, Jr. Since the defeat of his resolution was apparent, Byrd did not bring his resolution to
the floor of the Senate. Kissinger also began to comment
publicly on the treaty, and State Department news re-
leases contained more information on the negotiations
than they had in the past.

Even though the firing of Secretary Schlesinger by
President Ford in November 1975 was never tied in with
the conflict between Kissinger and Schlesinger over the
Canal, the Pentagon remained quiet on the Canal after
Donald Rumsfeld became secretary. The Defense Department
had lost its most outspoken opponent of a new treaty,
and the president now had his own appointee in the office
of secretary. This move did not lessen the hostility of
Congress directed at Kissinger and the State Department,
however.

1976 PRESIDENTIAL POLITICS

The risk the president ran in making any decision
on the negotiations during the summer of 1975 was that
the Canal issue could become a major campaign issue in
1976. As a congressional source explained the problem,
"Ford's listening to his political advisers now more than
his diplomats. They tell him that Reagan is breathing
down his neck and they don't want him coming out strong

publicly for the treaty."[29] During the campaign prior
to the Florida presidential primary held on 9 March,
Ronald Reagan found the Panama Canal a response-stirring
issue. "When it comes to the Canal, we bought it, we
paid for it; it's ours and we should tell Torrijos that
we are going to keep it." In response to the report
that the U.S. had secretly accepted a compromise formula
for a new treaty in which Panama would be given sovereignty over the Canal, Reagan commented, "If these reports are true it means the American people have been
deceived by a State Department preoccupied by secrecy."[30]
     The alignment of groups that took a public stand
on the Canal issue must also have been of concern to
President Ford. Both the American Legion and the Veterans of Foreign Wars passed resolutions in opposition to
a new treaty. The Canal Zone Central Labor Union affi-
liated with the AFL-CIO opposed any revision in the
existing treaties. This union alone did not carry great
weight, but the possibility of the AFL-CIO supporting
their position was of concern. The Panama Canal Pilots
Association, made up of 200 or so pilots, all but three
of whom were Americans, opposed a new treaty. Reminiscent of the argument over the Suez Canal pilots in 1956,
the American pilots said they would not work for Panama
and that the Panamanians could not do the piloting themselves. The American Institute of Merchant Shipping
(AIMS) wanted to keep the Canal tolls low and felt that
the only method of doing so was for the United States to
maintain control over the Canal. These pressures, plus
the reluctance of the U.S. military, provided substantial
political opposition to the conciliatory position.
     The positions of American multinational corpora-
tions on the Canal issue were mixed. One observer of
the Canal issue said that "U.S. corporate investors in
the Zone--such as ITT, which owns Central American Cables
and Radio, Inc. as well as Transoceanic Communications,
the zone-based communications system--are beginning to
register their unease at the prospect of coming under
direct Panamanian jurisdiction, although they are keeping
a low profile."[31] The overall pressure from the multinational corporations, however, seemed to be for a new
treaty.
     Late in 1975, a group of "more than two dozen"
large U.S. businesses and corporations started an extensive lobbying campaign for a new Canal treaty. These
multinational corporations feared that since Panama had
the support of virtually all of Latin America, retaliation against the multinational corporations was likely
not only in Panama but throughout Latin America. Representatives of the multinational corporations met at the
State Department and organized into the Business and
Professional Committee for a New Panama Canal Treaty.
Among the corporations listed as attending were the Ford
Motor Company, Chase Manhattan Bank, Pan American

Airways, Bankers Trust Company, Gulf Oil Company, and
Shell Oil Company.[32]   Nearly all of these corporations
had major facilities in Panama (Chase Manhattan had four
banks in Panama City alone), and all were active throughout Latin America.
    The principal nongovernmental group working against
a new treaty was the Committee for Continued U.S. Control of the Panama Canal. This group's statement in opposition to a new treaty bore twenty-nine signatures,
mainly from retired professors, military and government
officials, and representatives of major veterans groups.
Their memorial to Congress, introduced into the Congressional Record by Rep. Flood, called for modernization of
the present Canal through the Terminal Lake-Third Locks
Plan and other improvements and emphasized the strategic
and economic importance of the Canal to the United
States.[33]
    The Canal became the surprise issue of the presi-
dential campaign, after the attention the Canal issue
received during the campaign preceding the Florida primary. Ronald Reagan made the Canal's future a major
part of his campaign rhetoric.
    After his claim that the Canal belonged to the
U.S., Reagan then attacked the Torrijos government as
pro-communist with close ties to Castro and Cuba. On 31
March, in a nationally televised speech, Reagan described
the Canal Zone as "sovereign U.S. territory every bit the
same as Alaska and all the states that were carved from
the Louisiana Purchase."[34]   The State Department responded by describing Reagan's claim of U.S. sovereignty as
"totally wrong."
    In April, President Ford began to defend the nego-
tiations. While campaigning in Texas, Ford said that
the U.S. would "never give up its defense rights to the
Panama Canal and will never give up its operational
rights."[35]   Further, the president defended the negotiations as necessary to protect U.S. interests. He labeled
as "absolutely irresponsible" the Reagan demand that the
negotiations be ended.[36]
    In May, President Ford received support in his de-
fense of the negotiations from an unexpected source,
Senator Barry Goldwater (R., AZ). Goldwater described
Reagan's position as based on "either a lack of understanding of the facts or a surprisingly dangerous state
of mind." Goldwater felt that "unless we come to some
agreement with the Panamanian government there is going
to be a guerrilla war."[37]
    Late in May, Reagan proposed an alternative to a
new treaty. He wanted the Canal enlarged and modernized,
but no change in the status of the U.S. presence. This
proposal was similar to the Third Locks-Terminal Lake
Plan promoted by congressional opponents of a new treaty.
    The State Department, without mentioning Reagan,
responded to a number of Reagan's charges through

testimony of Deputy Assistant Secretary of State for
Inter-American Affairs William H. Luers before the House
Subcommittee on International Political and Military Affairs. He denied that the Torrijos government was under
communist influence. He labeled Torrijos as "nationalistic, pragmatic, and populist," and, in spite of claims
to the contrary, there was no sizable Cuban presence in
Panama, although Panama did recognize Cuba. The only
other communist countries with which Panama had diplomatic or economic relations were Yugoslavia and Poland.[38]
    When the Republican convention met in August, a
fight developed in the platform committee over the Canal
issue. The Reagan-supported proposal, which called for
the United States never to surrender its sovereignty
over the Zone, was defeated. The following compromise
plank was adopted by the committee and, on 18 August,
accepted by the convention:

> The present Panama Canal treaty provides that
> the United States has jurisdictional rights in the
> Canal Zone as "if it were the sovereign." The
> United States intends that the Panama Canal be
> preserved as an international waterway for ships
> of all nations . . . .
>   In any talks with Panama, however, the United
> States negotiations should in no way cede, dilute,
> forfeit, negotiate, or transfer any rights, power,
> authority, jurisdiction, territory or property
> that are necessary for the protection and security
> of the United States and the entire Western
> Hemisphere.[39]

As was the Canal plank in the Democratic platform,
the Republican plank was intended to unite the party and
was seen as such by the Panamanian press. The Panamanian
press was delighted, however, when President Ford received his party's nomination. Reagan's campaign statements had resulted in attacks on Reagan and support for
Ford in the Panamanian press. During the campaign following the conventions, the press in Panama leaned toward
Ford but openly attacked Carter only when he stated in
October, during the Carter-Ford televised foreign policy
debate, that the U.S. must "never give up complete control or practical control of the Panama Canal Zone, but
I would continue to negotiate with the Panamanians."[40]
    The Panamanian press, after Carter's election, was
cautious but optimistic that the negotiations would continue. The appointments of Sol Linowitz as co-negotiator
and former senator Gale McGee as ambassador to the OAS
were reassuring to Panama, since both men were well known
advocates of a new treaty. In July 1977, however, Panama was upset when President Carter stated, during an appearance in Yazoo City, Mississippi, that the U.S. might
need a sea-level canal in Panama sometime in the future.

This would be necessary, the president said, in order to accommodate large warships and oil tankers. Later in the same month, Carter said that before the year 2000 he thought that a "larger, wider, deeper" sea-level canal might be necessary.[41] This speculation about a sea-level canal without consultation with Panama was disturbing to Panama.

The issue within the executive was settled, however. The completion of a new treaty appeared imminent by the Summer of 1977. The next struggle was apparent. The new treaty had to be sold to the Congress.

NOTES

1. Stephen S. Rosenfeld, "The Panama Negotiations--A Close-Run Thing," Foreign Affairs 54 (October 1975):1-2.
2. New York Times (24 January 1972), p. 11.
3. Congressional Record (1 August 1975), p. E4396.
4. Thomas M. Franck and Edward Weisband, "Panama Paralysis," Foreign Policy 21 (Winter 1975-76):177.
5. Ibid., p. 169.
6. See U.S., Congress, House, Committee on Foreign Affairs, Hearings before the Subcommittee on Inter-American Affairs on H.R. 74, 154, 156 and others, 92d Cong., 1st sess., 1976.
7. The extent of Representative Flood's concern over the status of the Canal and the time he devoted to the question was reflected in the publication of a 523-page House Document of speeches Flood delivered on the Canal between 1958 and 1966. U.S., Congress, House, House Document 474, 89th Cong., 2d sess., 1966.
8. Hearings before the Subcommittee on Inter-American Affairs, p. 3.
9. U.S., Congress, House, Committee on Merchant Marine and Fisheries, Hearings before Subcommittee on Panama Canal, 91st Cong., 2d sess., 1970, p. 13.
10. Franck and Weisband, "Panama Paralysis," p. 168.
11. New York Times, 16 March 1972, p. 14.
12. American attitudes toward Panamanians and their ability to run the canal developed out of the construction period. Few Panamanians worked on the construction; most of the manual labor was done by imported labor. For many years, nearly all of the non-Americans working for the Canal Company were drawn from those who had helped construct the Canal or from their descendents.
13. Wall Street Journal, 21 August 1975, p. 1.
14. Ibid., p. 10.
15. U.S., Congress, Senate, Senate Resolution 301, 93rd Cong., 2d sess., 29 March 1974.
16. Congressional Record, 24 September 1975, p. H9044.
17. Ibid.
18. Congressional Record, 29 October 1975, p. H10418.
19. Congressional Record, 18 June 1976, p. H6173.
20. New York Times, 9 July 1975, p. 2.
21. New York Times, 16 September 1975, p. 11.
22. New York Times, 5 September 1975, p. 8; Franck and Weisband, "Panama Paralysis," p. 175.

23. Franck and Weisband, "Panama Paralysis," p. 177.
24. Christian Science Monitor, 8 October 1975, p. 7.
25. New York Times, 16 September 1975, p. 11.
26. Franck and Weisband, "Panama Paralysis," pp. 168-69, 176.
27. Rosenfeld, "Panama Negotiations," pp. 8-9.
28. Ibid., p. 9.
29. Wall Street Journal, 21 August 1975, p. 10.
30. Christian Science Monitor, 1 March 1976, p. 3.
31. Franck and Weisband, "Panama Paralysis," p. 174.
32. Wichita Eagle, 5 November 1975, p. 8B.
33. Congressional Record, 29 October 1975, pp. H10409-20.
34. U.S., Congress, Senate, Committee on Foreign Relations, A Chronology of Events Relating to Panama Canal. Prepared for the Committee on Foreign Relations by Congressional Research Service, Library of Congress, 95th Cong. 1st sess., p. 16.
35. Ibid., p. 17.
36. Ibid.
37. Ibid., p. 18.
38. Ibid., p. 19.
39. Ibid., p. 21.
40. Ibid., p. 22.
41. Ibid., p. 32.

10
The Fight for Ratification

When Sol Linowitz was appointed co-negotiator by
President Carter in February 1977, the appointment was
for six months. The president could, of course, extend
Linowitz's appointment for a longer period, but Carter
clearly had placed a deadline on the negotiations and
wanted them concluded by August. Bunker's appointment,
made in 1973, carried no time limitation.
In the early summer of 1977, rumors circulated in
both the United States and Panama that a new treaty would
soon be announced. Such optimistic speculations had developed a number of times before during the negotiations,
especially in 1974 following the Kissinger visit to Panama. The first strong indication that the rumors were
true this time came on 8 August when President Carter
telegraphed all members of Congress that a new treaty
"may be concluded very soon."[1] He asked Congress to reserve judgment on the treaty until they had a chance to
study the new agreement. On 10 August, the negotiators
announced that the negotiations had been successful and
two treaties would be signed at the Organization of
American States headquarters in Washington on 7 September. The long wait for the new treaties was ended.
What had not been resolved by the August announcement was the actual content of the treaties. The treaties had been agreed to in principle only. The completed
text was released only two days before the 7 September
signing. The signing ceremony went off as scheduled
with a maximum of diplomatic pomp. The heads of state,
or their representatives, of twenty-six Latin American
countries attended. Mexico's president, Jose Lopez
Portillo, and Brazil's president, Ernesto Geisel, did
not attend, saying they had previous commitments. Opponents of the treaties in the United States cited their
absence as evidence that Latin America was not united
behind the treaties. Both countries had expressed complete support for the treaties, however.
The signing was dominated by the emotional display
of General Torrijos, with his embraces of President

Carter and the tears he shed over at last obtaining a
new agreement with the United States. It seemed apparent
that the 1903 treaty would soon be only a part of the
history of United States-Panamanian relations.
To many Americans, the signing ceremony raised questions. Since most Americans are not familiar with the
process of treaty ratification, some saw the signing as
a final and hurried step that would formally implement
the treaties. The signing actually was only a necessary
first step before the treaties were subject to the domestic ratification procedures of the two countries.

PANAMA

The campaign to ratify the treaties in Panama began
almost immediately after their signing in Washington,
D.C., on 7 September. Shortly thereafter, Torrijos announced that a plebiscite would be held in Panama on 23
October to seek ratification of the treaties. Few observers doubted that Torrijos could obtain a majority
within his authoritarian regime in which the government
either owned or closely controlled the mass media. However, simply obtaining a majority was not enough. Torrijos had to convince the United States and the world
that a treaty concluded with a military regime, in power
as a result of a coup d'état, would have both legality
and durability. It was necessary to reassure the U.S.
and major Canal users that a post-Torrijos regime would
not be able to unilaterally abrogate the 1977 treaties
by claiming they were concluded with an illegitimate
regime.
To legitimize the treaties, Torrijos had to "demonstrate to the world that the results of the plebiscite
represented the feeling of the Panamanian people, as expressed through a truly democratic process."[2] Such a
demonstration required that Torrijos relax the political
controls which had been in effect since the National
Guard had assumed power in 1968. The Panamanian ruler
was taking a risk by opening up the political process to
an extent greater than at any other time during the nine
years he had ruled Panama, but Torrijos was counting
upon his personal popularity with the Panamanian people,
especially rural Panamanians, as well as the desire of
most Panamanians to settle the Canal issue once and for
all.
The problem of ratification had been anticipated by
Torrijos when he drafted Panama's new constitution in
1972. Article 274 of the new constitution specifically
provided for a plebiscite to approve or disapprove any
new treaties dealing with the status of the Canal and
the Canal Zone.[3] The plebiscite was to take the place
of the usual procedure established by the Panamanian
constitution, which called for a vote of the Assembly of
Corregimientos to approve all international agreements.

In a matter this important, however, Torrijos did not
want to give treaty critics the opportunity to besmirch
the legitimacy of the treaties by questioning their approval by a handpicked and tame representative body.
Ultimately, the Corregimientos would play only a small
role in the ratification process other than passing a
resolution expressing its wholehearted support for the
Canal treaties.

The plebiscite would be conducted in the following
manner.[4] Voters would receive two ballots of different
colors--one color for "yes," the other color for "no."
On each ballot was printed the following statement:

> I am in agreement with the Panama Canal
> Treaty, the treaty on permanent neutrality of the
> Canal and the operation of the Canal, the appended
> agreements and annexes signed between the Govern-
> ment of Panama and the United States on 7 September
> 1977.[5]

To diminish the possibility of fraud, each voter was
thumbprinted; and his cedula, or identity card, was
punched. In addition, academics from several countries
were invited to come to Panama and vouch for the integrity of the electoral process.

Torrijos also felt constrained to respond to those
critics who charged his regime with human rights violations by inviting both Kurt Waldheim, secretary general
of the United Nations, and Andres Aguilar, director of
the Inter-American Human Rights Commission, to visit Panama and observe the plebiscite. Later in the campaign,
spokesmen for the government also would forcefully respond to the Inter-American Press Association (IAPA),
which had been highly critical of the human rights record
of the Torrijos regime.

Opponents of the military regime quickly took advantage of the political opening provided by the plebiscite debate. Panama's Liberal Party met publicly for
the first time in the nine years since Torrijos had out-
lawed all political parties. The ostensible purpose of
the meeting was to discuss the Liberal Party's position
regarding the new treaties; but David Samudio, Liberal
Party president, used the opportunity to castigate both
the military regime and the Corregimientos.[6]

Another individual who took advantage of the opening
was former president Marco Robles, who announced that
he would support the treaties, but who, at the same time,
called for the return of political expatriates and the
re-establishment of political freedoms in Panama.[7]

The broad strategy which Torrijos used to offset
opposition to the treaties was essentially fourfold:

First: Conduct the plebiscite as quickly as possible before treaty opponents were able to mobilize
their opposition. The Torrijos regime did not intend to

emulate the lengthy period of debate which had occurred after the signing of the 1967 Draft Treaties and which probably contributed in large part to those treaties never coming up for ratification in Panama.

Second: Send government spokesmen, primarily the treaty negotiators, throughout the country to explain and defend the various provisions of the new treaties. In addition, the government used both radio and television to present their case for the treaties.

Third: Create an international political climate which was supportive of the new treaties. Torrijos made several trips abroad during the pre-plebiscite period, where he met with foreign leaders to explain the significance of the treaties to Panama.

Fourth: Organize and use pro-government groups to counter the most significant opposition to the treaties. For example, an organization called the Broad Front of Lawyers was developed during the campaign to more effectively answer the criticism of the Independent Lawyers Movement.

The linkage between domestic politics and the foreign policy process was clearly shown in the Panamanian plebiscite. As the tenor of the ratification campaign was established, it soon became clear that treaty opponents were, as one newspaper commentator noted, "basically not judging the treaties but the government." Despite this, the opposition did put forth several procedural arguments in their efforts to delay or block the ratification of the treaties.

The Independent Movement of Lawyers sought to delay the plebiscite by claiming that forty-six days was an insufficient length of time for the electorate to become informed about the treaties. The lawyers also demanded copies of the minutes of the negotiations so they might better assess how negotiators for both sides interpreted the meaning of the more controversial treaty provisions. The minutes of the secret negotiations were never made available to the lawyers; and the government spokesmen ridiculed the call for a plebiscite delay, arguing that the treaties should be a surprise to no one since their basic provisions had been known for several years, dating back to the Kissinger-Tack Agreement. The government also claimed that they planned to distribute 300,000 copies of the treaties before the plebiscite to better inform the electorate. Eventually, the Independent Movement of Lawyers took their case to the Panamanian Supreme Court, where they petitioned it to suspend the plebiscite.[8] Not surprisingly, this petition was rejected by the court.

Students, particularly from the University of Panama, were in the forefront of the opposition to the treaties. Although the students burned a U.S. embassy car which had come onto the university campus during the campaign, the majority of their opposition was

nonviolent.[9] Early in the campaign, Torrijos met with
the students and allowed them to present their demands.[10]
These demands included (1) an increased freedom of expression, (2) freedom to discuss the Canal treaties for
no less than ninety days before a plebiscite and (3)
permission for political exiles to return to Panama.
Students got much less than they demanded, although Torrijos assured them they would be given a full page in
the newspapers, an hour per day on radio and an hour
per week on television to present their case against the
treaties. However, the students' opposition was muted
by a pro-government student group, the Federation of Panamanian Students (FEP), which actively supported the
treaties.

The recently resurrected political parties were unable to have a major impact on the ratification of the
treaties. The Liberals expressed no opposition to the
treaties, claiming that they were little different from
the ones they had negotiated in 1967.[11] The Christian
Democrats issued an ambivalent statement which neither
supported nor opposed the treaties, while the Panameñista
party of former president Arnulfo Arias found itself divided between opposing positions. Although Arias issued
a statement, from exile, late in the campaign calling
for a categorical "no" to the treaties, the youth wing
of the party passed a resolution urging support for the
treaties.[12] Finally, the Communist party, possibly because of Torrijos' friendship with the Castro regime in
Cuba, urged Panamanian voters to erase the continuing
affront to the Panamanian people represented by the 1903
treaty.

Torrijos played a relatively subdued role in the
treaty ratification campaign in Panama, as he spent much
of his time traveling abroad, from where he sent back
lengthy statements describing his travels and his meetings with various foreign leaders. Two days before the
plebiscite was scheduled, Torrijos appeared on national
television to discuss the treaties and what they represented for Panama. Admitting the treaties did not give
Panama everything it wished for, he argued that the new
treaties would unify Panama for the first time in its
history as the Canal Zone passed under Panamanian control. Although Torrijos appeared to have accepted the
possibility of defeat, he did not establish any fixed
percentage of the votes which would be necessary to ratify the treaties.

Ultimately, when Panamanian voters went to the polls
to register approval or disapproval for the treaties, it
seemed that the majority accepted the government's claim
that the new treaties were less than perfect but that
the new ones were infinitely better than the old 1903
treaty, which had frustrated them for so many years.

October 23rd, election day, dawned bright and clear,
without the heavy rain clouds which had been predicted.

Torrijos took their absence as a good sign and declared, "Even the rain clouds are anti-imperialist."[13] When final returns from the plebiscite were tabulated, the results showed that 766,232 Panamanians had cast ballots, with only 14,310 being voided. Of the remaining valid ballots, 506,805 indicated approval for the treaties, while 245,117 voted "nay," for an approval rate of 67.4 percent.[14]

Although Torrijos expressed his satisfaction with the plebiscite results, only two out of every three Panamanians had voted to approve the treaties. Other observers saw the vote as a message of disapproval for the Torrijos regime. One opposition lawyer explained the negative vote by stating, "Some people voted 'no' because they want the U.S. to remain in Panama. Most took the opportunity to try to repudiate the Torrijos dictatorship."[15] His statement was echoed by a student who declared, "Our quarrel is more with Torrijos than with the United States. We know these treaties are the best we can get."[16]

Torrijos chose to interpret the results as providing additional support for the treaties, since they clearly demonstrated that the opposition had been allowed to express its arguments openly. In addition, he claimed that a two-thirds approval was comparable to the sixty-seven votes that would be required for the treaties' approval in the U.S. Senate. Despite Torrijos' claim, if the negative votes truly represented a repudiation of the military regime, it presented him with a difficult dilemma. On the one hand, Torrijos could not afford to allow the opposition too much freedom; but, on the other hand, he could not forcefully reinstate the previous controls for fear of giving U.S. treaty opponents additional ammunition to use against him in the ratification process in the United States.

Other clouds which darkened Torrijos' horizon were a lingering concern over the fate of the treaties in the U.S. Senate and the negative vote that the treaties received in the San Blas Islands, home of the Cuna Indians. Not only did the Cunas vote against the treaties by a slim margin, 4,605 to 4,149, they lowered the Panamanian flag and raised the American flag.[17] Apparently, the Cunas were persuaded that if they voted "yes" for the treaties, they would lose their jobs because the Americans would leave after closing the hospitals and the tourist hotels upon which the Indians depended for their livelihood.

THE UNITED STATES

In the United States, the treaty ratification process would take longer than the six weeks Panama had assigned to it. The U.S. Constitution requires that treaties receive Senate approval by a two-thirds vote

before they can be ratified. The review of the treaties
in the Senate was sure to take several months. Following
the Senate's approval and a majority vote in Panama in
support of the treaties, the formal exchange of ratifications between the two countries would complete the process.

General Torrijos' task was a simple one compared to
the one faced by President Carter. President Carter was
in the position of entering a new and lengthy set of negotiations, this time with the U.S. Congress. Congress
had not waited for the completion of the treaties to begin its activities, and hearings were already taking
place even before the treaties were signed. Opposition
to the new treaties in Congress was active and had been
gaining momentum in its drive to defeat any new agreements with Panama.

The role of the Senate in the ratification process
was not questioned, but what was not clear was the role
of the House of Representatives. The U.S. Constitution
states that whenever property of the United States is
disposed of, it has to be done by a vote of both houses
of Congress. The new treaties contained much that did
not pertain to the disposal of U.S. property, but, clearly, property then owned by the United States was either
to be transferred to Panama shortly after the completion
of the ratification process, or at some later date.
Eventually, all of the Canal Zone and its facilities
would be Panamanian-controlled.

Many members of the House of Representatives felt
that those provisions of the treaties dealing with the
transfer of property had to be approved by a vote of the
House. This view had been expressed in numerous resolutions introduced, but never voted on, by individual members of the House, and in committee hearings of the
Subcommittee on the Panama Canal and the Subcommittee on
Inter-American Affairs. Also, opponents of the new
treaties in the Senate favored a role for the House,
since it was generally felt that there was more opposition to the treaties in the House than in the Senate.
Certainly, in the past, opposition in the House had been
more vocal than had the Senate opposition, perhaps because of the uncertainty about the role of the House relative to new Canal treaties that had existed since the
1967 draft treaties.

Hearings on participation by the House had first
been held in the Senate in July, as the rumors circulated
that new treaties were forthcoming. The forum was the
Subcommittee on the Separation of Powers of the Judiciary
Committee.[18] The chairman of the subcommittee was James
B. Allen (D., AL), who was to prove to be a leader among
those opposing the treaties.

At their opening, Senator Allen made apparent the
intention of the hearings. "Inasmuch as Section 3 Article IV of the Constitution provides that Congress, that

is, both houses of Congress, shall have power 'to dispose of and make all needful rules and regulations respecting the territory or other property belonging to the
United States,' the subcommittee is concerned that serious constitutional issues involving the doctrine of
separation of powers are raised by the continued secret
negotiations of the executive branch for the disposition
of U.S. territory and property in the Canal Zone."

The legal argument presented to support a role for
the House was that since the Zone was obtained by a congressional act, the Spooner Act, it could be transferred
to Panama only by another act of Congress. Also cited
was Sierra Club v. Hickel, a decision of the Ninth Cir-
cuit Court of Appeals in 1973, which was affirmed by the
Supreme Court: "Article IV, Section 3 of the United
States Constitution commits the management and control
of the lands of the United States to Congress. That
Congressional power is unlimited."

The administration's case was presented by a Department of State legal advisor. He argued that the treaty
power was not intended to be restricted by the power of
Congress relative to the disposition of property. He
further argued that "all treaties made under the authority of the United States which are self-executing take
effect as the law of the land without further legislation."[19] He also pointed out that there were a number
of precedents for the transfer of property by treaty
without supporting legislative action.

The subcommittee, in one respect, expressed disappointment in the hearings. Senators Allen and Jesse
Helms (R., N.C.), the latter a witness, felt that the
hearings received little media coverage. Allen made the
charge that the media were so biased in favor of the
treaties that a fair amount of coverage was not possible.
The subcommittee held no further hearings until after
the treaties were released and signed.

At about the same time Allen's subcommittee was
holding hearings, the Subcommittee on the Panama Canal
of the House Merchant Marine and Fisheries Committee was
also holding hearings. These hearings dealt with the
economic and military value of the Canal to the United
States.[20] The subcommittee had the reputation of being
against new treaties, but its ranking minority member
Gene Snyder (R., KY), refused to participate in the hearings on the grounds they were hastily called and too
many witnesses were pro-treaty.[21]

Governor Parfitt of the Canal Zone was the opening
and star witness. He summarized several of the studies
done on the economic value of the Canal and projections
on Canal usage. A 1971 study done by the Economic Commission for Latin America (ECLA) estimated the savings
to have been $540 million annually from 1960 to 1970 and
projected an average annual savings of $805 million from
1970 to 1980. Another study, done by the Maritime

Administration, estimated that a Canal closure would increase the cost of U.S. exports "by $932 million and the
price of imports $583 million."[22] Only one study, Gov.
Parfitt reported, done in 1973 by International Research
Associates, had taken into account both alternatives to
the Canal and the current rate schedule. Between 1975
and 1985, the annual economic value to all users would
"build from $93 million to $141 million, with an average
economic value, or user's surplus, of $117 million."[23]
However, if the tolls were to be doubled, the revenues
would double initially, but as more economic routes were
explored, the revenues would decline.

After the decline in both the number of transits
(down to 12,300 in 1976 compared to about 15,500 transits
in 1974) and tonnage, Canal usage was again increasing,
but modestly. Governor Parfitt's explanation for the
decline in Canal usage after 1974 was the recession of
1975 and 1976 and the reopening of the Suez Canal in
1975. Projections were for 33.4 transits a day in 1977,
with an increase up to 40.6 transits a day in 1990.
Toll revenue would increase from $166.6 million in 1977
to $240 million in 1990 at the present toll rates. The
overall conclusion drawn by the governor was that the
Canal was of major economic importance to the United
States and would continue to be until the end of the
century. No projections were made beyond that date.[24]
This basic information on the Canal was referred to frequently as the hearings progressed.

Various other witnesses substantiated Governor Parfitt's analysis, but one witness in particular added information that resulted in some controversy. Dr. Margaret Hayes had recently completed a study of the Canal
for the Office of International Security Affairs in the
Department of Defense. She pointed out that much of the
U.S. traffic was bulk commodities such as petroleum,
grains, and coal. Such shipments accounted for fifty
percent of the Canal tonnage, although Dr. Hayes projected a decline.

> There has already been a noticeable drop in
> coal traffic through the Canal as the coal trade
> shifts to carriers too large to pass through the
> Canal. Alaskan oil production will soon supply
> West Coast U.S. needs, eliminating the need for
> shipments from the East. Latin American intercoast-
> al petroleum traffic will decline as domestic re-
> finery capacity increases in Ecuador and Peru.
> U.S. petroleum imports from Latin America have been
> declining steadily as a percentage of total petro-
> leum imports. . . . Currently, most U.S. imports
> from Latin America do not pass through the Canal.
> In the future, Mexico is likely to become a major
> supplier to the U.S. in petroleum. Of the major
> commodities currently transiting the Canal, only

grains shipped from U.S. Gulf ports to Pacific
Ocean destinations are expected to continue to
increase in volume.[25]

Dr. Hayes felt that Canal traffic overall would increase but at a much slower rate than had occurred before
1974. She also observed that with the exception of petroleum, no raw materials critical to the U.S. went
through the Canal in significant quantities. Alternative
routes, such as transcontinental rail shipments, were
available for nearly all commodities. Japan, however,
would remain heavily dependent on the Canal, as would
many of the Latin American countries.
Dr. Hayes also pointed out that revenues from the
Canal provided thirteen percent of Panama's GNP and was
Panama's most important economic asset. "It is therefore highly unlikely that Panama would purposely engage
in actions to threaten traffic flow through the waterway."[26] While the Canal would remain an important facility in international trade to the end of the century,
"the Panama Canal can hardly be considered vital to the
United States. It is neither essential nor indispensable
to the movement of U.S. commerce. Were it not available,
adjustments would occur as they did when the Suez Canal
was closed."[27] Various other witnesses supported Hayes'
conclusion. This sort of testimony was, of course, in
direct conflict with treaty opponents' arguments that
the Canal was a vital economic asset to the United
States.
Subcommittee members Robert Leggett (D., CA) and
Robert Dornan (R., CA), in particular, took exception to
this conclusion. They emphasized the total value of the
Canal, generally set at about $5 billion, and the small
amount of the investment in the Zone that had been amortized. The amount of unamortized value set by Governor
Parfitt was $752 million. This figure did not include
the expense of defense facilities in the Zone. The
question of the total investment the U.S. had made in the
Zone remained an issue throughout the ratification process.
One witness, James J. Reynolds, president of the
American Institute of Merchant Shipping, approached the
economic value of the Canal from the U.S. shipping industry's perspective. He pointed out that the Canal was
attractive to the U.S. and world shipping mainly because
of the toll structure. Alternative ocean routes would
become economically desirable if the tolls were to increase. He also mentioned that some Far East ports could
be reached more economically from New Orleans and New
York by the Suez Canal, or even around Cape Hope, than
by going through the Panama Canal if tolls were increased.
Before the hearings began, the subcommittee staff
submitted a list of questions to the witnesses asking

whether the Canal was vital to U.S. economic interests.
The testimony was strongly in the direction that the Canal was important to U.S. economic interests, but not
vital. The subcommittee then turned to the issue of the
importance of the Canal to United States defense interests. On this point, the opponents of new treaties were
more effective. Their most effective weapon was a statement issued on 8 June 1977 by four former chiefs of naval
operations, Robert Carney, George Anderson, Arleigh
Burke, and Thomas H. Moorer, all retired from active
duty. They had stated:

> The Panama Canal represents a vital portion of
> our U.S. naval and maritime assets, all of which
> are absolutely essential for free world security.
> It is our considered individual and combined judg-
> ment that you [the president] should instruct our
> negotiators to retain full sovereign control for
> the United States over both the Panama Canal and its
> protective frame, the U.S. Canal Zone, as provided
> in the existing treaty.[28]

These admirals based their statements on the importance of the Canal during times of crisis and, in particular, cited World War II, the Korean War, the Cuban
Missile Crisis and the war in Vietnam.

While no member of the Joint Chiefs of Staff (JCS)
testified, a representative was sent. He appeared as a
member of a panel of witnesses on U.S. defense interests.
The panel pointed out the declining importance of the
Canal during the Vietnam War as compared to previous
wars. They also concluded that most of the military activities carried on in the Zone could take place elsewhere. Their assessment was that the Canal was not a
vital defense interest of the U.S.

The hearings were concluded with the appearance of
a panel of witnesses that testified on the foreign policy aspects of the Canal. A principal spokesman for a
new arrangement with Panama was William D. Rogers, president of the Council of the Americas and former assistant
secretary of state for Inter-American Affairs. "The
reason [for approving the treaty] is simple. The pragmatic consideration, that a new treaty is needed to keep
the Canal open, appeals to business considerations and
to our national economic interests."[29] He argued that
the dispute between the United States and Panama over
the Canal was not an isolated one, but had far-reaching
impact throughout the rest of the world. He felt that
the issue had been internationalized to the point that
the U.S. had little choice but to conclude a new treaty.

The Council of the Americas was a major and important interest in support of the new treaties. Its membership included over 220 corporations that represented
ninety percent of U.S. investment in Latin America. A

second witness from the council took the position that the best means of keeping the Canal open was to have a new treaty with Panama. If anti-U.S. feelings continued to grow in Panama, not only might the Canal be closed but U.S. business interests throughout Latin America would be affected. The Canal issue had become the most important symbolic issue in U.S.-Latin America relations, and failure to resolve it would result in an "unfavorable trade and investment environment." [30]

Except for a brief hearing on the treaties before the Subcommittee on Inter-American Affairs, Congress held no further hearings until after the treaties were signed on 7 September. The activities of the executive between the 10 August announcement of the new treaties and their signing on 7 September were devoted primarily to developing a coalition of support for the treaties. On 11 August, the JCS gave the president their full support and promised to aid the executive in its efforts to have the treaties ratified.[31] Bunker and Linowitz appeared on "Meet the Press" on 14 August and appealed for bipartisan support for the new treaties. They also pointed out the danger of violence in Panama if the treaties were not approved by the Senate. On 17 August, former secretary of state, Henry Kissinger, after meeting with President Carter and Ambassador Bunker, said that it was his "strong view that the new treaty is in the national interest of the United States."[32] A few days later, former president Gerald Ford, after a meeting with Ambassador Linowitz and General George Brown, chairman of the JCS, in Vail, Colorado, announced that he was "absolutely convinced it's in the national interest of the United States that the two treaties be approved."[33] President Ford also attended the 7 September signing ceremonies.

The pattern of personal briefings on the treaties was not successful in gaining Ronald Reagan's support for the treaties, however. Following a private briefing by Ambassadors Bunker and Linowitz, Reagan said, "I do not believe we should ratify this treaty."[34] The president did receive support from another quarter, however. AFL-CIO president George Meany threw his support to the treaties after being given assurances that the rights of Panama Canal Company employees were adequately protected in the treaties.

If President Carter hoped for a swift ratification of the treaties, his hopes were dashed when, on 17 August, Senate Majority Leader Robert Byrd announced that debate on the treaties would not begin until January or February. Byrd felt that a debate sooner was premature, especially since public opinion in the United States was not yet ready. Byrd said that the energy bill, already scheduled to come before the Senate, had higher priority than the treaties.

The delay in the debate was probably to the treaties' and the executive's advantage. The public opinion

polls were running about three to one against the treaties, with a substantial percentage undecided. Senators'
offices were reporting that their mail was heavily a-
gainst the treaties. An immediate review of the treaties
presented no particular advantage for the proponents,
since the opposition appeared to be better organized and
certainly more vocal than were treaty proponents. Delay
in holding debate would give the executive an opportunity
to turn public opinion around and rally support in the
Senate. Reports were also circulating that various
senators who wanted to vote for the treaties were concerned about their constituents' reaction if they did so.
Privately, the administration was being told that if
public opinion could be changed, the votes would be there
in the Senate, but, otherwise, the treaties were in serious trouble. The delay until early 1978 provided the
time to conduct a campaign in support of the treaties.
    In the Senate, the opposition moved first. On 8
September--three days after the treaties were made public, two days after they were initialed by the negotiators, and the day after the formal signing ceremony--the
Subcommittee on Separation of Powers reopened hearings
on the treaties. When the subcommittee had held hearings earlier, they had been reasonably balanced, even
though the questions from the subcommittee were generally critical of any testimony in support of new treaties.
This time, the witnesses and the questioning were pointedly anti-treaties. The witnesses were Ronald Reagan,
Daniel Flood, and Representative Phillip M. Crane (R.,
IL), all longstanding opponents of a new treaty with Panama.
    Earlier, the opponents had had to attack a new trea-
ty in the abstract, based on rumors as to what the treaties would contain; but now the specifics were available.
In his opening statement, Senator Allen charged that the
"substance of the deal struck with Panama" was in the
"very lengthy executive agreements" that accompanied the
treaties. Allen claimed that the executive agreements
could be renegotiated every two years, thus giving the
executive the capacity to revise any agreement approved
by the Senate. The executive, Allen felt, "would be
given a blank check."[35]
    Senator Allen was also upset with the economic ar-
rangements outlined in the treaties. In all, Allen said,
Panama would receive $2.262 billion in cash payments in
the next twenty-two years. Other economic arrangements
included a $200 million loan from the Export-Import Bank,
a loan of $75 million for housing from the Agency for
International Development and a $20 million loan guaran-
teed by the Overseas Private Investment Corporation.
Panama would also receive $50 million in military aid.
Allen said the subcommittee was aware of these arrangements before the treaties were made public but had obtained its information from Panamanian sources because

the State Department and the Defense Department would
tell the subcommittee nothing.

Governor Reagan insisted that the United States had
obtained the right of sovereignty over the Zone in 1903,
to "the exclusion of the exercise of such rights by the
Republic of Panama."[36] He granted that this right of
sovereignty was not the same as the United States had received in the purchase of Alaska or Louisiana, but a legal base had been established for our use of the Zone to
operate a canal. The support of the JCS for the treaties, he felt, was more than offset by the opposition of
four former chiefs of naval operations (CNO), especially
since the latter were no longer obligated to the president.

Further, Governor Reagan felt that the United States
had nothing to apologize for in its treatment of Panama.
Panama had received considerable economic benefit from
the Canal that it would not have had if the United States
had not built the Canal. Panama had the highest per
capita income of any of the Central American countries,
and the United States had dealt fairly with both Colombia
and Panama. Rather than new treaties, the United States
should continue under the 1903 treaty and move toward
carrying out the Third Locks-Terminal Lake plan to expand use of the Canal.

In the course of his testimony, Reagan brought up
the Freedom House rating of Panama on human rights, a
judgment that was to be mentioned many times in future
hearings and on the floor of the Senate. Freedom House,
Reagan said, "which is recognized internationally as an
impartial monitor of the status of human freedom, rates
Panama as one of the 67 nations of the world that is
'not free.'"[37] Freedom House rated countries on a scale
of one to seven on both civil and political rights, with
seven the lowest rating. Panama had been given a seven
in both categories.

During questioning, Reagan discussed the support
Panama had from other Latin American countries. He said
that while the leaders of these countries did indeed
publicly support the new treaties, if members of the
Senate would discuss the matter with them privately, the
senators would find that many were concerned over the
future of the Canal if it were controlled by Panama. He
discounted the 1964 riots as "largely engineered and
stirred up and kept going by political leaders of the
left."[38] The Canal could be defended from Panamanians,
and the United States had already proven its ability to
do so during the 1964 riots.

Rep. Flood took, as he had often done before, what
was essentially a conspiratorial view of the development
of the new treaties. He said that the announcement of
the treaties "was a high point in the plan long in preparation to present the Nation and the Congress with a
fait accompli,"[39] and that since the announcement, the

news media in the United States had given considerable
coverage to the Canal question, but most of it was in
"support of the projected surrender of U.S. sovereignty
over the Canal Zone and, ultimately, the giving away of
the Panama Canal itself, all without compensation."[40]
The overall tone of this day of hearings was that
the United States was "giving away" the Canal because of
meaningless threats from Panama and Latin America. The
Canal could be defended from the Panamanians without the
use of 100,000 U.S. troops, which, among the proponents,
had become the size of force necessary to defend the Canal if guerrilla warfare developed. Latin American
leaders were not, in fact, anxious for the Canal to come
under Torrijos' control. The "give away" was actually a
massive payoff to Panama to take the Canal, whereas Panamanians should be paying us for it if they were to
have it. The Canal was of major military significance
to the United States, in spite of the State and Defense
Departments' statements to the contrary. Torrijos was
corrupt, and Panama was not a free country. And on the
domestic level, the opposition argument was not being
presented to the American public because of the media's,
especially television's, support of the treaties.
The subcommittee held no further hearings until after the all-important hearings before the Senate Foreign
Relations Committee began. The subcommittee saw its role
as presenting the opposition's arguments, since, in their
view, the Foreign Relations Committee hearings would be
weighted in favor of the treaties. The subcommittee in-
terspersed four days of hearings in October and November
to answer arguments presented before the Foreign Relations Committee.
The Foreign Relations Committee began its hearings
on 26 September. In all, the committee held fifteen
days of hearings before the committee's mark-up of the
treaties began on 26 January 1978. The committee completed its mark-up on 30 January and reported the two
treaties favorably to the Senate. The committee vote,
on both treaties, was fourteen in favor, with one member,
Senator Robert P. Griffin (R., MI), voting against the
treaties. The sixteenth member of the committee, Sen.
Hubert H. Humphrey, missed the hearings due to illness
and died on 13 January, before the committee voted on
the treaties.
The committee had, since World War II, supported the
executive on virtually every major foreign policy issue
that came before it. The only important exception was
during the Vietnam War, when the committee was chaired
by Sen. William Fulbright (D., AR). The war split the
committee, as it did the nation as a whole, as no other
issue had done since the committee developed an inter-
nationalist view of the world following World War II.
When Fulbright was defeated in the 1974 elections, the
committee came under the less forceful leadership of

Sen. John Sparkman (D., AL). The change in leadership
came in January 1975; and in April, South Vietnam col-
lapsed and the war came to an end. The committee once
more became a more united group.

In the Ninety-Fifth (1977-1979) Congress, the committee was divided, ten Democrats and six Republicans.
This ratio on the committee between parties was determined by the overall strength of the parties in the Senate, which was sixty-two Democrats and thirty-eight Republicans. The relationship between party strength in
the Senate and on the standing committees was a provision
of the Legislative Reorganization Act of 1946. The committee had, since Sen. Vandenberg's service on the committee following World War II, committed itself to conducting its affairs on a bipartisan basis. Even though
bipartisanship seemed to have a variety of meanings to
the committee membership, over the years it most often
meant that the executive's requests were supported by
the committee. Even during the division of the committee
during the Vietnam War, party lines were not the line of
division.

In spite of the lack of a public commitment to the
treaties on the part of many of the committee's members
in September 1977, there was clearly more support for
the treaties on the committee than in the Senate as a
whole. Most of the committee membership had visited Panama within the preceding twelve-month period or would
visit in the next few weeks. Both Sparkman and Sen.
Clifford Case (R., NJ), the ranking Republican on the
committee, along with several other committee members,
had been in Panama in February. The committee had prepared itself well for the hearings on the treaties and
viewed its review of them as a major foreign policy issue, perhaps the most important question to come before
the committee in a number of years.

The committee opened its hearings on 26 September
with four days of testimony from administrative witnesses, testimony which, as anticipated, was pro-treaty.
While hearing such witnesses first might appear to be a
pro-treaty move, the traditional procedure of the committee was to begin with administrative witnesses. The
hearings opened with the appearances of Secretary of
State Cyrus Vance and the co-negotiators, Ambassadors
Ellsworth Bunker and Sol Linowitz.

At the start of the hearings, several of the committee members made statements on the treaties. With the
exception of Sen. Claiborne Pell (D., RI), the statements
were noncommital, but with no overt anti-treaties comments. Pell supported the treaties. Sen. Robert P.
Griffin made no statement, although he had made statements previous to the hearings that he opposed the treaties. Although absent, a statement from Sen. Humphrey
was read into the record that announced his support for
the treaties.

Secretary of State Vance, in his testimony, argued
that the new treaties would "protect and advance the national interests of both the United States and Panama."[41]
The treaties would provide for an "open, neutral, secure
and efficiently operated canal for this hemisphere, and
for other nations throughout the world." The treaties
would gain respect for the United States and culminate
thirteen years of negotiations under four U.S. presidents.

Vance emphasized that the United States would have
the responsibility for operating the Canal until the
year 2000 under a new U.S. government agency, the Panama
Canal Commission. Until the year 2000, the U.S. could
keep its present military force of about 9,300 men in
Panama and could even increase it if this were felt to be
necessary. The U.S. would have all the military facilities necessary to defend the Canal and, after the year
2000, would have the permanent right to maintain the
neutrality of the Canal. This latter statement, and similar ones by other witnesses, became the source of major
controversy between Panama and the United States.[42]

Vance felt that the $.30 per Panama Canal ton that
Panama would receive in the future would more "fairly
reflect the fact that [Panama] is making available its
major national resource . . . ."[43] The $60 million that
Panama would receive annually from tolls would assure
that Panama would be most interested in the Canal remaining open and running efficiently. Vance also mentioned
the importance of the $200 million in credits from the
Export-Import Bank, the $75 million in AID housing guar-
antees, and a loan guarantee from the Overseas Private
Investment Corp. All of these were loans and required
repayment. Panama would also receive $50 million in
foreign military sales guarantees, so that the Panamanian
military forces could better defend the Canal.

As for the U.S. citizens currently working for the
Panama Canal Company, most of them would have their jobs
until retirement, and their civil and political rights
would be guaranteed under Panamanian law. Vance called
for support of the treaties by the Senate and assured
the committee that U.S. interests were well served by the
treaties.

In his testimony, Ambassador Bunker clarified the
nature of the new Panama Canal Commission that would run
the Canal until 2000. The composition of the commission
had been a problem up to the very end of the negotiations. Bunker said that the nine-man board would consist
of five Americans and four Panamanians. The administrator would be an American, and the deputy administrator
a Panamanian until 1990. After that, until 2000, the
administrator would be Panamanian, and the deputy American. All positions, including the administrator and deputy administrator (both before 1990 and after) and the
nine members of the board, would be appointed by the

United States. The Panamanian appointees would be proposed to the U.S. by Panama. The United States had won
this dispute, since Panama had wanted to make the appointment of Panamanians.

During the questioning of the witnesses, the issue
of the House's role in the transfer of property came up.
Ambassador Linowitz pointed out that the administration
did not intend to include the House in the review of the
treaties but that the House would review a number of
pieces of implementing legislation if the treaties were
approved by the Senate. This legislation was not to be
taken up until after the treaties were approved.

During the course of the hearings, there were several instances of the committee reacting to events that
occurred in Panama and instances of the Panamanian government responding to statements before the committee.
One example was the Panamanian interpretation of the
right of the United States to intervene in Panama after
1999 under the neutrality treaty. Torrijos insisted
that since the United States was so much more powerful
than Panama, it could intervene whenever it wished; thus,
a treaty provision was not necessary. Linowitz and Bunker both insisted that the United States had the right
to defend the Canal unilaterally, if necessary, until
2000. After that date, the U.S. could intervene to
maintain the neutrality of the Canal.[44]

Another such instance of cross-national interaction
was the interpretation of the phrase "expeditious passage." Article 6 of the neutrality treaty read that U.S.
"vessels of war and auxiliary vessels will be entitled
to transit the Canal expeditiously." The Panamanian interpretation was that U.S. naval vessels would take their
turn but would not be delayed unnecessarily in transit.
The United States read the clause to mean that our naval
vessels would move to the head of the line of any vessels
waiting to transit the Canal. Both of these issues were
debated at length before the committee and on the floor
of the Senate before the treaty was approved.

The questioning of Vance and the negotiators by committee members was sympathetic and designed to allow the
witnesses to develop their arguments in support of the
treaties. But when Sen. Griffin began his questioning,
the tone was more confrontive. He immediately put Linowitz on the defensive by pointing out that his commission
had expired on August 10 and that he was now appearing
as a private citizen. The senator also suggested that
the United States should follow the Panamanian example
and hold a national plebiscite on the treaties. Vance
pointed out that such a procedure would be a violation
of our own constitution and that these treaties should be
dealt with in the same way as any other treaty. Griffin
was also critical of the provision in the treaties that
allowed the construction of a sea-level canal only in

Panama. Sen. Griffin's questioning of witnesses on this
occasion, and of later witnesses, was brief.
The committee next turned to the defense issues
raised by the treaties. The witnesses were top officials
in the military and the Defense Department, including
Harold Brown, secretary of defense; General George S.
Brown, chairman of the JCS; Admiral Robert L. J. Long,
vice CNO; and Lt. Gen. D. P. McAuliffe, commander-in-
chief, Southern Command. Without exception, they argued
that the treaties were in the national interest of the
United States and would contribute to our national security. Our navy could use the Canal without interference,
and the Canal would be efficiently run. They stressed
that the Canal would be defended from both internal and
external threats and that while the treaties would allow
us to respond to both, the new agreements especially
would reduce the threat of internal interference.
    At this time, much was being written about the trea-
ties in the newspapers, news magazines and journals. Of
all the coverage, one article in particular attracted
the committee and raised concern. Hanson W. Baldwin,
longtime writer on military affairs for the New York
Times, now retired, had vigorously attacked the new
treaties in an article, "The Panama Canal: Sovereignty
and Security," in the American Enterprise Institute Defense Review.[45] His attack was less emotional than most
and developed the arguments of the opposition well.
Baldwin stressed the strategic importance of the Canal
to the U.S., particularly in times of crisis. He regarded the treaties as reflecting another retreat by the
United States and was concerned with the psychological
and political damage this would do.
    Baldwin felt that the administration was acting out
of a sense of guilt in granting the new agreements to
Panama, a guilt that was an outgrowth of the demise of
colonialism since World War II. In his view, none of
this reduced the importance of the Canal to the U.S.,
however. He attacked, at length, the argument that the
U.S. did not have sovereignty in the Zone. He said that
the United States had not exploited Panama over the
years, but, on the contrary, had done a great deal for
Panama. He denied that Latin America fully supported
Panama and doubted that Latin America could agree on any
single issue. He regarded the Torrijos regime as unstable and without the support of the Panamanian people.
The repeated threats made by Torrijos to attack the Canal, Baldwin surmised, could be dismissed as "breast-
beating machismo."[46]
    The Baldwin article was introduced into the record
of the hearings and was referred to often in the course
of the hearings and during the debate in the Senate. A
second article, written by Abraham F. Lowenthal and Milton Charlton, published in the same journal, presented

the arguments for the supporters of the treaties, but
received far less attention.[47]

The support of the JCS for the treaties was one of
the most troublesome sources of support for the opposition to counter. The opposition attempted to dismiss
this support by arguing that the members of the JCS were
not in a position to oppose the treaties as long as they
were on active duty and the president was their command-
er-in-chief. Opposition by retired members of the JCS,
they argued, was far more significant, since they had no
fear of losing their positions. General Brown countered
by saying that if the JCS acquiesced to the president's
wishes contrary to the needs of national defense, the
chiefs would be guilty of neglecting their duties. He
also pointed out that the JCS had opposed the president
on other matters, such as the cancellation of the B-1
program and on the withdrawal of the Second Division from
Korea unless certain conditions were met.

The dismissal of General Singlaub because of his opposition to the withdrawal of troops from Korea and the
cancellation of the neutron bomb project were cited by
the opposition as an example of what would happen to an
officer on active duty who opposed the president's position. General Brown insisted that such pressures did not
exist and also pointed out that although four former
CNO's opposed the treaties, not all former CNO's were
opposed. Admiral Zumwalt, also a former CNO, did support the treaties.[48]

Witnesses from the Defense Department were again
taken over much of the same ground that was covered earlier before the Allen subcommittee. The defensibility
of the Canal, the meaning of expeditious passage, neutrality of the Canal, Panama's ability to defend the Canal after 2000, declining use of the Canal by U.S. naval
vessels, and the absence of a Soviet presence in Panama
were all reviewed. As with the State Department witnesses, committee members posed Defense Department witnesses
few questions that would weaken the case for the treaties. The questioning was more of the "complete the
record" variety.

The committee next heard the attorney general, Griffin Bell, and State Department legal adviser Herbert
Hansell. Bell and Hansell developed once again the argument presented before the Allen subcommittee that a
self-executing treaty was a possible and constitutional
means of disposing of U.S. property. The committee also
heard Harold R. Parfitt, governor of the Canal Zone, and
William V. Jorden, U.S. ambassador to Panama. Both were
perennial witnesses before congressional committees and
were supportive of the treaties. Jorden was praised in
the Panamanian press for his testimony.[49]

The hearings before the Foreign Relations Committee
were carefully followed in Panama, with daily reviews
appearing in the press. On 27 September, Aristides Royo

attacked administrative witnesses for arguing that the
U.S. had the right to intervene in Panama. He conceded
that the U.S. had the right to defend the Canal but denied that the U.S. had the right to intervene in Panamanian affairs.[50] Actually, the witnesses had been careful to make the distinction that Royo made. Royo also
said that even Fidel Castro defended the treaties as the
best deal possible considering that President Carter
could grant Panama no more and still get the treaties
through the Senate.[51] The Panamanian press, however,
continued to be disturbed for several days over the right
of the U.S. to intervene.[52]

The hearings resumed with congressional witnesses
on 4 and 5 October. The four days of testimony by administrative witnesses had been totally supportive of the
treaties, but the congressional witnesses presented a
mixed view. This was the first opportunity for the opposition to present its views to the committee. Among
the opposition witnesses were Senators Allen, Robert
Dole (R., KS), Jesse Helms, Paul Laxalt (R., NV), William
Scott (R., VA) and Strom Thurmond (R., SC). This group
of senators later provided most of the debate against
the treaties when they came before the Senate in early
1978.

Senator Thurmond outlined the strategy of the opposition. His opening point of attack concerned the nature of the Torrijos government. Thurmond was opposed
to negotiating with a man who came to power by means of
a military coup. He also attacked the economic policies
of Torrijos that had increased the Panamanian national
debt from $167 million to over $1.5 billion and had resulted in thirty-nine percent of the Panamanian national
budget going to service the debt. Further, Thurmond opposed Panama's close relationship with Cuba and the Soviet Union and the absence of civil and political rights
in Panama. Thurmond also pointed out that in the prepared statements of Linowitz, Bunker, General Brown and
Secretary Brown, Torrijos' name did not appear once. In
general, Thurmond found the Torrijos government repre-
hensible, dictatorial, a friend of our enemies, economically unsound and unable to protect or run the Canal to
our satisfaction in the future.

Thurmond's second line of attack concerned the
sovereignty question. "We either have sovereignty or we
have the equivalent of sovereignty, and what difference
does that make?"[53] Those rights were granted in perpetuity, and "that means forever."

Thurmond also presented a number of other arguments.
Panama, Thurmond said, had rejected a military pact with
the United States during the negotiations (which it had)
for the period after 2000. Without such a pact, U.S.
interests were endangered. While the treaties prohibited
foreign troops after 2000, Thurmond pointed out that
they said nothing about foreign troops until that time.

Cuban and Soviet troops could be brought into Panama
shortly after the treaties went into effect, and the U.S.
would have no legal recourse under the treaties. Thurmond was also disturbed that the treaties prohibited a
new canal any place except in Panama and then only with
Panama's permission. Thurmond felt that privileged
passage of U.S. vessels should be assured in the treaties. Thurmond quoted, as did other opposition witnesses, from the controversial statements made by the Panamanian chief negotiator, Dr. Escobar, before the Assembly of Corregimientos on 19 August. Thurmond pointed out
that Dr. Escobar had said that "Those people [the United
States] believe that the right to intervene is granted,
but nobody grants the big powers the right to intervene.
They intervene wherever they damn well please, with or
without a pact."[54] Also, Thurmond said that Escobar had
stated on Panamanian radio that the neutrality treaty
"does not establish that the United States had the right
to intervene in Panama. This word 'intervention' was
discussed and eliminated."[55] Thurmond also attacked the
economic benefits Panama had received from the United
States. "Panama was the recipient of $342 million in
total U.S. aid, more per capita aid than was granted to
any other country in the world."[56] In spite of this aid,
Panama's economy was in trouble.

Thurmond and other opposition witnesses cited three
sources at length during their testimony before the Foreign Relations Committee--the letter written by the four
former CNOs to show that those members of the military
free to speak openly were opposed to the treaties; the
Freedom House report, to show that Torrijos was a dictator, falling in the lowest category concerning political
and civil rights; and the speeches made before the Assembly of Corregimientos by various Panamanian officials
on 19 August. Quotes from these speeches were used to
show that the government of Panama held a much more restricted view of U.S. rights to the Canal than was held
by the State and Defense Departments.

The questioning of Senator Thurmond by members of
the committee produced what was probably the best discussion of the treaties to take place before the committee. As a fellow senator, he was accorded the courtesy
given to a respected colleague, but the questions directed to Thurmond were designed to show the weaknesses of
his position. The committee members especially stressed
the vulnerability of the Canal from a hostile Panamanian
people.

The other opponents from Congress to appear before
the committee added little to the arguments presented by
Thurmond. The lead witness before a committee has the
distinct advantage in presenting the choice arguments.
Supporting witnesses then can, for the most part, offer
only expansions on those arguments. Senator Allen, in
his testimony, summarized well the opposition's main

points of attack by pointing out what he regarded as the
five major flaws in the treaties: "(1) the failure of
the Canal treaty to provide for an adequate defense of
the Canal during the proposed 23-year term of the treaty;
(2) the failure of the neutrality treaty to grant to the
United States the unilateral right to intervene to assure
the neutrality of the Canal; (3) the astonishing provision of the Canal treaty which forbids the United States
even to negotiate with another nation for construction
of a second sea-level canal without the express consent
of Panama; (4) the decision embodied in the Canal treaty
and related loan agreements to pay to Panama some $2.262
billion; and (5) the failure of the Canal treaty to require congressional authorization for its proposed cession to Panama of the United States territory and property."[57]   Since Senator Allen was to bear much of the argument against the treaties on the floor of the Senate,
his testimony was particularly important. Most of the
changes in the treaties offered on the floor of the Senate by the opposition dealt with one or another of these
points.

Senator Allen also made an important announcement
concerning the strategy the opposition would follow on
the Senate floor. He said that he did not foresee a
filibuster directed at the treaties. He reasoned that a
filibuster would be pointless "both because a filibuster
could be stopped by 60 senators whereas the treaties
could be stopped by 34 senators and because both treaties
present questions which should be disposed of without
undue delay . . . [If] the treaty should be defeated by
a filibuster, it really would not decide the basic question because the treaty would remain on the executive
calendar for the remainder of that Congress and for suc-
ceeding Congresses."[58]   As long as the treaties were on
the calendar, the executive could bring the treaties up
whenever it felt it had the necessary two-thirds majority
to pass the treaties. The issue best be settled now,
Senator Allen said, and he intended to offer amendments
to the treaties in an effort to make them more acceptable.

Senator Robert Dole offered his testimony in a
somewhat different fashion than had the other opposition
witnesses. On 23 September, Dole had been the first
senator to offer amendments to the treaties, and his
testimony before the committee was in defense of those
amendments. Several of the witnesses had mentioned that
they would introduce amendments to the treaties, but
only Senator Dole had done so.

Dole attacked the State Department's opposition to
any amendments to the treaties and insisted that his
amendments were designed to strengthen the treaties, not
kill them. Dole also pointed out that the Senate often
amended treaties before they were ratified, and there
was no reason why such should not be done in this case.

In all, Dole introduced six amendments and two reservations. (The content of these changes will be discussed
when the Senate floor debate is reviewed later in this
chapter.)
Senator Dole was also critical of what he described
as the administration's strategy of grouping all of
those who opposed the treaties as "off in right field,
somewhere in some extremist group."[59] He argued that
there were many valid reasons for opposing the treaties.
Although respectful of a fellow senator, the committee was less interested in Dole's reasons for opposing
the treaties than in a confidential cable, written by
the charge d'affaires of the United States embassy in
Panama, that Dole had released on 4 October. This cable
reported a private conversation between the U.S. diplomat
and the Panamanian negotiator, Carlos Lopez Guevera.
The cable made clear that the Panamanian interpretation
of "neutrality regime" and "expeditious passage" were
different from what had been presented to the committee
by administration witnesses. The Panamanian diplomat's
view was that the United States did not have the right
to intervene in Panama after 2000 and that "expeditious
passage" did not mean priority or preferential passage.
The U.S. would not be given "head of the line" privileges. To do so, the Panamanian negotiator argued, would
be a violation of the neutrality provisions of the treaty by giving the U.S. vessels special advantages.
To counter the impact of this cable, Senator Church
read into the record a letter from the State Department
stating that both the United States and Panama had the
"right to take any appropriate measures to defend the
Canal against any threat to the regime of neutrality established in the treaty." The United States was not
granted the right to intervene in the internal affairs
of Panama, however.[60]
The members of the committee, in their questioning
of Dole, did not raise the propriety of Dole's releasing
the contents of a confidential cable until Senator John
Glenn (D., OH) questioned Dole. Glenn accused Dole of
making no attempt to declassify the cable before releasing it, and wondered if Dole felt he was in a position
to declassify material on his own. This charge resulted
in a heated exchange between Senators Dole and Glenn.
Glenn also pointed out that this cable reflected one Panamanian diplomat's opinion and was not an official
statement of the Panamanian government. On 6 October,
State Department spokesman Hodding Carter III also attacked Dole for releasing the cable.
Beginning on 10 October, the committee began hearing
private witnesses. In all, nearly sixty witnesses appeared, not counting individuals accompanying the principal witness. The witnesses generally fell into two cate-
gories--either retired military and State Department
officials or representatives of organizations. Admiral

Thomas H. Moorer (former chairman of the JCS) strongly
opposed the treaties, but Admiral Elmo R. Zumwalt, (former CNO) and General Maxwell D. Taylor (former chairman
of the JCS) supported the treaties. Two former secretaries of state, Henry Kissinger and Dean Rusk, testified
in favor of the treaties.

The committee imposed a ten-minute limitation on
the less prominent private witnesses. The committee had
employed a similar practice in previous hearings to expedite proceedings, but the net effect was to reduce
considerably the time per witness as compared to the
time allotted earlier witnesses.

Among the most vehemently opposed witnesses were
representatives from the civic councils in the Canal
Zone. The civic councils were the nearest thing to an
organization in the Zone for the public articulation of
the residents' demands. Since the Zone was administered
through only appointed officials, there was no civil
government or elected officials. The representatives of
these councils were particularly upset with assertions
about the feelings of residents of the Zone made by witnesses who had never been to the Zone or had "spent one
to three days in the Canal Zone."[61] Also, they rejected
comments made by Ambassador Jorden on the grounds that
he had "no expertise in representing accurately what we
feel as a people in the Canal Zone because his contacts
are confined to the highest level of Canal Zone official-
dom."[62] It was also pointed out that Presidents Carter
and Ford, Henry Kissinger, and Sol Linowitz had never
been in the Zone and that Senator Hollings and Ellsworth
Bunker had been there only briefly. Their arguments
were, without exception, opposed to the new treaties.
They insisted that there was considerable opposition to
the treaties in Panama and that the upcoming plebiscite
would be a fraud; thus, the treaties would not resolve
the outstanding conflicts between Panama and the United
States. Property turned over to Panama in the past had
been poorly maintained and, they asserted, the money Panama would receive would go only to Torrijos and his
friends.

Both in their written statement and testimony, the
representatives insisted that there was considerable
communist influence in Panama. Soviet planes had been
seen on the Rio Hato airstrip, and Panamanian students
were studying in Cuba and in the Soviet Union. Panama
had requested Cuban advisors, and the Soviets were planning to build a hydroelectric plant in Panama, and a
Soviet bank was to be opened in Panama. These assertions
were largely unsubstantiated, however. Further, the Panamanians were charged with violating the present treaty;
therefore, they could not be expected to honor new treaties. The government of Panama was described as a reign
of "fear and terror." The representatives felt that no
new agreement should be made as long as Torrijos was in

power. They were particularly worried about living conditions in the Zone under Panamanian jurisdiction as was
provided for under the new treaties. The representatives
felt that the State Department had imposed a giant hoax
on the American people in the form of the new treaties.
Other opposition witnesses included the Liberty
Lobby. This conservative organization claimed a 25,000-
member board of policy categorically opposing the treaties. The Lobby took the view that the treaties were
mainly for the purpose of rescuing U.S. banks that had
overextended themselves in loans to Panama. A representative from the Canal Zone Non-Profit Public Information
Corporation, an organization created in the Zone to inform residents of the Zone on the treaty negotiations
and activities in the Zone, also opposed the treaties.
Rose Marie Aragon, the widow of Leopoldo Aragon, who had
immolated himself in September in front of the U.S. embassy in Stockholm, appeared as the representative of
the Panamanian Committee for Human Rights. She testified
that her husband had killed himself in protest of the
violation of human rights in Panama and the signing of
treaties with the Torrijos dictatorship. The Young Americans for Freedom opposed the new treaties and charged
President Carter with changing his position on a treaty
with Panama after his successful electoral campaign. A
representative of the United States Labor Party opposed
the treaties on the grounds that they would limit Panamanian sovereignty. He also opposed what he felt were
the controls the treaties would place on the economy of
Panama.

The representatives of several religious denomina-
tions testified in support of the treaties. The president of the National Council of Churches (who was also
the Stated Clerk of the United Presbyterian Church in
the U.S.A.), the archbishop of Philadelphia (representing
the United States Catholic Conference), the vice-president of the Synagogue Council of America, and a representative of the Church of the Brethren--all expressed
their support for the treaties.

Organized labor also supported the treaties. A delegation of officials from the AFL-CIO and representatives
of the United Auto Workers appeared in support of the
treaties. George Meany did not testify but had publicly
expressed his support for the treaties in September, before the hearings began. A representative of the National Maritime Union of America, AFL-CIO, also supported
the treaties.

In each instance, the labor witnesses felt that the
union members working in the Canal Zone would have their
interests protected under the new treaties. Witnesses
from the labor councils in the Zone, however, took a less
encouraging view of the treaties. Representatives from
the Canal Zone Central Labor Union and Metal Trades
Council said that "for the most part the employee

privileges and immunities written into the treaty are
satisfactory."63 Concern was expressed for the futures
of the non-U.S. citizen employees in the Zone, although
the unions were ninety-eight percent U.S. citizens and
represented few of the Panamanians employed in the Zone.
The representatives asked for protection for the 5,000
non-citizens that would lose their jobs under the new
treaties but did not insist on such a provision in the
treaties. The president of the Panama Canal Pilot's
Association indicated that his union took no position on
the treaties but estimated that between five and ten
pilots would resign if the treaties went into effect.
The union had a membership of about 210, all but two of
whom were U.S. citizens.

Some of the additional witnesses who testified a-
gainst the treaties were John Fred Schafly, chairman of
the Emergency Task Force on the Panama Canal of the American Council for World Freedom, and Gary Jarmin of the
American Conservative Union. The latter organization was
engaged in a nationwide program expressing its opposition
to the treaties. A representative from Radio Free America of the American Security Council and Hamilton Fish,
former congressman from New York and longtime anti-
communist during his twenty-five years' tenure in the
House, also opposed the treaties.

The week of testimony by public and expert witnesses
concluded with the appearances of the former secretaries
of state, Dean Rusk and Henry Kissinger. Their testimony was essentially a review of the administration's
case for the treaties. While the testimony of the former
secretaries was an important aspect of the administration's campaign to sell the treaties to the Senate, a
much more important development had taken place the same
week. General Torrijos had paid a brief visit to President Carter, and during their consultations the two heads
of state agreed on an understanding concerning the key
issues of expeditious passage and U.S. right to defend
the Canal after 2000. The understanding was delivered
to the Foreign Relations Committee on Friday, 14 October,
and the committee brought Linowitz and Bunker back on
the following Monday to explain its meaning.

The agreement was not signed by either Carter or
Torrijos, thus making it possible for Torrijos to return
to Panama less than ten days before the Panamanian plebiscite and boast that he had not signed any agreement
while in Washington that would weaken Panama's interests
in the treaties.64 Torrijos had agreed, however, to a
statement that supported the administration's arguments
before the Foreign Relations Committee. The "Statement
of Understanding" pertained to the neutrality treaty,
and it said that the principle in the treaty that both
Panama and the United States were responsible for the
Canal remaining open and secure should be interpreted to
mean that "each of the two countries shall, in accordance

with their respective constitutional processes, defend
the Canal against any threat to the regime of neutrality,
and consequently shall have the right to act against any
aggression or threat directed against the Canal or a-
gainst the peaceful transit of vessels through the Canal." This understanding made clear, with the language
"each of the two countries," that the United States could
act unilaterally in defense of the Canal.[65] The understanding said that the "vessels of war" and "naval auxi-
lary vessels of the United States and Panama will be entitled to transit the Canal expeditiously. This is intended, and it shall so be interpreted, to assure the
transit of such vessels through the Canal as quickly as
possible, without any impediment, with expedited treatment, and in case of need or emergency, to go to the
head of the line of vessels in order to transit the Canal
rapidly."[66] Torrijos said that he wanted all warships,
not just U.S. warships, to go to the head of the line
during times of emergency to get them away from Panama
as soon as possible for the sake of Panama's safety.[67]

These interpretations of the two controversial
clauses of the treaty had been what the administration
had been telling the committee were the correct interpretations. The administration hoped that the understanding would reduce the nationwide opposition to the
treaties and forestall amendments that were unacceptable
to the administration. Although the administration would
later change its mind, President Carter at this time
still insisted that the treaties be approved without a-
mendments. The committee greeted the understanding with
enthusiasm and support.

While the committee was reacting to this latest development, the new understanding was being explained to
the Panamanian people by Romulo Escobar Bethancourt, the
treaty negotiator. Dr. Escobar's earlier interpretations
of the treaties, particularly his comments before the
Assembly of Corregimientos on 19 August, had been used
by the opposition in the United States to show that Panama did not interpret "expeditious passage" to mean
head of the line during emergencies and that the United
States would not have the right to intervene in Panama
after 2000. Escobar was the logical one, therefore, to
explain the Carter-Torrijos agreement to the Panamanian
people, especially since his comments would be heard and
interpreted by audiences in the United States. In order
to avoid the impression that Torrijos had been summoned
to Washington to make concessions on the treaties, Escobar explained that President Carter had asked General
Torrijos to stop off in Washington to report on Torrijos'
trip to Western Europe and Israel.

Torrijos had, during the plebiscite campaign, spent
much of his time outside of Panama. He found considerable support for the treaties in Europe, and he used
this to build domestic support in Panama.[68] Escobar

said that Carter was interested in hearing the reactions
of the countries Torrijos had visited to the new treaties. Secondarily, Escobar explained, the two heads of
state met "to clarify some matters which were causing
confusion in Panama as well as in the United States."[69]
Escobar said that "President Carter pointed out that, in
spite of the fact that both he and General Torrijos
clearly understood the points concerning the Neutrality
Treaty, the following had occurred: The U.S. Senate
Foreign Affairs [sic] Committee was interpreting articles
4 and 6 of the Neutrality Treaty in a manner different
or contrary to the way it was being interpreted in Panama by us, the government's spokesmen, and that this was
causing confusion in both countries."[70] Escobar said
that Torrijos was anxious to clear up any confusion before the plebiscite was held on 23 October. Since some
senators maintained, Escobar said, that the right of defense of the Canal gave the U.S. the right to intervene
in the internal affairs of Panama, Panama wanted to make
clear that the U.S. had no such right, thus the Carter-
Torrijos agreement. Escobar granted that if Panama were
attacked, the United States had the right to defend the
Canal and insisted that Panama had always interpreted
the neutrality treaty in that fashion.[71]
     On the second point, the right to put U.S. warships
at the head of the line in times of emergency, Escobar
said it was in Panama's best interests. He pointed out
that the head-of-the-line provision applied to both Panamanian and U.S. warships, and even though Panama did
not have warships, it someday might. The U.S. was
granted nothing that Panama did not also have.
     Escobar also said that Panama was anxious to get
U.S. warships out of Panamanian waters as soon as possible, especially during times of emergency, the point
Torrijos had made. If head-of-the-line privileges were
necessary to accomplish this end, then it should be done.
He pointed out that "a prolonged delay could make that
ship an object of reprisal within our territorial waters."[72] In addition, he said, the prolonged stay of
foreign sailors in Panama "would have negative social
consequences," such as "social problems, problems of
disrespect for women, drunkenness, fights, scandals and
so forth." Since the U.S. was anxious to transit its
ships quickly during an emergency, it served the interests of both countries to do so.[73] (Escobar's news
conference also appeared in the Congressional Record, 20
October 1977).
     On 13 October, the day before the announcement of
the understanding, Senator Dole renewed the charge that
Moise Torrijos, brother of General Torrijos and Panamanian ambassador to Spain, had been involved in drug
smuggling.[74] A few days later, Senator Byrd announced
that Attorney General Bell had assured him that there
was "no direct connection between General Torrijos and

the narcotics trade."[75]   The question of his brother,
however, remained open. The committee did not take up
the charge, but during the Senate debates, the charge
was discussed at length.

The Foreign Relations Committee held no further
hearings on the treaties until after the Christmas recess. The final three days of hearings were held between
19 and 26 January, 1978. On the first day of the resumed
hearings, historians and legal scholars were heard; on
the second, representatives of various businesses and
corporations; and on the third, additional congressional
and public witnesses. Among the witnesses was David
McCullough, author of the best selling Path Between the
Seas, who supported the treaties, as did most of the expert witnesses. One such witness, however, did oppose
the treaties, but for different reasons than those the
committee was accustomed to hearing. Richard Falk, from
the Center for International Studies at Princeton University, argued that the treaties did not grant Panama
enough and that the United States was insisting on the
right to intervene in Panama when such a right was out-
moded in the world today. Falk was also concerned about
the one-third of the Panamanians who had voted against
the treaties in the 23 October plebiscite. This heavy a
vote against the position taken by an authoritarian government, he felt, was an indication that many Panamanians
recognized that the treaties were not in Panama's interests.

The central issue, however, perhaps was whether the
treaty vote was based exclusively on the approval or disapproval of the treaties or whether it was also a refer-
endum on the Torrijos regime. By this point in the hearings, witnesses were hard-pressed to say anything the
committee had not heard a number of times before, but
one witness was able to do so. Ely M. Brandes, president
of International Research Associates, a research group
that had conducted numerous studies concerning the Canal,
testified about the results of a just-completed study
done by his firm for the State Department and the Panama
Canal Company. The study dealt with the projected traffic of the Canal, the sensitivity of Canal traffic to
toll increases, and estimates on how much tolls could
practically be increased. The new estimates were $163
million revenue in 1977 with about a two percent increase
per year with revenues of $264 million in 2000. In-
creases in tolls from fifteen percent to fifty percent
would result in additional revenues from thirteen percent
to thirty-three percent. Toll increases over fifty percent would result in little additional revenue. The
maximum increase in revenues obtainable was forty percent, if no toll increases took place. Brandes concluded
that the Canal would produce enough revenue to be self-
supporting for the next five to ten years but had doubts

about the Canal remaining on a self-sufficient basis after that time.

This study was more pessimistic about the future ability of the Canal to pay its own way, even with toll increases, than had been previous studies. The committee wanted to know if the U.S. negotiators had had this information available to them during the negotiations. Brandes indicated that the study had been completed too late for use during the negotiations, and the study used by the negotiators was one completed three years earlier. Later in the hearings, the State Department notified the committee that this latest study did not seriously affect the economic arrangements of the treaties.

One congressional witness, Eldon Rudd (R., AZ), in addition to a routine attack on the treaties, introduced into the record of the hearings some of the campaign literature used by the Panamanian government to sell the treaties to the Panamanian people. All of the literature was labeled as "secretly taken out of Panama." Such surreptitious efforts hardly were necessary, since such literature was readily available to anyone in Panama during the campaign that preceded the plebiscite. One piece of literature was done cartoon style and showed the change the new treaties would make compared to the 1903 treaties. Uncle Sam was shown in somewhat neutral terms with a strong emphasis on the benefits Panama would derive from the treaties. Compared to cartoons and editorials attacking the United States in the Panamanian press in the past, this literature was mild and reasonably well-balanced.

One of the pro-treaties witnesses to appear before the committee was William D. Rogers, former assistant secretary of state for Inter-American Affairs and under-secretary of state for Economic Affairs, and more recently, from 1974 to 1977, a member of the Panama Canal Company Board. He did not appear in his capacity as an expert on Latin America, however, but, rather, as a member of the Committee of Americans for the Canal Treaties (COACT), the principal nongovernmental organization actively campaigning for the ratification of the new treaties.

Since the treaties had been completed, the administration had been conducting a nationwide campaign to obtain public support for them. The negotiators, Bunker and Linowitz, made a number of speeches in major cities, and the State Department sponsored several regional meetings whose purpose was to develop support for the treaties. The efforts of this campaign were concentrated in the states where both senators were not already committed. The objective of these efforts was to reduce adverse opinion about the treaties so that undecided senators could minimize the political risks of voting for the treaties. Although COACT had the full blessing of the administration, it was financed by private contributions.

The COACT campaign to support the treaties had been launched with a Washington conference of invited state and community leaders from all over the United States. The costs of attending the conference were borne by the individuals attending. The conference leaders expected about 400, but 1,200 attended. The conference included speeches by Vice President Mondale, Henry Kissinger, Ambassador Linowitz, Averell Harriman, and Graham Clayton, secretary of the navy. The program was to be climaxed with a speech by President Carter that was to be delivered during a White House reception. Although such a large crowd presented security and space problems at the White House, the reception took place as scheduled.

It is doubtful that the COACT conference changed many minds, since most attendees were pro-treaty already. The conference was essentially an effort to mobilize support among opinion leaders who were expected to return to their individual states and create support for the treaties.

The Committee on Foreign Relations closed its public hearings on the treaties on 25 January. Majority Floor Leader Robert C. Byrd (D., WV) had asked the committee on 1 December to attempt to report the treaties by 25 January. The committee had concluded the hearings by that date, but still had the markup of the treaties to do. The markup concluded on 30 January.

In many respects, the hearings the committee held were typical of previous hearings held on major foreign policy questions. The procedures followed by the committee in hearing the administrative witnesses first, followed by congressional witnesses and private witnesses, were routine ones for the committee. There were more congressional witnesses than was usually the case, but this reflected the high emotional pitch generated by this particular issue. The hearings were long, but the committee had held longer ones. The dismissal of General MacArthur hearings were longer, and the committee's hearings, under Senator William Fulbright's chairmanship, on the Vietnam War occupied considerably more time. As for the large number of administration witnesses, the Marshall Plan hearings had produced nearly all of President Truman's cabinet as witnesses. As for treaties, the committee had held extensive hearings when the treaty creating NATO came before the committee.

The committee had attempted to compile as complete a record on the Canal treaties as possible and had heard most of the arguments, pro and con, many times in the course of the hearings. As the hearings progressed, a consensus on the treaties seemed to develop among the committee members, with the obvious exception of Senator Griffin. This, too, was typical of the committee, as long hearings often had developed agreement among the

members of the committee. Senator Baker, as committee
member and minority floor leader, had still not expressed
his position on the treaties, although his questions and
comments were not hostile toward them.

The administration maintained good communications
with the committee throughout the hearings. The president had kept in touch with Senate leaders and had responded to the opposition with the Carter-Torrijos agreement. The State Department also had been most cooperative, particularly through the department's liaison with
Congress, the Office of Congressional Affairs and the
assistant secretary of state for Congressional Affairs.
When the committee had requested information of the Department of State, the department had responded with
quicker-than-usual promptness. It was certainly in the
interests of the department to maintain a good relationship with the committee, but the department was also reacting to the longstanding congressional charge that the
department would tell Congress nothing of what was going
on concerning Panama. Now that the treaties were completed, the State Department was more than willing to
provide information to further the cause of the treaties
before the Senate.

But in other respects, the hearings were far from
typical for the committee. Never before had so many
members of the committee, or of the Senate for that matter, visited the country involved in a question before
the committee. By February 1978, forty-two senators had
visited Panama, and nearly all of the committee had visited Panama within the previous year. The visits usually
lasted about three days and included an aerial trip of
the Canal, plus talks with Canal Company officials. Often, meetings with Panamanian officials were included as
well. While none of the trips could be characterized as
in-depth investigations of Canal problems, an unprecedented number of the Senate had some firsthand knowledge
of the country with which the United States had negotiated a major international agreement.

Perhaps because Panama was close to the United
States geographically, or because the presence of so many
Americans in Panama allowed for easier reporting on what
was said there, the Canal treaties hearings produced an
unusual number of reactions in the committee to what was
being said in Panama. The 19 August statements explaining the treaties to the Assembly of Corregimientos was
the most apparent example in the United States, but the
hearings were closely watched by Panama as well. The 14
October Carter-Torrijos agreement was a direct result of
such close observation of the hearings.

The markup of the treaties by the committee also
produced two unusual developments. In an unprecedented
move, the committee released its deliberations during
the markup. The committee wanted to avoid the normal
procedure of doing the markup of a treaty or bill in

executive session. Until the congressional reforms of
the early 1970s, such markups ordinarily took place behind closed doors, but the combination of a more open
Congress and the public attention focused on the treaties
resulted in the decision to make a public record of the
markup of the Canal treaties.

The procedure the committee adopted for the markup
was also unusual, but not without precedent. The committee included amendments to, reservations about, and understandings of the treaties in the committee report to
the Senate rather than as specific proposals in the resolution of ratification the committee passed on to the
Senate. The chairman of the committee, Senator Sparkman,
felt that this procedure would "allow the committee to
make its views known to the Senate on specific amendments, reservations, and understandings, and at the same
time permit all members of the Senate to have maximum
participation in the shaping of the Senate's action of
these treaties."[76] The committee would make recommendations to the Senate, but as Senator Church put it, the
resolution of ratification "will be a clear instrument
of consent."[77]

The markup sessions began with the appearance of
Majority Leader Byrd. Byrd had visited Panama in mid-
November, during which he had advised Torrijos of the extent of Senate opposition to the treaties and that changes in the treaties would be necessary if they were to
pass. Torrijos was reported to have said that he would
resign if that would improve the treaties' chances.[78]

In early January, Byrd's Republican counterpart,
Minority Leader Senator Baker, visited Panama. He also
told Torrijos of the problems the treaties had and that
without changes the treaties had little chance of approval. Clarifications were particularly necessary on the
key disputes of defense of the Canal after 2000 and head-
of-the-line privileges for U.S. naval vessels during
emergencies.

Shortly after his return, Senator Baker informed
President Carter that he would support the treaties if
amendments incorporating the Carter-Torrijos agreement
were adopted. On 18 January, following a two-hour meeting with a visiting delegation of several members of the
Foreign Relations Committee, Torrijos announced that he
would accept amendments that incorporated the Carter-
Torrijos agreement into the treaties.[79] Torrijos said
that such changes would be accepted without another plebiscite because the Panamanian people knew of the agreement before the 23 October plebiscite.[80]

When Byrd appeared before the committee, he announced that the senatorial leadership felt that amendments to the neutrality treaty clarifying U.S. guarantees
of neutral access to the Canal after 2000 and head-of-the
line passage for U.S. naval vessels during emergencies
were necessary. Byrd said that he had made the need for

these amendments clear to both President Carter and General Torrijos and that the amendments were no more than formal amendments expressing the intent of the Carter-Torrijos agreement. An unamended treaty was no longer politically possible. Byrd indicated that both he and the minority leader, Howard Baker, agreed on this point. While stating that the treaties did need these revisions, Byrd also made it clear that other revisions were not desirable, and, certainly, not revisions that would make a second plebiscite in Panama necessary.

In a further move to reduce the opposition to the treaties, Byrd released to the committee correspondence between Byrd and Torrijos. The human rights issue had been brought up repeatedly during the hearings, and, in recent weeks, Torrijos had taken several actions to indicate that his regime was less repressive than was the description of it before the committee. During the campaign before the plebiscite, the opposition was given access to the mass media in Panama to present its position on the treaties. Torrijos promised that political exiles would be allowed to return to Panama. Political parties had been allowed to hold meetings and present their positions on the treaties and other public policy issues. Byrd released to the committee a letter he had received from Torrijos in which Torrijos stated that decrees issued by his government restricting constitutional guarantees and prohibitions against public meetings in Panama City and Colón had been repealed. Torrijos also promised that further actions to expand human rights were forthcoming.

The committee had been functioning one member short during the illness and subsequent death of Senator Hubert Humphrey. Muriel Humphrey was appointed by the Minnesota governor to fill her husband's seat and, in an unusual move, the Democratic Steering Committee and the Democratic Caucus had appointed Mrs. Humphrey to the Foreign Relations Committee. The appointment was unusual in that appointments to the committee are ordinarily made after several years' service in the Senate. Mrs. Humphrey did not take her seat in the Senate until 4 February and thus did not participate in any of the hearings or the treaties' markup.

The committee approved the incorporation of the Carter-Torrijos agreement into the neutrality treaty by a thirteen to one vote, with Senator Griffin in opposition. Senator Baker abstained. Several other amendments to the neutrality treaty had been proposed by noncommittee members and had been referred to the committee for consideration. The committee judged that a total of seven of these proposed amendments were efforts to change the treaty to conform to the Carter-Torrijos agreement and thus were now moot.

The State Department opposed all amendments to the neutrality treaty, including those that would incorporate

the Carter-Torrijos agreement. The department felt the
"Statement of Understanding . . . to be an authoritative
and legally binding interpretation of the relevant provisions of the Neutrality Treaty. Accordingly, we do not
believe that any amendment of the treaty is required."[81]
The committee had incorporated the agreement into the
treaty in spite of the State Department's objections.
The administration's objection to any amendment was that
if the amending process once began amendments could be
incorporated into the treaties that would make the treaties unacceptable to Panama or would require Panama to
hold a second plebiscite.

The plebiscite in Panama had been held some three
months earlier. There had been some risk involved in
having Panama act on the treaties first. Once they were
approved, any changes made by the Senate would produce
drafts that differed from those approved by Panama. How
much change by the Senate was possible without General
Torrijos feeling it necessary to hold another plebiscite?
The safest course of action, as the administration saw
it, was to make no changes in the treaties.

The committee felt that the inclusion of the Carter-
Torrijos agreement in the treaties would present no problem, since it had been arrived at before the plebiscite
was held in Panama. The voters in Panama knew of the
agreement and knew of the interpretations it placed on
the terms "regime of neutrality" and "expeditious passage." Torrijos agreed with this contention.

In addition to the several amendments the committee
felt were now moot, the committee rejected others. One
proposed for the Canal treaty by Senators Dole and Goldwater called for a provision prohibiting the stationing
of any non-Panamanian or non-U.S. troops in Panama until
2000. The neutrality treaty had a provision preventing
non-Panamanian troops after 2000, but nothing was said
about the period until then. The committee tabled the
amendment on the grounds that U.S. troops would be in
Panama until 2000 and that the current treaties with Panama held no such provision; therefore, a new restriction
on Panama was uncalled for.[82]

The committee also tabled an amendment introduced
by Senator Dole concerning a sea-level canal. The treaty
prevented the U.S. from negotiating for a new canal route
outside of Panama without the permission of Panama. The
Dole amendments would have struck this prohibition.

The committee did add an understanding that the
United States could confer with states other than Panama
about the construction of a new canal but could not conclude an agreement without Panama's consent. This provision was introduced by the committee chairman, Senator
Sparkman, and had been recommended by the committee
staff.

Dole also had introduced an amendment and reservation concerning human rights in Panama. Both were

opposed by the State Department and gave the committee
some difficulty because of a general concern over human
rights in Latin America. The State Department argued
that on 12 November, following a visit by a group of
senators who had raised the human rights issue, Torrijos
had announced that he would revise the Panamanian press
code to allow greater freedom of expression, end summary
detention without trial for alleged terrorist acts, and
allow the return of political exiles following the ratification of the treaties. In addition, the Inter-American Human Rights Commission was conducting an investigation of human rights in Panama at Torrijos' invitation.[83]
Also, on 16 November 1977, Freedom House, the organization often quoted by the opposition and long a critic of
Panama's record on human rights, had announced that there
had been some improvement in Panama. It recommended that
the U.S. ratify the treaties because action to the contrary would be to refuse "to restore rights in the Canal
area to the sovereign." Amnesty International, the State
Department pointed out, had not included Panama in its
reports on human rights violations for several years.

Further, the department objected to a bilateral legal obligation by Panama on the question of human rights.
Such an obligation, State argued, would hamper investigations by international organizations looking into human
rights violations. Panama had already shown considerable
progress, as demonstrated during the plebiscite campaign,
but it was highly improbable that Panama would accept
human rights provisions in the treaties.

The department also pointed out that rejection of
the treaties by Panama because of human rights amendments
and reservations would defeat one of the major purposes
of the treaties. "It has been our experience that human
rights tend to be observed in countries where political
and social stability prevail and economic growth is
present, and that violations become prevalent in situations of political turmoil and chaos. . . . Perpetuation
of the Canal issue, however, would almost certainly usher
in a period of political turmoil as radical elements
attempted to use this inflammatory issue to their advantage." The way to solve the need for better human rights
in Panama was through the economic stability the new
treaties would provide.[84] The committee accepted the
State Department's arguments, and both the amendment and
reservation were tabled.

When the committee voted on the treaties themselves, the roll call was anticlimactic and predictable.
With Sen. Baker now committed to the treaties, the vote
on the neutrality treaty was fourteen to one, with Sen.
Griffin the lone dissenter. When the committee voted on
the Panama Canal treaty a few minutes later, the vote was
the same. The only amendments approved by the committee
were those that incorporated the Carter-Torrijos agreement into the neutrality treaty, but, as agreed to by

the committee, these were not attached to the treaty but were recommended to the Senate. The Canal Treaty was approved without recommendations. The way was now clear for the Senate to begin its debate.

During the five months since the treaties had been signed, five sets of hearings had been held. In the House, the Subcommittee on the Panama Canal of the Committee of the Merchant Marine and Fisheries and the Foreign Affairs Committee had held hearings. In the Senate, the Subcommittee on the Separation of Powers of the Judiciary Committee, the Committee on Foreign Relations, and, during January, the Armed Services Committee belatedly held hearings with witnesses who, in most cases, had already appeared before other committees.

Since the Foreign Relations Committee had the sole responsibility to report on the treaties, its hearings were clearly the most important. Other committees and subcommittees held hearings to some extent to "get in on the act," but, generally, the additional hearings were held with the hope of bringing out testimony the Foreign Relations Committee might overlook or neglect. Certainly, this was the intent of Senator Allen's Subcommittee on the Separation of Powers and of his inquiries into the propriety of transferring U.S. property through treaties. He also investigated the charge of drug trafficking by high Panamanian officials and allegations that the U.S. had spied on the Panamanian negotiators and that, in turn, the Panamanians had blackmailed the U.S. for concessions in exchange for not making an issue of the spying charges. Neither charge was proven, but both were reviewed at length on the Senate floor in the coming weeks.

During all of this activity in Congress, the administration had not been idle. Back in August, the president had appointed Hamilton Jordan as White House coordinator for the promotion of the treaties, and, in late September, Jordan had headed a delegation to Panama. The purpose of the visit had been to inform Torrijos of the administration's strategy, which was to develop a gradual campaign of support for the treaties.[85] Thus, in December and January, the program of educating the Congress and the public was only beginning to gain momentum. The feeling among the supporters of the treaties was that treaties opponents had peaked too early in their campaign. This assessment, coupled with the assumption that support for the treaties increased in proportion to how well informed an individual was on them, provided the strategic impetus for an educational campaign that was to reach its peak as the Senate took up the treaties.

On 11 January, Secretary Vance launched a speaking tour, which included other members of the administration, to promote the treaties. Vance appeared in Wheeling, Louisville, New Orleans, and Los Angeles. Each of these

cities was in a state of a senator who was not committed
to the treaties but who was thought to be persuadable.
Vance continued the administration's admonition to not
amend the treaties. A few days after Vance's tour began,
a so-called "truth squad," made up of congressmen and
retired military men and headed by Senator Laxalt, began
a nationwide tour of the United States in opposition to
the treaties.[86]

The administration's strategy of peaking its campaign to coincide with the opening of the Senate's debate
on the treaties was illustrated by President Carter's low
profile early in the treaty fight. He had made supportive statements about the treaties from time to time but
delayed an all-out appeal of support from the American
public until shortly before the Senate debate began. On
1 February, a week before the debate was scheduled to
begin (on 8 February), President Carter utilized the
"fireside" chat technique of FDR to make his appeal.
His speech emphasized the theme that when the treaties
were carefully studied, the interests of the United
States were fully protected, and the treaties deserved
support. He also described the treaties as a fair and
just solution to a problem between a large and powerful
nation and a small, but proud nation.[87] The Panamanian
press reacted favorably to the Carter address.[88]

The opinion polls had been indicating that a majority of the American public still opposed the treaties but
that the margin between the supporters and opponents was
narrowing. On the day of Carter's speech, the latest
Gallup poll was released and showed that for the first
time a majority of the respondents now supported the
treaties. The margin was close--forty-five percent in
support, forty-two percent opposed, with the rest unde-
cided--but the balance of opinion had now shifted to the
supporters.[89]

From the time the treaties had been completed in
August, senators had from time to time announced their
support or opposition. Estimates of how the Senate was
lined up on the treaties were numerous as the debate
grew near. Generally, the estimates were fifty-eight to
sixty senators in support and twenty-three to twenty-
five in opposition. The remaining senators were considered to be about evenly divided between those leaning
one way or the other. The estimates were such that the
treaties could be ratified or rejected by one or two
votes.

The opposition made a last-minute attempt to delay
the opening of the debate. Senator Helms asked that the
debate be delayed until February 20. The argument for
delay was mainly to allow more information to become
available to the Senate before the debate opened. Helms
said the Foreign Relations Committee's report had not
yet been printed, the Panama Canal Company's report on
the costs of the new Panama Canal Commission had not yet

been released, and the Armed Services Committee had not
yet completed its hearings on the treaties. Helms' request was denied by the leadership.[90]

Even though the administration had not yet acquiesced to the need for amendments to the treaties, the day
before the Senate opened its debate, seventy-eight senators, including Byrd and Baker as well as the majority
and minority whips, Senators Cranston and Stevens, introduced two amendments to the neutrality treaty that
would incorporate the Carter-Torrijos agreement.[91] Even
though it would be weeks before these amendments could
be voted upon, the administration's "no amendment" policy
clearly would not be adhered to by the Senate. These
were the same amendments the Foreign Relations Committee
had recommended to articles 4 and 6 of the treaty.
Sparkman, as committee chairman, and Case, as the ranking
minority member of the committee, also were among the
sponsors of the amendments introduced in the Senate.
Since the committee had approved the treaties without a-
mendments and had only recommended changes in the treaties, it was essential that the amendments be formally
introduced in the Senate if the committee's recommendations were to be followed. Byrd again warned against
crippling amendments, but he did not regard these amendments as such.

The Senate debate on the treaties did have a unique
quality about it in one respect. The Senate Rules Committee had recommended and the Senate had adopted a resolution allowing live radio broadcasts of the upcoming
debate. The debates were subsequently carried by National Public Radio. Television coverage was refused,
however.

Treaties, when they are sent to the Senate by the
administration, are assigned a letter designation. The
alphabetic listing of treaties starts with the beginning
of each session of Congress. The two treaties, since
they were treated as being one issue and delivered with
a single presidential message, were known as Executive N,
95th Congress, 1st session, and were so referred to
throughout the debate. The treaties were debated sepa-
rately, however, with the neutrality treaty coming first.

When the Senate began the debate, each treaty was
considered article by article in the Committee of the
Whole. The Senate rules of procedure called for the
reading of each article, but, ordinarily, the reading
was waived by unanimous consent. The opposition made it
clear that on this occasion it would object. The last
treaty to have been reviewed with each article read was
in 1922. The opposition felt that this procedure would
make it easier to introduce its amendments.

The procedural skirmishes at the beginning of the
debate were led by Senator Allen, but the debate on 8,
9, and 10 February was made up mainly of general statements of support or opposition to the treaties that had

already been heard before the Foreign Relations Committee. During the testimony before the Foreign Relations
Committee, administration witnesses had stressed that
the financial arrangements of the treaties would be paid
out of the revenues of Canal tolls. The administration
conceded on 10 February that there would be costs that
did not come from these revenues. The United States
would have to bear the expense of relocation of defense
installations and early retirement for Canal employees.

The senators returned to the treaties debate on 20
February, following a ten-day Lincoln's birthday recess.
The debate on 20 February was again of a general nature,
but the Senate held more than nine hours of closed debate on 21 February and four hours on 22 February. The
purpose of the closed sessions was to review charges
that (1) "because of some of the U.S. intelligence operations in Panama" (reference to the charge that the U.S.
had electronically eavesdropped on the Panamanian negotiators), Panama had coerced our negotiators to make
concessions they would not otherwise have made; (2) members of the Torrijos family had been involved in drug
trafficking and "these charges in some way had a bearing
on the outcome of the treaty negotiations"; and
(3) "high-level executive and legislative branch officials in return for arranging certain increases in the
annuity to be paid Panama under the treaty," had received
bribes.[92] The Senate Select Committee on Intelligence
had investigated the charges, and the committee's report
was the subject of the closed session of the Senate.

Later, the closed sessions were printed in the Congressional Record, although substantial sections of the
debate were deleted as classified. The discussion that
was available revealed that the Senate took the charges
of wrongdoing by U.S. and Panamanian officials seriously
and that the Intelligence Committee had conducted an extensive investigation into the various matters at hand.
The intent of the opposition senators appeared to be to
discredit the Torrijos government and thus cast doubt on
the trustworthiness of that government. The charges,
particularly those pertaining to narcotics smuggling,
were directed at the Torrijos family. In the course of
the debate, forty-nine members of Torrijos' family were
identified as present or past members of the Torrijos
government.[93] The principal target, however, was Torrijos' brother, Moises, the Panamanian ambassador to Spain.
Just before the closed sessions began, General Torrijos
had offered to surrender his brother to the United States
for prosecution if the U.S. could produce sufficient
evidence that his brother had been involved in drug smuggling.[94]

The charges of attempts to bribe U.S. officials to
obtain a treaty more favorable to Panama and efforts by
Panamanians to blackmail the U.S. negotiators with the
threat to reveal U.S. intelligence operations in Panama

were unsupported by hard evidence. Byrd reported that
there was no evidence that any U.S. official had received any payoff in regard to the negotiations. This
seemed to end the discussion. Back in September, Ambassador Bunker had denied that telephone electronic surveillance by U.S. intelligence had taken place and asserted that at no time had the U.S. negotiators been pressured by Panama.[95] Hodding Carter III, spokesman for
the State Department, had supported Bunker's statement
at the time.

In Panama, the charges against Moises Torrijos were
bitterly attacked.[96] The press personally attacked
Senators Dole and Allen for pushing the investigation of
the charges.[97] Dole had first aired the charge in October. In December, General Torrijos had addressed a message directly to Dole. Torrijos said he had learned from
the press of a visit by Dole and Laxalt to the Zone, but
had not seen them in the Republic. He wondered why they
refused to meet with Panamanian officials during their
visit, as other senators had done.[98]

On 1 March, Moises Torrijos resigned as ambassador
to Spain. The Panamanian government denied that the drug
charges were a factor. The official explanation was
Torrijos' poor health and that he had reached retirement
age.[99] He was sixty years of age. Moises Torrijos was
replaced with Hugo Torrijos, his brother.

The first roll call vote concerning the treaties
came on February 22. Senator Allen had introduced the
procedural motion that consideration of the treaties be
reversed, so that the Panama Canal treaty would be considered before the neutrality treaty. The administration
had requested that the neutrality treaty be considered
first; thus, Allen's request would be a test of the
Senate's support of the administration. The Allen proposal was defeated sixty-seven to thirty. This vote was
very close to the final vote on each of the treaties,
sixty-eight to thirty-two. Of the three senators who
missed the vote, two voted ultimately for treaty passage
and one against. One senator who voted for the proposal voted for the treaties, and two senators who voted
against the resolution voted against the treaties. This
vote thus was somewhat prophetic of the final result.

The Senate debate was one of the most extensive and
penetrating debates ever conducted on a treaty. Even
though little was added to the arguments that had been
expressed, in some instances several times, before committees and subcommittees, the Senate environment for the
debate was somewhat different from that of the hearings.
The opposition felt that the hearings, especially those
before the Foreign Relations Committee, were weighted in
favor of the treaties. The opposition could appear only
as witnesses, and even though their arguments became a
part of the record of the committees, the opposition was
not in a debater's position. Even when courtesy for a

fellow senator was carefully adhered to, the situation of witnesses answering questions did not allow for the free-ranging debate available on the Senate floor. On the Senate floor, the time was equally divided between the proponents and opponents of the treaties, and, unlike Senator Griffin's lone opposition vote in the Foreign Relations Committee, a number of senators were active participants in opposition. Senators Allen, Dole, Laxalt, Griffin, Harry Byrd, Jr., Helms, Hatch, Stennis, Tower, and Goldwater provided most of the opposition debate. Members of the Foreign Relations Committee--Church, Sparkman, Sarbannes, Javits, Baker, and Pearson--with the support of Senators Robert Byrd, Gravel, Hollings, and Muskie, provided much of the defense of the treaties.

Even though the debate did not provide any particularly new insights into the treaties, it did serve a variety of other purposes. While the estimate of undecided senators varied usually about a dozen were so classified. Both sides had to have additional votes in order to prevail. The debate, while not the only source of influence on those who were undecided, was regarded as an important one. Also, the debate was providing a public record that was, on this occasion, available to those interested enough to listen to the debate on radio. Any appearance that the Senate was putting forth anything less than a maximum effort to review the treaties in detail could do serious damage to the confidence the American public had in the institution.

The debate also brought an additional influence to bear that did not ordinarily exist when treaties were reviewed by the Senate. Besides the Canal treaties being the most important treaties that had come before the Senate in a number of years, the decision was in doubt. Ordinarily, treaties, even major ones, faced little opposition in the Senate, and rarely was the opposition sufficient to threaten the passage of a treaty. This time, the chance of defeat of one or both of the treaties was a real one, and the debate could be the deciding factor.

The opposition introduced a total of eleven amendments to article 1 alone. One was withdrawn, and the others were defeated, usually with the motion to table. Article 1 declared the Canal, as well as any future canal constructed in Panama, neutral. All of the amendments were defeated by a substantial margin (only a simple majority is necessary to pass or reject an amendment to a treaty). The number of votes opposing the amendments, if interpreted to be potential votes for the treaties, was in only one instance sufficient to have passed the treaty.

The attempted amendments seemed designed to better the position of the United States, although each would have made a change that probably was unacceptable to Panama. In the debate, this sort of amendment was referred to as a "killer" amendment. The amendments, if passed, would have extended the presence of U.S. troops in Panama as late as 2019; made the English text of the treaty binding, if there were a dispute between the Spanish and English texts; allowed U.S. troops to stay in Panama beyond 1999 if the U.S. were at war at that time; allowed the U.S. to intercept enemy warships bound for the Canal if the U.S. were at war; provided that Panama would commit itself to abide by the Monroe Doctrine and not aid any European power to expand its influence in Latin America; and would not allow warships of nations with which the U.S. was at war to use the Canal undisturbed. The Panamanians were adamant that U.S. troops be out of Panama by 2000, were sensitive about the use of only the English text of the treaty as the official text, saw the Monroe Doctrine as, historically, an excuse for the United States to interfere in the internal affairs of Latin American nations, and strongly opposed United States interference with the passage of warships of any nation. The United States, if at war with a nation, could, under international law, intercept that nation's warships in international waters but not interfere with that vessel if it were in Panamanian waters or in the Canal. Some of the amendments were introduced more than once as changes to other articles in the treaties. This was true of amendments to extend the presence of U.S. troops beyond 1999, which was the principal "killer" amendment.[100]

Article 2 attracted only one amendment, and it was tabled.[101] This amendment would have allowed the U.S. to retain its naval base on Galeta Island after 1999. This base was described as a top-secret intelligence-gathering base. Two amendments proposed for article 3 had been defeated earlier when introduced as amendments to article 1.[102] They were both tabled this time as well. The first amendment to pass was one introduced by the Senate leadership and attached to article 4 and was one of two amendments that incorporated the Carter-Torrijos agreement into the treaty. It passed eighty-five to five. Efforts by the opposition to strengthen the wording of the amendment were tabled.[103] A part of the agreement was also amended to article 6 by an eighty-five to three vote. These two amendments were known throughout the treaty process as the leadership amendments and were the same amendments proposed by the Foreign Relations Committee. An amendment to make the U.S. the sole judge of when an emergency existed and, thus, when U.S. vessels would go to the head of the line was tabled, as was an amendment that would have allowed U.S. warships to transit the Canal toll-free.[104]

After the article-by-article review of the treaty, Senator Schmitt offered a substitute treaty that would have established an inter-American regional organization called Intersea that would run the Canal. During the negotiations, both Panama and the United States had

opposed the Canal being run by an international organization. The substitute treaty was tabled sixty-five to
thirty.[105]

When the resolution of ratification came before the
Senate following the article-by-article review, a number
of reservations, understandings and conditions were introduced and several were adopted by the Senate. Senator
Nunn introduced the condition that nothing in the treaty
would preclude the United States and Panama from making
an agreement that would allow U.S. troops to be stationed
in Panama after 1999. This condition would not allow
U.S. troops to be in Panama without Panama's permission;
thus, it presented no problems in Panama and was adopted
eighty-two to sixteen.[106] A reservation introduced by
Senator Randolph stated that the U.S. and Panama would,
before the treaty went into effect, begin negotiations
on an agreement for the American Battle Monuments Commission to administer the section of Corozal Cemetery
containing U.S. citizens, that the U.S. flag would fly
there, and that the commission would administer that
section of the cemetery after 1999. Senator Thurmond
had failed in an effort to amend the treaty to this effect by adding a new article to the treaty, but as a reservation it was adopted ninety-five to one. An understanding that would make all toll increases reasonable
and consistent with U.S. and Panamanian economic interests was adopted by a voice vote.

A reservation, introduced by Senator Bartlett, stating that prior to the exchange of the instruments of
ratification, the president of the United States would
have to determine that Panama had ratified the amended
treaty in accordance with its constitutional procedures
of a plebiscite, was tabled sixty to thirty-seven. A
condition offered by Senator DeConcini and a number of
other senators provided that if the Canal were closed,
or its operations interfered with, both Panama and the
United States had the unilateral right to take any actions necessary, including the use of armed force, to
reopen the Canal. Although this condition caused considerable consternation in Panama, the Senate adopted it
seventy-five to twenty-three. An effort by Senator
Allen to make this condition a reservation was tabled.[107]

The DeConcini condition had been agreed to by the
president and Senator Byrd only after their survey of
the Senate determined that the supporters of the treaty
did not have enough votes to ratify it. This condition
was commonly referred to in the Senate, by the press,
and in Panama as a reservation, but its status was that
of a condition of ratification. At this stage, the proponents were about three or four votes shy of the necessary sixty-seven votes. Senator DeConcini, plus Senators
Ford, Long, Nunn, and Talmadge, were considered necessary
votes in order to pass the treaty.[108] All but Senator
Ford eventually voted for the treaties. Senator

DeConcini met with the president on 15 March, and the two agreed to the condition.[109] The DeConcini condition was adopted on 16 March, the date the Senate leadership had agreed would be the final vote on the resolution of ratification. Even then, the issue was in doubt, and neither side had sufficient votes committed to it to insure victory. Three additional reservations and understandings were also adopted, but they were minor in nature.

Also on March 16, the Panamanian government announced that General Torrijos had received a letter, and then a phone call, from Carter explaining to Torrijos that some changes in the treaty would occur.[110]

The final effort to defeat the treaty came when the opposition proposed that the Senate return the treaty to the president with the instructions that negotiations between the United States and Panama be reopened.[111] This was tabled sixty-seven to thirty-three. The Senate then approved the resolution of ratification by a vote of sixty-eight to thirty-two, one vote more than necessary for approval.[112] The first treaty had resulted in an administration victory, but its passage did not guarantee the passage of the Panama Canal treaty, since some of the senators had qualified their support of the neutrality treaty by saying that they would not necessarily support the second treaty.

Panama did not greet the ratification with great enthusiasm. The DeConcini condition, as Panama read it, allowed the United States to intervene in Panamanian affairs to keep the Canal open. This was undoubtedly the single most sensitive point with Panama. Torrijos was most outspoken in his opposition to the condition.

In a press conference in Panama, Dr. Escobar said that although the DeConcini condition was offensive, official reaction to the treaty as passed would be reserved until the treaty process was complete.[113] Panama apparently was attempting to minimize the Panamanian opposition to the changes being made by the Senate. Escobar said that the changes did not alter the important provisions of the treaty, especially the one that the U.S. would leave the Zone in 1999. Demonstrations in Panama against the DeConcini condition were surprisingly small.[114]

The day after approving the neutrality treaty, the Senate began its debate on the second treaty, the one dealing with the future operations and administration of the Canal and the legal jurisdiction of Panama and the United States in the Canal Zone. The second treaty was as important as the first in that if it were not approved, the neutrality treaty could not stand alone. The Senate followed the same procedure used with the first treaty, an article-by-article consideration in the Committee of the Whole.

The general statements were fewer on the second treaty than on the first, and the amending process on

article 1 began on 20 March with an amendment offered by
Dole. This amendment, rejected by a forty-five to
thirty-nine vote, provided for only U.S. or Panamanian
troops to be stationed in Panama for the duration of the
treaty.[115] The same day, an amendment by Wallop was defeated fifty to thirty-seven. This amendment said that
if Panama abrogated any provision of either treaty, both
treaties would be abrogated, and earlier treaties between
the United States and Panama would again go into effect.[116] The next day, an amendment by Allen was rejected that would have allowed the United States to prevent
any other country from building a canal in Panama and
that would have given the United States the right to
build a canal in any country it wished.[117] The Senate
also rejected, by a seventy-five to fifteen vote, a
Bartlett amendment that would have allowed the U.S. a
ninety-nine-year lease on land and installations for
operation of a sea-level canal with an option for a
ninety-nine-year renewal.[118]

An amendment by Hatch would have prevented Panama
from nationalizing any property owned by the Panama Canal Company, U.S. citizens or corporations owned by U.S.
citizens. This, too, was defeated.[119] Another Allen
amendment, defeated fifty-six to thirty-six, would have
allowed all U.S. citizens employed by the Canal Company
to retain their positions until they retired.[120] Hatch
again brought up the issue of the role of the House by
offering an amendment that would prevent the treaty from
going into effect until both houses had acted on the
disposition of U.S. property in the Zone. This was
tabled fifty-eight to thirty-seven.[121] No amendment was
successfully attached to article 1. On 22 March, the
Senate leadership and Helms, as the representative of
the opposition, met and set the date for the vote on the
treaty as no later than April 26.[122]

Two proposed amendments to article 2, both defeated,
would have granted the U.S. the use of the American sector of the Corozal Cemetery in perpetuity and would have
required Panama to hold another plebiscite before the
treaty would go into effect. The latter, by Allen, was
certainly a "killer" amendment. Article 3 also attracted
few amendments. Allen attempted to require confirmation
by the Senate of all nine members of the board of the
new Panama Canal Commission. Hatch wanted all revenues
from the Canal put in the U.S. Treasury, which, rather
than the Canal Commission, would pay Panama for services
provided in the Canal Zone. Both were defeated. Senator
Cannon wanted to reduce the payment to Panama for services provided in the Zone from $10 to $5 million. This
also failed.[123]

Article 4, which contained provisions for protection
and defense of the Canal by the U.S. and Panama, also
was left unamended, although several amendments were
proposed. Helms introduced an amendment to allow U.S.

forces free movement through Panamanian airspace, territory, and waters. Helms also wanted amendments that
would allow the U.S. to conduct separate military operations when it deemed them necessary and would allow the
transport of nuclear weapons through the Canal. The latter was prohibited under the Treaty for the Prohibition
of Nuclear Weapons in Latin America.[124]
     Two attempts were made to amend article 5, which
prohibited any involvement by U.S. citizens in the internal affairs of Panama. A Hatch amendment would have
required Panama to respect freedom of speech and press;
and a Helms amendment, which was a substitute for article
5, included a restriction on any consideration of U.S.
citizens as Panamanian citizens if they were born in the
Zone. Additional civil rights guarantees would be granted U.S. citizens above and beyond those specified in the
original article.[125] Both were defeated. No attempts
were made to amend articles 6-9.
     Article 10 received one proposed Hatch amendment
which would have given federal jobs to Canal employees
who lost their positions or chose to leave the Zone after the treaty went into effect. The amendment was defeated.[126] Dole wanted to amend article 11, which dealt
with the thirty-month transitional period to Panamanian
control of the Zone, by extending that period until at
least 1990. The amendment failed.[127] Article 12, which
discussed a sea-level canal or a third set of locks, also
was not amended, but several senators sponsored an amendment that would have allowed the U.S. to negotiate with
a third country for a construction site.[128] The attempts
to amend remaining articles were either new versions of
previously defeated amendments or were of little consequence. The treaty remained unamended at the end of the
article-by-article review.
     As was the case with the neutrality treaty, the most
controversial changes in the Canal treaty came when the
resolution of ratification was debated. In all, twenty-
one reservations and understandings were offered, and
twelve were adopted by the Senate. The strategy of the
supporters of both treaties was, with the exception of
the incorporation of the Carter-Torrijos agreement into
the neutrality treaty, to leave the wording of the treaties unchanged. Senate sentiments on both treaties were
expressed in understandings, conditions, and reservations. This method of expressing the Senate's views
honored the president's request to not change the treaties and lessened the chances of Torrijos calling for a
new plebiscite.
     The first reservation by Long and others, which the
Senate adopted, voiced restrictions on the U.S. and Panama to construct or negotiate for rights to construct
a new interoceanic canal. The vote was sixty-five to
twenty-seven. The opposition to the reservation was made
up mainly of those senators who wanted as clean a treaty

as possible. An understanding by Brooke and Byrd of Virginia, which had been tried earlier as an amendment, indicated that nothing in the treaty would obligate the U.S. to provide economic or military assistance to Panama. This was adopted by a voice vote.[129]

Several of the adopted reservations and understandings were noncontroversial and were adopted with only two or three votes in opposition or by voice vote. Efforts by Dole, Thurmond, and others to adopt stronger provisions were defeated. A number of the adopted reservations and understandings dealt with the specific financial arrangements of the treaty, especially payments to Panama.

One reservation adopted was proposed by the bipartisan leadership and by DeConcini and was designed to counter the growing opposition in Panama to the DeConcini condition attached to the neutrality treaty. The leadership reservation stated that any actions taken by the U.S. under the treaties would be for the sole purpose of keeping the Canal open and would not imply a right to intervene in the internal affairs of Panama. It passed seventy-three to twenty-seven. Efforts by Allen to narrow the interpretation of this reservation were tabled. Allen wanted to clarify that this reservation did not limit or diminish U.S. rights under the controversial DeConcini condition attached to the neutrality treaty. The leadership hoped to take the sting out of the DeConcini condition with this new reservation, especially since DeConcini was a co-sponsor.

Even though the Panamanian government had announced it would reserve judgment on the treaties until the treaty ratification process was completed, pressure against the DeConcini condition had been increasing in Panama. By early April, various groups and the press in Panama were calling for the rejection of the DeConcini condition.

Lopez Guevara, speaking for the government, explained that a reservation (the condition was so labeled in Panama) was actually a counter-proposal that was still to be negotiated. He also said that the so-called leadership amendments that incorporated the Carter-Torrijos agreement into the neutrality treaty were acceptable, but, in his opinion, the DeConcini condition was unacceptable.[130] In the U.N., Jorge Illueca explained the Panamanian position on the neutrality treaty and its reservations and appealed for the membership's support.[131] Torrijos had also written to heads of state of several Latin American countries.[132]

During the first part of April, there were reports that Panama would reject the DeConcini condition, but the Panamanian Foreign Ministry denied it.[133] Torrijos, also hoping to calm the situation, announced, "I believe everything is going to be all right."[134] He had been in communication with Carter and apparently felt confident that the DeConcini condition would be modified.

Efforts by the administration to persuade DeConcini to modify his condition were initially unsuccessful, but on 12 April DeConcini, "reluctantly" accepted "some language to modify or clarify" his condition.[135] The modification in the DeConcini condition was attached to the Canal treaty the day the treaty was passed.

Senators Griffin and Wallop attempted to substitute for the resolution of ratification a resolution that would return the treaty to the president for further negotiations. This was tabled sixty-four to thirty-six.

On 18 April, the Senate voted on the resolution of ratification. The vote was the same as for the neutrality treaty, sixty-eight to thirty-two, with no senators shifting from the position they had taken on the neutrality treaty.[136] Each of the treaties had passed with one extra vote, but the narrowness of the margin of victory may have been deceptive in that the leadership probably had other votes it could have called upon if necessary. One or two of the opposition votes had privately indicated that if their votes were needed they would vote for the treaty, but that to do so probably would have meant their defeat at the next election. Since their votes were not needed, they were free to vote against the treaty.

In Panama, following the Senate's approval, the government announced that the "interventionist language" of the DeConcini condition had "clearly been modified."[137] The treaty was acceptable as it was, and a second plebiscite would not be necessary.

Torrijos also announced that he would not have accepted the treaty if the DeConcini condition had not been neutralized. He said that the Panamanian armed forces had decided, if the treaty had been rejected or the DeConcini condition left unchanged, to not reopen negotiations but, rather, to destroy the Canal. He promised that in the future Panama would never lose its capacity to destroy the Canal, and if the U.S. ever attempted to intervene in Panama, the Canal would be destroyed. This bravado was reminiscent of Torrijo's rhetoric in the early 1970s. The issue was now moot and safe, since the treaty has passed, and the DeConcini condition had been modified.[138]

A week after passage, the Panamanian foreign ministry issued a fifty-three-page document that examined the treaties in detail. The conclusion drawn in the document was that the treaties were acceptable to Panama.[139]

NOTES

1. U.S., Congress, Senate, Committee on Foreign Relations, A Chronology of Events Relating to Panama Canal, by Congressional Research Service, Library of Congress, 95th Cong., 1st sess., 1977, p. 33.

2. FBIS, 1 September 1977, p. N-1, La Estrella de Panama, 31 August 1977, p. 2.

3. Article 274. Treaties which may be signed by the Executive Organ with respect to the Panama Canal, its adjacent zone, and the protection of the said Canal, and for the construction of a new canal at sea level or a third set of locks, shall be submitted to a national plebiscite. Constitution of Panama 1972, General Secretariat, Organization of American States, Washington, D.C., 1974.

4. FBIS, 16 September 1977, p. N-9, La Estrella de Panama, 14 September 1977, pp. 1, 25.

5. Ibid.

6. FBIS, 6 September 1977, p. N-3, ACAN, 3 September 1977.

7. FBIS, 2 September 1977, p. N-1, Star and Herald, 1 September 1977.

8. FBIS, 17 October 1977, p. N-6, Circuita RPC, 15 October 1977.

9. FBIS, 5 October 1977, p. N-2, ACAN, 4 October 1977.

10. FBIS, 16 September 1977, p. N-1, Critica, 15 September 1977, pp. 12, 20.

11. FBIS, 21 October 1977, pp. N-16, N-17, Domestic Television Network, 20 October 1977.

12. FBIS, 20 October 1977, pp. N-4, N-5, Radio MIA Network, 19 October 1977.

13. FBIS, 26 October 1977, p. N-5, ACAN, 23 October 1977.

14. FBIS, 31 October 1977, N-1, Domestic Service Radio, 28 October 1977.

15. U.S. News and World Report, 7 November 1977, p. 61.

16. Ibid.

17. FBIS, 26 October 1977, p. N-9, Critica, 24 October 1977, p. 1.

18. U.S., Congress, Senate, Committee on the Judiciary, Panama Canal Treaty (Disposition of United States Territory). Hearings before the Subcommittee on Separation of Powers of the Committee on the Judiciary, 95th Cong., 1st sess., 22 and 29 July 1977.

19. Ibid., p. 4.

20. U.S., Congress, House, Committee on Merchant Marine and Fisheries, U.S. Interest in Panama Canal. Hearings before a subcommittee of the House Committee on Merchant Marine and Fisheries, 95th Cong., 1st sess., 25, 26, 27 July 1977.

21. Ibid., pp. 3-5.

22. Ibid., pp. 8, 14-15.

23. Ibid., p. 9.

24. Ibid., pp. 14, 17.

25. Ibid., p. 34.

26. Ibid., p. 36.

27. Ibid.

28. Ibid., p. 127.

29. Ibid., p. 182.

30. Ibid., p. 207.

31. Ibid., pp. 250-55.

32. Chronology of Events, p. 34.

33. Ibid.

34. Ibid., p. 35.

35. Treaty, Disposition of Territory, p. 18.
36. Ibid., p. 10.
37. Ibid., p. 15.
38. Ibid., p. 27.
39. Ibid., p. 33.
40. Ibid.
41. U.S., Congress, Senate, Committee on Foreign Relations, Panama Canal Treaties. Hearings before the Committee on Foreign Relations, Executive N, Part 1, 95th Cong., 1st sess., 26, 27, 29, and 30 September, October 19, 1977, p. 10.
42. Ibid., p. 12.
43. Ibid.
44. Ibid., p. 30.
45. Reprinted in Ibid., pp. 107-27.
46. Ibid., p. 122.
47. "The United States and Panama: Confrontation or Cooperation," reprinted in Ibid., pp. 140-48.
48. Ibid., pp. 154-58.
49. FBIS, 3 October 1977, Dominical, 2 October 1977, p. 4.
50. FBIS, 28 September 1977, Televisora Nacional, 27 September 1977.
51. Ibid.
52. FBIS, 30 September 1977, Televisora Nacional, 29 September 1977.
53. Panama Canal Treaties, Part 2, p. 4.
54. Ibid., p. 5.
55. Ibid.
56. Ibid., p. 6.
57. Ibid., p. 119.
58. Ibid., p. 126.
59. Ibid., p. 220.
60. Ibid., p. 228.
61. Panama Canal Treaties, Part 3, p. 73.
62. Ibid.
63. Ibid., p. 439.
64. FBIS, 17 October 1977, Televisora Nacional, 15 October 1977.
65. Panama Canal Treaties, Part 1, p. 454.
66. Ibid.
67. FBIS, 26 October 1977, Domestic Service, 21 October 1977.
68. FBIS, 3 October 1977, Dominical, 2 October 1977, p. 4.
69. Panama Canal Treaties, Part 1, p. 457.
70. Ibid.
71. Ibid., p. 458.
72. Ibid., p. 459.
73. Congressional Record, 20 October 1977, pp. S17599-602.
74. Compendium of Major Statements, p. 510.
75. Ibid., p. 511.
76. Panama Canal Treaties, Part 5, p. 37. An amendment adds to or removes wording from a treaty. Since an amendment changes the treaty as it was originally negotiated, the change must be accepted by the other party or parties to the treaty. Reservations and understandings provide the United States' interpretation of the treaty or aspects of the treaty. These appendages to a treaty do

not necessarily mean that the other party or parties to the treaty accept the interpretation or that the treaties are opened to further negotiations. Conditions to a treaty, although their status is unclear, seem to differ little from reservations and understandings. The Foreign Relations Committee staff, however, argued that all changes and attachments to a treaty were equally binding under international law. Memorandum to All Members, Norvil Jones, Staff Director, U.S. Senate Foreign Relations Committee, Subject: "Treaty Procedure: Legal Aspects of Changes," 12 January 1978. Quoted in Franck and Weisband, Foreign Policy, p. 276.

77. Ibid., p. 38.

78. FBIS, 14 November 1977, pp. N2-3, Circuito RPC Television 12 November 1977.

79. FBIS, 19 January 1978, N1, ACAN, 18 January 1978.

80. Ibid.

81. Comparing Ex. N., 95-1, the Panama Canal Treaty and the Treaty Concerning the Permanent Neutrality of the Panama Canal to the Amendments, Reservations and Understandings Thereto (markup document used by the Foreign Relations Committee during consideration of the treaties), p. 19. Hereafter referred to as Markup.

82. Panama Canal Treaties, Part 5, pp. 77-78; Markup, p. 4.

83. FBIS, 14 September 1977, p. N2, Televisora Nacional, 13 September 1977.

84. Markup, pp. 13, 15.

85. FBIS, 3 October 1977, p. N1-2, Domestic Service, 1 October 1977.

86. Compendium of Major Statements, p. 518.

87. Ibid., p. 521.

88. FBIS, 2 February 1978, Televisora Nacional, 1 February 1978.

89. Compendium of Major Statements, p. 522.

90. Ibid.

91. Congressional Record, 7 February 1978, p. S1407.

92. Ibid., 22 February 1978, p. S1995.

93. Ibid., 3 March 1978, p. S2910.

94. Compendium of Major Statements, p. 524.

95. FBIS, 19 September 1977, p. N1, Televisora Nacional, 7 September 1977.

96. FBIS, 15 February 1978, pp. N1-4, Critica, p. 4, Matutino, p. 6, Televisora Nacional, all 14 February 1978.

97. FBIS, 17 February 1978, pp. N1-3, La Estrella de Panama, p. 4, Televisora Nacional, 16 February 1978.

98. FBIS, 29 December 1977, p. N1, Televisora Nacional, 28 December 1977.

99. FBIS, 2 March 1978, p. N1, Televisora Nacional, 2 March 1978.

100. Congressional Record, 24 February 1978, p. S2276; 27 February 1978, pp. S2371-72, S2383; 28 February 1978, pp. S2503-04; 1 March 1978, pp. S2602, S2619, S2636; 2 March 1978, pp. S2728-29, S2755, S2759; 3 March 1978, p. 2842; 6 March 1978, p. S2973; 14 March 1978, p. S3635; Compendium of Major Statements, pp. 348-59.

101. Congressional Record, 7 March 1978, pp. S3113, S3133; Compendium of Major Statements, pp. 360-61.

102. Congressional Record, 7 March 1978, p. S3133; 8 March 1978, p. S3230.

103. Ibid., 9 March 1978, pp. S3298-99, S3324, S3330; 10 March 1978, pp. S3389, S3396, S3414-16; Compendium of Major Statements, pp. 365-69.

104. Congressional Record, 10 March 1978, pp. S3422-23, S3426-27; 13 March 1978, pp. S3504, S3512, S3515, S3520, S3522; 14 March 1978, p. S3624; Compendium of Major Statements, pp. 370-78.

105. Congressional Record, pp. S3626-30, S3633-34; Compendium of Major Statements, pp. 382-97.

106. FBIS, 3 April 1978, p. N5, Televisora Nacional, 30 March 1978.

107. Congressional Record, 14 March 1978, p. S3649; 15 March 1978, pp. S3735-36, S3740-41; 16 March 1978, pp. S3812, S3816-17, S3819, S3824-25, S3827-31, S3856; Compendium of Major Statements, pp. 398-408.

108. Compendium of Major Statements, p. 527.

109. Ibid.

110. FBIS, 17 March 1978, p. N2, Domestic Service, 16 March 1978.

111. Congressional Record, 16 March 1978, p. S3831; Compendium of Major Statements, p. 408.

112. Congressional Record, 16 March 1978, p. S3857; Compendium of Major Statements, p. 413.

113. FBIS, 17 March 1978, pp. N2-7, Domestic Service, 16 March 1978.

114. Compendium of Major Statements, pp. 530-31.

115. Congressional Record, 20 March 1978, pp. S4075, S4109; Compendium of Major Statements, p. 416.

116. Congressional Record, 20 March 1978, pp. S4102-03; Compendium of Major Statements, p. 417.

117. Congressional Record, 20 March 1978, pp. 4256-57; 22 March 1978, pp. S4336, S4351; Compendium of Major Statements, pp. 418-19.

118. Congressional Record, 22 March 1978, pp. S4352-53, S4356; Compendium of Major Statements, pp. 420-21.

119. Congressional Record, 22 March 1978, pp. S4356, S4359; Compendium of Major Statements, pp. 421-22.

120. Congressional Record, 23 March 1978, p. S4459; 5 April 1978, p. S54814; Compendium of Major Statements, p. S4814.

121. Congressional Record, 23 March 1978, p. S4463; 5 April 1978, pp. S4795-96; Compendium of Major Statements, pp. 423-24.

122. Compendium of Major Statements, p. 532.

123. Congressional Record, 6 April 1978, pp. S4920, S4928, S5083; 11 April 1978, pp. S5246-47, S5249; 13 April 1978, pp. S5481, S5486, S5491, S5500; Compendium of Major Statements, pp. 426-35.

124. Congressional Record, 11 April 1978, pp. S5229, S5239, S5241, S5246; Compendium of Major Statements, pp. 436-40.

125. Congressional Record, 11 April 1978, pp. S5249, S5253-54; 12 April 1978, pp. S5345-46. Compendium of Major Statements, pp. 441-45.

126. Congressional Record, 12 April 1978, pp. S5348, S5354; Compendium of Major Statements, pp. 453-54.

127. Congressional Record, 13 April 1978, p. S5473; Compendium of Major Statements, pp. 456-57.

128. Congressional Record, 10 April 1978, pp. S5138-39, S5151; Compendium of Major Statements, pp. 458-59.

129. Congressional Record, 17 April 1978, pp. S5606, S5620, S5630-31, S5635-41, S5649-50, S5655, S5657; 18 April 1978, S5732, S5734-36, S5738-41, S5744-46, S5761, S5765, S5768-69, S5771-72; Compendium of Major Statements, pp. 467-92.

130. FBIS, 3 April 1978, p. N5, Televisora Nacional 30 March 1978.

131. FBIS, 4 April 1978, p. N1, Critica, 3 April 1978, p. 1.

132. Compendium of Major Statements, p. 534.

133. FBIS, 10 April 1978, p. N1, Circuito RPC Television, 7 April 1978.

134. FBIS, 17 April 1978, p. N1, ACAN, 17 April 1978.

135. Compendium of Major Statements, pp. 535-56.

156. Congressional Record, 18 April 1978, p. S5796; Compendium of Major Statements, p. 495.

137. FBIS, 19 April 1978, p. N1, Domestic Service 18 April 1978.

138. Ibid., pp. N3-4.

139. FBIS, 26 April 1978, pp. N1-2, Circuito RPC Television, Televisora Nacional, both 25 April 1978.

11
Aftermath and Possibilities

With the Senate debate over and the resolutions of ratification approved, the Carter administration claimed a major victory. Victories in Congress had been few for President Carter during his first fifteen months in office, but on this occasion not only had the treaties been approved, they were approved with no major changes. The most controversial change had been the DeConcini condition attached to the neutrality treaty, and it had been neutralized by a reservation to the second treaty.

What success Carter had had with Congress in the past had produced legislation considerably altered before the administration's proposals became law. The package of energy legislation taken up by Congress shortly before the Canal treaties was a typical example. With the Panama Canal treaties, such was not the case. Not only were the treaties close to what had been their wording when first offered to the Senate, but Torrijos had announced the treaties were acceptable in the form passed by the Senate.

President Carter's victory was clouded, however, in that much of the credit for the victory belonged to the Senate bipartisan leadership rather than the administration. Senators Byrd and Baker had played an important role through their contacts with Torrijos in the writing of the Carter-Torrijos agreement in October 1977 and had successfully supported the amendments to articles 4 and 6 of the neutrality treaty that incorporated the Carter-Torrijos agreement in the treaty. Baker's trip to Panama in January 1978, along with other senators, was seen as instrumental in convincing Torrijos that the agreement had to be included in the treaty in order for the treaties to pass the Senate.[1] "Baker's achievement was stunning. Rarely has a senator, especially a member of the minority party, succeeded in acting overseas as if he were Secretary of State."[2]

During the voting on the treaties, the numerous attempts to introduce "killer" changes in the treaties had all been beaten back, but credit for this was generally given to the Senate leadership, plus Senators Church, Sarbanes, and Cranston, floor leaders for the treaties.[3] Also, the most effective support for the treaties from within the executive did not come from the White House. The State Department, with the assistance of the Defense Department, was constantly available during the debate with information to refute the opposition's arguments.[4] Experts from State and Defense maintained an office near the Senate chamber and either answered the questions as they arose or found an answer as soon as possible. Such efforts had taken place also during the hearings before the Committee on Foreign Relations. Off the record, State Department personnel complained that the White House staff was of little assistance with the Senate, especially during the hearings and the early stage of the floor debate.

The White House received criticism in another respect as well. When the treaties were first introduced in the Senate, public opinion polls clearly indicated that a majority of the public opposed the new treaties.[5] The White House strategy was to delay the Senate debate until public opinion could be turned around. This strategy was, in a sense, forced on the administration in that Byrd had made it clear that both the Senate's calendar and opposition in the Senate would not allow for consideration or approval of the treaties until early 1978.[6] With this delay, the administration had from September 1977 to April 1978 to carry out its task of swinging public opinion around to support for the treaties.

The administration did set up the Committee for Ratification of the Panama Canal Treaties (COACT) under the leadership of the highly respected Averell Harriman and other well-known private citizens once prominent in U.S. foreign policy-making. Many business groups such as the National Association of Manufacturers and the U.S. Chamber of Commerce supported the treaties. Corporations doing business in Latin America were virtually unanimous in their support. Labor and church groups were also supportive. Opinion and civic leaders from a number of states were invited to the White House for personal briefings by Carter. Over 800 appearances were made by State Department personnel in support of the treaties.

The White House campaign for the treaties was managed by Hamilton Jordan. Even though the campaign was a good one, all of this effort had little effect on public opinion through the vote on the first treaty, which came on 16 March. It was not until early April that a Louis Harris poll showed that for the first time a slim margin supported both treaties. This was after the leadership amendments and the DeConcini condition had been attached to the neutrality treaty, actions that made the treaties more acceptable to some, but actions that, to a great extent came from the Senate.

A study of polls taken on the Canal question, done

by the State Department's senior opinion analyst, points up some interesting problems in interpreting the results of the many polls taken.[7] The first nationwide poll on the Canal question was taken in June 1975 by Opinion Research Corporation (ORC) for the American Council for World Freedom. The results of the poll, which contained a number of questions, revealed that the public had little in-depth knowledge about the Canal and that twenty-nine percent gave responses favorable to Panama, about fifty percent gave answers unfavorable to Panama, with about twenty percent "don't knows."[8] The overall results formed a pattern that remained consistent for the next two years. Unfortunately, the questions designed to test the depth of knowledge the public held on the question were not repeated on subsequent polls by the same firm.

In this 1975 poll, after eleven years of negotiation with Panama, eighty-two percent of the respondents admitted that they did not know that the Panama Canal was an issue. This did not prevent about the same percentage from having an opinion on the subject, however. This poll was used by the American Council for World Freedom to indicate that only twelve percent of the public favored a new treaty with Panama, since only that percentage favored turning the Canal over to Panama. An additional seventeen percent indicated that they would not be disturbed if Panama should receive the Canal, but the Council chose to ignore this later percentage when reporting the results of the poll.

ORC conducted additional polls in April 1976, May 1977, and February 1978. On the question of whether the United States should turn the Canal over to Panama, a question asked on all four polls, the result in May 1977 was seventy-eight percent in opposition. Only eight percent favored turning over the Canal to Panama. This degree of opposition was not found in other polls, however. A CBS poll in May 1976 found that twenty-four percent favored, fifty-two percent opposed, and twenty-four percent were undecided as to whether the Canal should "eventually" be turned over to Panama. The ORC question did not allow for any time period before control would be transferred. Other polls received results similar to those found in the CBS poll (Roper, January 1977; Yankelovich, March 1977; Caddell, May 1977). The results of these polls were twenty-four to twenty-nine percent favorable to Panama, fifty-one to fifty-three percent opposed, and eighteen to twenty-three percent undecided.[9]

The seventy-eight percent opposition found in the May 1977 ORC poll was widely mentioned in the press and the Senate. It was this percentage that Majority Leader Byrd referred to in the fall of 1977 when he said that the Senate should not take up the treaties until public opinion was turned around. This percentage apparently was later transposed by the New York Times (February 1, 1978) to eighty-seven percent when the newspaper reported that the percentage of opposition had been reduced by the administration's campaign from eighty-seven percent to fifty-five percent. The Christian Science Monitor ran a similar story (February 2, 1978) using the same percentages to indicate the progress made by the administration. No poll ever reported a percentage of opposition higher than seventy-eight percent; thus, the typographical-error explanation of the source of eighty-seven percent seems to be well-founded.

In January 1978, just before the treaties were reported out of committee, CBS conducted a second poll. Twenty-nine percent favored the treaties, fifty-one percent opposed, and twenty percent had no opinion. In the same month, an NBC poll found twenty-eight percent in support and sixty-two percent in opposition. Variations in questions, especially questions containing some qualification as to the time involved before the Canal would be turned over to Panama, seemed to be an important element in the different results between the CBS and NBC polls and the ORC results.

In October 1977, Gallup asked a question explaining that the Canal would remain under U.S. control until 2000 before it turned the Canal over to Panama, after which time the U.S. could intervene to defend the Canal. The results were thirty-six percent in support of the treaties and forty-six percent opposed. When the question was repeated in January 1978, the percentages were forty-three percent in support and thirty-seven percent in opposition to the treaties. This was the first poll to indicate more support for the treaties than opposition. The ORC question about whether the Canal should be turned over to Panama that had produced the seventy-eight percent opposition back in May still produced seventy-two percent opposition in February 1978. Harris, also polling in February 1978, asked specifically about support for the treaties and found thirty-one percent in support and forty percent opposed. On a question that discussed the changes made in the neutrality treaty, Harris found that the changes were supported fifty-six percent in favor, twenty percent in opposition.[10] After the first treaty was approved by the Senate, Harris found that forty-nine percent approved of the Senate's action, and forty-one percent opposed it.

After the Senate had voted on both treaties, Harris, Roper, and NBC conducted polls asking whether the Senate should have passed the treaties (Harris, April and June 1978; Roper in June 1978; and NBC in September 1978). The results were thirty to thirty-five percent approved, forty-nine to fifty-six percent disapproved, and ten to eighteen percent "don't know" or "not sure." These percentages were close to the percentages found in the polls taken before the treaties were submitted to the Senate.

The extensive polling on this issue certainly produced
no trends, and the variation in the questions, even by
the same polling firm, made comparison of results difficult. Regardless, the polls were watched carefully by
both the opposition and supporters of the treaties and
cited often as the results supported their positions.

The confusion over the meaning of the various polls
thus made it difficult to assess the success of the administration's campaign for the treaties. A comparison
of the early polls with the final ones indicates a trend
that "could have been graphed with a straight horizontal
line."[11] The administration's campaign for treaty support appeared to have had little effect on public opinion.

If coordination were lacking between the White House
staff, the State Department, and the Senate leadership,
all three approved of what the Senate did. In the final
stages, the president used Vance, Mondale, Harold Brown,
and National Security Advisor Zbigniew Brzezinski, as
well as Deputy Secretary of State Warren Christopher,
Bunker and Linowitz, to lobby for the treaties. Frank
Moore headed the White House's liaison with Congress.
The president lobbied with frequent phone calls to waver-
ing or undecided senators and personally invited a number of such senators for a personal visit. Anyone in
the administration associated with the treaties was a-
vailable to any senator who wished to see him.[12] The
White House wanted the treaties approved; and, regardless
of what errors were attributed to the White House staff,
the treaties were approved. In this sense, the passage
of the treaties was a victory for the administration.

Nor had the White House carried on its campaign for
the treaties without opposition. So-called "truth
squads" often followed White House and State Department
personnel on their speaking tours to counter their pro-
treaty arguments. Efforts by the Conservative Caucus,
the American Conservative Union, the American Legion,
Veterans of Foreign Wars, American Security Council, the
Committee to Save the Panama Canal, and the Emergency
Coalition to Save the Panama Canal to defeat the treaties were extensive. Their campaign reached its zenith
with an all-out effort between 16-20 January. If the
White House made little progress in swinging public o-
pinion around to support of the treaties, the opposition,
which, by all accounts, outspent the treaty supporters,
did no better.

The question of which institution could claim credit
for the success of the treaties, the Senate and its
leadership or the White House, was being asked in the
environment of the post-Vietnam and post-Watergate period. Fights between the two institutions were seen as a
zero-sum game; what one lost, the other gained. The
question of who "won" on the treaties could best be answered by pointing out the support the Senate leadership

gave the president and the subsequent success that both shared. Senators had introduced 192 changes in the treaties, and eighty-eight were voted on in the Senate.[13] All but a few were defeated through the combined efforts of the administrative and the Senate leadership. The practice of assigning a decision into the categories of either a congressional or a presidential victory simply was not appropriate in the instance of the treaties.

The confusing element in an analysis of who won is the DeConcini condition. The president had insisted on an unaltered set of treaties. The amendments to the neutrality treaty were accepted by both Carter and Torrijos and thus presented no problem for the Carter policy of no changes. But the DeConcini condition ran contrary to the president's position. Did the president, not fully recognizing how Panama might react, agree to the condition in order to obtain what Carter thought to be a deciding vote in the Senate? DeConcini was only one vote, but the president knew that he had few, if any, votes to spare. The condition did, whatever the president's reasons, cause a crisis that was alleviated only by some quiet diplomacy.

Changes in the treaties were proposed by senators for a variety of reasons. Some changes were presented in the hope that, if adopted, the treaties would be rejected by the Panamanian government or, at least, a new and unsuccessful plebiscite would be held. These were the "killer" amendments. A second category of changes were more of a housekeeping nature and were not controversial. Most of the adopted changes were in this latter category and took the form of reservations, understandings, and conditions.

A third category of change was an attempt to put an individual senator's mark on the treaties. In some cases, the change would allow the senator to explain to his constituents that his change now made it possible for him to vote for the treaties. In other instances, the treaties, as widely discussed as they were, were an excellent opportunity to gain attention by sponsoring a change in the treaties. Even an unsuccessful effort could gain this end.

The DeConcini condition seemed to fall in this latter category. As a freshman senator, the attention DeConcini received from Carter, Christopher, and the Senate leadership indicated the advantages of being both an undecided vote and the sponsor of a controversial change. The DeConcini condition apparently was not intended to be a "killer" change, although it was the one change approved by the Senate that was very nearly a "killer." DeConcini personally favored the treaties, even though his constituents were heavily against them.[14] His condition was his price for voting for the treaties as well as his explanation to his constituents. In the process, he received a great deal of attention.

The DeConcini condition evolved from other changes that the senator had considered. Christopher and the Senate leadership persuaded DeConcini not to submit his earlier changes, but, ultimately, DeConcini introduced his condition, which read as if the U.S. was resuming its right to intervene in the internal affairs of Panama to keep the Canal open, a right the U.S. had given up in the 1936 changes to the 1903 treaty.[15]

When it became apparent in February and March that the treaties were short of the necessary sixty-seven votes, the White House added Robert Beckel, a public relations specialist, to its primary team working with the Senate. Frank Moore continued as White House congressional liaison. A week before the neutrality treaty vote, Beckel reported that the treaty was still short several votes.[16]

Christopher attempted to persuade DeConcini to soften the language of his condition, but was unsuccessful. DeConcini asked for a meeting with the president, and Carter agreed. On 15 March, the meeting took place, and Carter agreed to the condition. Beckel had told the president that the choice was "between going with DeConcini or losing the treaty."[17] The condition was attached to the treaty on the day the treaty was approved by the Senate.

When the neutrality treaty with the DeConcini condition attached was approved by the Senate, Torrijos' reaction was unambiguous: "This is not a day of celebration. There is nothing to celebrate."[18] Only after Torrijos sent letters to the heads of state of about three-fourths of the membership of the United Nations did Carter persuade Torrijos to issue a statement that he would reserve judgment on the treaty until after the second treaty was passed. This meant that the United States had to come up with a proposal for the second treaty to counteract the DeConcini condition on the neutrality treaty. Such a proposal was worked out just two days before the vote in the Senate on the second treaty on 18 April.

On 16 April--a Sunday morning--Senators Byrd, Church, and Sarbanes, Christopher, and former assistant secretary of state, William D. Rogers, met with Gabriel Lewis, Panamanian ambassador to the United States. The topic of their discussion was the wording of a reservation to the Canal treaty that would undo the damage caused by the DeConcini condition. DeConcini had been excluded from the negotiations, probably because he had been so uncompromising during the discussion of his condition. He did approve the new reservation the following day.[19]

If there were a hero in these negotiations, it was William Rogers. Rogers had been an active lobbyist for the treaties from the beginning as the spokesman for the Council of the Americas. In working out the compromise, he had served as the intermediary.

When it became clear in both countries that the De-
Concini condition jeopardized both treaties even if the
second treaty were approved by the Senate, the Panamanian
government sought out Rogers, then a lawyer in private
practice, to serve as its advocate. Whereas the State
Department approved of Roger's role in representing Panama, the Justice Department thought Rogers might be
guilty of conflict of interest because of his previous
position in the State Department. As a compromise,
Rogers played the role of intermediary between the two
governments. In this role, he received no pay for his
services. Both governments agreed that Rogers would be
"the sole channel of communication."[20] Rogers undertook
his delicate task with the approval of Torrijos, Byrd,
Baker, and Christopher. Rogers' only condition was that
the White House staff stay out of the negotiations.[21]
The treaties were saved by excluding the White House from
the rescue effort.

Although there can be no final determination as to
whether the passage of the treaties was a presidential or
a congressional victory, similar problems arise in deciding if the treaties were a victory for the United States
or for Panama. The opponents of the treaties, with few
exceptions, viewed the treaties as a sellout by the
United States; thus, the treaties were, to them, a major
victory for Panama. But from Panama's perspective the
treaties, if a victory, were far from a complete one.

For decades, Panama wanted to do away with the perpetuity and sovereignty clauses of the 1903 treaty. The
new treaties returned fifty-eight percent (although Panama asked for about eighty-five percent) of the Canal Zone
to Panama, but the United States would still control the
operation of the Canal until 2000. The number of U.S.
bases was reduced, but the main base complexes remained
under U.S. control, and U.S. troops would be in Panama
until 2000. Even after that date, the U.S. reserved the
right to intervene to keep the Canal open. The Panamanian government saw the treaties as ultimately giving
Panama most of what it had asked for, but such was not
to be granted immediately. Of additional concern to Panama was how the United States would implement the treaties. The United States was hardly viewed by Panamanians
as trustworthy, since in the eyes of many Panamanians the
United States had exceeded the limits of past agreements
many times.

In addition, Panama had backed off from its original
demands for economic aid. The opponents of the treaties
in the U.S. could not understand why any economic settlement was due Panama; indeed, in their view, Panama
should be paying the United States for the Canal. But
from Panama's perspective, compensation was due Panama
for past exploitation of its resources. Panama accepted a much smaller settlement because what was offered

in the treaties was considerably more than Panama had
received before--an increase from $2.3 million annual
payment to $60 million. With Panama's large national
debt, much of which was owed to foreign private banks,
the money was needed now, even if longer negotiations
might have produced a larger settlement. Economically,
Panama could wait no longer for a settlement of the Canal issue. Panama received part of what it wanted economically, part of the Zone and a share in the administration of the remainder of the Zone and operation of
the Canal. The rest was deferred until 2000. To Panama,
this was a limited victory.

Proponents of the treaties in the U.S. thought of
the new treaties more in terms of what the treaties would
do for U.S.-Latin American relations than within the
context of what the treaties themselves contained. The
settlement would improve, it was hoped, the climate for
U.S. business in Panama and throughout Latin America by
the removal of the single biggest issue causing conflict.
The economic package for Panama would come out of future
revenues from the Canal or from loans that Panama would
have to repay one day. In addition, the economic importance of the Canal was declining and might be of even
less importance by the year 2000. What the United States
had given up primarily was complete control of the Canal
and the Zone.

Thus, were the treaties a United States or a Panamanian victory? The answer probably rests with the economic importance of the Canal in the year 2000. If the
Canal is worth little at that time, then Panama struck a
poor bargain; but if the importance of the Canal remains
significant in foreign commerce, then Panama was wise in
entering into the treaties. From the United States perspective, it can only be hoped that Panama is willing to
wait until 2000 before receiving full control of the Canal and the removal of U.S. troops from Panama.

The new treaties did not provide Panama with an immediate solution to its problems. Torrijos had long told
the Panamanian people that the solution to Panama's problems rested with Panama's receiving its fair share of
the Canal revenues. Even while the treaties were being
debated in the Senate, riots occurred against internal
policies, especially food prices, of the Torrijos government. As was the case with earlier riots prompted by
rises in the prices of milk and rice, Torrijos found it
difficult to shift the blame to the United States for the
failure of his domestic economic policies.

Both the business community and the left wing were
unhappy with Torrijos. Business leaders felt that Torrijos, through his populist policies, discouraged private
investment in Panama. Leftists saw the treaties as a
sellout by Torrijos to obtain economic assistance from
the United States and to receive a portion of the economic benefits Panama was entitled to, but certainly not

254

all that Panama should receive. The leftists wanted immediate Panamanian control of the Canal and the immediate withdrawal of the United States. The year 2000 was much too far in the future.

It was, of course, unreasonable to expect the new treaties to have an immediate impact on the Panamanian economy; indeed, the transfers of property and the thirty-month transition period were not even scheduled to begin until 1 October 1979. Nevertheless, the Canal issue was no longer an issue on which Torrijos could hang the blame for the failures of his government. He had supported the negotiations and proclaimed the new treaties a solution to his country's problems; he now had to live with the results. With Panama's economic problems still very serious, with a heavy foreign debt and serious inflation, and with the Canal issue removed as a scapegoat issue, Torrijos' political future was cloudy.

Torrijos, who in recent years had left the day-to-day operations of government to others and devoted much of his time to the Canal negotiations, had now nearly worked himself out of a job. He had a weak reputation as an administrator and showed little interest in becoming an active chief administrative officer of Panama. His solution to his future was to enter into semi-retirement, thus avoiding any of the detail of day-to-day administration. This move also allowed Torrijos to stay out of domestic controversies, permitting his stature to be somewhat that of the elder statesman overseeing the destiny of Panama. Torrijos did leave behind a major domestic issue, however. When he withdrew from the domestic scene following the October 1978 elections for the Assembly of Corregimientos, military men were also removed from the bureaucracy and replaced with civilians. All of this was in preparation for promised elections for a true legislative body scheduled for 1981. Torrijos postponed the elections until 1984, and, even then, only one-third of the legislature would be elected. Presidential elections would be held at the same time. Torrijos' domestic opposition felt betrayed.

The constitutional head of state was Aristides Royo, former minister of economic planning, who had replaced Lakas as president of Panama. The daily operations of government were turned over to Royo. However, there was little question in the mind of any observer of Panamanian affairs but what Torrijos still held the ultimate authority. Also, Torrijos continued to remain the principal decision-maker of Panama's foreign policy, especially on such issues as the conflicts in Nicaragua and El Salvador. The Torrijos family nepotism, which was an issue during the Senate debate, continued as an issue in Panamanian politics. Thirty or more of General Torrijos' relatives were in middle- or upper-echelon positions in the government. Torrijos' influence was obviously still very strong even in his semi-retired status.

EVALUATION OF SENATE DEBATE

One observer of the Senate floor debate, Steve Ropp,
wrote, "Listening to the floor debate that preceded ratification proved to be a thankless task for anyone interested in understanding the full range of issues involved."[22] Ropp evaluated the debate overall as "muted."
He did concede, however, that "not . . . all important
matters were ignored. The central tenets of the treaties
were fully and tediously elaborated."[23] His explanation
for the "muted" nature of the debate was that the

> relative shallowness of the debate stemmed to some
> extent from the difficulty that the foreign policy
> establishment had in finding the proper "face" with
> which to present the Canal issue. If the American
> public were exclusively mercenary, it would have
> been sufficient to state that major U.S. corpora-
> tions have direct investments totaling $23.5 billion
> in Latin America today . . . and that the canal is
> a relatively small and unprofitable venture by com-
> parison. However, lacking this popular orientation,
> the arguments of the corporations were couched in
> the rhetoric of fair play.[24]

The security issue, he felt, was not the security of the
Canal, but security of the U.S. investments in Latin
America.

The assumption that there is a foreign policy establishment and that, if there is one, it can speak with
one voice is questionable, but of greater importance is
the observation that the Senate debate lacked a sense of
completeness and depth. In one sense, no debate before
Congress or any other deliberative body is complete in
the minds of both the observers and participants. But
how does the debate on the Canal treaties bear up under
comparison with other treaty debates?

The floor debate did not cover the range of issues
covered before the Foreign Relations Committee. This
observation would, however, be true of virtually any issue that received an extended review before a committee.
Because a committee has a smaller membership than the
Senate and can call witnesses to aid in bringing out a
variety of viewpoints, a committee thus can allow its
members to pursue a point more extensively. One such
instance was the degree to which the committee went into
the economic future of the Canal. The floor debate did
not develop this point nearly as well as the hearings
did, but the public record of the hearings and the floor
debate together constituted considerable analysis. To
reasonably assess the Senate's attention to an issue,
both the hearings and the floor debate should be evaluated. On the issue that Ropp raises concerning the security of investments in Latin America by U.S. corporations,

the hearings repeatedly brought out the need for settling
the Canal issue in order to make those investments more
secure in the future.

The proponents of the treaties used any argument
available to promote the treaties, but, at the same time,
the opposition did not overlook any means available to
attack the treaties. An argument could be made that all
of the arguments pro and con did not seem appropriate to
the issues at hand, but not that the issues were over-
looked.

The debate on the two Canal treaties was one of the
longest held on any treaty to come before the Senate.
While in this instance there were two treaties, whereas
other major treaty reviews such as the Treaty of Versailles and the North Atlantic Treaty involved only one
treaty, the combined debate on the floor occupied the
Senate for over ten weeks. The debate was preceded by
sixteen days of hearings over a three-month period by the
Foreign Relations Committee. Over 2,400 pages of hearings were published by the committee. "Every aspect of
the treaties was examined in exhaustive, repetitive detail."[25] In addition to this were the hearings by the
Subcommittee on the Separation of Powers of the Judiciary Committee and the Armed Services Committee. All
of this together amounted to more attention being paid
to a single foreign policy issue by the Senate than to
any other since World War II.

LaFeber attacks the hearings from a different perspective. He felt that the debate "droned" on; even
though the "discussion thoroughly examined details of the
treaties, . . . it soon became repetitious and produced
no memorable speech-making. . . . The Senate leadership's
objective, however, was not memorable speech-making but
ending the debate as soon as the members made a record
for the folks back home. Byrd and Baker had the necessary 67 votes well in hand at the start of the Senate
sessions."[26] LaFeber's argument that the votes to pass
the treaties were there from the beginning is based on
the vote taken in the Senate on 22 February to reverse
the consideration of the treaties and take up the Canal
treaty first. That vote was sixty-seven to thirty to
not make the change. A vote against the change was considered pro-treaty.

To draw the conclusion that that vote was indicative
of how the Senate would vote ultimately on the treaties
is to indicate little understanding of the behavior of
the Senate. Eventually, the Senate took many roll call
votes that affected either an entire treaty or part of
one. Some of those roll calls were also close to the
final vote on the treaties, but others were far off. The
leadership could not have been confident that any one of
the roll call votes was indicative of how the final vote
would go. Even after the neutrality treaty was approved,
there was doubt that the full sixty-eight votes could be

mustered again in support of the Canal treaty. Senator
Brooke specifically stated that he might vote against
the Canal treaty even though he had voted for the neutrality treaty. Senator Hayakawa made a similar statement.

In comparing the first roll call with the final
votes on the treaties, LaFeber states that only one senator shifted his vote--Senator Henry Roth shifted from
support to opposition. Actually, three senators changed
their positions. In addition to Roth, Senator Jennings
Randolph (D., WV) also shifted to the opposition, and
Senator Cannon (D., NV) shifted to support on the final
votes. To assume that those sixty-seven senators would
vote the same way in the final vote is to assume that
there was no indecision or bargaining after 22 February.

The sixty-seven pro-treaty votes on that early roll
call were exactly the number of votes necessary to pass
the treaties if the entire Senate voted. No responsible
leader could have rested on the security of such a minimum margin of victory, especially since so many members
of the Senate had not yet declared themselves on the
treaties. If the leadership had been certain of the
votes from 22 February on, then the DeConcini condition
agreed to by Carter was unnecessary, as were the quid
pro quo's Carter was accused of making with various senators to secure their votes for the treaties.

The charge that the debate "droned" on and that the
senators "produced no memorable speech-making" is hardly
proof that the debate's only purpose was to give opportunity "to make a record for the folks back home." Senate debates typically are repetitious, especially those
that involve a substantial number of senators. Merely
because a point has been made once does not prevent other
senators from making it again. Repetition is not a basis
for ruling a senator out of order. Memorable speeches
before the Senate are rare, and to observe that this debate produced no great speeches is not unusual. No doubt
the charge that much of the speech making was for the
folks back home is true, but, again, this is hardly unusual behavior in the Senate.

In comparison to other debates in the Senate on
legislation or other treaties, the debate on the Canal
treaties was extensive, thorough, and generally to the
point. If the debate did nothing else, it allowed the
leadership and the White House the opportunity to try to
marshal support for the treaties in the Senate.

Before leaving an evaluation of the Senate's handling of the treaties, one additional observation is in
order--one that is not necessarily critical of the Senate
but, rather, one that notes a deviation from the Senate's
usual practices in handling a foreign policy issue. In
April 1977, the administration informed the Foreign Relations Committee that a breakthrough was likely in the
negotiations. Up until that time, communication between

the Senate and the executive concerning the treaties had
been very limited. Close communication between the executive and the Foreign Relations Committee had been traditional in the post-World War II period, and the Foreign
Relations Committee was respected by the Senate for its
special access to the administration and the State Department.[27] The chairman of the committee was critical
in this relationship. In 1977, John Sparkman, as committee chairman, was generally regarded as a weak leader,
and the committee's communication with the State Department had waned. The principal means of contact shifted
to Majority Leader Byrd.[28] Throughout the treaty review
process, the Senate's leadership, plus some members of
the committee, though not its chairman, provided the
guidance necessary to gain the Senate's approval of the
treaties. The committee as an institution was not as
centrally important on the Canal question as the committee had been during so many foreign policy questions in
the past.

THE AFTERMATH

     With approval of the treaties in the Senate, the
casual observer of the Canal controversy might have
thought it was ended, at least as far as the new treaties
were concerned. Actually, two further steps were necessary before the treaties were to go into effect. One,
essentially a formality, was the exchange of the instruments of ratification of the treaties, and the second,
the passage of the implementing legislation by Congress,
which proved to be far from a formality.
     The rumor had circulated in Panama in August 1977
that President Carter would come to Panama for the signing of the treaties. Instead, the treaties were signed
in Washington at the OAS headquarters. The only other
ceremonial occasion concerning the treaties would be the
exchange of ratifications between the governments of Panama and the United States following their respective
domestic approval procedures. Considering the Panamanian
sensitivities about seemingly always having to go to
Washington to consult with the United States and the concerted effort by the United States to dispel this feeling
by carrying on most of the negotiations in Panama after
the Kissinger-Tack Agreement in early 1974, it followed
that the exchange of ratifications would take place in
Panama. This was agreed to by the United States, and
President Carter flew to Panama on 15 June for a two-day
visit.
     Carter's visit was a mixed experience of jubilation
by the Panamanians and hostility by the Zonians. The
presence in Panama of an American Panama and a Panamanian
Panama was never more pointedly demonstrated. The president's appearance in the Cinco de Mayo Plaza in Panama
City just across from the Zone was greeted by a huge

celebrating crowd of Panamanians. The president's visit
was not without controversy in the Republic, however.
Before he arrived, Panamanian students staged demonstra-
tions opposing Carter's visit and the treaties. These
demonstrations were stopped by the Panamanian National
Guard, and the University of Panama was once more closed.
Two Panamanians were killed in the action by the National
Guard.

The president also visited the Zone, where his wel-
come was subdued. The Zonians knew they had lost their
fight to keep the Zone as an American enclave, and morale
in the Zone was low. Carter attempted to explain the
need for the new treaties and to assure Zonians that the
rights of the American workers would be protected. The
mood in the Zone was hostile nevertheless, and Carter
probably never had faced a more disagreeable audience.
After a stay in Panama through 17 June, Carter returned
to the United States. The exchange of ratifications
formally committed Panama and the U.S. to start the implementation of the treaties on 1 October 1979.

In anticipation of the considerable planning and
preparation necessary to meet the 1 October 1979 date,
President Carter asked Congress to pass the legislation
necessary to implement the treaties by 31 May 1979. This
deadline for implementing legislation would occur more
than thirteen months after the approval of the treaties
by the Senate and would allow four months after the legislation was passed in which to prepare for the implementation deadline. The president's proposal for the implementation procedures was encompassed in HR 1716. The
House did not begin its deliberations on the legislation
until the beginning of the Ninety-Sixth Congress in January 1979. While the schedule for implementation appeared to be reasonable, it did not allow for the substantial number of House members who still opposed the
treaties.

The House was particularly unhappy with the manner
in which the administration excluded the House from the
treaty approval process in late 1977 and early 1978. The
administration's argument that treaties were self-executing and could transfer U.S.-owned property to Panama
without congressional, and, thus, House, approval was
particularly offensive to many members of the House.
Now the president was asking the House for the legislation necessary to implement the treaties, and the House
was ready to express its resentments in its opposition
to the powers the president requested in HR 1716.

Aspects of or all of the legislation were referred
to four committees--Merchant Marine and Fisheries, Foreign Affairs, Judiciary, and Post Office and Civil Service. Through its chairman, John M. Murphy (D., NY),
the Merchant Marine and Fisheries Committee wrote its own
legislation, HR 111. This version of the implementing
legislation was managed by Chairman Murphy and David R.

260

Bowen (D., MS). An even worse bill, from the administration's viewpoint, was introduced by Congressman George Hanson (R., ID). Both Hansen and Murphy were long-standing critics of the treaties. When the three versions of the implementation legislation were reported to the Rules Committee, Rules rejected both Hansen's and the administration's versions in favor of HR 111. The administration ultimately supported the Murphy bill, after it found that HR 1716 had no chance. Overall, the Murphy bill and the administration's bill differed in the flexibility granted the president. Even after it decided to support the committee version, the administration objected to aspects of HR 111 as violating the treaties.

HR 111 passed the House on 21 June, three weeks after the deadline the administration had imposed on the legislation. The delay resulted mainly from efforts by supporters of the administration to find the votes in the House for the president's position. The key vote on HR 111 came when the House rejected an amendment by George Hansen that called for Panama to bear the full costs of implementing the treaties. His amendment reflected the main tenet of his rejected legislation. This amendment was defeated 200-220. The administration argued that the amendment violated the treaties and, by so doing, gave Panama the legal right to take over the Canal on 1 October. Hansen supported his amendment with the argument that the administration had claimed during the treaty process that implementation would not cost the American taxpayer; all costs would come from Canal tolls. Since such a pledge had been made, all transition funds should come from Panama. Hansen claimed that the transfer of the Canal to Panama would cost $4,000,000,000 before it was completed. The administration's estimate was $871,000,000, upped from an earlier estimate of $350,000,000. Bowen put the cost at $830,000,000 and pointed out that most of the funds, $757,000,000, would go for moving U.S. military facilities and providing services for Canal employees and dependents, and thus were not Panama's responsibilities. Hansen's amendment would have shifted all of these costs to Panama by prohibiting "any cost to U.S. taxpayers." An amendment, offered by G. V. Montgomery (D., MS), which would have required Panama to pay $75,000,000 of the costs, was narrowly defeated 210-213. A motion to recommit the bill to committee with instructions that the committee report the bill with the Hansen amendment attached was defeated 210-216. The bill passed 224-202. The issue of implementation in the House appeared to be settled.

In the Senate, the legislation was sent to the Armed Services Committee rather than to the Foreign Relations Committee. The new Foreign Relations Committee chairman, Frank Church, must have been relieved not to have to deal directly with the legislation, as he was under heavy attack from conservatives in his home state of Idaho.

One of the points made by his detractors was his support of the treaties.[31] The Armed Services Committee reported the legislation favorably, but nine of the ten Democratic members refused to floor-manage the bill. This task thus fell to the most junior Democratic member of the committee, Carl Levin (D., MI).[32] The committee vote was nine to eight. On 26 July, the Senate approved the legislation sixty-four to thirty.

Since the Senate's version differed from the House's, the measure was sent to a conference committee. The controversy was revived when the conference report was rejected in the House on 20 September by eleven votes, 192-203. The Senate approved the compromise sixty to thirty-five. The vote in the Senate on the conference report was close to that the treaties had received when approved by the Senate, but some change in membership had occurred due to retirements, death, and the results of the 1978 election. The Senate had twenty new members. Nine of the new members voted for the report, and eleven against. Their predecessors had voted thirteen to seven in favor of the treaties. Of those who were members of both the 1978 and 1979 Senates, several changed their votes or were absent. The five senators who missed the vote—Senators Bentsen, Biden, Cranston, Stafford, and Weicker—had all voted for the treaties. Two senators who had voted against the treaties, Senators Stennis and Zorinsky, voted for the report; and Senator Cannon, who had voted for the treaties, voted against the report.[33]

Comparison of the Senate votes on the treaties and the conference report shows that the Senate had undergone some change in attitude since 1978 on the Canal question; but such a comparison presents problems. Since only a majority vote was necessary to pass the conference report, little effort by the administration to recruit votes was necessary. Evidence that the vote was not anticipated to be a close one was the absence of five senators who had voted for the treaties, including Cranston and Biden, who had been among the hard-core of support for the treaties. It is also interesting to note that Senator Zorinsky, who had voted against the treaties, voted for the report. He became a member of the Foreign Relations Committee at the beginning of the Ninety-Sixth Congress (1979), and the influence of socialization to that committee's norms may have been reflected in his vote on the report. He was also the chairman of the committee's Subcommittee on Latin American Affairs.

Time was now critical. When the House rejected the conference report, only ten days remained before the 1 October date to begin the implementation of the treaties. Many House members were now making clear their resentment that the president had denied a role for the House when the treaties had been before the Senate. The conference committee had attempted to allay these resentments by

making changes in the legislation and including changes
favored by treaty critics without producing provisions
that would be regarded as treaty violations. Not only
was the implementing legislation facing a deadline, but
a $467 million authorization to run the Canal in fiscal
1980 needed to be passed by 1 October, the beginning of
the new fiscal year. The authorization cleared the House
Rules Committee on 20 September.

Earlier in June, during the debate on the legislation, an unusual event had taken place--the House held a
closed session. There had not been a closed session in
the House since 1830. Closed sessions of the Senate were
not that unusual--twenty between 1945 and 1978--but the
House had avoided them for nearly a century and a half.
The House closed session was to hear charges that Panama
was involved in the Nicaraguan civil war then going on.
The treaty opponents charged that Panama was supplying
arms to the rebels. This charge, still being heard in
September, was regarded as a factor in the vote rejecting
the conference report. Also, the recently announced
presence of Soviet troops in Cuba contributed to many
members' feelings that the U.S. should continue control
of the Canal.

When the conference report was rejected in the
House, treaty supporters and opponents differed as to
what would be the result if the implementing legislation
was not approved by 1 October. The floor leader for the
legislation, Representative John Murphy, said that the
United States would no longer have a legal basis to operate the Canal and that Panama would be entitled to take
over the Canal on that date. Murphy also said that Carter might implement the treaties by executive order if
the House did not approve legislation. In Panama, Diogenes de la Rosa, one of the negotiators of the treaties,
said that if the United States did not pass the legislation, Panama "could immediately assume all functions of
the canal and denounce the United States for being in
violation of the treaties."[34] Opponents of the legislation, on the other hand, felt that the United States
would simply continue to operate the Canal under the
procedures applied in the past. Rejecting the legislation, Representative Bauman argued, was the only means
the House had available to it to show its, and the American public's, disapproval of the new treaties.

The implementing legislation was needed to carry out
several provisions in the treaties. The most important
was the establishment of a new U.S. government agency,
the Panama Canal Commission, and the procedures for the
appointment of members to that commission. Also, the
legislation would establish the basis for setting tolls;
establish arrangements for U.S. participation on various
binational committees; authorize the employment system
for employees working for the new commission; spell out
the procedures for phasing out the U.S. court system in

the Zone and establish the arrangements to implement the thirty-month transition period from American to Panamanian law; and make provisions for the migration to the United States of long-term employees of the old Canal company who were non-U.S. citizens.

The margin necessary for passage of implementing legislation in the House seemed to rest with those representatives who, while opposing the treaties, recognized that implementing legislation had to be passed. Those members, plus supporters of the treaties, had to find the appropriate compromise that did not, as interpreted by the State Department and Panama, violate the treaties. The conference report had failed to do this on a number of issues.

On the question of property transfers, the House wanted Congress to have the authority to stop transfers of property to Panama, up to and including the transfer of the Canal in 1999. The Senate argued that the Canal treaty itself provided for all transfers and that further congressional action was unnecessary. The compromise offered in the conference report allowed for congressional approval of the transfer of U.S. property, but it also allowed the president to transfer Canal property in compliance with the treaty.

The House was also concerned about wartime control of the Canal. The House version of the legislation allowed the president to place the U.S. military in control of the Canal during wartime. The conference report authorized the president to order the Canal administrator to comply with orders issued by the military charged with defense of the Canal. Compliance was thus at the discretion of the president. The House did not think this arrangement strong enough, especially since the Canal administrator would be a Panamanian citizen beginning in 1990. The House versions of both property transfers and wartime control were labeled by Carter as violations of the treaties. The House and Senate also remained divided on the question of who would pay the costs of implementation. The Senate rejected the House plan that Panama bear any of the costs of transfer or property.

Certainly, one of the most difficult issues to decide was the status of the new Panama Canal Commission. The House wanted it to be a government agency, and the Senate wanted it to be a quasi-governmental corporation, much as the old Panama Canal Company had been. The House felt that its position on the commission would allow for more congressional supervision of the commission than would the Senate's proposal. The Senate accepted the House's position on the commission in exchange for the removal from the legislation of those provisions that the Carter administration felt were violations of the treaties. In addition to transfers and wartime control, these violations included requiring Panama to reimburse the United States for the costs of transfer before Panama

would receive the $10 million per year from Canal tolls.
The conference committee removed this provision. The
House version placed the Canal Commission under the Defense Department. This was replaced in the conference
report with a statement that the president would exercise
his authority over the commission through the Defense Department.

Wages and benefits for Canal Zone employees were
also an issue in the conference report. The administration, and the Senate, wanted employees of the new commission placed under the wage scales of the Defense Department. This would have been a considerable reduction
in wages and benefits for Canal employees, especially
the 500 or so teachers in the Zone. Under the Canal
Company, they were paid the same as teachers in Washington, D.C., which had one of the highest pay scales in
the United States. The House wanted the same pay scales
for employees, including teachers, that they had received
under the Canal Company. The effort to reduce the pay
scale brought threats from labor unions to oppose the
implementing legislation overall. The conference report
adopted the Senate version, but did allow the continuation of the generous leave and travel benefits the employees enjoyed under the Canal Company.

Additional issues included the composition of the
U.S. membership on the Canal Commission. The House version, at Murphy's urging, provided that three of the five
members represent shipping, ports, and maritime labor.
The Senate version had no such arrangement, and the administration opposed the special representation of those
interests. The conference report specified that three
members would be private individuals, but did not say
what interests they would represent. The other two members would be Defense Department officials.

The special immigration quotas for non-citizen Canal
Company employees and their families also caused difficulty. The House version allowed up to 7,500 persons to
immigrate to the United States, but the Senate version
replaced the limit at 25,000. These immigrants would be
mainly West Indians who wanted to come to the United
States after Panama took over the Canal. The conference
report placed the limit at 15,000, with no more than
5,000 in any given year.

Following the rejection of the conference report by
the House, new conferees were appointed and a new compromise presented. The second conference report was
voted on in the Senate on 25 September and was adopted
sixty-three to thirty-two. The next day, the House a-
dopted the new report 232-188. The adoption of the second report allowed Vice President Mondale and Secretary
of State Vance to go to Panama for the 1 October ceremonies marking the beginning of the transition period.

The second report was adopted after a number of
compromises were offered the treaty opponents and after

a substantially stepped-up lobbying effort by the administration. The administration had been criticized earlier for not making a greater effort when the legislation and the first conference report had been before the House. Even Congressman Bauman, the outspoken opponent of the treaties and the leader of the opposition to the legislation, said that the second report should be passed, although he eventually voted against it. The second report no longer contained any of the treaty violations that the Carter administration claimed were in the first report.

The mood in the House seemed to be that some implementing legislation had to be passed and that the second conference report was the best the opposition would receive. On property transfers, a provision was included that the president could not transfer the Canal before the 31 December 1999 date called for in the Canal treaty. This was designed to satisfy the suspicions of those members who thought the president might give in to Panamanian pressures for an earlier transfer. While both versions of the conference report required the president to notify the Congress 180 days before a transfer of property to Panama, the second report denied Congress the right to veto property transfers.

The second report did contain the provision that three members of the commission would include representatives from shipping, ports, and labor. At least three of the commission members could not be government officials, but the report did not specify that all of the special-interest representatives had to be private individuals. In a move to satisfy the demand that Panama pay some of the costs of transition, the second report required that $10 million a year from tolls be used to operate the schools and hospitals under commission control. The second conference report spelled out that a threat to the Canal, under which wartime conditions would go into effect, included the presence of foreign combat forces in Panama. This was to satisfy the fears of some that Panama would invite in Cuban troops.

The second report also prohibited payments to Panama from tolls if Panama imposed retroactive taxes on U.S.-owned businesses in the Zone. Such a provision was already in the treaty. The congressional phase of the implementation of the treaties was now complete when the second report was adopted by both houses. The legislation was quickly signed into law by the president.

The essence of the new law established the Panama Canal Commission, which, along with the U.S. military, would run and protect the Canal and about forty-two percent of the old Zone through 1999. The president's authority over the commission would be exercised through the Defense Department, and all tolls collected by the commission would be deposited in the U.S. treasury; all funds expended by the commission had to be appropriated

by Congress. The legislation authorized payments to Panama as provided for in the treaties, but if U.S. tax
money were used to implement the treaties, it must first
be authorized and appropriated by Congress. The president would appoint all nine members of the commission,
including the four Panamanians; and all U.S. members had
to vote as instructed by the secretary of defense. The
legislation also established three top administrative
positions, including a chief administrator, a deputy administrator and a chief engineer.

Various other aspects of the future conduct of the
United States in Panama were also covered. The legislation brought up once more the issue of a sea-level canal
in Panama and authorized the president to negotiate with
Panama concerning such a canal. The president was also
authorized to negotiate the possibility of stationing
U.S. military forces in Panama after 1999.

One characteristic that virtually all political issues share is that they never come to a final and complete resolution of the dispute at hand. Even with the
transition under way following the 1 October 1979 ceremonies, much remained to be done. In November 1979, Panama charged the United States with failing to start up
the new Canal commission. Carlos Lopez Guevara, Panamanian ambassador to the United States, said that the Panamanian foreign minister, Carlos Ozores, had delivered
a protest to the United States in November charging the
United States with violations of the treaties by failing
to make the U.S. appointments. The protest was not mentioned publicly by either government until December.[35]
The Panamanians had long since made available to the
United States the Panamanian nominations for the four
positions. They had nominated Gabriel Lewis Galindo and
Robert Huertematte, both former ambassadors to the United
States; Edwin Fabrega, former Canal negotiator and foreign policy advisor; and Ricardo Rodriquez, former minister of justice. The chief administrator had been appointed by the United States--Lieutenant-General Dennis
P. McAuliffe, former governor of the Zone. The Panamanian deputy administrator was Fernando Manfredo. The
Manfredo appointment was viewed by the State Department
as Panama's way of assuring the United States of the
Panama's good intentions. Manfredo was viewed as a moderate in Panamanian politics. His appointment was also
seen as a means of balancing off the left and right forces in Panama. Some of the other Panamanian appointments
to the Panama Canal Commission and other joint committees
were known leftists.

The delay in the U.S. appointments was attributed
in part to the cumbersome and complicated qualifications
set up by the Panama Canal Act. Finding persons qualified under the provisions of the act proved to be no easy
task. Also, the Carter administration was, after 4 November, preoccupied with the seizure of the American

hostages in the U.S. embassy in Tehran and could devote
little time to the search for American members of the
Canal commission.

But, in addition to the lack of time for the appointments, another issue concerning the appointments
had developed. Since 1961, the State Department had had
a position on the Panama Canal Company board. The list
of appointees the Department of Defense sent the White
House had included two names from the Defense Department
but none from State. The State Department felt the precedent had been set for their having a representative
and insisted on having a member from State on the new
commission.

Other than the appointments question, however, the
transition in Panama was going well. The State Department took the view that most of the major issues remaining between the United States and Panama could be resolved during the thirty-month transition period. The
single most important issue, as seen by the department,
was to make the implementation of the Canal treaties as
smooth and efficient as possible in order to assure un-
interrupted operation of the Panama Canal. One State
Department official, involved in the implementation process, noted that the process proceeded more smoothly than
the department had anticipated.

To carry out representation of the two countries
during the implementation process, each country established an administrative agency. The United States set
up the Panama Review Committee, which included the United
States ambassador to Panama, Chief Administrator
McAuliffe and General Nutting of the Southern Command.
The task of this group was to alert the State Department
as problems in implementation arose. The Panamanians
set up what amounted to a super-ministry, the Panama Canal Authority. Inter-agency squabbles lessened the ef-
fectiveness of the authority, however. In addition,
thirty-six bilateral subcommittees were established to
handle the myriad of specific issues to be settled.
Also, joint commissions for environmental problems and
military affairs were established.

The range of pending problems at the beginning of
implementation was long. The State Department identified
nearly fifty. Not all presented an immediate need for
attention but did need to be dealt with by the end of the
transition period, 1 April 1982. The following presents
a sampling of these problems: the adaptation of U.S.-
owned businesses to Panamanian laws, entry and exit permits for U.S. citizens, transfer of social security
funds, taxation of imported liquor, certification and
authentication of documents, the status of U.S. Army
post offices, the granting of diplomatic privileges to
U.S. citizens on the Panama Canal Commission, Panamanian
civil court treatment of Panama Canal Commission employees, treaty-prescribed payments to Panama and Panamanian

debt payments, property transfer procedures, further negotiation of a sea-level canal, military sales to Panama,
expansion of the Colón Free Zone and a prisoner exchange
between Panama and the United States.

LINKAGE FACTORS

The overall theme followed in this study of United
States-Panamanian relations relative to the Panama Canal
has been to establish the linkage factors involved in
this relationship. The easiest of the linkages to analyze undoubtedly was that between the domestic and foreign policies of Panama. Through the crisis before and
after the 1964 riots, the rejection of the 1967 draft
treaties, the revolution that brought Torrijos to power,
the renewed negotiations in 1971, the Kissinger-Tack
Agreement, and the subsequent conclusion of the new treaties in 1977, the single most important issue in Panama
was the Panama Canal and its future. Other problems,
both domestic and foreign, developed for Panama, such as
the growing economic crisis in Panama and disputes involving Belize, El Salvador, and Nicaragua; but even if
these issues temporarily gained the limelight, the future
of the Panama Canal remained the enduring and central issue of Panamanian politics. Torrijos and his predecessors built their political constituencies by promises of
a better life for Panama when Panama gained its fair
share of Canal revenues. Panama was truly a penetrated
society in that a foreign policy question was also the
main domestic question. In fact, the Canal was neither
a domestic nor foreign policy issue; it was simply the
issue of the Panamanian political system.
    Linkage between the domestic and foreign policy
spheres of politics in the United States is a somewhat
different story. Before 1976, the domestic concern over
the future of the Canal was limited virtually to a few
members of Congress, but with the 1976 primary elections,
the American public became aware of the issue. From that
time until the implementing legislation was passed, the
behavior of the United States in its negotiations with
Panama was strongly influenced by what was going on domestically in the United States. At no time did the
United States approach being a penetrated society on the
issue, however.
    Linkages between the United States and Panamanian
domestic political systems became closer throughout the
negotiations, but particularly so in 1974 and after. The
publics in both countries were very sensitive to comments
made by the decision-makers of the other country. More
often than not, the remarks made by decision-makers were
interpreted in the other country as more hostile than was
intended by the speakers. Publics and decision-makers
alike often seemed to have difficulty in understanding
when statements were made for domestic consumption and

when the remarks were intended for the other country.
This was especially true of the manner in which Torrijos'
statements to the Panamanian public were interpreted in
the United States. Often, what he said was to maintain
himself in power, but his remarks were heard in the United States as bravado, if not threats. During the Senate's review of the treaties, virtually any public statement by a Panamanian official entered into the debate
and was interpreted to be contrary to the manner in which
the senatorial proponents of the treaties were interpreting the treaties.

Linkages between the Organization of American States
and the United States and Panama were also frequent.
Although the OAS had little to do with the final outcome
of the negotiations other than providing the building in
which the treaties were signed, meetings of the organization were frequently used by both countries to present
their positions on the issue.

Even though Panama used the OAS as a means of stating its demands and internationalizing the Canal question, the United Nations was more frequently and more
effectively used as a forum by Panama than was the OAS.
The United Nations did not participate in the actual negotiations of the new treaties any more than did the OAS,
however.

An important linkage for Panama, and perhaps the
most important one, was the internationalization of the
Canal issue. This diplomatic success was actually the
development of several linkages. It began with the
firming up and expansion of the linkage Panama had with
other Latin American countries. Mainly, this was done
outside the OAS. The Security Council meetings in Panama expanded this linkage further. The socialist nations
and non-Latin, Third World nations lined up behind Panama
during and following these meetings. Panama subsequently was itself categorized as a Third World, non-aligned
nation when it was admitted to the Non-aligned Conference. This provided an additional linkage and forum for
Panama's position on the Canal issue. By 1975, Panama
had both the ear and the sympathies of most of the nations of the world in regard to the Canal. Panama had
successfully branded the United States as a colonial
master and marked the Canal Zone as a U.S. colonial possession.

The linkages between the United States and Panama
did not end with the new treaties. The two countries
had a number of problems during the implementation period
and undoubtedly will continue to have conflicts through
the years until 2000, even if both nations continue to
seriously attempt to make the treaties work.

While the thirty-month implementation period went
well, by both U.S. and Panamanian accounts, political
and economic problems continued in Panama. The first
significant internal political development came on 31

July 1981 when General Omar Torrijos died in a plane
crash in western Panama. The political stability Torrijos had maintained in Panama for years, even after his
semi-retirement from public life in 1978, did not come
to an abrupt end, however. President Royo was able to
remain as national leader nearly a year in spite of
his lack of support from both the Panamanian public and
the National Guard. On 30 July 1982, the National Guard
forced Royo to resign, and he was replaced with Ricardo
de la Espriella, who had been vice president. The real
power, it was generally conceded, rested with General
Rubin Dario Paredes, commander of the National Guard.[36]
     The death of Torrijos probably produced mixed feel-
ings among officials in Washington. On the one hand,
although he had taken a consistently nationalistic view
of the Canal issue, he had proven cooperative during the
implementation period. Also, he had granted asylum to
the Shah of Iran at the request of President Carter. On
the other hand, Torrijos had, since his semi-retirement,
become an activist in Central American affairs by supporting the Sandinistas in Nicaragua and the guerrillas
in El Salvador.
     The economic situation in Panama did not improve,
notwithstanding the increased payments Panama received
under the new treaties. By 1983, Panama's foreign debt
approached $3 billion, and unemployment officially was
at fifteen percent. The agricultural sector of the economy was in serious straits. The new treaties had not
solved Panama's economic troubles. In spite of the
smooth transition during the implementation period, Panama was protesting various aspects of the implementation
process. Panama was unhappy with the implementation
legislation Congress had passed. It argued that the
treaties had been violated by placing the Canal commission under the direct control of the secretary of defense
and by requiring congressional approval of the Canal
budget. Panama further complained about the hiring practices of the Canal commission. New employees hired under
the new treaty arrangement were mainly Panamanians and
were paid only about half as much as were employees hired
earlier. Panama brought these complaints to the United
Nations in September 1981 and charged in the General Assembly that U.S. treaty violations would cause Panama to
lose $4 billion by the year 2000. Panama also charged
that the U.S. was not modernizing the Canal as promised
and that by the time the Canal was transferred, it might
be worthless.[37] Despite these charges, no significant
changes in the practices of the Canal commission resulted.
     Of greater concern to Panama was the decline in Ca-
nal traffic. For a time after the treaties were approved, Canal transits had increased appreciably; but in
1982, traffic began to fall. The decline was attributed
to the loss of shipments of Alaskan oil. A new pipeline,

which crossed Panama, now allowed tankers to unload on
the Pacific side and pump their oil to tankers on the
Atlantic side. Although tolls were increased by nine
and eight-tenths percent in March 1983 to compensate for
the loss of revenue, the increase did not cover the previous losses.[38] All of these issues have aggravated U.S.-
Panamanian relations, but the greatest threat to future
relations between the two countries will depend upon
whether Panama is willing to wait another seventeen years
before receiving control of the Canal.

NOTES

1. Walter LaFeber, The Panama Canal: The Crisis in Historical Perspective (Oxford University Press, 1979), pp. 236-37; also
New York Times, 5 January 1978, sec. 2, p. 10 and 8 January 1978,
p. 19.
2. LaFeber, The Panama Canal, p. 237.
3. Ibid., p. 239.
4. In September 1977, the State Department had assigned
fifteen officers to work with Congress and the public to develop
support for the treaties.
5. Congressional Record, 8 September 1977, p. S14437.
6. New York Times, 11 September 1977, p. 3 and 22 September
1977, p. 5.
7. Bernard Roshco, "The Polls: Polling on Panama-Si; Don't
Know; Hell, No!" Public Opinion Quarterly 42 (Winter 1978):551-62.
8. Ibid., pp. 552-54.
9. Ibid., pp. 554-55.
10. Ibid., pp. 557-60.
11. Ibid., p. 562.
12. Congressional Record, 18 March 1978, p. S678.
13. Cecil V. Crabb, Jr. and Pat M. Holt, Invitation to
Struggle: Congress, the President and Foreign Policy (Congressional
Quarterly Press, 1980), p. 75.
14. Thomas M. Franck and Edward Weisband, Foreign Policy by
Congress (Oxford University Press, 1979), p. 278.
15. Ibid., p. 276.
16. Ibid., p. 278.
17. Quoted in Ibid., p. 279.
18. LaFeber, The Panama Canal, p. 246.
19. Crabb and Holt, Invitation to Struggle, p. 79; see also,
Franck and Weisband, Foreign Policy, pp. 281-83.
20. Crabb and Holt, Invitation to Struggle, p. 79.
21. Franck and Weisband, Foreign Policy, p. 282.
22. Steve C. Ropp, "Ratification of the Panama Canal Treaties:
The Muted Debate," World Affairs 141 (1978):283.
23. Ibid.
24. Ibid., p. 287.
25. Crabb and Holt, Invitation to Struggle, p. 73.
26. LaFeber, The Panama Canal, pp. 239-40.
27. Crabb and Holt, Invitation to Struggle, p. 69.
28. Ibid., p. 71.

29. William L. Furlong, "The President, Congress and the Panama Canal," paper presented at the International Studies Association meetings, Los Angeles, 19-22 March 1980, pp. 52-54.

30. History of HR 111 can be found in Congressional Quarterly, 23 June 1979, pp. 1207-09; 22 September 1979, pp. 2035, 2059-60; 29 September 1979, pp. 2119-20, 2181; 6 October 1979, pp. 2196-98.

31. Crabb and Holt, Invitation to Struggle, p. 84.

32. Ibid.

33. Twenty-four senators ran for re-election in 1978. These senators voted fifteen to nine in favor of the treaties. Seven of those who voted for the treaties were defeated, but only one senator who opposed the treaties was defeated.

34. Christian Science Monitor, 24 September 1979, p. 1.

35. New York Times, 7 December 1979, p. 7.

36. New York Times, 19 December 1982, p. 10.

37. New York Times Magazine, 22 November 1981, p. 122.

38. Christian Science Monitor, 6 April 1983, p. 5.

Appendix A:
Treaty Concerning the Permanent Neutrality and Operation of the Panama Canal

The United States of America and the Republic of Panama have agreed upon the following:

ARTICLE I

The Republic of Panama declares that the Canal, as an international transit waterway, shall be permanently neutral in accordance with the regime established in this Treaty. The same regime of neutrality shall apply to any other international waterway that may be built either partially or wholly in the territory of the Republic of Panama.

ARTICLE II

The Republic of Panama declares the neutrality of the Canal in order that both in time of peace and in time of war it shall remain secure and open to peaceful transit by the vessels of all nations on terms of entire equality, so that there will be no discrimination against any nation, or its citizens or subjects, concerning the conditions or charges of transit, or for any other reason, and so that the Canal, and therefore the Isthmus of Panama, shall not be the target of reprisals in any armed conflict between other nations of the world. The foregoing shall be subject to the following requirements:

(a) Payment of tolls and other charges for transit and ancillary services, provided they have been fixed in conformity with the provisions of Article III(c);

(b) Compliance with applicable rules and regulations, provided such rules and regulations are applied in conformity with the provisions of Article III;

(c) The requirement that transiting vessels commit no acts of hostility while in the Canal; and

(d) Such other conditions and restrictions as are established by this Treaty.

ARTICLE III

1. For purposes of the security, efficiency and proper maintenance of the Canal the following rules shall apply:

(a) The Canal shall be operated efficiently in accordance with conditions of transit through the Canal, and rules and regulations that shall be just, equitable and reasonable, and limited to those necessary for safe navigation and efficient, sanitary operation of the Canal.

(b) Ancillary services necessary for transit through the Canal shall be provided;

(c) Tolls and other charges for transit and ancillary services shall be just, reasonable, equitable and consistent with the principles of international law;

(d) As a pre-condition of transit, vessels may be required to establish clearly the financial responsibility and guarantees for payment of reasonable and adequate indemnification, consistent with international practice and standards, for damages resulting from acts or omissions of such vessels when passing through the Canal. In the case of vessels owned or operated by a State or for which it has acknowledged responsibility, a certification by that State that it shall observe its obligations under international law to pay for damages resulting from the act or omission of such vessels when passing through the Canal shall be deemed sufficient to establish such financial responsibility;

(e) Vessels of war and auxiliary vessels of all nations shall at all times be entitled to transit the Canal, irrespective of their internal operation, means of propulsion, origin, destination or armament, without being subjected, as a condition of transit, to inspection, search or surveillance. However, such vessels may be required to certify that they have complied with all applicable health, sanitation and quarantine regulations. In addition, such vessels shall be entitled to refuse to disclose their internal operation, origin, armament, cargo or destination. However, auxiliary vessels may be required to present written assurances, certified by an official at a high level of the government of the State requesting the exemption, that they are owned or operated by that government and in this case are being used only on government non-commercial service.

2. For the purposes of this Treaty, the terms "Canal," "vessel of war," "auxiliary vessel," "internal operation," "armament" and "inspection" shall have the meanings assigned them in Annex A to this Treaty.

ARTICLE IV

The United States of America and the Republic of Panama agree to maintain the regime of neutrality established in this Treaty, which shall be maintained in order that the Canal shall remain permanently neutral, notwithstanding the termination of any other treaties entered into by the two Contracting Parties.

ARTICLE V

After the termination of the Panama Canal Treaty, only the Republic of Panama shall operate the Canal and maintain military forces, defense sites and military installations within its national territory.

ARTICLE VI

1. In recognition of the important contribution of the United States of America and of the Republic of Panama to the construction, operation, maintenance, and protection and defense of the Canal, vessels of war and auxiliary vessels of those nations shall, notwithstanding any other provisions of this Treaty, be entitled to transit the Canal irrespective of their internal operation, means of propulsion, origin, destination, armament or cargo carried. Such vessels of war and auxiliary vessels will be entitled to transit the Canal expeditiously.
2. The United States of America, so long as it has responsibility for the operation of the Canal, may continue to provide the Republic of Colombia toll-free transit through the Canal for its troops, vessels and materials of war. Thereafter, the Republic of Panama may provide the Republic of Colombia and the Republic of Costa Rica with the right of toll-free transit.

ARTICLE VII

1. The United States of America and the Republic of Panama shall jointly sponsor a resolution in the Organization of American States opening to accession by all nations of the world the Protocol to this Treaty whereby all the signatories will adhere to the objectives of this Treaty, agreeing to respect the regime of neutrality set forth herein.
2. The Organization of American States shall act as the depositary for this Treaty and related instruments.

ARTICLE VIII

This Treaty shall be subject to ratification in accordance with the constitutional procedures of the two Parties. The instruments of ratification of this Treaty shall be exchanged at Panama at the same time as the instruments of ratification of the Panama Canal Treaty, signed this date, are exchanged. This Treaty shall enter into force, simultaneously with the Panama Canal Treaty, six calendar months from the date of the exchange of the instruments of ratification.

DONE at Washington, this 7th day of September, 1977, in the English and Spanish languages, both texts being equally authentic.

ANNEX A

1. "Canal" includes the existing Panama Canal, the entrances thereto and the territorial seas of the Republic of Panama adjacent thereto, as defined on the map annexed hereto (Annex B),[1] and any other interoceanic waterway in which the United States of America is a participant or in which the United States of America has participated in connection with the construction or financing, that may be operated wholly or partially within the territory of the Republic of Panama, the entrances thereto and the territorial seas adjacent thereto.

2. "Vessel of war" means a ship belonging to the naval forces of a State, and bearing the external marks distinguishing warships of its nationality, under the command of an officer duly commissioned by the government and whose name appears in the Navy List, and manned by a crew which is under regular naval discipline.

3. "Auxiliary vessel" means any ship, not a vessel of war, that is owned or operated by a State and used, for the time being, exclusively on government non-commercial service.

4. "Internal operation" encompasses all machinery and propulsion systems, as well as the management and control of the vessel, including its crew. It does not include the measures necessary to transit vessels under the control of pilots while such vessels are in the Canal.

5. "Armament" means arms, ammunitions, implements of war and other equipment of a vessel which possesses characteristics appropriate for use for warlike purposes.

6. "Inspection" includes on-board examination of vessel structure, cargo, armament and internal operation. It does not include those measures strictly necessary for admeasurement, nor those measures strictly necessary to assure safe, sanitary transit and navigation, including examination of deck and visual navigation equipment, nor in the case of live cargoes, such as cattle or other livestock, that may carry communicable diseases, those measures necessary to assure that health and sanitation requirements are satisfied.

---

[1]Not printed here.

Appendix B:
Panama Canal Treaty

The United States of America and the Republic of Panama,

Acting in the spirit of the Joint Declaration of April 3, 1964, by the Representatives of the Governments of the United States of America and the Republic of Panama, and of the Joint Statement of Principles of February 7, 1974, initialed by the Secretary of State of the United States of America and the Foreign Minister of the Republic of Panama, and

Acknowledging the Republic of Panama's sovereignty over its territory,

Have decided to terminate the prior Treaties pertaining to the Panama Canal and to conclude a new Treaty to serve as the basis for a new relationship between them and, accordingly, have agreed upon the following:

ARTICLE I

ABROGATION OF PRIOR TREATIES AND ESTABLISHMENT OF A NEW RELATIONSHIP

1. Upon its entry into force, this Treaty terminates and supercedes:

(a) The Isthmian Canal Convention between the United States of America and the Republic of Panama, signed at Washington, November 18, 1903;

(b) The Treaty of Friendship and Cooperation signed at Washington, March 2, 1936, and the Treaty of Mutual Understanding and Cooperation and the related Memorandum of Understandings Reached, signed at Panama, January 25, 1955, between the United States of America and the Republic of Panama;

(c) All other treaties, conventions, agreements and exchanges of notes between the United States of America and the Republic of Panama concerning the Panama Canal which were in force prior to the entry into force of this Treaty; and

277

(d) Provisions concerning the Panama Canal
which appear in other treaties, conventions, agreements
and exchanges of notes between the United States of
America and the Republic of Panama which were in force
prior to the entry into force of this Treaty.

2. In accordance with the terms of this Treaty and
related agreements, the Republic of Panama, as territorial sovereign, grants to the United States of America,
for the duration of this Treaty, the rights necessary to
regulate the transit of ships through the Panama Canal,
and to manage, operate, maintain, improve, protect and
defend the Canal. The Republic of Panama guarantees to
the United States of America the peaceful use of the land
and water areas which it has been granted the rights to
use for such purposes pursuant to this Treaty and related
agreements.

3. The Republic of Panama shall participate increasingly in the management and protection and defense of
the Canal, as provided in this Treaty.

4. In view of the special relationship established
by this Treaty, the United States of America and the Republic of Panama shall cooperate to assure the uninter-
rupted and efficient operation of the Panama Canal.

ARTICLE II

RATIFICATION, ENTRY INTO FORCE,
AND TERMINATION

1. This Treaty shall be subject to ratification in
accordance with the constitutional procedures of the two
Parties. The instruments of ratification of this Treaty
shall be exchanged at Panama at the same time as the instruments of ratification of the Treaty Concerning the
Permanent Neutrality and Operation of the Panama Canal,
signed this date, are exchanged. This Treaty shall enter
into force, simultaneously with the Treaty Concerning
the Permanent Neutrality and Operation of the Panama
Canal, six calendar months from the date of the exchange
of the instruments of ratification.

2. This Treaty shall terminate at noon, Panama time,
December 31, 1999.

ARTICLE III

CANAL OPERATION AND MANAGEMENT

1. The Republic of Panama, as territorial sovereign,
grants to the United States of America the rights to
manage, operate, and maintain the Panama Canal, its com-
plementary works, installations and equipment and to provide for the orderly transit of vessels through the Panama Canal. The United States of America accepts the grant
of such rights and undertakes to exercise them in

accordance with this Treaty and related agreements.
2. In carrying out the foregoing responsibilities,
the United States of America may:
(a) Use for the aforementioned purposes, without cost except as provided in this Treaty, the various
installations and areas (including the Panama Canal) and
waters, described in the Agreement in Implementation of
this Article, signed this date, as well as such other
areas and installations as are made available to the
United States of America under this Treaty and related
agreements, and take the measures necessary to ensure
sanitation of such areas;
(b) Make such improvements and alterations to
the aforesaid installations and areas as it deems appropriate, consistent with the terms of this Treaty;
(c) Make and enforce all rules pertaining to
the passage of vessels through the Canal and other rules
with respect to navigation and maritime matters, in accordance with this Treaty and related agreements. The
Republic of Panama will lend its cooperation, when necessary, in the enforcement of such rules;
(d) Establish, modify, collect and retain tolls
for the use of the Panama Canal, and other charges, and
establish and modify methods of their assessment;
(e) Regulate relations with employees of the
United States Government;
(f) Provide supporting services to facilitate
the performance of its responsibilities under this
Article;
(g) Issue and enforce regulations for the effective exercise of the rights and responsibilities of
the United States of America under this Treaty and related agreements. The Republic of Panama will lend its
cooperation, when necessary, in the enforcement of such
rules; and
(h) Exercise any other right granted under this
Treaty, or otherwise agreed upon between the two Parties.
3. Pursuant to the foregoing grant of rights, the
United States of America shall, in accordance with the
terms of this Treaty and the provisions of United States
law, carry out its responsibilities by means of a United
States Government agency called the Panama Canal Commission, which shall be constituted by and in conformity
with the laws of the United States of America.
a) The Panama Canal Commission shall be super-
vised by a Board composed of nine members, five of whom
shall be nationals of the United States of America, and
four of whom shall be Panamanian nationals proposed by
the Republic of Panama for appointment to such positions
by the United States of America in a timely manner.
(b) Should the Republic of Panama request the
United States of America to remove a Panamanian national
from membership on the Board, the United States of America shall agree to such request. In that event, the

Republic of Panama shall propose another Panamanian national for appointment by the United States of America to such position in a timely manner. In case of removal of a Panamanian member of the Board at the initiative of the United States of America, both Parties will consult in advance in order to reach agreement concerning such removal, and the Republic of Panama shall propose another Panamanian national for appointment by the United States of America in his stead.

(c) The United States of America shall employ a national of the United States of America as Administrator of the Panama Canal Commission, and a Panamanian national as Deputy Administrator, through December 31, 1989. Beginning January 1, 1990, a Panamanian national shall be employed as the Administrator and a national of the United States of America shall occupy the position of Deputy Administrator. Such Panamanian nationals shall be proposed to the United States of America by the Republic of Panama for appointment to such positions by the United States of America.

(d) Should the United States of America remove the Panamanian national from his position as Deputy Administrator, or Administrator, the Republic of Panama shall propose another Panamanian national for appointment to such position by the United States of America.

4. An illustrative description of the activities the Panama Canal Commission will perform in carrying out the responsibilities and rights of the United States of America under this Article is set forth at the Annex. Also set forth in the Annex are procedures for the discontinuance or transfer of those activities performed prior to the entry into force of this Treaty by the Panama Canal Company or the Canal Zone Government which are not to be carried out by the Panama Canal Commission.

5. The Panama Canal Commission shall reimburse the Republic of Panama for the costs incurred by the Republic of Panama in providing the following public services in the Canal operating areas and in housing areas set forth in the Agreement in Implementation of Article III of this Treaty and occupied by both United States and Panamanian citizen employees of the Panama Canal Commission: police, fire protection, street maintenance, street lighting, street cleaning, traffic management and garbage collection. The Panama Canal Commission shall pay the Republic of Panama the sum of ten million United States dollars ($10,000,000) per annum for the foregoing services. It is agreed that every three years from the date that this Treaty enters into force, the costs involved in furnishing said services shall be reexamined to determine whether adjustment of the annual payment should be made because of inflation and other relevant factors affecting the cost of such services.

6. The Republic of Panama shall be responsible for providing, in all areas comprising the former Canal Zone,

services of a general jurisdictional nature such as customs and immigration, postal services, courts and licensing, in accordance with this Treaty and related agreements.

7. The United States of America and the Republic of
Panama shall establish a Panama Canal Consultative Committee, composed of an equal number of high-level representatives of the United States of America and the
Republic of Panama, and which may appoint such subcommittees as it may deem appropriate. This Committee shall
advise the United States of America and the Republic of
Panama on matters of policy affecting the Canal's operation. In view of both Parties' special interest in the
continuity and efficiency of the Canal operation in the
future, the Committee shall advise on matters such as
general tolls policy, employment and training policies
to increase the participation of Panamanian nationals in
the operation of the Canal, and international policies on
matters concerning the Canal. The Committee's recommendations shall be transmitted to the two Governments,
which shall give such recommendations full consideration
in the formulation of such policy decisions.

8. In addition to the participation of Panamanian
nationals at high management levels of the Panama Canal
Commission, as provided for in paragraph 3 of this Article, there shall be growing participation of Panamanian
nationals at all other levels and areas of employment in
the aforesaid commission, with the objective of preparing, in an orderly and efficient fashion, for the assumption by the Republic of Panama of full responsibility for
the management, operation and maintenance of the Canal
upon the termination of this Treaty.

9. The use of the areas, waters and installations
with respect to which the United States of America is
granted rights pursuant to this Article, and the rights
and legal status of United States Government agencies
and employees operating in the Republic of Panama pursuant to this Article, shall be governed by the Agreement
in Implementation of this Article, signed this date.

10. Upon entry into force of this Treaty, the United
States Government agencies known as the Panama Canal
Company and the Canal Zone Government shall cease to
operate within the territory of the Republic of Panama
that formerly constituted the Canal Zone.

ARTICLE IV

PROTECTION AND DEFENSE

1. The United States of America and the Republic of
Panama commit themselves to protect and defend the Panama Canal. Each Party shall act, in accordance with its
constitutional processes, to meet the danger resulting
from an armed attack or other actions which threaten the

security of the Panama Canal or of ships transiting it.

2. For the duration of this Treaty, the United States of America shall have primary responsibility to protect and defend the Canal. The rights of the United States of America to station, train, and move military forces within the Republic of Panama are described in the Agreement in Implementation of this Article, signed this date. The use of areas and installations and the legal status of the armed forces of the United States of America in the Republic of Panama shall be governed by the aforesaid Agreement.

3. In order to facilitate the participation and co-operation of the armed forces of both Parties in the protection and defense of the Canal, the United States of America and the Republic of Panama shall establish a Combined Board comprised of an equal number of senior military representatives of each Party. These representatives shall be charged by their respective governments with consulting and cooperating on all matters pertaining to the protection and defense of the Canal, and with planning for actions to be taken in concert for that purpose. Such combined protection and defense arrangements shall not inhibit the identity or lines of authority of the armed forces of the United States of America or the Republic of Panama. The Combined Board shall provide for coordination and cooperation concerning such matters as:

(a) The preparation of contingency plans for the protection and defense of the Canal based upon the cooperative efforts of the armed forces of both Parties;

(b) The planning and conduct of combined military exercises; and

(c) The conduct of United States and Panamanian military operations with respect to the protection and defense of the Canal.

4. The Combined Board shall, at five-year intervals throughout the duration of this Treaty, review the resources being made available by the two Parties for the protection and defense of the Canal. Also, the Combined Board shall make appropriate recommendations to the two Governments respecting projected requirements, the efficient utilization of available resources of the two Parties, and other matters of mutual interest with respect to the protection and defense of the Canal.

5. To the extent possible consistent with its primary responsibility for the protection and defense of the Panama Canal, the United States of America will endeavor to maintain its armed forces in the Republic of Panama in normal times at a level not in excess of that of the armed forces of the United States of America in the territory of the former Canal Zone immediately prior to the entry into force of this Treaty.

ARTICLE V

PRINCIPLE OF NON-INTERVENTION

Employees of the Panama Canal Commission, their dependents and designated contractors of the Panama Canal Commission, who are nationals of the United States of America, shall respect the laws of the Republic of Panama and shall abstain from any activity incompatible with the spirit of this Treaty. Accordingly, they shall abstain from any political activity in the Republic of Panama as well as from any intervention in the internal affairs of the Republic of Panama. The United States of America shall take all measures within its authority to ensure that the provisions of this Article are fulfilled.

ARTICLE VI

PROTECTION OF THE ENVIRONMENT

1. The United States of America and the Republic of Panama commit themselves to implement this Treaty in a manner consistent with the protection of the natural environment of the Republic of Panama. To this end, they shall consult and cooperate with each other in all appropriate ways to ensure that they shall give due regard to the protection and conservation of the environment.
2. A Joint Commission on the Environment shall be established with equal representation from the United States of America and the Republic of Panama, which shall periodically review the implementation of this Treaty and shall recommend as appropriate to the two Governments ways to avoid or, should this not be possible, to mitigate the adverse environmental impacts which might result from their respective actions pursuant to the Treaty.
3. The United States of America and the Republic of Panama shall furnish the Joint Commission on the Environment complete information on any action taken in accordance with this Treaty which, in the judgment of both, might have a significant effect on the environment. Such information shall be made available to the Commission as far in advance of the contemplated action as possible to facilitate the study by the Commission of any potential environmental problems and to allow for consideration of the recommendation of the Commission before the contemplated action is carried out.

ARTICLE VII

FLAGS

1. The entire territory of the Republic of Panama, including the areas the use of which the Republic of Panama makes available to the United States of America

pursuant to this Treaty and related agreements, shall be under the flag of the Republic of Panama, and consequently such flag always shall occupy the position of honor.

2. The flag of the United States of America may be displayed, together with the flag of the Republic of Panama, at the headquarters of the Panama Canal Commission, at the site of the Combined Board, and as provided in the Agreement in Implementation of Article IV of this Treaty.

3. The flag of the United States of America also may be displayed at other places and on some occasions, as agreed by both Parties.

ARTICLE VIII

PRIVILEGES AND IMMUNITIES

1. The installations owned or used by the agencies or instrumentalities of the United States of America operating in the Republic of Panama pursuant to this Treaty and related agreements, and their official archives and documents, shall be inviolable. The two Parties shall agree on procedures to be followed in the conduct of any criminal investigation at such locations by the Republic of Panama.

2. Agencies and instrumentalities of the Government of the United States of America operating in the Republic of Panama pursuant to this Treaty and related agreements shall be immune from the jurisdiction of the Republic of Panama.

3. In addition to such other privileges and immunities as are afforded to employees of the United States Government and their dependents pursuant to this Treaty, the United States of America may designate up to twenty officials of the Panama Canal Commission who, along with their dependents, shall enjoy the privileges and immunities accorded to diplomatic agents and their dependents under international law and practice. The United States of America shall furnish to the Republic of Panama a list of the names of said officials and their dependents, identifying the positions they occupy in the Government of the United States of America, and shall keep such list current at all times.

ARTICLE IX

APPLICABLE LAWS AND LAW ENFORCEMENT

1. In accordance with the provisions of this Treaty and related agreements, the law of the Republic of Panama shall apply in the areas made available for the use of the United States of America pursuant to this Treaty. The law of the Republic of Panama shall be applied to matters or events which occurred in the former Canal Zone prior to the entry into force of this Treaty only to the

extent specifically provided in prior treaties and agreements.

2. Natural or juridical persons who, on the date of entry into force of this Treaty, are engaged in business or non-profit activities at locations in the former Canal Zone may continue such business or activities at those locations under the same terms and conditions prevailing prior to the entry into force of this Treaty for a thirty-month transition period from its entry into force. The Republic of Panama shall maintain the same operating conditions as those applicable to the aforementioned enterprises prior to the entry into force of this Treaty in order that they may receive licenses to do business in the Republic of Panama subject to their compliance with the requirements of its law. Thereafter, such persons shall receive the same treatment under the law of the Republic of Panama as similar enterprises already established in the rest of the territory of the Republic of Panama without discrimination.

3. The rights of ownership, as recognized by the United States of America, enjoyed by natural or juridical private persons in buildings and other improvements to real property located in the former Canal Zone shall be recognized by the Republic of Panama in conformity with its laws.

4. With respect to buildings and other improvements to real property located in the Canal operating areas, housing areas or other areas subject to the licensing procedure established in Article IV of the Agreement in Implementation of Article III of this Treaty, the owners shall be authorized to continue using the land upon which their property is located in accordance with the procedures established in that Article.

5. With respect to buildings and other improvements to real property located in areas of the former Canal Zone to which the aforesaid licensing procedure is not applicable, or may cease to be applicable during the lifetime or upon termination of this Treaty, the owners may continue to use the land upon which their property is located, subject to the payment of a reasonable charge to the Republic of Panama. Should the Republic of Panama decide to sell such land, the owners of the buildings or other improvements located thereon shall be offered a first option to purchase such land at a reasonable cost. In the case of non-profit enterprises, such as churches and fraternal organizations, the cost of purchase will be nominal in accordance with the prevailing practice in the rest of the territory of the Republic of Panama.

6. If any of the aforementioned persons are required by the Republic of Panama to discontinue their activities or vacate their property for public purposes, they shall be compensated at fair market value by the Republic of Panama.

7. The provisions of paragraphs 2-6 above shall

apply to natural or juridical persons who have been engaged in business or non-profit activities at locations
in the former Canal Zone for at least six months prior
to the date of signature of this Treaty.

8. The Republic of Panama shall not issue, adopt or
enforce any law, decree, regulation, or international
agreement or take any other action which purports to regulate or would otherwise interfere with the exercise on
the part of the United States of America of any right
granted under this Treaty or related agreements.

9. Vessels transiting the Canal, and cargo, passengers and crews carried on such vessels shall be exempt
from any taxes, fees, or other charges by the Republic of
Panama. However, in the event such vessels call at a
Panamanian port, they may be assessed charges incident
thereto, such as charges for services provided to the
vessel. The Republic of Panama may also require the passengers and crew disembarking from such vessels to pay
such taxes, fees and charges as are established under
Panamanian law for persons entering its territory. Such
taxes, fees and charges shall be assessed on a nondis-
criminatory basis.

10. The United States of America and the Republic of
Panama will cooperate in taking such steps as may from
time to time be necessary to guarantee the security of
the Panama Canal Commission, its property, its employees
and their dependents, and their property, the Forces of
the United States of America and the members thereof, the
civilian component, and their property, and the contractors of the Panama Canal Commission and of the United
States Forces, their dependents, and their property. The
Republic of Panama will seek from its Legislative Branch
such legislation as may be needed to carry out the foregoing purposes and to punish any offenders.

11. The Parties shall conclude an agreement whereby
nationals of either State, who are sentenced by the
courts of the other State, and who are not domiciled
therein, may elect to serve their sentences in their
State of nationality.

ARTICLE X

EMPLOYMENT WITH THE PANAMA CANAL
COMMISSION

1. In exercising its rights and fulfilling its responsibilities as the employer, the United States of A-
merica shall establish employment and labor regulations
which shall contain the terms, conditions and prerequi-
sites for all categories of employees of the Panama Canal
Commission. These regulations shall be provided to the
Republic of Panama prior to their entry into force.

2. (a) The regulations shall establish a system of
preference when hiring employees, for Panamanian

applicants possessing the skills and qualifications required for employment by the Panama Canal Commission.
The United States of America shall endeavor to ensure
that the number of Panamanian nationals employed by the
Panama Canal Commission in relation to the total number
of its employees will conform to the proportion established for foreign enterprises under the law of the Republic of Panama.

(b) The terms and condition of employment to be
established will in general be no less favorable to persons already employed by the Panama Canal Company or Canal Zone Government prior to the entry into force of this
Treaty, than those in effect immediately prior to that
date.

3. (a) The United States of America shall establish
an employment policy for the Panama Canal Commission that
shall generally limit the recruitment of personnel outside the Republic of Panama to persons possessing requi-
site skills and qualifications which are not available in
the Republic of Panama.

(b) The United States of America will establish
training programs for Panamanian employees and apprenti-
ces in order to increase the number of Panamanian nationals qualified to assume positions with the Panama
Canal Commission, as positions become available.

(c) Within five years from the entry into force
of this Treaty, the number of United States nationals
employed by the Panama Canal Commission who were previously employed by the Panama Canal Company shall be at
least twenty percent less than the total number of United
States nationals working for the Panama Canal Company
immediately prior to the entry into force of this Treaty.

(d) The United States of America shall periodically inform the Republic of Panama, through the Coordi-
nating Committee, established pursuant to the Agreement
in Implementation of Article III of this Treaty, of
available positions within the Panama Canal Commission.
The Republic of Panama shall similarly provide the United
States of America any information it may have as to the
availability of Panamanian nationals claiming to have
skills and qualifications that might be required by the
Panama Canal Commission, in order that the United States
of America may take this information into account.

4. The United States of America will establish qualification standards for skills, training and experience
required by the Panama Canal Commission. In establishing
such standards, to the extent they include a requirement
for a professional license, the United States of America,
without prejudice to its right to require additional
professional skills and qualifications, shall recognize
the professional licenses issued by the Republic of
Panama.

5. The United States of America shall establish a
policy for the periodic rotation, at a maximum of every

five years, of United States citizen employees and other
non-Panamanian employees, hired after the entry into
force of this Treaty. It is recognized that certain exceptions to the said policy of rotation may be made for
sound administrative reasons, such as in the case of employees holding positions requiring certain non-transfer-
able or non-recruitable skills.

6. With regard to wages and fringe benefits, there
shall be no discrimination on the basis of nationality,
sex, or race. Payments by the Panama Canal Commission
of additional remuneration, or the provision of other
benefits, such as home leave benefits, to United States
nationals employed prior to entry into force of this
Treaty, or to persons of any nationality, including Panamanian nationals who are thereafter recruited outside
of the Republic of Panama and who change their place of
residence, shall not be considered to be discrimination
for the purpose of this paragraph.

7. Persons employed by the Panama Canal Company or
Canal Zone Government prior to the entry into force of
this Treaty, who are displaced from their employment as
a result of the discontinuance by the United States of
America of certain activities pursuant to this Treaty,
will be placed by the United States of America, to the
maximum extent feasible, in other appropriate jobs with
the Government of the United States in accordance with
United States Civil Service regulations. For such persons who are not United States nationals, placement efforts will be confined to United States Government activities located within the Republic of Panama. Likewise,
persons previously employed in activities for which the
Republic of Panama assumes responsibility as a result of
this Treaty will be continued in their employment to the
maximum extent feasible by the Republic of Panama. The
Republic of Panama shall, to the maximum extent feasible,
ensure that the terms and conditions of employment applicable to personnel employed in the activities for which
it assumes responsibility are no less favorable than
those in effect immediately prior to the entry into force
of this Treaty. Non-United States nationals employed by
the Panama Canal Company or Canal Zone Government prior
to the entry into force of this Treaty who are involun-
tarily separated from their positions because of the discontinuance of an activity by reason of this Treaty, who
are not entitled to an immediate annuity under the United
States Civil Service Retirement System, and for whom
continued employment in the Republic of Panama by the
Government of the United States of America is not prac-
ticable, will be provided special job placement assistance by the Republic of Panama for employment in positions for which they may be qualified by experience and
training.

8. The Parties agree to establish a system whereby
the Panama Canal Commission may, if deemed mutually

convenient or desirable by the two Parties, assign certain employees of the Panama Canal Commission, for a limited period of time, to assist in the operation of activities transferred to the responsibility of the Republic of Panama as a result of this Treaty or related agreements. The salaries and other costs of employment of any such persons assigned to provide such assistance shall be reimbursed to the United States of America by the Republic of Panama.

9. (a) The right of employees to negotiate collective contracts with the Panama Canal Commission is recognized. Labor relations with employees of the Panama Canal Commission shall be conducted in accordance with forms of collective bargaining established by the United States of America after consultation with employee unions.

(b) Employee unions shall have the right to affiliate with international labor organizations.

10. The United States of America will provide an appropriate early optional retirement program for all persons employed by the Panama Canal Company or Canal Zone Government immediately prior to the entry into force of this Treaty. In this regard, taking into account the unique circumstances created by the provisions of this Treaty, including its duration, and their effect upon such employees, the United States of America shall, with respect to them:

(a) determine that conditions exist which invoke applicable United States law permitting early retirement annuities and apply such law for a substantial period of the duration of the Treaty;

(b) seek special legislation to provide more liberal entitlement to, and calculation of, retirement annuities than is currently provided for by law.

ARTICLE XI

PROVISIONS FOR THE TRANSITION PERIOD

1. The Republic of Panama shall reassume plenary jurisdiction over the former Canal Zone upon entry into force of this Treaty and in accordance with its terms. In order to provide for an orderly transition to the full application of the jurisdictional arrangements established by this Treaty and related agreements, the provisions of this Article shall become applicable upon the date this Treaty enters into force, and shall remain in effect for thirty calendar months. The authority granted in this Article to the United States of America for this transition period shall supplement, and is not intended to limit, the full application and effect of the rights and authority granted to the United States of America elsewhere in this Treaty and in related agreements.

2. During this transition period, the criminal and

civil laws of the United States of America shall apply
concurrently with those of the Republic of Panama in
certain of the areas and installations made available for
the use of the United States of America pursuant to this
Treaty, in accordance with the following provisions:
(a) The Republic of Panama permits the authorities of the United States of America to have the primary
right to exercise criminal jurisdiction over United
States citizen employees of the Panama Canal Commission
and their dependents, and members of the United States
Forces and civilian component and their dependents, in
the following cases:
(i) for any offense committed during the
transition period within such areas and installations,
and
(ii) for any offense committed prior to that
period in the former Canal Zone.
The Republic of Panama shall have the primary right
to exercise jurisdiction over all other offenses committed by such persons, except as otherwise provided in this
Treaty and related agreements or as may be otherwise
agreed.
(b) Either Party may waive its primary right to
exercise jurisdiction in a specific case or category of
cases.
3. The United States of America shall retain the
right to exercise jurisdiction in criminal cases relating
to offenses committed prior to the entry into force of
this Treaty in violation of the laws applicable in the
former Canal Zone.
4. For the transition period, the United States of
America shall retain police authority and maintain a
police force in the aforementioned areas and installations. In such areas, the police authorities of the United States of America may take into custody any person
not subject to their primary jurisdiction if such person
is believed to have committed or to be committing an offense against applicable laws or regulations, and shall
promptly transfer custody to the police authorities of
the Republic of Panama. The United States of America and
the Republic of Panama shall establish joint police pa-
trols in agreed areas. Any arrests conducted by a joint
patrol shall be the responsibility of the patrol member
or members representing the Party having primary jurisdiction over the person or persons arrested.
5. The courts of the United States of America and
related personnel, functioning in the former Canal Zone
immediately prior to the entry into force of this Treaty,
may continue to function during the transition period
for the judicial enforcement of the jurisdiction to be
exercised by the United States of America in accordance
with this Article.
6. In civil cases, the civilian courts of the United
States of America in the Republic of Panama shall have no

jurisdiction over new cases of a private civil nature,
but shall retain full jurisdiction during the transition
period to dispose of any civil cases, including admiralty
cases, already instituted and pending before the courts
prior to the entry into force of this Treaty.

7. The laws, regulations, and administrative authority of the United States of America applicable in the
former Canal Zone immediately prior to the entry into
force of this Treaty shall, to the extent not inconsistent with this Treaty and related agreements, continue
in force for the purpose of the exercise by the United
States of America of law enforcement and judicial jurisdiction only during the transition period. The United
States of America may amend, repeal or otherwise change
such laws, regulations and administrative authority. The
two Parties shall consult concerning procedural and sub-
stantive matters relative to the implementation of this
Article, including the disposition of cases pending at
the end of the transition period and, in this respect,
may enter into appropriate agreements by an exchange of
notes or other instrument.

8. During this transition period, the United States
of America may continue to incarcerate individuals in the
areas and installations made available for the use of the
United States of America by the Republic of Panama pursuant to this Treaty and related agreements, or to transfer them to penal facilities in the United States of
America to serve their sentences.

ARTICLE XII

A SEA-LEVEL CANAL OR A THIRD LANE OF LOCKS

1. The United States of America and the Republic of
Panama recognize that a sea-level canal may be important
for international navigation in the future. Consequently, during the duration of this Treaty, both Parties
commit themselves to study jointly the feasibility of a
sea-level canal in the Republic of Panama, and in the
event they determine that such a waterway is necessary,
they shall negotiate terms, agreeable to both Parties,
for its construction.

2. The United States of America and the Republic of
Panama agree on the following:

(a) No new interoceanic canal shall be constructed in the territory of the Republic of Panama during the
duration of this Treaty, except in accordance with the
provisions of this Treaty, or as the two Parties may
otherwise agree; and

(b) During the duration of this Treaty, the United States of America shall not negotiate with third
States for the right to construct an interoceanic canal
on any other route in the Western Hemisphere, except as
the two Parties may otherwise agree.

3. The Republic of Panama grants to the United States of America the right to add a third lane of locks to the existing Panama Canal. This right may be exercised at any time during the duration of this Treaty, provided that the United States of America has delivered to the Republic of Panama copies of the plans for such construction.

4. In the event the United States of America exercises the right granted in paragraph 3 above, it may use for that purpose, in addition to the areas otherwise made available to the United States of America pursuant to this Treaty, such other areas as the two Parties may agree upon. The terms and conditions applicable to Canal operating areas made available by the Republic of Panama for the use of the United States of America pursuant to Article III of this Treaty shall apply in a similar manner to such additional areas.

5. In the construction of the aforesaid works, the United States of America shall not use nuclear excavation techniques without the previous consent of the Republic of Panama.

ARTICLE XIII

PROPERTY TRANSFER AND ECONOMIC
PARTICIPATION BY THE REPUBLIC OF PANAMA

1. Upon termination of this Treaty, the Republic of Panama shall assume total responsibility for the management, operation, and maintenance of the Panama Canal, which shall be turned over in operating condition and free of liens and debts, except as the two Parties may otherwise agree.

2. The United States of America transfers, without charge, to the Republic of Panama all right, title and interest the United States of America may have with respect to all real property, including non-removable improvements thereon, as set forth below:

(a) Upon the entry into force of this Treaty, the Panama Railroad and such property that was located in the former Canal Zone but that is not within the land and water areas the use of which is made available to the United States of America pursuant to this Treaty. However, it is agreed that the transfer on such date shall not include buildings and other facilities, except housing, the use of which is retained by the United States of America pursuant to this Treaty and related agreements, outside such areas;

(b) Such property located in an area or a portion thereof at such time as the use by the United States of America of such area or portion thereof ceases pursuant to agreement between the two Parties.

(c) Housing units made available for occupancy by members of the Armed Forces of the Republic of Panama in accordance with paragraph 5(b) of Annex B to the Agreement in Implementation of Article IV of this Treaty at such time as such units are made available to the Republic of Panama.

(d) Upon termination of this Treaty, all real property and non-removable improvements that were used by the United States of America for the purposes of this Treaty and related agreements and equipment related to the management, operation and maintenance of the Canal remaining in the Republic of Panama.

3. The Republic of Panama agrees to hold the United States of America harmless with respect to any claims which may be made by third parties relating to rights, title and interest in such property.

4. The Republic of Panama shall receive, in addition, from the Panama Canal Commission a just and equitable return on the national resources which it has dedicated to the efficient management, operation, maintenance, protection and defense of the Panama Canal, in accordance with the following:

(a) An annual amount to be paid out of Canal operating revenues computed at a rate of thirty hundredths of a United States dollar ($0.30) per Panama Canal net ton, or its equivalency, for each vessel transiting the Canal after the entry into force of this Treaty, for which tolls are charged. The rate of thirty hundredths of a United States dollar ($0.30) per Panama Canal net ton, or its equivalency, will be adjusted to reflect changes in the United States wholesale price index for total manufactured goods during biennial periods. The first adjustment shall take place five years after entry into force of this Treaty, taking into account the changes that occurred in such price index during the preceding two years. Thereafter, successive adjustments shall take place at the end of each biennial period. If the United States of America should decide that another indexing method is preferable, such method shall be proposed to the Republic of Panama and applied if mutually agreed.

(b) A fixed annuity of ten million United States dollars ($10,000,000) to be paid out of Canal operating revenues. This amount shall constitute a fixed expense of the Panama Canal Commission.

(c) An annual amount of up to ten million United States dollars ($10,000,000) per year, to be paid out of Canal operating revenues to the extent that such revenues exceed expenditures of the Panama Canal Commission including amounts paid pursuant to this Treaty. In the event Canal operating revenues in any year do not produce a surplus sufficient to cover this payment, the unpaid balance shall be paid from operating surpluses in future years in a manner to be mutually agreed.

ARTICLE XIV

SETTLEMENT OF DISPUTES

In the event that any question should arise between the Parties concerning the interpretation of this Treaty or related agreements, they shall make every effort to resolve the matter through consultation in the appropriate committees established pursuant to this Treaty and related agreements, or, if appropriate, through diplomatic channels. In the event the Parties are unable to resolve a particular matter through such means, they may, in appropriate cases, agree to submit the matter to conciliation, mediation, arbitration, or such other procedure for the peaceful settlement of the dispute as they may mutually deem appropriate.

DONE at Washington, this 7th day of September, 1977, in duplicate, in the English and Spanish languages, both texts being equally authentic.

ANNEX

PROCEDURES FOR THE CESSATION OR TRANSFER
OF ACTIVITIES CARRIED OUT BY THE PANAMA
CANAL COMPANY AND THE CANAL ZONE
GOVERNMENT AND ILLUSTRATIVE LIST
OF THE FUNCTIONS THAT MAY BE PERFORMED
BY THE PANAMA CANAL COMMISSION

1. The laws of the Republic of Panama shall regulate the exercise of private economic activities within the areas made available by the Republic of Panama for the use of the United States of America pursuant to this Treaty. Natural or juridical persons who, at least six months prior to the date of signature of this Treaty, were legally established and engaged in the exercise of economic activities in the former Canal Zone, may continue such activities in accordance with the provisions of paragraphs 2-7 of Article IX of this Treaty.
2. The Panama Canal Commission shall not perform governmental or commercial functions as stipulated in paragraph 4 of this Annex, provided, however, that this shall not be deemed to limit in any way the right of the United State of America to perform those functions that may be necessary for the efficient management, operation and maintenance of the Canal.
3. It is understood that the Panama Canal Commission, in the exercise of the rights of the United States of America with respect to the management, operation and maintenance of the Canal, may perform functions such as are set forth below by way of illustration:
   a. Management of the Canal enterprise.
   b. Aids to navigation in Canal waters and in proximity thereto.

c. Control of vessel movement.

d. Operation and maintenance of the locks.

e. Tug service for the transit of vessels and dredging for the piers and docks of the Panama Canal Commission.

f. Control of the water levels in Gatun, Alajuela (Madden) and Miraflores Lakes.

g. Non-commercial transportation services in Canal waters.

h. Meterological and hydrographic services.

i. Admeasurement.

j. Non-commercial motor transport and maintenance.

k. Industrial security through the use of watchmen.

l. Procurement and warehousing.

m. Telecommunications.

n. Protection of the environment by preventing and controlling the spillage of oil and substances harmful to human or animal life and of the ecological equilibrium in areas used in operation of the Canal and the anchorages.

o. Non-commercial vessel repair.

p. Air conditioning services in Canal installations.

r. Engineering design, construction and maintenance of Panama Canal Commission installations.

s. Dredging of the Canal channel, terminal ports and adjacent waters.

t. Control of the banks and stabilizing of the slopes of the Canal.

u. Non-commercial handling of cargo on the piers and docks of the Panama Canal Commission.

v. Maintenance of public areas of the Panama Canal Commission, such as parks and gardens.

w. Generation of electric power.

x. Purification and supply of water.

y. Marine salvage in Canal waters.

z. Such other functions as may be necessary or appropriate to carry out, in conformity with this Treaty and related agreements, the rights and responsibilities of the United States of America with respect to the management, operation and maintenance of the Panama Canal.

4. The following activities and operations carried out by the Panama Canal Company and the Canal Zone Government shall not be carried out by the Panama Canal Commission, effective upon the dates indicated herein:

(a) Upon the date of entry into force of this Treaty:

(i) Wholesale and retail sales, including those through commissaries, food stores, department stores, optical shops and pastry shops;

(ii) The production of food and drink, including milk products and bakery products;

(iii) The operation of public restaurants and cafeterias and the sale of articles through vending machines;

(iv) The operation of movie theaters, bowling alleys, pool rooms and other recreational and amusement facilities for the use of which a charge is payable;

(v) The operation of laundry and dry cleaning plants other than those operated for official use;

(vi) The repair and service of privately owned automobiles or the sale of petroleum or lubricants thereto, including the operation of gasoline stations, repair garages and tire repair and recapping facilities, and the repair and service of other privately owned property, including appliances, electronic devices, boats, motors, and furniture;

(vii) The operation of cold storage and freezer plants other than those operated for official use;

(viii) The operation of freight houses other than those operated for official use;

(ix) The operation of commercial services to and supply of privately owned and operated vessels, including the construction of vessels, the sale of petroleum and lubricants and the provision of water, tug services not related to the Canal or other United States Government operations, and repair of such vessels, except in situations where repairs may be necessary to remove disabled vessels from the Canal;

(x) Printing services other than for official use;

(xi) Maritime transportation for the use of the general public;

(xii) Health and medical services provided to individuals, including hospitals, leprosariums, veterinary, mortuary and cemetery services;

(xiii) Educational services not for professional training, including schools and libraries;

(xiv) Postal services;

(xv) Immigration, customs and quarantine controls, except those measures necessary to ensure the sanitation of the Canal;

(xvi) Commercial pier and dock services, such as the handling of cargo and passengers; and

(xvii) Any other commercial activity of a similar nature, not related to the management, operation or maintenance of the Canal.

(b) Within thirty calendar months from the date of entry into force of this Treaty, governmental services such as:

(i) Police;

(ii) Courts; and

(iii) Prison system.

5. (a) With respect to those activities or functions described in paragraph 4 above, or otherwise agreed upon by the two Parties, which are to be assumed by the

Government of the Republic of Panama or by private persons subject to its authority, the two Parties shall
consult prior to the discontinuance of such activities
or functions by the Panama Canal Commission to develop
appropriate arrangements for the orderly transfer and
continued efficient operation or conduct thereof.

(b) In the event that appropriate arrangements
cannot be arrived at to ensure the continued performance
of a particular activity or function described in paragraph 4 above which is necessary to the efficient management, operation or maintenance of the Canal, the Panama
Canal Commission may, to the extent consistent with the
other provisions of this Treaty and related agreements,
continue to perform such activity or function until such
arrangements can be made.

Selected Bibliography

Allison, Graham T. "Conceptual Models and the Cuban Missile Crisis." American Political Science Review 63 (September 1969):689-718.
Baxter, Richard R. and Doris Carroll. The Panama Canal: Background Papers and Proceedings of the Sixth Hammarskjold Forum. Dobbs Ferry, N.Y.: Oceana Publications, Inc., 1965.
Biesanz, John B. and Mavis Biesanz. The People of Panama. New York: Columbia University Press, 1955.
Biesanz, John B. and Luke M. Smith. "Panamanian Politics." Journal of Politics 14 (August 1952):386-402.
Bray, Wayne D. The Common Law Zone in Panama. San Juan: Inter-American University of Puerto Rico, 1977.
Cochrane, James D. "Costa Rica, Panama and Central American Economic Integration." Journal of Inter-American Studies and World Affairs 7 (July 1965):331-44.
Costrell, E. S. "U.S. Policy towards Panama, 1903-Present." Department of State Bulletin 70 (April 22, 1974):438-40.
Crabb, Cecil V., Jr., and Pat M. Holt. Invitation to Struggle: Congress, the President and Foreign Policy. Washington, D.C.: Congressional Quarterly Press, 1980.
Dubois, Jules. Danger Over Panama. New York: Bobbs-Merrill Co., 1964.
Ealy, Lawrence O. Yanqui Politics and the Isthmian Canal. University Park, Penn.: Pennsylvania State University Press, 1971.
_____. The Republic of Panama in World Affairs, 1903-1950. Philadelphia: University of Pennsylvania Press, 1951.
Farrell, R. Barry, ed. Approaches to Comparative and International Politics. Evanston, Ill: Northwestern University Press, 1966.
Franck, Thomas M. and Edward Weisband. Foreign Policy by Congress. New York: Oxford University Press, 1979.
_____. "Panama Paralysis." Foreign Policy 21 (Winter 1975-76).
Goldrich, Daniel. Sons of the Establishment: Elite Youth in Panama and Costa Rica. Chicago: Rand McNally & Co., 1966.
Halperin, Morton H. and Arnold Kanter, eds. Readings in American Foreign Policy: A Bureaucratic Perspective. Boston: Little, Brown, 1973.

Hanrieder, Wolfram F. "Dissolving International Politics: Reflections on the Nation-State." American Political Science Review 72 (December 1978):1276-87.
_____. West German Foreign Policy 1949-1963: International Pressure and Domestic Response. Palo Alto: Stanford University Press, 1967.
Howard, Harry N. Military Government in the Panama Canal Zone. Norman: University of Oklahoma Press, 1931.
Hoyt, Edwin C. "Law and Politics in the Revision of Treaties Affecting the Panama Canal." Virginia Journal of International Law 6 (April 1966).
Kinzer, Stephen. "The New Panama." The New Republic (February 10, 1979), pp. 21-23.
Kissinger, Henry A. American Foreign Policy. New York: W. W. Norton and Co., 1969.
Klette, Immanuel J. From Atlantic to Pacific: A New Interocean Canal. New York: Harper & Row, 1967.
Langley, Lester. "U.S.-Panamanian Relations Since 1941." Journal of Inter-American Studies 12 (July 1970):339-66.
_____. "The World Crisis and the Good Neighbor Policy in Panama, 1936-1941." Americas 24 (October 1967).
LaFeber, Walter. The Panama Canal: The Crisis in Historical Perspective. New York: Oxford University Press, 1979.
Liss, Sheldon B. The Canal: Aspects of United States-Panamanian Relations. South Bend, In.: University of Notre Dame Press, 1967.
Mallett, John W. "Group Conflict in the Panamanian Coup d'Etat of 1968." Master's essay, University of Texas at Austin, 1972.
McCain, William. The United States and the Republic of Panama. Durham, N.C.: Duke University Press, 1937.
McCullough, David. The Path Between the Seas: The Creation of the Panama Canal, 1870-1914. New York: Simon and Schuster, 1977.
Mellander, G. A. The United States in Panamanian Politics. Danville, Ill.: The Interstate Printers & Publishers, Inc., 1971.
Pippin, Larry L. The Remón Era: An Analysis of a Decade of Events in Panama, 1947-1957. Palo Alto: Stanford University Press, 1964.
Ropp, Steve C. "Ratification of the Panama Canal Treaties: The Muted Debate." World Affairs 141 (1978).
_____. "Military Reformism in Panama: New Directions or Old Inclinations?" Caribbean Studies 12 (October 1972).
Rosenau, James N. "Foreign Policy as Adaptive Behavior: Some Preliminary Notes for a Theoretical Model." Comparative Politics 2 (1970).
Rosenau, James N., ed. Linkage Politics: Essays on the Convergence of National and International Systems. New York: The Free Press, 1969.
Rosenfeld, Stephen S. "The Panama Negotiations—A Close-Run Thing." Foreign Affairs 54 (October 1975).
Roshco, Bernard. "The Polls: Polling on Panama—Si; Don't Know; Hell, No!" Public Opinion Quarterly 42 (Winter 1978)551-62.

U.S., Congress, House, Committee on Foreign Affairs. Hearings before the Subcommittee on Inter-American Affairs on H.R. 74, 154, 156 and others, 92d Cong., 1st sess., 1971.

U.S., Congress, House, House Committee on Foreign Affairs. Report on United States Relations with Panama, H.R. #2218, 86th Cong., 2d sess., 1960.

U.S., Congress, House, Committee on Merchant Marine and Fisheries. Hearings before a subcommittee of the House Committee on Merchant Marine and Fisheries, 95th Cong., 1st sess., 1977.

U.S., Congress, House, Committee on Merchant Marines and Fisheries, Panama Canal Finances. Hearings before the Subcommittee on on Panama Canal of the Committee on Merchant Marines and Fisheries, H.R. #12641, 94th Cong., 2d sess., 1976.

U.S., Congress, House, Committee on Merchant Marine and Fisheries. Hearings before the Subcommittee on Panama Canal, 91st Cong., 2d sess., 1970.

U.S., Congress, Senate, Committee on Foreign Relations. Background Documents Relating to the Panama Canal, 95th Cong., 1st sess., 1977.

U.S., Congress, Senate, Committee on Foreign Relations. A Chronology of Events Relating to Panama Canal, by Congressional Research Service, Library of Congress, 95th Cong., 1st sess., 1977.

U.S., Congress, Senate, Committee on Foreign Relations. Panama Canal Treaties. Hearings before the Committee on Foreign Relations, Executive N, 5 Parts, 95th Cong., 1st sess., 1977.

U.S., Congress, Senate, Committee on Foreign Relations. Senate Debate on the Panama Canal Treaties: A Compendium of Major Statements, Documents, Record Votes and Relevant Events, by Congressional Research Service, Library of Congress, February 1979.

U.S., Congress, Senate, Committee on the Judiciary. Panama Canal Treaty (Disposition of United States Territory). Hearings before the Subcommittee on Separation of Powers of the Committee on the Judiciary, 95th Cong., 1st sess, 1977.

Index

Adair, Charles W., Jr., 45
Adaptive behavior, 55, 56
    convulsive, 9, 10
    definition, 9
Agency for International Development, 92, 101, 102, 205
Agreements 1974, 2, 3, 142, 143, 144
Ahumada, Adolfo, 159
Air Panama, 92
Air space, 91
Alaskan oil, 271
Aleman, Roberto, 51
Allen, James, 195, 196, 201, 210, 211, 226, 228, 230
    amendment, 235
Allen, Richard, 157
Alliance for Progress, 37, 39
Allison, Graham, 12
    bureaucratic politics model, 8
    Essence of Decision, 8
    rational policy model, 8
Amador, Manuel, 19, 68
Amendments, 222, 224, 228, 231
    housekeeping, 251
    killer, 228, 231, 235, 245, 251
    leadership, 231, 246
American Conservative Union, 215, 250
American corporations, 86
American Council for World Freedom, 215, 247
American Enterprise Institute Defense Review, 207
American Institute of Merchant Shipping, 183, 198

American Legion, 183, 250
American Security Council, 215, 250
Amnesty International, 225
Anderson, Jack, 154
Anderson, Robert, 44, 142, 143
Annuity, 26, 30, 85, 95, 96
Anti-colonialism, 121, 132, 134, 135
Anti-racism, 121
Aquilar, Andres, 191
Aragon, Leopoldo, 214
Aragon, Rose Marie, 214
Argentina, 132
Arias, Arnulfo, 28, 44, 51, 53, 54, 55, 70, 71, 79, 89, 142, 193
    impeachment 1951, 44
    National Union candidate, 53
Arias, Harmodia, 26
Aristocracy, 120
Armed Services Committee, 228, 257
Assembly of Corregimientos, 149, 158, 163, 190, 191, 210, 216, 220, 255
Atlantic-Pacific Interoceanic Canal Study Commission, 97, 105, 108, 109, 112, 115, 170, 172
Atomic Energy Commission, 110
Australia, 133

Baker, Howard, 220, 222, 225, 245, 253
Balboa Heights, 38
Balboa Heights High School, 97
    U.S. students, 40

Baldwin, Hanson, 207
Barletta, Nicholas, 152, 159
Battelle Memorial.Institute, 116
Bauman, Robert 263, 266
Beckel, Robert 252
Bell, Griffin, 208
Bell, Morey, 147, 150
Benedetti, Eloy, 50
Biddle, Alexander, 14
Bidlack-Mallorino Treaty, 15,
    16, 21, 32
Biesanz, John, 79
Biesanz, Mavis, 79
Bilateral linkages, 59
Bogota, 20
Bolivar, Simon, 14
Borah, Hugh, 24
Bowen, David, 261
Boyd-Roosevelt Highway, 100
Boyd, Aquilino, 36, 41, 124,
    125, 133, 137, 151, 152,
    153, 154
Bray, Wayne D., 15, 32
Bridge of the Americas, 38
Broad Front of Lawyers, 192
Brown, George, 149, 181, 200,
    207
Brown, Harold, 207, 250
Bryan-Chamarro Treaty 1916,
    112, 170
Brzezinski, Zbigniew, 250
Bunau-Varilla, Philippe, 19,
    20, 21
Bunker, Ellsworth, 2, 41, 137,
    143, 147, 148, 149, 151,
    152, 153, 155, 157, 178,
    179, 181, 182, 250
Bureaucratic politics model, 8
Bush, George, 125, 126, 131
Business & Professional Commit-
    tee for a New Panama Canal
    Treaty, 183
Byrd, Robert, 200, 222, 228,
    230, 245, 247, 253, 259
Byrnes, James, 28

Callaway, Howard, 180
Campesinos, 73
Canal, 67, 137
    alternatives, 11
    construction costs, 84
    decline in traffic, 271
    defense installations, 84
    international control, 120

Isthmian Commission, 60, 61
    jobs, 85
    land acquisition, 84
    Panama Canal Act 1912, 62
    proposed Third Locks, 172, 184
    replacement cost, 84
    revenues, 84, 111
    tolls, 48, 85, 94, 95
    traffic limitations, 106
    transits, 197
    wartime control, 264
Canal Company, 101, 106, 168
Canal issues, 10
    defense, 222
    human rights, 223, 224
    internationalization, 270
    property transfer, 264, 266
    security, 256
    wartime control, 264
Canal Treaty, 234, 258
    administration, 234
    legal jurisdiction, 234
    operations, 234
Canal Treaty debates, 228, 230,
    231, 256, 257
    closed, 229
Canal Zone, 2, 23, 59, 63, 65,
    67, 68, 73, 80, 100, 126,
    172, 184
    air space, 91
    American law, 87
    civil government, 62
    commissaries, 23, 24, 28, 63,
    68, 101
    depopulation policy, 63
    employees' wages and benefits,
    265
    government, 61, 66, 106
    jurisdiction, 88
    labor unions, 183, 214
    leases, 28
    legal jurisdiction, 87
    license plates, 92
    military governor, 87
    penitentiary, 88
    police, 40, 43
    schools, 97
    smuggling, 28, 66
    students, 40
    training sites, Jungle Survival
    School, 90
    United States courts, 87
    United States postal system, 92
    1964 riots, 55, 70, 122

Canal Zone Bus Company, 98
Canal Zone Commissary Incident,
    88
Carter-Ford debate, 153
Carter, Hodding III, 212
Carter, Jimmy, 153, 156, 158,
    163, 184, 189, 195, 215,
    216, 217, 227, 245, 259
Case, Clifford, 155, 204
Castro, Fidel, 60, 77, 151, 209
Central American Common Market,
    66, 120
Central Intelligence Agency,
    54, 147
Cerro Colorado, 73
Chapman, Guillermo, 51
Charlton, Milton, 207
Chiari, Roberto, 41
    inaugural speech, 37
    U.S. visit, 38
Chicago Tribune, 46, 170
Chiefs of Naval Operations,
    202, 210
Chile, 131
China, 132
Chiriqui, 24
Christian Democratic Party, 53
Christopher, Warren, 250, 253
Church of the Brethren, 214
Church, Frank, 212, 222, 261
Cinco de Mayo Plaza, 259
CINCSOUTH, 62
Civic Councils, 213
Clayton-Bulwer Treaty, 16, 17,
    32
Clements, William Jr., 149,
    180, 181
Coalition to Save the Panama
    Canal, 250
Colombia, 17, 22, 51, 131, 148
Colón, 20, 66, 105
Colón Free Trade Zone, 73, 144
Colonialism, 129, 270
Commercial activity, 101
Commission, Isthmian Canal, 60,
    61
Committee for Continued U.S.
    Control of the Panama
    Canal, 184
Committee for Ratification of
    Panama Canal Treaties, 246
Committee of Americans for the
    Canal Treaties, 219, 220

Committee of the Whole, 228, 234
Communist Party, 193
Comparative Studies, 5
CONEP, 155
Conference Committee, 262
Conference Report, 264
    First, 264
    Second, 265, 266
Congress, 168, 171, 178, 179
    reaction, 11
    unrepresentative of Zonians, 8
Congressional Record, 46, 229
Conservative caucus, 250
Constitutional Reform Commission,
    74
Contadora Island, 147
Costa Rica, 25, 132, 148
Costa Rica-Panama boundary dis-
    pute, 24
Council of Foreign Relations, 50,
    51
Council of the Americas, 199, 200,
    252
Crane, Phillip, 201
Cranston, Alan, 171
Cristobal, 38
Cuba, 131, 148, 184, 263
    economic boycott, 122
Cuban Missile Crisis 1962, 106
Cuna Indians, 194

Darien, 117
Declaration of Ilatelolco, 138
DeConcini condition, 233, 234,
    237, 238, 245, 246, 251, 252,
    253, 258
Defense of Canal issue, 222
Defense Department, 152, 177, 178,
    179, 180, 181, 208, 265, 266
    International Security Affairs,
    167
Defense facilities, 111
Defense sites, 28
    agreement 1942, 28, 29
Deliberative behavior definition,
    9
Dingley Tariff, 23
Discrimination, 98, 102
Dole amendments, 224, 235
Dole, Robert, 209, 211, 217, 224,
    230
Dolvin, Welborn, 151
Domestic influence on foreign
    policy, 5

Domestic interests, 83
Domestic support, 86
Domestic system, 5
Dornan, Robert, 198
Draft treaties 1967, 66, 93, 96
Drug smuggling, 100, 217, 229
Drug traffic, 173
Dual-flag policy, 39, 40
Dubois, Jules, 32
Dulles, John Foster, 31
Dungan, Ralph, 41

Ealy, Lawrence, 32
Ecological opponents, 115
Economic aid, 85, 167, 253
Economic Commission for Latin
    America, U.N., 94, 196
Eisenhower-Remón Treaty, 30
Eisenhower, Dwight, 29, 36, 172
Eisenhower, Milton, 31, 36, 172
El Salvador, 131
Election, Panama 1964, 44
Elections, 74
Eleta, Fernando, 45, 50, 51
Ellsworth, Robert, 180
Emergency Task Force on the
    Panama Canal, 215
Employment for Panamanians, 47
Enclave psychology, 96
Entrepreneurial elite, 65
Escobar, Romulo B., 155, 156,
    157, 158, 159, 160, 210,
    216, 217, 234
Espriella, Ricardo de la, 271
Ethnic composition, 98
Expeditious passage, 160, 206,
    216
Export-Import Bank, 201, 205
Expropriations, 23
Extradition, 89

Fabrega, Octavio, 38, 50
Falk, Richard, 218
Farland, Joseph S., 38, 39
Farrell, Barry, 12
Federation of Panamanian
    Students, 193
Federation of Revolutionary
    Students, 150
Federation of Trade Unions of
    Panama, 128
Figueres, Jose, 132
Filibuster, 211
Filos-Hines Treaty 1947, 52

Fish, Hamilton, 215
Flag incident, 40
Flag issue, 160
Fleming, Robert J., 38, 40, 41
Flood, Daniel, 79, 171, 172, 176,
    184, 201, 202
Ford, Gerald, 152, 154, 181, 182,
    183, 184, 200
Foreign Affairs Committee, 168
Foreign Policy, 5, 11
    product of domestic political
    system, 11
Foreign policy establishment, 256
France, 133
Franck, Thomas, 12, 169
Free medical care, 63
Freedom House, 202, 210, 225
French Canal Company, 18

Galeta Island, 231
Galindo, Lewis, 267
Gallegos, Father Hector, 74
Gallup Poll, 227
Gatun Lake, 106
Geisel, Ernesto, 189
General Assembly, 122, 123
Glenn, John, 212
Goethals, G. W., 61, 78
    appeal from, 62
    arbitrary authority, 61
Goldwater, Barry, 184, 224
Gonzales, Geraldo, 153
Good Neighbor Policy, 26, 27, 65
Griffin, James, 206
Griffin, Robert, 203, 204, 220,
    225
Gringo, 63
Guadalupe-Hidalgo, Treaty of, 15,
    32
Guardia Nacional, 69, 70, 78
    Remón, Jose Antonio, 29
Guardia, Ernesto de la, 98
Guevaria, Carlos Lopez, 117, 147,
    149, 212, 237, 267

Halperin, Morton, 12
Hanrieder, Wolfram, 10, 12
    definition of penetration, 10
Hansell, Herbert, 208
Hansen Amendment, 261
Harris Poll, 246, 247
Hay-Herran Treaty, 18, 21
    Spooner Act, 19
    United States pressure, 19

Hay-Pauncefote Treaty, 18
Hay/Bunau-Varilla Treaty, 32,
    60, 65, 68, 102
    article 3, 21
    article 2, 27
Hay, John, 21
Hayes, Margaret, 197
Head-of-line privilege, 216,
    217, 222
Helms, Jesse, 196, 227
Hennessy, John, 99
Hickenlooper Amendment, 130
Hilton, Ronald, 64
Hollings, Ernest, 213
Hotel Tivoli, 64
House Appropriations Committee,
    155
House enabling legislation, 170
House Foreign Affairs Commit-
    tee, 171, 177, 260
    report, 37
House Judiciary Committee, 260
House of Representatives, 36,
    195, 206, 260
    closed session, 263
    enabling legislation, 170
    implementing legislation,
    206
House Post Office and Civil
    Service Committee, 260
House Rules Committee, 261,
    263
House Subcommittee on the
    Panama Canal, 99, 151
Hoyt, Edwin C., 22, 33
HR 111, 260, 261
HR 1716, 260, 261
Huertas, Esteban, 68
Huertematte, Robert, 267
Hull-Alfaro Treaty, 27, 65,
    172
    article 10, 65, 66
    provisions, 26
Hull, Cordell, 26
Human rights issue, 60, 223,
    224
Humphrey, Hubert, 203, 204
Humphrey, Muriel, 223

Illueca, Jorge, 44, 128, 149,
    151, 237
Immigration quotas, 265
Imperialism, 84, 85, 102

Implementing problems, 268, 270,
    271
Implementing legislation, 259,
    263, 264, 266, 269
    threats from labor unions, 265
Independent Lawyers Movement, 192
Indonesia, 133
Ingersoll, Robert, 181
Instituto Nacional (Panamanian
    High School), 40
Instruments of Ratification, 259
Inter American Conference 1825,
    14
Inter-American affairs, 137
Inter-American Development Bank,
    99
Inter-American Human Rights Com-
    mission, 225
Inter-American Peace Committee,
    41
Inter-American Press Association,
    74, 191
International Commission of
    Jurists, 43
International law, 87
International Organization and
    Movements, 137
International Research Associates,
    218
Intervention, 210, 234
Irwin, John, 45, 143
Isthmian Canal Commission, 60, 61,
    62, 63
    chairman, 61
    chief engineer, 61
    governor, 61
    Spooner Act 1902, 61

Jefe Maximo, 75
Job discrimination, 133, 134
Johnson, Lyndon, 40, 41, 43, 45,
    93, 97, 105, 142, 172
Joint Chiefs of Staff, 199, 200,
    202, 208
Jordan, Hamilton, 226, 246
Jorden, Vernon, 92, 152, 154, 213
Jorden, William, 147, 208
Judiciary, 67
Junta, 71, 72
Jurisdiction, 48
Justice Department, 253

Kanter, Arnold, 12

Kellogg-Alfaro Treaty, 25
Kennedy, John, 37, 38
  assasination, 39
  Latin America, 1
Kissinger-Tack Agreement,
  145, 146, 147, 154, 174,
  178, 180, 259
Kissinger, Henry, 1, 12, 137,
  138, 146, 148, 149, 150,
  151, 179, 180, 181, 182
  200, 213, 215
  Agreement, 2
  Middle East, 1
  Nixon's foreign policy, 1
  political scientist, 6
  remarks at Governors'
    Conference, 4
  Tack, 2

La Estrella de Panama, 126, 147,
  155
Labor unions, 68, 265
LaFeber, Walter, 31, 257, 258
Lakas, Demetrio, 72, 149
Langley, Lester, 31, 32
Latin America, 1, 86, 125,
  179, 180, 183
Latin American constitutions,
  75
Latin American Nuclear Free
  Zone Treaty, 109
Leadership amendments, 231,
  246
Leadership Reservation, 237
League of Nations, 25, 122
Leggett, Robert, 198
Legislative Reorganization
  Act, 175
Lesseps, Ferdinanc de, 16, 17
Levin, Carl, 262
Lewis, Gabriel, 252
Liberals, 193
Liberty Lobby, 214
Linkage, 3, 11, 59, 192, 269
Linowitz, Sol, 155, 156, 157,
  184, 189, 200, 204, 206,
  250
Locks canal, 48, 105, 108
  traffic projections, 106
  vulnerability to sabotage,
    109, 111
Long, L. J., 207
Low-cost housing, 63

Lowenthal, Abraham, 207
Luers, William, 184

Manfredo, Fernando, 267
Mann, Thomas C., 41
Martin, Edwin, 41
Martinez, Boris, 54, 72
Martinique, 18
Martyrs Day, 35
McAuliffe, Dennis, 207, 267
McCain, William, 31
McClellan, John, 145, 147
McCullough, David, 31, 218
McGee, Gale, 184
Meany, George, 200, 214
Media restrictions, 60
Mellander, Gustavo, 22, 31
Memorandum of Understanding, 26
Merchant Marine & Fisheries Com-
  mittee, 168, 173, 177, 196,
  260
Merchant, Livingston T., 36
Metal Trades Council, 214
Mexico, 130
Miami Herald, 72, 129
Military regime, 60, 76
Military use of Panamanian terri-
  tory, 87
Miner, Dwight C., 31
Mondale, Walter, 250, 265
Monroe Doctrine, 14, 16
Montgomery amendment, 261
Moore, Frank, 250, 252
Moorer, Thomas, 213
Mora, Gustavo Tepada, 50
Morgan, Thomas, 177
Multi-national corporations, 183
Mundt, John, 143
Murphy, John, 99, 100, 151, 173,
  260

Nasser, Gamel Abdul, 31
National Assembly, 50, 67
  Robles impeachment, 54
National Assembly of Corregimien-
  tos, 74, 75
National Association of Manufac-
  turers, 246
National Council of Churches, 214
National Council of Private
  Enterprises, 128
National Federation of Democratic
  Women, 128

National Guard, 44, 54, 55, 68, 74, 90, 260
National Maritime Union of America, AFL-CIO, 214
National Security Council, 181
National Union Party, 53
  demands, 54
Negotiations, 2, 11, 86, 167
  bilateral, 119, 121, 130, 131, 138
  international, 120
  secrecy, 143, 149, 150, 168, 169
Neutrality Pact, 160
Neutrality Treaty, 206, 215, 222, 223, 245, 246, 251, 252, 257
New Granada, Republic of, 14
  Bidlack-Mallorino Treaty, 15
New Panama Movement, 73, 74
New York Times, 72, 129, 247
Nicaragua canal site, 18
Nixon, Richard, 143
  foreign policy, 1
  Latin America, 1
  mobilization order 1973, 6
No-amendment policy, 227, 228
Non-aligned Conference, 270
Non-aligned nations, 139
Non-intervention policy, 65
Nuclear excavation, 48, 109
Nuclear Test Ban Treaty, 109

O'Meara, Andrew, 41
Occupational differential, 98
Office of International Security Affairs, 197
Old France Field, 148
Operation Sovereignty, 36
Opinion Research Corporation, 247
Oregon, USS, 17
Organization of American States, 4, 11, 35, 41, 43, 122, 126, 189, 259, 270
  council, 41, 43
  reform movement, 123, 124
  Special Committee, 154
Overseas Private Investment Corporation, 201, 205
Ozores, Carlos, 267

Panama, 148, 181
  business community, 254
  commercial elite, 30
  concessions, 27
  Council of Foreign Relations, 50, 51
  counterpart funds, 102
  custom officials, 100
  demonstrations, 50
  dependency on Canal, 73
  election 1964, 44
  elections, 255
  elites, 65, 67, 68
  foreign debt, 255, 271
  foreign policy, 255
  general development plan, 102
  governing aristocracy, 120
  Independence Day, 55
  inflation, 255
  Instituto Nacional High School, 40
  judiciary, 67
  labor unions, 68
  leadership, 9
  leftists, 49, 255
  middle class, 67
  military, 68
  National Assembly, 28, 49, 50, 67, 71
  national debt, 209
  National Guard, 1, 35, 41, 54, 90
  national lottery, 144
  nationalism, 9
  negotiators, 50
  news media, 125, 126, 129
  penetrated society, 11, 21, 269
  people, 9
  police force, 69
  political parties, 68
  political system, 11, 83
  President Roberto Chiari, 37
  relationship between political system and Canal, 11
  rural poor, 67
  seeking support from Latin America, 4
  seeking support from Third World, 4
  sovereignty, 48
  students, 68
  Supreme Court, 54, 70
  titular sovereignty, 36
  United Front, 49

Panama (continued)
  use of territory for military
    purposes, 87
  views geography as benefit, 84
  1904 constitution, article
    136—22, 23, 65, 68
  1946 constitution, 75
  1972 constitution, 75, 76, 190
Panama Bar Association, 43, 52,
  157
  treaty objections, 52
Panama Canal Act 1912, 62, 267
Panama Canal Authority, 268
Panama Canal Commission, 205,
  227, 263, 264, 265, 266, 267
  administrator, 205
  composition of U.S. members,
    265
  deputy administrator, 205
Panama Canal Company, 62, 150,
  205
  report, 227
Panama Canal Company Board, 268
Panama Canal Pilots Association,
  183, 215
Panama City, 66, 73, 105
Panama Declaration, 148
Panama Interoceanic Canal Com-
  mission, 48
Panama railroad, 16, 160
Panama Review Committee, 268
Panama Supreme Court, 192
Panama-Costa Rica boundary
  dispute, 24
Panamanian Power and Light Com-
  pany, 99
Panamanians, 11, 60, 63, 79, 259
  urban, 73
  working in Zone, 97
Panameñista Party, 53, 193
Paredes, Rubin Dario, 271
Parfitt, Harold, 148, 151, 156,
  196, 197, 208
Parker, Gen. David, 148
Path Between the Seas, 218
Peace Corps, 102
  expulsion, 101
Pell amendment, 130
Pell, Claiborne, 204
Penetrated society, 10, 269
  Penama, 11, 55
Penetrated system, definition,
  10, 22
  Panama, 21

Pentagon, 182
Peron, Juan, 30
Perpetuity, 93, 134, 145, 253
Peru, 72, 128
Phillips, Christopher, 126
Pippin, Larry, 32, 64
Plaza, Galo, 123
Plebiscite, 162, 191, 192, 216,
  223, 224
  returns, 194
  second, 238
Police force, 69
Political asylum, 87, 88, 89
Political exiles, 223
Political parties, 68, 193
Polls, 247, 250
Portillo, Jose Lopez, 189
Postwar Defense Bases Pact 1947,
  28
Press, 167
  restrictions, 60
Priorities, Canal issue, 7
Private land ownership, 63
Protectorate, 65
Public opinion, 200, 201, 227,
  246, 250
Puerto Rico, 122

Rabiblancos, 70
Racial discrimination, 133
Radio Free America, 215
Rational policy model, 8
Reagan, Ronald, 152, 183, 184,
  200, 201, 202
Recession, 66
Reform movement of OAS, 123, 124
Regime, military, 60
Remón, Jose Antonio assassinated,
  30, 69
  Guardia Nacionale, 29
Republican platform, Canal plank,
  184
Reservations, Canal treaty, 234,
  236, 237
  leadership, 237
Resolution of Ratification, 234
Revilla, Nicolas Gonzalez, 139,
  155, 158, 169
Reynolds, James, 198
Richardson, William, 157
Rio Hato, 30, 91
Rio Pact 1947, 41

Riots, Canal Zone 1978, 254
Riots, Canal Zone 1964, 55, 70
    flag, 36
Riots, Canal Zone 1947, 36
Ritter, Eduardo Aislan, 123
Roa, Paul, 131
Robles, Marco, 44, 45, 49, 50,
    51, 55, 70, 142, 191
    impeachment attempt, 53, 54
Rogers, William, 149, 151, 179,
    181, 199, 219, 252, 253
Roosevelt-Boyd Highway, 178
Roosevelt, Franklin D., 26
Roosevelt, Theodore, 60, 61, 68
Roper Poll, 247
Ropp, Steve, 256
Rosa, Diogenes de la, 51, 263
Rosenau, James, 5, 9, 12, 32
    definition of penetration, 10
    penetrated system, 22
Royo, Aristides, 157, 160, 208,
    255, 271
Rumsfeld, Donald, 182
Rural poor, 67, 73
Rusk, Dean, 213, 215

Samudio, David, 51, 53, 54, 70
San Blas Islands, 194
Sanjur, Amado, 73, 89
Scali, John, 131, 135, 136, 137
Schlesinger, James, 180
Sea snake, 116
Sea-level canal, 17, 37, 39, 45,
    48, 51, 53, 94, 97, 105,
    106, 108, 112, 113, 114,
    134, 145, 267
    opposition, 114
    political and economic ques-
    tions, 11
Security Council, U.N., 41, 121,
    125, 126, 128, 147, 179
    Addis Ababa meeting, 121, 125
    advantage to Panama, 122
    disadvantage to U.S., 122
    nonpermanent members, 121
    Panama meetings, 124, 143, 270
    resolution, 135
    veto, 135, 136
    veto-bearing nations, 121
Security issue, 256
Segregation, 134
Senate Armed Services Committee,
    261, 262

Senate Foreign Relations Commit-
    tee, 65, 158, 175, 203, 204,
    217, 218, 220, 226, 227, 246
Senate Select Committee on Intel-
    ligence, 229
Seward, William, 16
Shont, Theodore, 61
Silvera, Ramiro, 73, 89
Snyder amendment, 169, 176, 178,
    180
Soles, Galileo, 38
South Vietnam, 148, 174
"Southern comfort," 63
Southern Command, 178
Sovereignty, 87, 89, 145, 202, 253
    titular, 93
Soviet Union, 174
Spanish-American War, 17
Sparkman, John, 155, 204, 224, 259
"Spiggoty," 63
Spooner Act 1902, 18, 19, 61, 196
State Department, 145, 150, 152,
    170, 177, 178, 179, 180, 181,
    182, 184, 220, 225, 246, 259
    Inter-American Affairs, 167
State Department Authorization
    Act, 177
Statement of Understanding, 215,
    220, 222, 223, 224
Status of Forces Agreement, 49,
    87, 159, 180
    definition, 87
Stevenson, Adlai, 41
Students, 68, 150, 152, 162, 213,
    260
    high school, 52, 68
    U.S., 40
    university, 52, 68
    University of Panama, 192, 193
Subcommittee on Inter-American
    Affairs, 171, 195, 200
Subcommittee on Latin American
    Affairs, 262
Subcommittee on the Panama Canal,
    172, 195, 196
Subcommittee on the Separation of
    Powers, 195, 201, 226, 257
Substitute treaty, 231
Sucre, Arturo, 72
Suez Canal, 117, 154, 197
    nationalization, 31, 93
    Users Conference, 31
Sullivan, Leonor, 151, 173, 177

312

Super tankers, 106
Supreme Court, Panama, 54
Symington, Stuart, 177
Synagogue Council of America, 214

Tack, Juan Antonio, 1, 88, 100, 123, 124, 128, 135, 136, 147, 148, 149, 151, 173
Taft, William H., 23, 61
Tariffs, 23
Terminal Cities, 105
Terminal Lake-Third Locks Plan, 114, 184, 202
Thatcher Ferry Bridge, 38
Third World, 120, 121, 122, 123, 124
Thirty-month transition period, 255, 264, 268
Thompson, Urritia Treaty, 25, 33, 155
Thurmond resolution, 175, 176, 177
Thurmond, Strom, 145, 147, 174, 209, 210
Titular sovereignty, 36, 93, 176
U.S. interpretation, 36
Tivoli Hotel, 41
Tobago, resort island, 23
Tocumen Airport, 2, 100
Tolls, 95, 106, 198, 205, 218, 219, 229, 261, 265, 266, 272
  increase, 94
  rates, 96
  structure, 94
  understanding, 233
Torrijos, Moise, 100, 173, 217, 229, 230
  drug smuggling, 217
Torrijos, Omar, 1, 54, 55, 60, 71, 72, 73, 74, 75, 76, 77, 78, 84, 124, 129, 130, 136, 138, 142, 151, 152, 153, 154, 155, 156, 157, 162, 163, 169, 171, 180, 189, 190, 191, 192, 193, 194, 215, 216, 217, 222, 223, 237, 238, 24 , 270, 271
  background, 77
  executive secretary, National Guard, 71
  family of, 229
  government, 86

Training facilities, 69
Trans-Isthmian Canal Commission, 168
Trans-Isthmian pipelines, 109
Transition cost, 261, 266
Treaties, Draft 1967, 45, 46, 47, 51, 93, 96, 120, 143, 170
  financial benefits, 145
  joint administration, 145
  rejection, 120
  statement of objectives, 45
Treaty, Canal 1977, 234
  defense, 181
  defense 1967, 51
  Filos-Hines 1967, 52
  hearings, 226
  Neutrality, 206, 215, 222, 223, 245, 246, 251, 252, 257
  Nunn condition, 233
  prohibition of nuclear weapons, 236
  Randolph reservation, 233
  Schmitt substitute, 231
  violations, 261
Treaty for the Prohibition of Nuclear Weapons, 236
Treaty implementation, 260, 262
Treaty markup, 220, 222
Treaty secrecy, 46
Treaty violations, 263, 264, 267
Treaty, Hay/Bunau-Varilla, 60

U.S.-Latin American relations, 254
Understandings, 234, 236, 237
United Kingdom, 133
United Nations, 4, 11, 35, 121, 124, 157, 237, 270
  General Assembly, 121, 122, 123
United States Army Corps of Engineers, 62
United States Chamber of Commerce, 246
United States Constitution, disposal of property, 194, 195
United States corporations, 86
United States Defense Department, 79, 85
United States embassy, 89
  1974 attack on, 39
  1963 attack on, 4
United States Information Agency, 41
United States Labor Party, 214

United States Military Assistance Program, 69, 70
United States Southern Command, 91
  Quarry Heights HQ, 91
United States State Department, 54, 79, 85, 99
United States-Latin American Relations Commission, 155
Universal Declaration of Human Rights, 43
University of Panama, 260
Urban guerrilla movement, 89
Urban Panamanians, 73
USSR, 132

Vallarino, Bolivar, 54, 70, 71
Valle, Miguel Angel de la Flor, 130
Vance, Cyrus, 41, 154, 157, 204, 205, 206, 226, 250, 265
Vaughan, Jack H., 43, 45
Venezuela, 148
Veterans of Foreign Wars, 183, 250

Waldheim, Kurt, 126, 191
Wallace, George, 149
Wallop, Malcom, 235
Ward, David, 143
Wartime control, 264, 266
Water rights, 87, 92
Weil, Thomas, 31
Weisband, Edward, 12, 169
Welles, Sumner, 26
West Indians, 98
White, Edward T., 24
  decision, 25
Wilson, Woodrow, 25
Wiseman, Frederick, 80
World Bank, 99
Wyse, Lucien Napoleon Bonaparte, 17

Young Americans for Freedom, 214
Yugoslavia, 132

Zero-sum game, 250
Zonians, 11, 38, 39, 40, 43, 59, 60, 64, 79, 80, 97, 145, 171, 178, 179, 213, 214, 259, 260
Zumwalt, Elmo, 208